AVICENNA

GREAT MEDIEVAL THINKERS

Series Editor
Brian Davies
Fordham University

DUNS SCOTUS
Richard Cross

BERNARD OF CLAIRVAUX
Gillian R. Evans

JOHN SCOTTUS ERIUGENA
Deirdre Carabine

ROBERT GROSSETESTE
James McEvoy

BOETHIUS
John Marenbon

PETER LOMBARD
Philipp W. Rosemann

ABELARD AND HELOISE
Constant J. Mews

BONAVENTURE
Christopher M. Cullen

AL-KINDĪ
Peter Adamson

JOHN BURIDAN
Gyula Klima

ANSELM
Sandra Visser and Thomas Williams

JOHN WYCLIF
Stephen E. Lahey

HUGH OF SAINT VICTOR
Paul Rorem

AVICENNA
Jon McGinnis

AVICENNA

Jon McGinnis

OXFORD
UNIVERSITY PRESS

2010

OXFORD
UNIVERSITY PRESS

Oxford University Press

Oxford University Press, Inc., publishes works that further
Oxford University's objective of excellence
in research, scholarship, and education.

Oxford New York
Auckland Cape Town Dar es Salaam Hong Kong Karachi
Kuala Lumpur Madrid Melbourne Mexico City Nairobi
New Delhi Shanghai Taipei Toronto

With offices in
Argentina Austria Brazil Chile Czech Republic France Greece
Guatemala Hungary Italy Japan Poland Portugal Singapore
South Korea Switzerland Thailand Turkey Ukraine Vietnam

Copyright © 2010 Oxford University Press, Inc.

Published by Oxford University Press, Inc.
198 Madison Avenue, New York, New York 10016
www.oup.com

Oxford is a registered trademark of Oxford University Press

Library of Congress Cataloging-in-Publication Data

McGinnis, Jon.
Avicenna / Jon McGinnis.
p. cm.
ISBN 978-0-19-533147-9; 978-0-19-533148-6 (pbk.)
1. Avicenna, 980–1037. 2. Philosophy, Islamic—History. I. Title.
B751.Z7M4 2010
181'.5—dc22   2009016862

Printed in the United States of America
on acid-free paper

To Celina,
My other great passion

SERIES FOREWORD

Many people would be surprised to be told that there *were* any great medieval thinkers. If a *great* thinker is one from whom we can learn today, and if "medieval" serves as an adjective for describing anything that existed from (roughly) the years 600 to 1500 AD, then, so it is often supposed, medieval thinkers cannot be called "great."

Why not? One answer often given appeals to ways in which medieval authors with a taste for argument and speculation tend to invoke "authorities," especially religious ones. Such invocation of authority is not the stuff of which great thought is made—so it is often said today. It is also frequently said that greatness is not to be found in the thinking of those who lived before the rise of modern science, not to mention that of modern philosophy and theology. Students of science are nowadays hardly ever referred to literature earlier than the seventeenth century. Students of philosophy in the twentieth century have often been taught nothing about the history of ideas between Aristotle (384–322 BC) and Descartes (1596–1650). Contemporary students of theology are often encouraged to believe that significant theological thinking is a product of the nineteenth century.

Yet the origins of modern science lie in the conviction that the world is open to rational investigation and is orderly rather than chaotic—a conviction that came fully to birth, and was systematically explored and developed, during the middle ages. And it is in medieval thinking that we find some of the most sophisticated and rigorous discussions in the areas of philosophy and theology ever offered for human consumption—not surprisingly, perhaps, if we note that medieval philosophers and theologians, like their contemporary counterparts, were often university teachers (or something like that) who participated in an ongoing worldwide debate and were not (like many seventeenth-, eighteenth-, and even nineteenth-century philosophers and theologians) people working in relative isolation from a large community of teachers and students with whom they were regularly involved. As for the question of appeal to authority: it is certainly true that many medieval thinkers believed in authority (especially religious authority) as a serious court of appeal; and it is true that many people today would say that they cannot do this. But as contemporary philosophers are increasingly reminding us, authority is as much an ingredient in our thinking as it was for medieval thinkers (albeit that, because of differences between thinkers, one might reasonably say that there is no such thing as "medieval thought"). For most of what we take ourselves to know derives from the trust we have reposed in our various teachers, colleagues, friends, and general contacts. When it comes to reliance on authority, the main difference between us and medieval thinkers lies in the fact that their reliance on authority (insofar as they had it) was often more focused and explicitly acknowledged than it is for us. It does not lie in the fact that it was uncritical and naive in a way that our reliance on authority is not.

In recent years, such truths have come to be recognized at what we might call the "academic" level. No longer disposed to think of the Middle Ages as "dark" (meaning "lacking in intellectual richness"), many university departments (and many publishers of books and journals) now devote a lot of their energy to the study of medieval thinking. And they do so not simply on the assumption that it is historically significant, but also in the light of the increasingly developing insight that it is full of things with which to dialogue and from which to learn. Following a long period in which medieval thinking was thought to be of only antiquarian interest, we are now witnessing its revival as a contemporary voice—one with which to converse, one from which we might learn.

The Great Medieval Thinkers Series reflects and is part of this exciting revival. Written by a distinguished team of experts, it aims to provide substantial introductions to a range of medieval authors. And it does so on the assumption that they are as worth reading today as they were when they wrote. Students of medieval "literature" (e.g., the writings of Chaucer) are currently well supplied (if not oversupplied) with secondary works to aid them when reading the objects of their concern. But those with an interest in medieval philosophy and theology are by no means so fortunate when it comes to reliable and accessible volumes to help them. The Great Medieval Thinkers Series therefore aspires to remedy that deficiency by concentrating on medieval philosophers and theologians, and by offering solid overviews of their lives and thought coupled with contemporary reflection on what they had to say. Taken individually, volumes in the series will provide valuable treatments of single thinkers, many of whom are not currently covered by any comparable volumes. Taken together, they will constitute a rich and distinguished history and discussion of medieval philosophy and theology considered as a whole. With an eye on college and university students, and with an eye on the general reader, authors of volumes in the series strive to write in a clear and accessible manner so that each of the thinkers they write on can be learned about by those who have no previous knowledge about them. But each contributor to the series also intends to inform, engage, and generally entertain even those with specialist knowledge in the area of medieval thinking. So, as well as surveying and introducing, volumes in the series seek to advance the state of medieval studies both at the historical and the speculative level.

Nobody seriously concerned with medieval philosophy and theology, whether done from the Islamic, Jewish, or Christian perspective, can afford to ignore Avicenna (Ibn Sīnā). Born at the end of the tenth century in what is now modern day Uzbekistan, Avicenna became a profound influence not only on Islamic thinking but also on that of Jews (such as Maimonides) and Christians (such as Thomas Aquinas). If a great thinker is one whose thought can be assimilated and developed by people of very different intellectual traditions, then Avicenna was, without doubt, a great thinker.

In the present volume, Jon McGinnis provides a detailed introduction to all of the issues on which Avicenna wrote. He puts Avicenna into his historical intellectual context (Greek and Islamic). He also explains how Avicenna thought on topics such as logic, physics, psychology, metaphysics, politics, and medicine (Avicenna has often been said to be the founder of modern medicine). Professor McGinnis aims to provide philosophers, historians of science, and students of medieval thought with a starting point from which to assess the place, significance, and influence of Avicenna and his philosophy within the history of ideas. He does so very well, and his book should prove to be extremely useful to anyone concerned with medieval thinking in general, and with Islamic thinking in particular.

Brian Davies

PREFACE

When I first began the present work, I took as my model the excellent volumes in this series by John Marenbon and Peter Adamson on Boethius and al-Kindī respectively. What I admired most about their works was both the careful analysis of the philosophical arguments and the concise nature of the texts. This seemed the right approach: One could pick up their books and in a very short time have some genuine sense of the philosophical thought of Boethius or al-Kindī. Moreover, unlike the concern that Marenbon and Adamson raised about whether their figures were "great medieval thinkers," I had no such problem, for I think I can say with complete confidence and without prejudice that Avicenna is indeed a great medieval thinker (especially if we understand "medieval" as strictly a chronological designation). Thus, my task seemed relatively clear: Present the high points of Avicenna's philosophical system and do it concisely.

This turns out to be easier said than done. Nearly three hundred works have been attributed to Avicenna. Moreover, even if one limits oneself to Avicenna's philosophical encyclopedias, he wrote no less than three (extant) *summas*, whose content, organization, and presentation can at times differ significantly. Additionally, recent scholarship has begun making a case that Avicenna's thought underwent an evolution, and so the problems of dating his works (even the encyclopedias) and determining what are his "mature" views arise. In order partly to address this last issue, I decided to focus primarily on Avicenna's philosophical system as it appears in his most extensive and well-known encyclopedic work, the *Cure* (*ash-Shifā'*), albeit in places drawing significantly on his other extant encyclopedias—particularly the *Salvation* (*an-Najāt*), and to a lesser extent *Pointers and Reminders* (*al-Ishārāt wa-t-tanbīhāt*) as well as his *Canon of Medicine* (*Qānūn fī ṭ-ṭibb*). Unfortunately, this meant that I gave rather short shrift to Avicenna's shorter specialized treatises as well as his *Discussions* (*Mubāḥathāt*) and *Glosses* (*Ta'līqāt*), even though I recognize that these works frequently have a more fully developed presentation of certain technical and tricky points. Also because of this self-imposed limit, I have thought it prudent not to take up the issue of intellectual development, not because I deny that it occurred or that it is not important, but because in the end I think that presenting a roughly unified Avicennan system of thought as it is appears predominantly in the *Cure* will be more useful for those readers who are interested primarily in getting some initial sense of Avicenna's overall philosophy as well as providing a starting point for scholars who want to explore systematic developments in his thought.

Even limiting myself to the *Cure*, however, presented problems, for what one quickly discovers is that Avicenna is indeed a systematic thinker, weaving and interlacing a few very basic concepts, ideas, and arguments throughout a legion of diverse philosophical topics and problems. Consequently, in order to appreciate some move he makes, for example, in metaphysics, one must first understand the problem that he is addressing, which might have arisen initially in physics or medicine. Similarly, the value of some Avicennan notion, which might seem peculiar or even gratuitous—such as his doctrine of the Giver of Forms, which is virtually unique to his system—can be fully grasped only by seeing how it provides him with a single solution to a score of seemingly diverse philosophical problems that in fact Avicenna reveals to have a common ailment and so require a common cure. Moreover, often one cannot properly appraise Avicenna's philosophical contribution without first understanding the historical context and problematic to which he is responding. In short, what I had hoped to be a relatively concise presentation of Avicenna's philosophical system quickly grew into a somewhat lengthy tome as I tried to provide the necessary pieces needed to get some sense of the beautiful and, were it possible, almost seamless mosaic that is his system. I can only hope that the present work does justice to the systematic nature of Avicenna's unique philosophical mind.

Despite the need in places to give an extended discussion of Avicenna's own thought and context, I still wanted to keep this volume relatively short. It is for this reason that I have not addressed the secondary literature in a way that some might find adequate, and for this I can only beg the reader's indulgence. I additionally should confess that there are certain Avicennan scholars that I have simply been reading and being enriched by since my graduate school days, and their astute insights and observations have simply become blended in my mind with the very thought of Avicenna himself. In this category are those scholars who have pioneered and advanced the field of Avicennan studies: Herbert Davidson, Thérèse-Anne Druart, Amélie Marie Goichon, Dimitri Gutas, Ahmad Hasnawi, Jules Janssens, Michael Marmura, and Yahya Michot. As often as not their thought has simply become my own. So, if their names do not appear as frequently as they ought in my notes, my only defense is to say that imitation is the sincerest form of flattery. I genuinely owe them a great intellectual debt.

In a related vein, it is also my pleasant responsibility to acknowledge the numerous organizations and individuals who have contributed in varying ways to my understanding of Avicenna and the completion of this work. Among the institutions, I would like to acknowledge, first, the University of Missouri Research Board for providing me with financial support for a semester off to write. Additionally, I would like to thank the Center for International Study at UM-St. Louis for the significant travel support that they have provided me in past years that has allowed me to present my work on Avicenna at conferences both here and abroad. I am also very grateful for the support of my department, which not only graciously granted me research leaves, but also has allowed me to teach some pretty arcane courses on Avicenna. Beyond the local level, I was blessed with two National Endowment for the Humanities Fellowships and a membership at the Institute for Advance Study (Princeton, NJ), all of which allowed me to focus on various aspects of Avicenna's thought.

At the individual level, there are the numerous scholars and students who have willingly (or perhaps not so willingly) spent countless hours talking with me about Avicenna, reading earlier drafts of chapters and papers, attending and responding at conference presentations that I have given, and in general just giving of themselves. I particularly want to thank Peter Adamson and David C. Reisman whom I got to know when we were all still graduate students and with whom I have been having ongoing dialogues since that time. I also am exceptionally grateful for the willingness of senior scholars—such as Idit Dobbs-Weinstein, Thérèse-Anne Druart, Lenn Goodman, Dimitri Gutas, Jules Janssens, Yahya Michot, and Richard C. Taylor—for listening and talking with me about Avicenna. Also, I have been blessed by a number of scholars in my hometown of St. Louis with whom I have been able to discuss finer points of medieval and Arabic philosophy, particularly Asad Ahmed of Washington University in St. Louis and Eleonore Stump of St. Louis University. I was particularly pleased to have an opportunity to teach a class jointly with Professor Stump on Aquinas and the Arabs during which I feel that I may have learned more than anyone else in the class. A special "obrigado" also goes out to my Brazilian colleague and friend Tadeu Verza, who meticulously went through an earlier version of this book. His keen sight and insight certainly saved me from making a number of errors. I further want to acknowledge the countless number of undergraduate and graduate students who enrolled and positively contributed to courses that I have deliberately created to try out some of the material presented in this book. It speaks highly of the genuine intellectual curiosity of the UM-St. Louis students that those courses were always full and the questions always thought provoking. In particular, however, I would like to note four such students for their relentless enthusiasm and piercing questions, comments, and observations: Joe Brutto, Josh Hauser, Stuart Reeves, and Dan Sportiello. Sue Bradford Edwards did a beautiful job creating the map specifically for this volume. I am also grateful to Brian Davies for providing me the opportunity to contribute a volume on Avicenna to the Great Medieval Thinkers Series, and his comments on an early draft of this work. Finally, I want to thank my family: my wife for seeing that I got the time to work on this project; my boys for seeing that I got enough play time away from this project.

CONTENTS

AVICENNA

I

AVICENNA'S INTELLECTUAL AND HISTORICAL MILIEU

Historical Background: From
Athens to Baghdad

Ex nihilo nihilo fit: Nothing comes from nothing, and Avicenna and his philosophy are no exception. Indeed, multiple influences were at work in the formation of his thought. In this chapter, I consider a few of these influences so as to provide a general backdrop against which to situate the intellectual and political-historical milieu within which Avicenna worked.[1] To this end, I begin the odyssey that was Avicenna's life with a brief look at the Greek scientific and philosophical course curriculum being taught at the Academies in Athens and Alexandria, which in turn became the standard regimen of study for those practitioners of *falsafa*, that is, the Arabic philosophical tradition that saw itself as the immediate heir and continuation of a Neoplatonized Aristotelianism. I then consider the reception and appropriation of this Greek scientific and philosophical heritage into Arabic, which in its turn also offers an opportunity to consider the Islamic political situation just prior to and during the time of Avicenna. In addition to the Graeco-Arabic scientific tradition, Avicenna also took inspiration from influences indigenous to the culture in which he lived. These include, but are certainly not limited to, the religion of Islam itself and particularly its philosophical-theological articulation (*kalām*), the Persian Renaissance, and of course mathematical, scientific, and philosophical developments that were being done in Arabic as well. Once having provided this background, I turn to the life and works of Avicenna himself and the political turmoil of the region that haunted him and constantly forced him to be on the move throughout his life.

The Greek Milieu

While Avicenna was born outside of Bukhārā in what is now modern-day Uzbekistan in 980 of the Common Era, a significant part of his story begins some 1,300 years earlier in Athens. For it is the fourth century BCE Greek philosopher, Aristotle, and his works on logic, science, and philosophy that would provide the starting point for much of Avicenna's own unique vision of philosophy.[2] Indeed, it was the works of Aristotle—ordered and supplemented by later thinkers—that provided what might be called the school curriculum for most philosophers working in the late Hellenistic world—whether in the academy at Athens until it was closed in 529 CE or thereafter in the academy at Alexandria.[3] Moreover, most philosophers working in the earlier medieval Islamic period up to the time of Avicenna received their philosophical and scientific training following this curriculum.[4] Thus, I should look at it in some detail.

The first element of the Greek Academic course curriculum in Athens and Alexandria was logic. The logic segment began with the *Isagoge* of Porphyry (ca. 232–ca. 305 CE), which, as its name implies (it literally means "introduction") introduces the uninitiated to certain key concepts in Aristotle's logic, namely, genus, difference, species, property, and accidents, the so-called five predicables or most basic pieces of informative data from which scientific and philosophical propositions are built. After the *Isagoge*, the student took up the logical works of Aristotle himself, beginning with the *Categories*, with its substance-accidents ontology, and going through his works on deductions generally (the *Prior Analytics*) and scientific deductions or demonstrations specifically (the *Posterior Analytics*), all the way through to the *Rhetoric* and *Poetics*, topics that were seen as part of logic's propaedeutic nature. (Although strictly speaking mathematics was viewed as a theoretical science standing between physics and metaphysics, it, like logic, was also viewed as sharpening the promising philosopher's mind and training him to think abstractly. Here, however, it was not Aristotle but Euclid (ca. 325–ca. 270 BCE) and his *Elements of Geometry* that provided

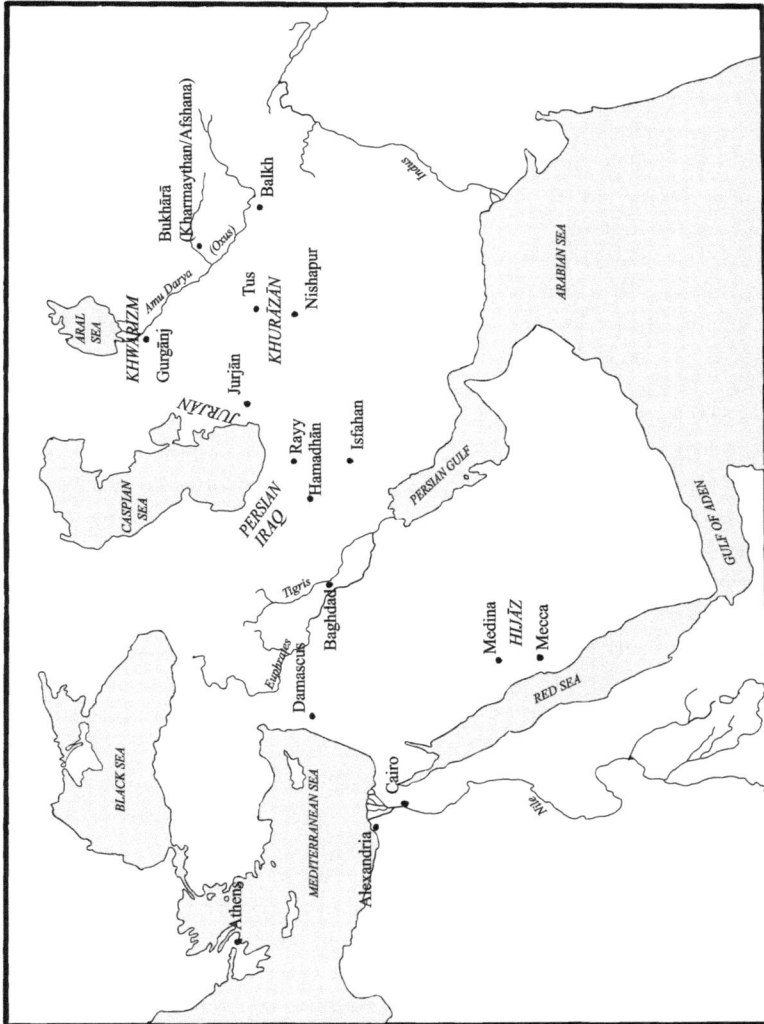

the preliminary and primary training.) The main reason for starting one's intellectual training with logic was that it was seen as a tool—an *organon*—for undertaking the exploration of the world and/or organizing one's findings about it, both activities that lie at the very heart of science and philosophy.

Indeed, whether one calls it "science" or "philosophy," the goal of these enterprises was a deeper understanding (Gk. *epistēmē*, Ar. *'ilm*, Lat. *scientia*) of the world in which we live and our place in it. To the ancient and medieval mind, such understanding involved two criteria: one, knowing the causal explanation for some given phenomenon, and, two, knowing that that explanation is a necessary one (as opposed to merely being an accidental one). Aristotle himself identifies four causes that must be discovered if one is to provide a complete causal explanation of a given phenomenon. One must identify (1) the material cause, (2) the formal cause, (3) the efficient cause, and (4) the final cause. The matter might be thought of as whatever has the potentiality to become a certain natural kind or be accidentally modified in some way, such as the wood that might make up a desk, bed, chair, or the like; form is that by which something actually is the sort of thing that it is, such as the bedlike structure that shapes and informs the wood so that it is a bed; the efficient cause is that which explains a given form's coming to be in the matter in which it comes to exist, so, for example, the carpenter, who imposes the bedlike structure on the wood; and finally, the final cause is that end or good that the efficient cause intends from or for the form-matter composite, such as, in the case of the bed, to provide a comfortable and safe place to sleep. Of course, most cases of genuine scientific explanation are not as jejune as the example just given. Instead, the whole causal structure of most scientifically interesting cases is considerably more complex and so more difficult to uncover. Still, this was the ideal that most philosophers sought: to understand, in a rich and complete sense, the very causal structure of the cosmos.

To this end, Aristotle's *Physics* provided the most basic and general concepts for understanding natural or physical things, that is, things that in some way change or move owing to some internal principle. Such general concepts include nature, motion or change, place, time, and the like. The course curriculum follows up this general discussion of natural things with Aristotle's *De Caelo*, which is an investigation into the makeup and motion of the heavens. The heavens were themselves thought to be of a different material kind than the things that make up the Earth, for, to the ancient and medieval mind, the heavens from the Moon and beyond were thought to involve perfectly regular circular motion, unlike the erratic, primarily rectilinear motions—such as rising and falling—that typify the movements here on Earth. The quite sketchy account of the *De Caelo* was significantly supplemented with the astronomical works of Ptolemy (ca. 100–ca. 175 CE), and particularly his *Almagest*, which provided the basic planetary hypothesis (albeit modified and corrected for accuracy) up until the time of Copernicus. After treating the heavens, the student would study Aristotle's *On Generation and Corruption*, which provides a general discussion of the makeup of the sublunar realm with its specific emphasis on the generation and corruption of those things that we find around us. This general discussion was in turn followed by an investigation of inanimate natural things, which Aristotle treated in his *Meteorology*. The natural sciences conclude with Aristotle's psychological and biological works. It was Aristotle's *De anima* that provided the most basic and general concepts associated with an investigation of living things, such as the soul (Gk. *psuchē*, Ar. *nafs*, Lat. *anima*), which was viewed as simply that principle of animation that explains why living things perform those functions unique to them as living things. A study of the *De anima* was then followed by the *parva naturalia* of Aristotle, which is a series of shorter works on nature, that deal with increasingly more specific topics in the life sciences. As with astronomy, much of Aristotle's biological and anatomical works were later supplemented and sometimes corrected by the voluminous writing of the second-century physician Galen (ca. 129–199 CE), particularly for those students who would go on to pursue medicine. Still, having said that, the Galenic corpus (and indeed medicine more generally) never fully came to be incorporated into the ancient and medieval course curriculum in the way, say, Ptolemy's astronomical writings, were.

Next on the curriculum was the science of metaphysics, literally "that which is after physics." Here, the student would read both Aristotle's *Metaphysics* and additionally the writings of Plato. In fact, at least during the late antique period, it was primarily the Platonic corpus, especially as read through the lens of Plato's later interpreters such as Plotinus (204–270 CE) and Proclus (411–485 CE), that provided the core texts for the student of metaphysics. In part owing to this Platonic, or more exactly Neoplatonic, understanding, metaphysics, which Aristotle had envisioned as a science of being qua being, was reenvisioned as theology or the study of immaterial beings. In fact, as will become clear when I consider Avicenna's metaphysical system,[5] it was only when he rediscovered that Aristotle's *Metaphysics* was intended to provide a science of being qua being, which subsumed theology as one of its proper subtopics, that he came to understand and fully appreciate Aristotle's contribution to this science.

Even then Avicenna remained impressed by at least two Neoplatonic elements that were to feature prominently in his own metaphysical system as well as those of medieval philosophers writing in Arabic more generally. These were the notions of the One and emanation. The Neoplatonic One, which loosely might be viewed as the divinity, is absolutely and completely simple. In fact, the One is the principle or cause of all unity in the cosmos. As such, it is also the source of being or existence, for already as early as Plato and Aristotle, a thing's being or existence was viewed as closely linked with the unity inherent in it. Here, just think of a cloud of chalk particles, which neither is nor exists as a piece of chalk, but only becomes one insofar as the particles have been brought together to form a unified whole. Consequently, given that the One is the principle of unity coupled with the notion that to be or to exist is to be unified, the One must also be the ultimate principle of being and existence itself. As for the One itself, it is beyond or above being and existence. So much so, argued the Neoplatonists, that the very existence or being of the cosmos overflows or emanates from the One: first in the form of Intellect, from which then emanates the World Soul—that is, the animating principle of nature and the cosmos, analogous to the soul in a human—and the world then emanates from the World Soul.

Ironically, despite the influence that Neoplatonists such as Plotinus and Proclus played on the formation of the *falsafa* tradition, Aristotle was most often credited with their innovations while they stood in the proverbial shadows. This is in no small part due to the fact that in the medieval Arabic-speaking world the two primary works in which much of the Neoplatonic metaphysical machinery was laid out were falsely ascribed to Aristotle.[6] Thus, for example, the Arabic redaction of large sections of Plotinus's *Enneads* IV–VI went under the title *The Theology of Aristotle (Uthūlūjiyā)*, while a redaction of Proclus's *Elements of Theology*—which in Arabic was titled the *Pure Good (al-Khayr al-maḥḍ)* and subsequently became the Latin *Liber de Causis* ("The Book of Causes")—was believed to come from the pen of Aristotle. In addition to these two pseudepigrapha, numerous Neoplatonic philosophers commented on the Aristotelian corpus and read into Aristotle's text Neoplatonic doctrines. These commentaries were in turn translated together with the works of Aristotle into Arabic. Given these false ascriptions and the (Neoplatonic) commentary tradition that grew up around Aristotle's works, it is no wonder that many subsequent thinkers in the medieval Islamic world thought that Aristotle actually authored these Neoplatonic innovations. The net effect of this confusion was that by the time that the Arabic Aristotle reached Avicenna, he had been thoroughly Neoplatonized.

The study of metaphysics, whether Aristotelian or Platonic, was then followed by ethics, which drew upon Aristotle's *Nicomachean Ethics* as well as a number of Plato's dialogues and the ethical writings of the Stoics, such as the *Enchiridion* of Epictetus (ca. 35–ca. 135 CE). Ethics, as Aristotle himself says at the beginning of the *Nicomachean Ethics*,[7] is itself subordinate to the science of politics. Here, it was not Aristotle that provided the basis of political studies but again Plato, both in the Greek- and Arabic-speaking worlds. In fact, only the first (or at most the first two) books of Aristotle's *Politics* were translated into Arabic, whereas it seems that both Plato's *Republic* and *Laws* were available in Arabic translation (or at the very least they were thoroughly summarized and explained in Arabic). This fact is notable in itself since, in general, most of the Platonic dialogues were not translated into Arabic, which may perhaps be owing to the high literary and even poetic style of Plato's writings, which makes it often difficult, if nigh impossible, to capture in translation. Instead, most frequently only philosophical synopses of Plato's works were available. As for why Plato's *Republic* may have appealed more to the medieval Muslim intellectual than Aristotle's *Politics*, the most obvious reason is that Plato's Philosopher-King can with relative ease be interpreted as either a Prophet-Lawgiver, such as Muḥammad, or an ideal Caliph, as in Sunni Islam, or an Imam, as in Shiite Islam.

This brief summary should hopefully provide the reader with a sense of the basic curriculum that was being taught at the end of the classical period of Greek philosophy. In general, and to summarize, the works of science and philosophy covered by the curriculum included texts on logic, natural philosophy (such as physics and biology), mathematics and astronomy, metaphysics, and then readings in practical philosophy (such as ethics and politics). Moreover, it was this curriculum that would be translated into Arabic and make up the educational basis for those thinkers, such as Avicenna, working in the *falsafa* or Arabic philosophical tradition. Thus, I should now turn to the Arabic translation movement and the general scientific and philosophical environment it created within the medieval Islamic world.

The Arabic-Islamic Milieu

Certainly, one of the great achievements of the human intellectual spirit was the Arabic translation movement.[8] Over the course of about one hundred years, virtually the entire Greek scientific and philosophical corpus was either translated or summarized into Arabic, and it was certainly in large part owing to the presence of this body of knowledge in Arabic translation that made possible Avicenna's own unique philosophical synthesis. The movement, which roughly occurred during the tenth century, had its intellectual center in Baghdad, the newly established religious and political capital of Islam. A brief account of the history leading up to the translation movements and key figures in it will offer one a glimpse into the sociopolitical situation immediately prior to Avicenna's own times, and so it is to that history that I now turn.

After the death of Muḥammad in 632, the political and religious leadership of Islam passed through a number of Caliphs, literally "successors." The first four of these successors—the so-called *Rāshidūn* or rightly guided Caliphs—had their power base in the Ḥijāz on the Arabian Peninsula. They were then followed by the Umayyad Caliphs, who were centered in Damascus and remained in power in the East from 661–750. In a series of battles between 749–750, Abū l-ʿAbbās (r. 749–754) wrenched control from the Umayyads, setting up his own dynasty, the ʿAbbāsids, which, at least in name, continued until the mid-thirteenth century. It was Abū l-ʿAbbās's immediate successor, al-Manṣūr (r. 754–775), who, on 30 July 762, laid the first foundation stone for the new ʿAbbāsid capital, Baghdad, and it would be at Baghdad—situated where the Tigris and Euphrates rivers run close to each other—that the Arabic translation movement would find its headwaters. Here, Greek, Persian, and even Indian sciences mixed with the study of Arabic grammar and literature, or *adab*, as well as Islamic law (*fiqh*), and Islamic speculative thought (*kalām*) all coming together to form *falsafa*, the Arabic-Islamic philosophical tradition of which Avicenna would be one of its most significant representatives.

Even while consolidating his power, al-Manṣūr was also initiating the translation of foreign philosophical, scientific, and literary works, including Sanskrit astronomical tables, Persian tales and fables, and, of course, Greek texts such as Ptolemy's *Almagest* and the logical writings of Aristotle. Still, it was under the Caliph al-Maʾmūn (r. 813–833) that the Arabic translation movement truly hit its stride, and the first Arabic philosopher, al-Kindī (ca. 800–ca. 870), emerged.[9] The contribution of al-Kindī to the development of the *falsafa* tradition comes from no less than three fronts. First, he assisted in the translation of Greek scientific and philosophical texts, not, it would seem, by himself actually undertaking any translation from the Greek, but by advising about the content and assessing the philosophical sense of the translations as well as suggesting works that should be translated. Second, he also ardently supported the so-called foreign sciences against certain Muslim theologians and intellectuals who were challenging their usefulness and value. Thus, in a very real way he helped to ensure the continuation and preservation of the Greek scientific and philosophical tradition within the medieval Islamic world. Third, and arguably most important, al-Kindī began to appropriate and to formulate the newly translated Greek learning into an Arabic-Islamic philosophical worldview, and, while perhaps not as well known as the philosophical systems of his successors, such as al-Fārābī and Avicenna, al-Kindī's philosophical vision nonetheless did set the agenda and present modes of argumentation that would come to typify *falsafa*.

Also at about the time that al-Kindī was at his peak, so too was the great Nestorian Christian translator Ḥunayn ibn Isḥāq (809–877) and his circle, which included his son Isḥāq ibn Ḥunayn (d. ca. 910), a nephew Ḥubaysh and disciple ʿĪsá ibn Yaḥyá. The output of this handful of men was immense, and had to number many hundreds of translated works if not more. (Ḥunayn himself translated around a hundred texts by Galen alone.) In addition, they revised many earlier cumbersome translations both for readability and content and helped to establish what would become the standard Arabic philosophical vocabulary. It was thus primarily these few men who provided the basic textual sources that would become the groundwork for *falsafa*. While the translation movement certainly continued on after Ḥunayn and his group by such thinkers as the Nestorian Christian Abū Bishr Mattá (d. 940) and the Jacobite Christian Yaḥyá ibn ʿAdī (d. 974),[10] much of the subsequent translation activity merely involved revising already existing translations.

In addition to the inestimable value of all of these translators in preserving and continuing Greek scientific and philosophic thought, many of these translators also contributed to the development of *falsafa* in their own right, themselves writing numerous independent medical and philosophical works and commentaries. Indeed, many of these translators, along with other luminaries of the time, were part of the circle of philosophers known collectively as the Baghdad Peripatetics, which was a loose affiliation of Aristotelians who would meet to read and discuss philosophy together. Because of their own philosophical and scientific interests, these thinkers, in conjunction with translating the Aristotelian corpus, as well as other works, often expounded and questioned that corpus too; so, for example, Ḥunayn produced a series of sixteen questions on Aristotle's cosmological work, the *De Caelo*, while Abū Bishr Mattá and Yaḥyá ibn ʿAdī commented on Aristotle's logical, physical, and metaphysical writings.

Arguably the most outstanding commentator and philosopher among the Baghdad Peripatetics was al-Fārābī (ca. 870–ca. 950). This was certainly Avicenna's opinion, who in general considered the Baghdad Peripatetics to be rather pedestrian thinkers, again with the notable exception of al-Fārābī. While Avicenna's assessment of the rest of these philosophers is open to question, his high praise of al-Fārābī is certainly warranted. Al-Fārābī's renown in logic was so complete that it earned him the moniker "the second teacher" (*al-muʿallim ath-thānī*), second that is only to Aristotle himself. In addition, to commenting and expounding on the logical works of Aristotle, al-Fārābī also made an epitome of Aristotle's *Physics* as well as writing a small treatise on the intentions of the *Metaphysics* (*Fī aghrāḍ*), which proved to be invaluable to Avicenna's own understanding of that science; al-Fārābī's interests in Aristotle even included a long commentary on the *Nicomachean Ethics*, which unfortunately is no longer extant.

Still, perhaps al-Fārābī's greatest contribution to the history of *falsafa* was that he was a system builder. Unlike so many of the earlier philosophers working in Arabic, who contented themselves with merely commenting on the works of earlier Greek philosophers, al-Fārābī wanted to organize the huge body of knowledge available to him into a synthetic whole, showing the dependence of all things on a First Cause, God, followed by the hierarchy that exists within the created order, and the place of humans as well as their moral and/or political obligations within that hierarchy. Two Alfarabian synthetic works are his *The Principles of the Opinions of the Inhabitants of the Perfect State* (*Mabādi ʾārā ʾahl al-madīna l-fāḍila*) and *The Principles of Existing Things* (*Mabādi ʾal-mawjūdāt*), both of which outline a metaphysical system in which the sciences of physics, psychology, ethics, and politics all find their place.[11] Avicenna would carry on this spirit of system building—but at an encyclopedic level that does not merely present the various philosophical and scientific theses but strenuously argues for and defends those positions.

While up to this point I have stressed the Greek philosophical and scientific traditions to which Avicenna would be heir, his worldview also included purely Islamic and Arabic elements as well. The most obvious influence is that of Islam itself as represented in the Qur'ān and the sayings of the prophet Muḥammad (sing. *ḥadīth*). While the Qur'ān never aspires to be a philosophical textbook that lays out arguments in syllogistic fashion, it, nonetheless, makes a number of claims that fall within the domain of subjects that ancient and medieval philosophers treated. Such claims include that God exists and has certain divine attributes, as, for example, being alive, knowing, powerful, and having a will; that there is but one God; that God created the cosmos; that there is an afterlife; and, of course, numerous dicta concerning how one should act (ethics) and interact with others (politics). No Muslim philosopher could simply ignore these claims; rather, he needed to incorporate or reinterpret them into his philosophical system. In fact, Avicenna frequently goes to great lengths to reinforce the idea that his philosophical system is really nothing more than the theoretical articulation of Islam itself.

Additionally shaping the world that surrounded Avicenna would have been the various schools of Islamic law (*fiqh*) and Islamic dialectical or speculative discourse (*kalām*), both of which provided their own interpretation of Islam, and sometimes interpretations quite at odds with the *falsafa* tradition. More like Judaism than Christianity, Islam frequently prizes right practice, or orthopraxy, more highly than (or at least as a necessary element of) right belief, or orthodoxy. In fact, in theory all one needs to believe to be a Muslim is the *Shahāda*, or profession of faith: "There is no god but God (Allah), and Muḥammad is the messenger of God." Consequently, the lawyer (*faqīh*) and judge (*qāḍi*) who interpret divine law (*Sharīʿa*) as revealed in the Qur'ān and sayings of the prophet have always had a more important place in the Islamic world than the theologian. At least among Sunni Muslims, four legal schools (sing. *madhhab*), all of which were considered equally valid, had emerged by Avicenna's time: These were the Ḥanifī, Mālikī, Shāfiʿī, and Ḥanbalī schools. Whatever the school it was often the job of lawyers to extend the application of the law to those cases not explicitly dealt with by the *Sharīʿa*. As a result Muslim lawyers developed rules of (analogical) reasoning (*qiyās*) that were in places quite different from Aristotelian logic. It would in fact seem that Avicenna received his first taste of logic from studying law, for he mentions in his autobiography that while still a young adolescent he had become quite adept at legal questioning and refutation.

Among the so-called Islamic sciences, however, it was *kalām* that exercised and challenged those working within the *falsafa* tradition most.[12] While *kalām* is frequently translated as "theology" or more expansively as "Islamic speculative theology," it is as much of a philosophical worldview as *falsafa* was. Whereas *falsafa* favored the logical system of Aristotle, the *mutakallimūn* (that is, proponents of *kalām*) saw Aristotelian logic, at least initially, as little more than Greek grammar, and thus preferred their own Arabic grammatical categories and analogical reasoning. While *kalām* preferred an ontology of atoms and accidents, *falsafa* favored continuous magnitudes, that is, ones that are potentially divisible infinitely. Despite obvious differences between the two traditions, both were nonetheless interested in roughly the same sets of issues and questions and their answers frequently even shared common intuitions. In this respect perhaps the greatest difference between the two was in their own perceptions of themselves and each other: The proponents of *falsafa* saw themselves as adopting, adapting, and generally extending the Graeco-Arabic philosophical and scientific tradition, while the advocates of *kalām* envisioned themselves as promoting a way of thought intimately linked with the Arabic language and the Islamic religion.

By the time of Avicenna there were broadly two general schools of *kalām*: the Mu'tazilites and the more traditionally inclined Ash'arites (there were additionally the Māturīdīs who fell loosely between the two, or, if anything, inclining slightly toward the Ash'arites). The Mu'tazilites rejected a literal reading of the Qur'ān, and maintained that it had to be read through the lens of what logic and reason require. Thus, for instance, while the Qur'ān ascribes a number of attributes to God, such as having sight, hearing, power, will, and others, the Mu'tazilites argued that if taken at face value these ascriptions would undermine divine unity, uniqueness, and simplicity (*tawḥīd*); for if there are distinct attributes in God and each one of them is divine, then there would be multiple divine things, all equally deserving of being a divinity. Remember, however, that the Muslim confession of faith adamantly asserts that there is but one God. For the same reason, the Mu'tazilites argued that the Qur'ān, despite its claims for itself, could not literally be the word of God but had to be created;[13] for if it were not created, then it too would have to be eternal and so worthy of being a god. Another doctrine in need of reinterpretation, or so the Mu'tazilites believed, was that of divine determinism, which reserved all power and all causality for God. Here, the Mu'tazilites argued that if God were to cause every act including human acts of volition, such as to sin or to submit to God, then divine justice would be jeopardized; for surely God could not punish or reward us based upon what God himself does. While the political heyday of the Muʿtazilites was during the Caliph al-Maʾmūn and his immediate successors, who tried to impose Muʿtazilism as religious orthodoxy, it was during Avicenna's own time in the work of ʿAbd al-Jabbār (935–1025) in Rayy, whom Avicenna most likely knew,[14] that Muʿtazilism reached its full intellectual maturity, even if politically it had waned.

Even then Muʿtazilism never seemed to have a broad theological appeal, and thus in response to what was viewed as the Muʿtazilites' overly rationalistic interpretation of Islam, certain traditionalists staunchly maintained a quite literal understanding of the Qurʾān even in the face of what reason purportedly demanded. Although this traditionalist movement is most frequently associated with the name of Aḥmad ibn Ḥanbal (780–855), it would be the more moderate vision of al-Ashʿarī (d. 935) that would come to dominate theology, at least in Sunni Islam. For unlike Ibn Ḥanbal, who completely distrusted reason and logic, al-Ashʿarī had originally been trained as a Muʿtazilite and appreciated the value of reason and logic, particularly in refuting the deficiencies he found in the Muʿtazilite system; however, unlike the Muʿtazilites, al-Ashʿarī also thought that there were limits to the application of reason beyond which it simply could not go. Those limits, he argued, were reached when it came to things divine. Concerning these issues one simply had to rely on what was revealed about God in the Qurʾān. Thus, al-Ashʿarī affirmed those attributes ascribed to God as well as the Qurʾān's being the uncreated word of God. Also, while God does in fact will and create every event here on Earth, we nonetheless, according to al-Ashʿarī, acquire (kasb) responsibility for those actions, good or bad, that are done through us. These doctrines, maintained al-Ashʿarī, simply have to be accepted without asking how (bilā kayf). By the time of Avicenna, falsafa too had come under the criticism of Ashʿarite theologians, and particularly by the judge and very able theologian al-Bāqillānī (d. 1013), whose critique of the philosophers would only be rivaled by the great Ashʿarite theologian al-Ghazālī (d. 1111) some hundred years later.

While Ashʿarite theology came to dominate in Sunni Islam, Muʿtazilite thought never completely died out among Shiite intellectuals, who always seemed somewhat more receptive to philosophical speculation. Additionally, one form of Shiite Islam, namely, that of the Ismāʿīlīs, would have a profound effect on the intellectual climate of Avicenna's time. By the beginning of the tenth century the Ismāʿīlī leader ʿUbayd-Allāh al-Mahdī

(910–934) conquered a stretch of North African and founded the Fāṭimid dynasty. Sixty years later the Fāṭimid army took control of Egypt and founded their new capital, Cairo, from which they sent missionaries throughout the ʿAbbāsid caliphate proclaiming their Ismāʿīlī theology, which was replete with intellectually subtle philosophical argumentation. One of the tools used by these Ismāʿīlī missionaries was a series of philosophical treatises, over fifty in all, that were written collectively by a group of men who referred to themselves simply as the Brethren of Purity (*ikhwān aṣ-ṣafāʾ*). The *Treatises of the Brethren of Purity* wove Ismāʿīlī theology together with Aristotelian and Neoplatonic elements as well as Neopythagorean thought. Avicenna himself testifies to knowing this Ismāʿīlī thought and quite possibly these treatises as well, although he is also quick to add that he was not convinced by their arguments.

Finally, perhaps the greatest source of inspiration for Avicenna would have been the general air of scientific and intellectual inquiry that permeated the environment in which he found himself. Thus, the young Avicenna undertook a series of correspondences with the greatest polymath and comparative scholar of the time, al-Bīrūnī (973–c. 1050). Avicenna was also an immediate contemporary of the greatest optical theorist in the medieval Islamic world, Ibn al-Haytham (965–1039) of Cairo, with whom Avicenna shared a similar optical theory. Moreover, in addition to knowing the traditional Greek mathematical sciences of geometry and arithmetic, Avicenna was also versed in Indian arithmetic and the new science of algebra, both of which he incorporated into the mathematical sections of his encyclopedic work, the *Cure*, in a way that set him apart from other philosophers working before him.[15] He was a contemporary of the great Persian poet Firdawsī (c. 939–1020), who through his epic *The Book of Kings* virtually single-handedly revived Persian as a language of high literature and culture, while Avicenna's own *The Book of Sciences* (*Dāneshnāme-yi ʿAlāʾī*) was the first work of philosophy written in Persian following the Islamic conquest of the East. In short, Avicenna was very much a product and part of his time, and it is to the specifics of his life that I now turn.

Avicenna's Life and Works

Like that of few others (and even fewer philosophers), Avicenna's life has all the elements for a best-selling novel: There is political intrigue, battles, imprisonment, harrowing escapes, alleged poisonings, drinking parties, and (if one is to believe Avicenna's biographer) lots of sex. One knows these details about Avicenna's life because at the bequest of one of his students, al-Jūzjānī, Avicenna dictated a brief autobiography of his early life, and thereafter al-Jūzjānī chronicled the events from the time of their meeting up to his master's death.[16]

Avicenna's Early Life

About fifty years before Avicenna's birth the ʿAbbāsid Empire began to collapse, even if the ʿAbbāsids retained the titular title "Caliph" long thereafter. In 945 Shiite Būyids captured Baghdad and made the ʿAbbāsid Caliph, al-Mustakfī (r. 944–946), a virtual puppet ruler. The fall of Baghdad was followed by the ever-increasing fragmentation of the empire with various generals, petty lords, and the like carving it up into a number of local autonomous states, albeit often ostensibly showing homage to the ʿAbbāsid Caliph. One such dynasty was that of the Sāmānids who controlled the region of Khurāsān. It was under the last great Sāmānid Amīr, Nūḥ ibn Manṣūr (r. 976–997), that Avicenna's father served as governor of the village of Kharmaythan, one of the more important villages around Bukhārā. While we are only told that his father was a man from Balkh, one of the four capitals of Khurāsān, two sources tell us that his mother's name was Sitāra.

The couple made their home in the small village of Afshana, which lay at the outskirts of Kharmaythan, where in 980 they were blessed with their first child, Abū ʿAlī l-Ḥusayn ibn Sīnā, the "Avicenna" of Latin medieval fame. Sometime after the birth of Maḥmūd, Avicenna's younger brother of five years, the family moved to Bukhārā proper, where teachers of both the Qur'ān and Arabic literature were found for the young Avicenna. He was clearly something of prodigy, for he recounts that by the age of ten he had memorized the entire Qur'ān as well as many works of Arabic literature. He also had even begun studying both Indian arithmetic with a local vegetable seller and Islamic law with the Ḥanafī jurist, Ismāʿīl az-Zāhid. At the age of ten he was given a private tutor, one Abū ʿAbd Allāh an-Nātilī, with whom he first began the philosophical course curriculum outlined earlier. Even before that, however, Avicenna had had a taste of philosophical thought, for he tells us that he would listen in as Ismāʿīlī missionaries spoke about the soul and intellect with his father, and, while he understood their arguments, he was not convinced by them, even though, he says, both his father and brother were.

Still, it was with an-Nātilī that Avicenna began his formal philosophical training, and it was an-Nātilī who encouraged Avicenna's father to steer his son toward only academic pursuits. The teacher and pupil began with Porphyry's *Isagoge*, and in fact Avicenna even impressed his tutor by independently verifying the definition of genus as that which is predicated of many species in answer to the question, "What is it?" doing so in a way that was completely new to an-Nātilī. Avicenna then went on and completed the course on logic, reading the primary and secondary texts mostly on his own, since apparently his tutor simply could not grasp the subtleties of logic. Also with an-Nātilī, Avicenna read Euclid's *Elements* and Ptolemy's *Almagest*, although again according to Avicenna it was in fact he who taught the teacher and an-Nātilī who was the student.

At some point after completing the *Almagest*, an-Nātilī departed from Bukhārā and Avicenna took up reading natural philosophy and philosophical theology (*Ilāhīyāt*) by himself as well as continuing his study of law and beginning the study of medicine. He tells us that at this time he was sixteen and that he spent the next year and half returning to logic and all parts of philosophy. Now, however, he studied these sciences in earnest, compiling for himself notecards on which he formalized all the arguments he came across, listing the premises, conclusions, and implications. During this time he remarks that he never slept an entire night through, but, like a child with a comic book, he would pour over philosophical texts by candlelight, and even when sleep did overtake him he would see the philosophical problems in his dreams. He continued in this way until the sciences of logic, natural philosophy, and mathematics were so deeply rooted within him that he understood them, he says, as far as was humanly possible.

Having reached this point in his self-education, Avicenna took up reading Aristotle's *Metaphysics*; however, he confesses that the intent of that work completely eluded him. In fact, he read the *Metaphysics* forty times to the point of memorizing it and yet he could make no sense of the text, and so he gave up on it altogether as being simply incomprehensible. As luck would have it, however, at about the same time that he was giving up on the *Metaphysics*, he happened to be in the bookseller's quarter where a man came up to him with al-Fārābī's *The Aims of Aristotle's* Metaphysics.[17] While Avicenna initially dismissed the small five-page treatise, the seller was persistent, saying that he was selling the book on consignment and that the owner was desperate for money and that he would take a mere three dirhams.[18] Avicenna reluctantly agreed, and once home he quickly read through the short work. Almost immediately, he says, the intention of the *Metaphysics* became clear to him and he was so grateful that the very next day he gave much in alms to the poor in order to show his gratitude to God.

While studying these philosophical sciences, Avicenna, as I noted, had also taken up medicine, which he mastered in a very short time, claiming that it is one of the easier disciplines. His study of medicine even extended to caring for the sick so as to gather practical clinical experience that could not be acquired through mere books. His knowledge of medicine must have been quite good, for he says that distinguished doctors would read medicine under him even though he was still a very young man. There would seem to be some element of truth to this boast, for at about the age of seventeen and a half Avicenna was called in to advise a number of court physicians about an illness from which the Amīr Nūḥ ibn Manṣūr was suffering.

The advice must have been helpful, since Nūḥ ibn Manṣūr recovered and took Avicenna into his service. While at court, the young Avicenna asked permission to browse the palace library. The library consisted of many rooms, each one of which was dedicated to a different science. Moreover, each room was filled with chests of books, many of which, Avicenna tells us, he had never heard of before or saw thereafter. From then until he was eighteen he read and mastered these books, claiming that upon reaching that point of his life he hit upon the basic elements of his own philosophical system, and while his understanding of those elements may have matured over time, he claims that he added nothing substantively new to them. By the age of twenty-one, Avicenna's knowledge of the sciences had certainly become locally well known; for he was asked to write a compilation of these sciences for one Abū l-Ḥasan 'Arūḍī, which he gave the title *Prosodic Wisdom* (*al-ḥikma l-'arūḍīya*), a pun on 'Arūḍī's name, which means "prosodist" (the work also goes under the name *Compendium*). The lawyer Abū Bakr al-Baraqī also asked Avicenna to comment on the books of science that he had read, the result of which was the twenty-volume *The Sum and the Substance* (*al-Ḥāṣil wa-l-maḥṣūl*); he also wrote for al-Baraqī *The Saintly and the Sinful* (*al-Birr wa-l-ithm*).

Sometime after that—reports have it in the year 1002 at the age of twenty-two—Avicenna's father died, and Avicenna took one of the administrative posts in Bukhārā. By this time Sāmānid power had all but vanished from the region, and so Avicenna tells us, in what would become a leitmotif of his life, that "necessity forced him to leave" Bukhārā for Gurgānj in Khwarizm, now the modern town of Kunya Urgench in northern Turkmenistan. In the garb of a lawyer, he was presented to the Amīr ʿAlī ibn Maʾmūn (r. 997–1009) and was found a position at a modest monthly salary.

Before or around 1012, necessity again forced Avicenna to flee, now for the court of Amīr Qābūs (r. 978–1012) in Jurjān on the Caspian Sea. His flight took him through Nasā, Bāward, Ṭūs, Samanqān, and Jājarm at the extreme limits of Khurāsān before ultimately reaching his destination. Legend has it that the necessity in question was the Sulṭān Maḥmūd of Ghazna (r. 998–1030), the virtual founder of the Turkish Sunni Ghaznavid dynasty, whose lands extended to nearly all of the present territory of Afghanistan and the Punjab.[19] The story goes that Maḥmūd requested that Amīr Maʾmūn send to him a number of scholars to adorn the new Ghaznavid court. The scholars in question included al-Bīrūnī and Avicenna among others. While al-Bīrūnī and most of the others (reluctantly) agreed to go, Avicenna feared the Sulṭān's ruthless treatment of anything that even hinted at unorthodoxy. Thus, he and a Christian scholar, Abū Sahl al-Masīḥī, with whom Avicenna was apparently quite close, chose to flee. The story continues that on the fourth day the two were caught in a sandstorm, becoming completely lost in the desert, and that al-Masīḥī finally died of heat exposure. Avicenna himself carried on, traveling through the various cities noted until finally reaching Jurjān. While nothing precludes the tale's harrowing flight across the desert, a matter of dates suggests that it may not have been in order to flee the clutches of Maḥmūd. For al-Bīrūnī, again one of the scholars who did agree to go to the Ghaznavid court, puts the date of his departure at 1017, five years after the death of Qābūs, who died in the winter months of 1013. Whatever the case, the flight was for naught, for in 1012, when Avicenna would have arrived in Jurjān, the Ghaznavids had already seized Qābūs and imprisoned him in one of his own fortresses, where he died.

Again on the run, Avicenna fled north to Dihistān near the border of Khwarizm, where he fell gravely ill. Upon recovering from his illness, Avicenna must have felt that the situation was safe enough to return to Jurjān, and so he did. It was here, at the age of thirty-two, that he met his disciple Abū ʿUbayd al-Jūzjānī, who would remain by Avicenna's side for the rest of his master's life chronicling the events that he witnessed.

Avicenna's Later Life

Avicenna's time in Jurjān, which could not have been more than three years, was apparently uneventful although productive. One Abū Muḥammad ash-Shīrāzī, of whom we know very little other than that he had a great appreciation for the sciences, purchased a house for Avicenna to live in. It was here that Avicenna composed his *Middle Summary on Logic* (*al-Mukhtaṣar al-awsaṭ al-manṭiq*), *The Origin and Return* (*al-Mabda' wa-l-ma'ād*), *Complete Astronomical Observations* (*ar-Arṣād al-kullīya*), *The Summary of the* Almagest (*Mukhtaṣar* al-Majistī), and many shorter treatises. Most notably, perhaps, it was during his time in Jurjān that Avicenna began his monumental *Canon of Medicine* (*Qānūn fī ṭ-ṭibb*). Avicenna's *Canon* distills into a relatively small handbook the medical knowledge of the Greeks, such as the voluminous works of Galen, and the new discoveries of physicians working in the Arabic-speaking world, such as Abū Bakr ar-Rāzī (ca. 864–ca. 930), as well as Avicenna's own contributions to medicine.

It would seem that some time before 1015 the lure of a rich patron finally enticed Avicenna to leave Jurjān for the mountain country (*arḍ al-jabal*), or what was known at the time as Persian Iraq, which makes up the central regions of modern Iran. Here Avicenna would remain for the rest of his life traveling between, sometimes fleeing from, the region's major cities such as Rayy, outside of modern-day Tehran, Qirmīsīn, which is modern Kirmanshah, Hamadhān, and Iṣfahān. In this first instance, the lure came from Rayy, the largest of the mountain country capitals, to where Avicenna and his disciple moved when the nominal ruler of that city, the Būyid Majd ad-Dawla (ca. 997–1029) was suffering from melancholia or what we would call major depression—which at the time was identified with an excessive buildup of "black bile" (Gk. *melan* [black] + *cholē* [bile]). Avicenna presented letters, presumably commending his medical expertise, to the actual power of the city, Majd ad-Dawla's mother (d. 1028), who simply went by the title "the Lady," and was then taken into her service. Sometime around 1015, the Sulṭān Maḥmūd of Ghazna—whom I mentioned when recounting Avicenna's flight to Jurjān—did in fact seem to have requested that Avicenna be sent to him so as to grace his court. Avicenna, feeling justifiably threatened by these advances, left Rayy first for Qazwīn, west of Rayy, and then for Hamadhān in the midwest part of Iran at the foothills of the Alvand Mountain, where it would appear that he once again took up service for the Lady.

While in Hamadhān, Avicenna became acquainted with its ruler, the Būyid Shams ad-Dawla (r. 997–1021), who was suffering from colic. Avicenna was able to cure him successfully and thereafter became one of his boon companions. In fact, Avicenna even accompanied the Amīr on one of his military expeditions. Upon returning to Hamadhān, the Amīr made Avicenna his vizier. Unfortunately, troops, apprehensive of the new vizier and their standing, rebelled against Avicenna, surrounding his house, ransacking his goods, throwing him in prison, and even demanding that Shams ad-Dawla execute him. The Amīr refused to have Avicenna killed, but was willing to banish him, which in the end involved nothing more than Avicenna's hiding himself away in an acquaintance's home for forty days. Upon suffering another bout of colic, Shams ad-Dawla called upon his old friend to cure him again, apologizing profusely, and even restoring Avicenna to the position of vizier. Avicenna agreed and this time he seems to have been accepted.

Between 1016 and 1021, while still in Hamadhān, al-Jūzjānī asked his master to comment on the works of Aristotle, and although Avicenna refused, he did agree to set out what he considered to be correct among all of the sciences. The result was that he began writing the "Physics" of his monumental work the *Cure* (*ash-Shifā'*), while also continuing to work on the *Canon*. The *Cure* was envisioned as an encyclopedia of science and philosophy consisting of all the theoretical sciences: nine books on logic, eight on natural philosophy, four on mathematical sciences, and one on metaphysics, whose final section also provides Avicenna's treatment of issues ethical and political. In the *Cure* Avicenna wove together the Greek course curriculum and indigenous Islamic influences seen in the previous sections so as to form an intellectual tapestry that was Avicenna's own unique philosophical system.

While serving as Shams ad-Dawla's vizier, Avicenna apparently spent his mornings writing and then spent the rest of the daylight hours attending the Amīr with matters of state. In the evening he would meet with his students, one reading from the newly completed pages of the *Cure* and another from those of the *Canon*, with Avicenna explaining and answering questions. The lessons were then followed by an almost certainly riotous symposium, replete with singers of varying classes, and wine, all with which Avicenna and his students busily occupied themselves. As a somewhat lurid aside, since most professional singers at this time were female slaves, and slave girls were viewed as being at their master's sexual disposal,[20] Avicenna's soirees probably involved a good bit of "adult entertainment," which would be consistent with al-Jūzjānī's own observation that Avicenna had an insatiable sexual appetite.

Sometime around 1021, Shams ad-Dawla set out on another military expedition, but was again overcome by his old colic as well as other ailments. He died in that year while in retreat. Power ultimately past to his son 'Alī ibn Shams ad-Dawla, who, at the request of his troops and the court, asked Avicenna to continue on as vizier. Avicenna, apparently not as impressed with the son as he had been with the father, delicately refused the offer and then began secret negotiations with the governor of Iṣfahān, 'Alā' ad-Dawla (d. 1041/42). During this time Avicenna secluded himself in the home of a druggist and busied himself with writing the *Cure*, completing over the course of two days an entire outline of the work, which he then began fleshing out, writing at a startling rate of some fifty folio pages a day. During this time he completed, with the exception of the book on animals (corresponding with Aristotle's biological works), the rest of the *Cure*'s books on natural philosophy, its metaphysics, and even started writing the sections on logic. Becoming suspicious of Avicenna's communiqués with 'Alā' ad-Dawla, the political powers in Hamadhān instigated a search for him, whereupon finding him they imprisoned him in the castle of Fardajān some fifty miles away, where he remained for four months, during which time he wrote *The Guidance* (*al-Hidāya*) and a philosophical allegory *Alive son of Awake* (*Ḥayy ibn Yaqẓān*).

As it so turns out, 'Alā' ad-Dawla attacked Hamadhān in 1023, bringing that city to its knees and forcing the prince and his vizier, who had had Avicenna imprisoned, to flee to the safety of Fardajān. Upon 'Alā' ad-Dawla's withdrawal from Hamadhān, the prince and vizier returned, bringing Avicenna with them, now redoubling their efforts to entice him into their service. During this time in Hamadhān, Avicenna stayed with a Shiite friend, to whom he dedicated a work on *Cures of the Heart* (*al-Adwiya l-qalbīya*)—a work whose opening sections provide a wonderful account and practical suggestions for dealing with certain mental or emotional disorders, which were thought at that time to be more closely associated with the heart than the brain—all the while Avicenna also continued to work on the logic of the *Cure*.

Apparently the situation in Hamadhān became unbearable, and so disguised as a Sufi along with his brother and al-Jūzjānī and two slaves, Avicenna and his party sneaked out of that city heading southeast for

Iṣfahān and the court of ʿAlāʾ ad-Dawla. Upon reaching Iṣfahān, Avicenna was greeted warmly, provided with a well-furnished place to stay in the city's district of the dome, and finally, al-Jūzjānī tells us, the master received the respect that he so richly deserved. While in Iṣfahān, Avicenna completed the logical works of the *Cure*, as well as the mathematical books: geometry, arithmetic, astronomy, and music (which, with its emphasis on harmonics and proportions, was included within the mathematical *quadrivium*). Thus, only the biological work of the *Cure* remained to be written. Avicenna finally completed it while accompanying ʿAlāʾ ad-Dawla on a campaign against the city of Sābūr Khwāst, to the west of Iṣfahān and south of Hamadhān. Since ʿAlāʾ ad-Dawla undertook multiple expeditions against Sābūr Khwāst, this would put the completion of the *Cure* at 1027, the traditional dating,[21] or perhaps as late as 1030, for which there is also good evidence.[22] Also during this campaign, Avicenna composed another, shorter, encyclopedia of philosophy and science, the *Salvation* (*an-Najāt*), which while drawing upon many of Avicenna's earlier works—such as *The Shorter Summary on Logic*, which he had written while still in Jurjān—in places also shows evidence of being every bit as, if not more, mature than the thought of the *Cure*. Other works Avicenna wrote while in Iṣfahān include: the *Fair Judgment* (*al-Inṣāf*), and, though only fragments are extant, al-Jūzjānī tells us that it was originally twenty volumes treating approximately 28,000 questions derived from Aristotelian and pseudo-Aristotelian texts;[23] a Persian philosophical encyclopedia for his patron ʿAlāʾ ad-Dawla, which has come to be called the *Book of Science for ʿAlāʾ ad-Dawla* (*Dāneshnāme-yi ʿAlāʾī*), and was the first philosophical work written in Persian following the fall of the old Persian Sassanian Empire; *Pointers and Reminders* (*al-Ishārāt wa-t-tanbīhāt*), which is yet another philosophical encyclopedia that merely provides key premises and main philosophical conclusions, while frequently leaving the actual construction of the arguments to the reader (while it is likely that this work was completed when in Iṣfahān, an earlier Hamadhān date has also been suggested);[24] the single volume work, the *Easterns* (*al-Mashriqīyūn*), which like *Fair Judgment* exists only in a fragmentary form, and which purportedly gave Avicenna's own philosophy without commenting on the tradition; and finally, while in Iṣfahān Avicenna completed the *Canon of Medicine*.

Far from spending all of his time in Iṣfahān with ink and paper at hand, Avicenna also quickly became one of the Amīr's confidants and a member at court. Indeed, every Friday the Amīr held a literary salon that included scholars who were experts in all the arts and sciences and by whom, al-Jūzjānī brags, Avicenna was never outclassed. Although, he relates, there was one evening when an expert in the Arabic language, Abū Manṣūr al-Jabbān, openly criticized Avicenna's knowledge of Arabic, protesting that, while Avicenna was a philosopher and physician, his remarks about philology showed that he was not literate in that subject. Loath to accept such a criticism, Avicenna began plotting a very elaborate joke on the philologist. He immersed himself in the study of philology, Arabic grammar, and rare words, sending as far away as Khurāsān for all the best works on the subject. At the end of three years he had mastered the subject such that few were his equal. He then wrote three odes in different styles of Arabic, brimming with rare and arcane words, which he had bound together and had the volume purposefully distressed so as to look aged. Avicenna then brought the Amīr in on his little joke and asked him to present the volume to al-Jabbān with the story that the Amīr had found the work while hunting in the desert and could al-Jabbān explain it to them. Al-Jabbān was nonplussed as he tried to work his way through the lines and began inventing things to cover up his ignorance, at which point Avicenna chimed in quoting philological authorities by page and line to explain the odes. Realizing that he had been made the butt of a joke, al-Jabbān publicly apologized to Avicenna.

Together with his love for a good laugh—admittedly at somebody else's expense—Avicenna was a bon vivant, enjoying all the pleasures that life has to offer whether intellectual or physical. I have noted that he held drinking parties well into the night, preferring food, drink, and companionship over sleep. When asked about his excesses, Avicenna purportedly said, "God, Who is exalted, has been generous concerning my external and internal powers, so I use every power as it should be used."

One can, however, only burn the proverbial candle at both ends for so long. Eventually Avicenna's lifestyle caught up with him, and probably sometime around 1034 he found himself afflicted with colic; for it was most likely in this year that the Ghaznavid army fought 'Alā' ad-Dawla at Karaj, forcing 'Alā' ad-Dawla to retreat to Īdhaj south of Iṣfahān. Not wanting to be left behind, Avicenna tried to cure himself of his intestinal complaint by administering enemas to himself, sometimes as many as eight times in one day. The result was that he developed ulcers and even began suffering seizures. His situation only deteriorated when, wanting to be done with the colic, he ordered a small measure of celery seed to be added to the enema to expedite its effect. One of the physicians assisting him, either intentionally or unintentionally (al-Jūzjānī is not sure), added more than twice the amount that Avicenna had prescribed, and the result was that it caused Avicenna to suffer internal bleeding. Avicenna's already declining condition was then further exacerbated when a slave, who, al-Jūzjānī alleges, was stealing from Avicenna, overdosed with opium an electuary that Avicenna was taking to help with the seizures. Avicenna collapsed and had to be carried back to Iṣfahān on a stretcher once it was safe to return.

At home, Avicenna continued to administer to himself, but no sooner was he able to walk than he presented himself to 'Alā' ad-Dawla ready for political life again. Moreover, he also once again took up his old habits of sensual excess. Al-Jūzjānī says that Avicenna never completely returned to his former state of health but spent the next four or so years suffering relapses followed by partial recoveries. In late spring of 1037, 'Alā' ad-Dawla set out for Hamadhān with his old friend accompanying him, when Avicenna was once again seized by his recurring complaint. By the time they reached Hamadhān, Avicenna was all but a corpse, and realizing that death was inevitable, he ceased treating himself. Avicenna passed from this world at the age of 58 in Hamadhān where one can still visit his tomb, a monument to one of the truly great intellectual spirits.

2

LOGIC AND SCIENCE

Introduction

Logic for Avicenna is primarily a tool for scientific discourse and discovery. It can perform its function, however, only if there is some connection linking the objects of logic, namely, the universal predicables such as, for example, genus, difference, and species, with the objects of which the practitioner of a given science has immediate access, namely, concrete particulars and their causal interactions. Establishing that there is a close association between the objects of logic and science is a necessary part of Avicenna's philosophic enterprise, inasmuch as Avicenna requires that the premises used in logic and the conclusions derived from them accurately capture the way that the world itself is. In this chapter, I focus primarily on how Avicenna envisions the relation between logic and the sciences. Thus, I do not deal with the technical points of Avicenna's syllogistic, that is to say, Avicennan logic considered as a formal language, except insofar as that is necessary for understanding how Avicenna sees logic as a tool of science.[1] One technical point, however, is worth noting here about Avicenna's system of logic: "Every proposition in Avicenna's system is either temporalized or modalized; there is no proposition which directly captures the non-modalized assertoric proposition used in introductory accounts of the categorical syllogistic."[2] So, for example, an assertoric statement such as

"(Every) human is a rational body" is only the implicit way of stating "(Every) possible human is necessarily a rational body." This fact, I believe, reflects Avicenna's conviction that the basic ontological structure of the world is inherently modal. In other words, everything, from the lowliest mote to the divinity itself, is either necessary or possible in itself, a point that I turn to in depth in chapters 6 and 7.

For now, however, I begin by sketching what might be thought of as Avicenna's metatheory of logic, which underlies his philosophy of science and theory of knowledge ('ilm). Here I consider how Avicenna supports his scientific realism and the theoretical foundation that he provides for the relation between logical notions (such as genus and difference) and the objects of scientific inquiry. Additionally, I look at the role that Avicenna has logical notions play in the scientific enterprise. After a brief consideration of how Avicenna divides the sciences, I turn to two of the most important logical tools that the medieval scientist and philosopher used, namely, definitions and demonstrations, and their relation to causes. In the final section of this chapter, I take up Avicenna's discussion of some of the empirical methods employed by the scientist for acquiring knowledge of definitions and the first principles of demonstrations, at least as those methods appear in his logical works.

The Relation between Logic and Science

When one considers the relation between logic and science, one may view logic as standing to science in the way that language, or perhaps better syntax, stands to a body of thought. Avicenna certainly seems to endorse such a view when he writes, "The relation of this field of study [that is, logic] to inner reflection, which is called 'internal reasoning' is like the relation of grammar to the explicit interpretation, which is called 'external reasoning,' and like the relation of prosody to the poem" (*Introduction*, I.3, 20.14–16). In this respect logic is a tool (*āla*) that guarantees a certain precision in scientific reasoning and even safeguards science against the introduction of hidden assumptions and formal fallacies.

Considered as such, logic, for Avicenna, is essential to a proper and scientific understanding of our world; however, in order fully to appreciate logic's role in the scientific enterprise, one must first understand what Avicenna means by "scientifically understanding a thing." "Science" or "scientific knowledge or understanding" translates the Arabic *ʿilm*, which itself is the common Arabic translation of the Greek *epistēmē*. For Avicenna, scientific knowledge involves two aspects: first, conceptualizing (*taṣawwur*) what is meant when either a term, premise, or even inference or syllogism is presented, and second, verifying (*taṣdīq*, literally "truth-making") what one is conceptualizing.[3] Avicenna describes these two aspects thus:

> Something is scientifically understood (*yuʿlamu*) in two respects: One of them is that it is conceptualized only, such that if it has a name and [the name] is uttered, then what [the name] means is exemplified in the mind, regardless of whether it is true or false, such as when "man" or "do such and such" is said, for when you attend to the meaning of that which you are discussing, then you have conceptualized it. The second is verification together with the conceptualization, and so, for example, when you are told that "all white is an accident," then from this not only do you conceptualize the meaning of this statement, but also you verify that it is such. As for when you have doubts whether or not it is such, you still have conceptualized what is said (for you do not have doubts about what you have neither conceptualized nor understood); however, you have not verified it yet. All verification, then, is together with a conceptualization, but not conversely. In the case of what this [statement] means, the conceptualization informs you that [both] the form of this composite [statement] and that from which it is composed (like "white" and "accident") occur in the mind, whereas [in] verification, this form's relation to the things themselves occurs in the mind, that is, [the form in the mind] maps unto (*muṭābiqa*) [the things themselves] (*Introduction*, 1.3, 17.7–17).

Conceptualization, on the one hand, simply involves understanding the meaning or intention (*maʿná*) of a word or a statement or even how statements work together to form an inference, with no reference to whether that term refers, or the statement is true, or the inference is sound. In verification, on the other hand, not only does the conceptualization of the meaning of a word or form of a statement or inference occur in the mind, but also the object of the conceptualization must map onto or "correspond"[4] with the thing itself.

Bearing in mind Avicenna's distinction between conceptualization and verification let me tentatively distinguish the discipline of logic from the sciences: Logic and the objects of logic, such as genus, difference, and species (the so-called second intelligibles), focus primarily on that aspect of knowledge that concerns conceptualization and the objects of conceptualization,[5] whereas science and the objects of science, such as extramental things and their causal relations, concern that aspect of knowledge that involves verification.

As for what the objects of conceptualization are, Avicenna mentions definitions, definite descriptions, exemplars, and the signs or terms of things (*Introduction*, I.3. 18.5). Most frequently, these objects of conceptualization are composite in nature. Thus, one first must conceptualize the simple or singular terms from which the more complex is composed in order to understand fully the sense of the term or statement in question (*Introduction*, I.4, 21.1–22.12). For Avicenna, following Porphyry's *Isagoge*, the most logically basic or simple terms are universals represented by the genus (*jins*), difference (*faṣl*), species (*naw'*), property (*khāṣṣa*), and accident (*'araḍ*), the so-called predicables.[6] So, for example, when one conceptualizes the term "human" one might recognize that what is meant by it is a composite of the simpler or more logically basic concepts, "animal" and "rational." Here, "animal" represents the genus, namely, that which is common to several individuals varying in species (*Introduction*, I.9), and "rational" represents the difference, namely that which specifies among the generically common things what kind of animal human specifically is (*Introduction*, I.13). Jointly, the genus and difference constitute the definition of the species "human." Similarly, one might conceptualize that humans have the capacity to laugh, where "the capacity to laugh" is a property of humans in that it is something unique to humans even though it does not make up part of the definition of "human." Also, one might conceptualize that "walking" or "black" might belong to humans, where "walking" and "black" are neither constitutive of the definition of human nor unique to humans, but are accidents of, that is, something nonessential to, a human. The propositions composed from the singular terms falling under these universal divisions are in turn constructed into syllogisms or, ideally, demonstrations, which are then used within the sciences.

Although later I shall need to clarify how Avicenna believes that the universal predicables—genus, species, difference, property, and accident—as well as the propositions, and then syllogisms composed from them, relate to the extramental world, let me now explain how he considers them as they exist in conceptualization and how the conceptualization of them is related to logic. To do this I must first consider a topic that might initially seem to have more to do with metaphysics than logic, namely, essences (*māhīyāt*), a topic, let me hasten to add, that is a recurring theme throughout Avicenna's thought. Still, since Avicenna himself introduces essences in his logical works in order to explain the relation between logic and the sciences, I consider this topic here as well. In his *Introduction* to the *Cure*, Avicenna writes about essences:

> The essences of things might be in the concrete particulars of the things or in conceptualization, and so they can be considered in three ways. [One] is the consideration of the essence inasmuch as it is that essence without being related to one of the two [ways] of existence [that is, either in the concrete particulars or conceptualization] and whatever follows upon it insofar as it is such. [Two] it can be considered insofar as it is in concrete particulars, in which case certain accidents that particularize its existing as that follow upon it. [Three] it can be considered insofar as it is with respect to conceptualization, in which case certain accidents that particularize its existing as that follow upon it, as, for example, being a subject and predicate, and also, for example, universality and particularity in predication, as well as essentiality and accidentality in predication, for being essential and being accidental are not in things existing in the external [world] by way of predication, nor is something [in the external world] a logical subject (*mubtada'*) and a logical predicate (*khabar*), nor a premise, a syllogism, and the like (*Introduction*, I.2, 15.1–8).

For now I concentrate on Avicenna's view of essences as they exist in conceptualization. He tells us that when one conceptualizes the essences of things, those essences acquire certain accidental features inasmuch as they are conceptualized, and that these accidental features need not belong to those essences considered either in themselves or as existing in concrete particulars. One of the things that accidentally occurs to essences during conceptualization is that they may be conceptually divided into a part that is a logical subject and a part that is a logical predicate; for example, in the definition of "human," one might consider "human" as the logical subject and "rational animality" as something predicated of that subject. Moreover, Avicenna tells us that during conceptualization essences may be considered as something universal or something particular, although, as will be seen, essences considered in themselves are, for Avicenna, paradoxically neither universal nor particular.

For Avicenna, logic, at least inasmuch as it is relevant to the various sciences, is related to essences precisely insofar as it considers those essences as existing in conceptualization together with the accidental features that accrue to essences when they are conceptualized. Avicenna, thus, continues:

> Now, when we want to think discursively (*natafakkara*) about things [that is, syllogistically] and know them, we must necessarily take them in conceptualization, in which case they necessarily happen to have states that involve the conceptualization. So, we must necessarily consider the states that they have in conceptualization, especially when we want to come to know things by way of discursive reasoning that were unknown, where that [proceeds] from things that are known. Inevitably, things are unknown and likewise known only in relation to the mind. Now, the state and accident that they happen to have so that we [can] move from what is known about them to what is unknown about them is a state and accident that they happen to have with respect to conceptualization, even if what belongs to them in themselves is also something existing together with that. Thus, it is necessary that we know these states: their quantity, quality, and how they are considered in this accidental [way]. . . . This kind of investigation is called the science of logic, namely, the investigation into the aforementioned things inasmuch as from them it leads to making the unknown known as well as what is accidental to them inasmuch as they are only like that (*Introduction*, I.2, 15.9–16.12).

Logic, inasmuch as it is a tool of the sciences, concerns essences along with the accidental features that follow upon their being conceptualized, and then ordering what is known in such a way that one can move from prior knowledge to a new knowledge about something, which was originally not known. Logic considered as a science in itself, however, is primarily interested in the accidental features that occur as a result of being conceptualized, such as being a logical subject or predicate, universal or particular, and the like. That is because it is the accidental features following upon conceptualization that allow logic to classify things under one of the five aforementioned universal predicables; to construct definitions and propositions from those predicables; and then to arrange those propositions so that they form valid syllogisms that allow one to move from the knowledge conveyed in those propositions to conclusions that convey something that had previously been unknown.

I have now considered how Avicenna envisions logic's relation to conceptualization, but this relation raises the deeper question for him about how logic is related to scientific knowledge in its fullest sense, that is, knowledge involving both conceptualization and verification. To put the same point slightly differently, the question is "How do the objects of logic—namely, second intentions, which at least for Avicenna are purely mental objects—relate to the objects that the sciences investigate, namely, things in the world and their causal interactions?"[7] In fact, the problem is even more acute; for Avicenna is a realist inasmuch as for him the goal of philosophical and scientific inquiry is ultimately a type of necessary certainty (*yaqīn*) about the way the world in fact is.[8] Thus, if one cannot be certain that the objects of logic and the conclusions derived from logic actually capture the way the world really is, then logic, for all the precision in reasoning it might bring, would fail to be an adequate tool for doing science. If logic is to play a role in the scientific enterprise, as Avicenna believes that it does, then there must be some bridge, or common element, linking the universal predicables treated in logic with the concrete particulars of immediate experience.

In order to answer this deeper question concerning the relation of logic and science, Avicenna returns to his account of essences. Recall that for him essences exist either in conceptualization or in concrete particulars. Inasmuch as an essence exists externally in concrete particulars, it has accidents different from those that follow upon its existing in conceptualization. More precisely, these accidents, at least in the case of the physical and natural kinds that we see around us here on Earth, follow upon the essence's existing in matter,[9] and by existing in matter, that essence becomes the essence of some concrete particular, as, for example, the essence of human that belongs to me. Among the accidents that follow upon an essence's existing in matter are such things as, for example, walking, being white, having this particularly bodily configuration, coming to be at this particular place and time, and the like. In this respect, the essence of human, for example, that exists in individuals such as Socrates, Plato, and Aristotle exists as a particular owing to the material conditions necessary for the existence of those individuals. Perhaps the most significant difference between the essence existing in matter and the essence existing in the mind, and so conceptualized, is that in the latter case the essence exists as something universal or general, whereas in the former case it exists as something particular or individuated.

In addition to essences' being considered as they exist either in concrete particulars or in conceptualization, Avicenna also believes that they can be considered merely in themselves. Considered in themselves, essences for Avicenna are neither universal nor particular, but potentially one or the other. Thus, Avicenna says, "The animal in itself is a certain thing (*ma 'ná*)— whether as something existing in concrete particulars or something conceptualized in the soul—but in itself it is neither general nor particular" (*Introduction*, I.12, 65.11–12). Despite the apparently paradoxical nature of claming that essences considered in themselves are neither universal nor particular, Avicenna believes that to assert otherwise leads to absurdities. To make his point he presents the following dilemma.

> If [animal] in itself were general [that is, universal]—so that animality is general because it is animality—then necessarily no animal is an individual; rather, every animal is something general. Again, if the animal— because it is animal—were an individual, then only a single individual [animal] would be possible, namely, that animal that animality requires, and it would be impossible that any other thing is an animal. (*Introduction*, I.12, 65.12–16)

The first horn assumes that animal is something essentially universal, that is to say, animal in itself would be the animality common to many animals. As such, being an animal would apply only to many animals, and so paradoxically being an animal could not apply to any animal taken singularly. In other words, given the assumption that animal in itself is necessarily and essentially universal and so holds only of many animals, and no animal taken individually is many animals, no individual animal could essentially be an animal, which Avicenna takes to be absurd. The second horn assumes that animal in itself is essentially particular and as such is not applicable to many, just as being the individual Socrates is not applicable to many. As such, being an animal would apply only to a single individual and anything other than that individual animal would not be an animal essentially, which again Avicenna finds absurd. Therefore, he concludes that to make animal in itself either universal or particular leads to absurd consequences. Thus, animal in itself cannot be either universal or particular. Since the argument can be generalized to any essence considered in itself, essences in themselves are neither general nor particular.

In fact, it is precisely because essences in themselves are potentially both universal and particular that logic is applicable to the scientific enterprise. That is because logical reasoning, which involves mental existents, maps onto scientific understanding, which involves extramental existents, precisely because the objects of logic and science are partially identical for Avicenna inasmuch as the essences of things considered in themselves are common to both types of existence. That follows because when, through a process of abstraction (which I discuss more thoroughly in chapter 4), one strips away various accidental features that follow upon essences inasmuch as they exist, either in the mind or the concrete particulars, and then one considers merely the essences in themselves, what exists in the mind exactly equates with what exists in the world. In a very real sense it is the exact same thing in the mind and in the world, namely, an essence in itself. The essence in itself, then, provides the link between the world as it is and the world as we conceptualize it, guaranteeing that the two in very important ways are identical.

Let me briefly summarize the most salient points thus far. For Avicenna essences exist in either one of two ways: They may exist in concrete particulars, that is to say, extramentally, or they may exist in conceptualization, that is to say, mentally. Although essences always and only exist according to one of these two modes of existence, both modes have something in common, namely, the essence considered in itself, which bridges the gap between the extramental and the mental. So, for example, the essence of animal may exist as instantiated in concrete particulars or it may exist as an intelligible in the mind, and yet, despite the difference between these two ways that animal might exist, both modes of existence have in common the essence of animal considered in itself. It is this commonality that guarantees that in salient ways the objects of the intellect map onto things in the world. Logic as a tool used in the sciences is for Avicenna concerned primarily with those accidental features that accrue to essences considered inasmuch as they are conceptualized. These features involve: the logical classification of things into subjects and predicates, as well as into genera, species, and the like; the various logical modes that hold of propositions formed from these predicables,[10] as, for example, being universal or particular, essential or accidental, necessary or possible, always or sometimes, and the like; and likewise the valid inferential structures that hold between propositions so as to lead to necessary conclusions.

The Division of the Sciences

In contrast with logic, the sciences are not concerned with the conceptual accidents that follow upon essences existing in the mind; rather, the sciences are concerned with the true natures (*ḥaqāʾiq*) of things as those things exist in the world. Consequently, in the *Introduction*, Avicenna divides the sciences according to the various ways that things can be said to exist. The first division Avicenna makes is between "things that either do not exist as a result of our choice and action and those that do exist as a result of our choice and action (*Introduction*, I.2, 12.6–5).[11] Those things over which we have no control belong to the theoretical sciences, while those over which we do have control belong to the practical sciences. Thus, the theoretical sciences seek knowledge simply for knowledge's sake, whereas the practical sciences seek knowledge for the sake of action.

Avicenna further divides theoretical sciences according to whether the object of the science (1) exists necessarily mixed with or involving motion or (2) is not necessarily mixed with motion. Those things that exist necessarily with motion Avicenna again divides into (1.a) those that neither can exist nor be thought of independent of motion and (1.b) those things that, although necessarily existing together with motion, can nonetheless be thought of as independent of motion. Those things that neither subsist nor are conceived without motion, (1.a), must furthermore exist with matter, claims Avicenna, since matter is required if something is to undergo motion or change. For example, a concrete particular animal cannot exist without flesh and blood, which is the matter from which there is an animal, and similarly one cannot conceptualize what an animal is without considering flesh and blood—one simply is not thinking of an animal if one is conceptualizing a bloodless and fleshless thing. In contrast, other things can be conceptualized without matter, (1.b), for example, square-ness, even though the actual existence of a square for Avicenna requires matter. The natural sciences study, (1.a), those existents that are necessarily mixed with motion and that neither can subsist nor be conceptualized without matter. Those existents, (1.b), that can be conceptualized without matter, even though they are necessarily mixed with motion and never subsist without matter, are the subject of the mathematical sciences.

In addition to the objects of the natural sciences and mathematical sciences, there are, (2), those things that are not necessarily mixed with motion. Some of these are necessarily separate from matter and motion, such as God and immaterial substances in general (what Avicenna calls "Intellects," which are akin to what we might think of as angels), while others can but need not be mixed with motion, such as being, unity, multiplicity, and causality. Although one might expect Avicenna to mark off two theoretical sciences given the difference he notes within this division, he in fact subsumes all things whose existence does not require motion under the single science of metaphysics, which simply studies being qua being, a point to which I return in more detail in chapter 6.

In short, for Avicenna, there are three major branches of theoretical sciences: the natural sciences, the mathematical sciences, and the science of metaphysics. These divisions correspond respectively with whether the objects investigated by the science must necessarily subsist as well as be conceptualized together with motion and matter; necessarily subsist together with matter and motion but need not be conceptualized as such; or need neither subsist nor be conceptualized together with matter and motion.

As for the practical sciences, Avicenna's comments are brief. He divides them according to the various spheres of human actions, whether at the state, home, or individual level (*Introduction*, I.2, 14.11–15). Thus, city management or generally politics concerns the concerted actions of a general human populace with shared interests. Home management (that is "economics" in the literal sense) concerns the concerted actions of a private group of humans with shared interests. Finally, ethics is concerned with the concerted actions of the single individual with respect to the flourishing of his or her own soul.

Theoretical Science and the Search for Causes: Definitions

Avicenna's overt interests lie with the theoretical sciences. The goal for Avicenna of these sciences, and what they all share in common, is that they aim at a type of certainty or certitude (*yaqīn*) about the way the world is or why, given the actual makeup of the world, it must be as it is.[12] For Avicenna the only way such certitude about the world can be obtained is through discovering the causes of and causal interrelations among things. Thus, while it is definitions that one conceptualizes, it is that the definitions reflect the true causal natures of things in the world that makes the definitions true, that is to say, the true causal natures of extramental things are the verifiers or truth-makers (*taṣdīq*) of one's definitions of those things. Similarly, while it is syllogisms that can lead one from what is known to knowledge of what was initially unknown, it is only when they map onto or mirror actual causal relations in the world that they are sound and that there is a verification of them. The theoretical sciences for Avicenna are concerned, then, with various kinds of existents, but even more specifically with the relations of causes to existence. In the case of things that have causes, the sciences are interested in uncovering those causes, whereas, should it turn out that something exists that has no cause, such as God, one would be concerned with it primarily as it is a cause of the existence of other things. Given the centrality of causality to Avicenna's conception of science and knowledge, I consider, first, the relation of causes to definitions, and then in the next section the relation of causes to syllogisms.

Avicenna says of scientific definitions that "the primary aim in defining is to indicate by the expression the essence of the thing" (*Introduction*, I.9, 48.3–4). Now, in the case of something absolutely simple or a singular term, Avicenna realizes that it cannot be defined in terms of essential or constitutive elements more basic than the very thing that is being defined. In these cases, one must appeal to relationships, accidents, concomitants, and necessities that belong to the thing in order to explain it. In contrast, Avicenna continues:

> If the account of the thing is something composed of [other] accounts, then it has a definition, namely, the statement that is composed of the accounts from which its essence occurs so that its essence occurs. Because the essential factors (*dhātīyāt*) most proper to the thing are either its genus or its difference ... the definition must be composed of the genus and the difference. So, when the proximate genus and the differences that follow it are present, then the definition occurs from them, as in our defining human as "rational animal." In the case where the genus has no name, [defining] is equally accomplished by means of the definition of [the genus itself], as, for example, if there were no word for animal, then [the definition of human] would be accomplished by the definition of [animal], namely, a body possessing a sensate soul, to which "rational" is then attached. The same holds on the part of the difference. (*Introduction*, I.9, 48.13–49.2)

Definitions, then, are for Avicenna, statements composed of a genus and difference that indicate a thing's essence. The genus, Avicenna defines, as "that which is said of many things varying in species in answer to the question, 'What is it?'" (ibid., 49.13–14); however, since the species is defined by reference to the genus, Avicenna realizes that there is at least the appearance of a circular definition. Thus, at the end of his chapter in the *Introduction* on the genus, he says that "species" can be replaced in the definition of the genus, in which case genus is defined as "that which is said of many things varying in true natures, essences, and essential forms in answer to the question, 'What is it?'" (ibid., 53.13–14).

The difference is the second essential element of a thing's definition; however, Avicenna observes that logicians have recognized three different sorts of differences: the general difference, the proper difference, and the strict difference (*Introduction*, I.13). A general difference is some distinguishing trait that might belong to something, x, at one time and so differentiate x from y, but that at another time might belong to y. For example, one might differentiate Peter from Paul at one time by saying, "Peter is the one sitting" and then later distinguish Paul from Peter, by saying, "Paul is the one sitting," where "sitting" is a general difference. A proper difference is some necessary accident[13] predicated of one sort of thing that differentiates it from another sort of thing, and since "the differentiation occurs by means of an inseparable accident belonging to what is differentiated by it, there never ceases to be a differentiation proper to it" (ibid., 73.9–10). Avicenna gives the example of humans' having "thin hair covering" (*bādī l-bashara*), for having a (relative) thin hair covering, for example, always differentiates a human (even a hirsute one) from, say, an orangutan.

Neither the general nor proper differences are elements in the definition of some natural kind; rather, only the strict difference is used in forming a scientific definition. Avicenna writes of it:

> The difference said in the strict sense constitutes the species, namely, it is that which when joined with the nature of the genus constitutes a species and thereafter whatever necessarily follows on or is accidental to [the difference] necessarily follows on or is accidental to [the species]. So, it is something essential to the nature of the genus constituting a species in existence, namely, it fixes, divides, and individuates [the nature of the genus], for example, like the rationality belonging to human. This difference is differentiated from all the other things that are together with it in that it is that which primarily encounters the nature of the genus and so makes it determinate and divides it; and [in] that the rest of those attach to that general nature only after this [difference] has encountered [the genus] and divides it. Thus, [that general nature] is prepared for the necessity of what necessarily follows upon it and the concomitance of what is concomitant with it, for they necessarily follow it and are concomitant with it only after the specification. This is like rationality's belonging to human; for after the potency [or "faculty"] called the "rational soul" is joined with the matter—and so at that time the animal becomes rational—[the animal] is prepared to receive scientific and technical knowledge, such as

navigation, husbandry, and writing. It is also prepared to wonder and so to laugh at oddities and to cry and to feel embarrassment and to do the other things that belong to being human. It is not the case that any one of these things was joined with animality in the mind first, and then on account of that the animal came to be prepared in order that it be rational; rather, the universal preparation and the universal human potency are that by which [the animal] is called "rational," whereas these latter are its nurslings and dependents. You know that by the least amount of reflection. Also, you can discover that were it not that some initial potency is something prepared to distinguish and to understand, which already belonged to the human, then [the animal] would not have these latter particular preparations. That potency is called "reason" and so by it one becomes rational. This is the difference that essentially constitutes the nature of the species. (*Introduction*, I.13, 74.11–75.9)

Avicenna goes on and technically defines the strict difference much as he defined genus, namely, as "the universal singular said of the species in answer to the question, 'What kind of thing is it in itself within its genus?'" (ibid., 76.8–9). The sciences again are primarily, although not exclusively, concerned with identifying those features of things that correspond with strict differences rather than the other types of differences.

As a general rule, since definitions are supposed to capture the way things actually are in the world, the elements constituting the definition of the species must indicate positive causal factors belonging to things rather than negative aspects.[14] Thus, Avicenna explicitly contradicts Porphyry, arguing that negative differences are not constitutive of a definition, but rather follow upon a consideration of the positive causal features that do in fact constitute the thing itself.[15] "Negations," Avicenna maintains:

> are concomitants belonging to things relative to a consideration of certain (positive) accounts that do not belong to [the things]. So, [for example], "irrational" is something intellectually understood by considering rational, in which case the species, its (positive) account, and its difference that belongs to it are in the thing itself, and thereafter it is entailed of it that it is not described by anything else. (*Introduction*, I.13, 79.3–5)

Predicating a negation, such as "irrational," of something, then, is subsequent on a consideration of those features or causal factors that actually belong to a thing. In other words, a negation is predicated of something just in case some positive account, such as "rational," fails to belong to that thing.[16]

The constitutive elements that go into making a definition, namely, the genus and difference, then, must for Avicenna be positive factors that mirror real features of the world. There is also an important corollary that can be drawn from Avicenna's point about the use of negations in defining the essences of things, namely, if something that purportedly has an essence cannot be defined in terms of positive factors, then, in fact, what one is conceptualizing is a vacuous concept. (This point becomes important when Avicenna attacks the notion of a void in his *Physics*, for, as will become clear, a key element in his critique of that notion is that no scientifically adequate definition can be given for a void in positive terms, and thus the name "void" does not refer.)

The positive features in the world with which genus and difference correspond are for Avicenna a thing's material and formal causes respectively. Still, Avicenna argues that one cannot simply identify the logical notions of genus and difference with the material and formal causes that exist in external concrete particulars. Indeed, doing so, observes Avicenna, has led to philosophical confusion. He relates two cases of such confusion.

> One of the greatest causes of confusion concerns how animal is a cause of the human's being corporeal, given what we have claimed about that, for as long as the human is not corporeal, then, neither is it an animal. Or, how is [animal] a cause of the human's having sensation, when as long as the human does not have sensation, then neither is it an animal, because corporeality and sensation are both causes of the existence of animal? As long as something does not exist, then the existence of whatever depends upon it does not exist. Also, when the account of the soul is joined with the account of body, such that it is the composite of the two that is an animal, not just one of them, then how can the body be predicated of the animal? In that case, it would be just like predicating the single thing of the two. Similarly, how can being animate be predicated of the animal, in which case it would be just like predicating the single thing of the two? (*Book of Demonstration*, I.10, 49.4-10)

Here, Avicenna notes two puzzles. The first puzzle arises from the fact that Avicenna believes that being an animal is a cause, of, and so prior to, the human's body, but if one considers the logical relations between "animal" and "body" it would seem that "body" is the cause, and so prior to "animal," for "animal" is defined as "a *body* having sensation," where "body" functions as the genus and "having sensation" functions as the difference. "Body" and "having sensation," then, seem to be explanatory and so prior to the species "animal" rather than animal's somehow being their cause. In the second puzzle, since again "animal" is defined as "a body having sensation," to predicate "body" of "animal" is logically equivalent to saying "sensate body is body." In this case the concern is that a certain whole, namely, "sensate-body," is being identified with a part, namely, "body," whereas a whole clearly cannot be identical with one of its parts.

The puzzles are resolved, claims Avicenna, once one distinguishes the body qua matter from the body qua genus, and similarly once one distinguishes sensation qua form and sensation qua difference.[17] In general, the distinction between matter/form and genus/difference concerns whether what is signified is taken in an exclusive way or nonexclusive way respectively. I focus primarily on Avicenna's discussion of body qua matter and body qua genus, although similar remarks can be made about form and difference.

The body as matter is for Avicenna body insofar as only length, breadth, and depth are signified and nothing else. It is, as it were, that which has bare corporeality. Any other qualifications are additional to the body as matter. In this respect, one might think of the body qua matter as the thinnest possible account of what it is to be a body, for, as will be seen in the next chapter, being three-dimensional is for Avicenna the hallmark of being a body. In contrast, the body considered qua genus is an account that signifies not only three dimensions, but also, according to Avicenna, every other possible description or account that one might associate with the term "body" when one conceptualizes various corporeal things. Indeed, Avicenna invites his reader to include within the meaning of "body," understood as genus, every possible account compatible with being a body, even if those accounts might mutually exclude one another in reality, such as being animate or inanimate, sensate or insensate, and rational or irrational. In this respect, one might think of the body qua genus as the thickest possible account of body that is still compatible with the notion of body.

Given this distinction between matter and genus (and the analogous one for form and difference), Avicenna claims that "whatever is in the sense of the matter or the form is simply not predicated and is not taken as middle terms in their essence and definition, but as causes are taken as middle terms,[18] namely, in the way we shall explain latter" (*Book of Demonstration*, I.10, 49.12–14). He argues for this point thus:

> Since the body in the first sense [that is, as matter] is a part of the substance composed of body and the forms that are posterior to the corporeality

that is in the sense of matter, it is not something predicated, because that whole is not some abstract substance possessing only length, breadth, and depth. This second [that is, body as genus], however, is something predicated of whatever is a composite of matter and form, whether one form or a thousand, among which will be [having] three dimensions. Thus, [the body qua genus] is predicated of what is composed of corporeality (which is like matter) and soul, because the whole of that is a substance. (*Book of Demonstration*, I.10, 50.4–8)

Body qua matter, and similarly sensation qua form, cannot be predicated of animal since both are constitutive parts or elements that jointly cause the animal, and so stand to the animal as constitutive or essential parts stand to the whole. Thus, to predicate body qua matter or sensation qua form of the animal is tantamount to making the part equivalent to the whole, which it obviously is not. In contrast, when one considers the body qua genus, one considers body in its thickest sense and as such it contains every possible account that is included in one's conceptualization of body. In other words, for Avicenna the logical notion of a genus implicitly contains all the ways that the genus can be differentiated and so implicitly contains all of its species. It is precisely because body qua genus does implicitly contain the species "animal" that "body" can be predicated of "animal," for such predication is similar to saying that the whole includes one of its parts. A similar account holds for difference as well.

Although Avicenna believes that one must distinguish the causal notions of matter and form from the logical notions of genus and difference, I noted in the first section of this chapter that he also insists that there is, nonetheless, a close relation between them as well, for he believes that the causal elements in the essences of concrete particulars furnish the content of the universal predicables conceptualized in the mind. It is precisely because one has discovered, for example, that animal body and rationality are the matter and form respectively of the essence of concrete particular humans that the essence of human conceptualized in the mind in terms of the genus "animal" and the difference "rationality" provides the scientific definition of "human" as "rational animal." In other words, because the logical ordering mirrors the causal ordering, logical definitions in terms of genus and difference map onto the true natures of thing, and thus can function as proxies in logical inferences. Since any given determinate kind existing in the physical world has certain material and formal causes, the effect of this mirroring of the ontological ordering by the logical ordering is that that kind must likewise have a definition in terms of the logical counterparts of matter and form, namely, in terms of genus and difference. Avicenna observes, "These differences, though trivial in themselves, are useful in the sciences, and should not be undervalued" (*Book of Demonstration*, I.10, 52.22). How they can be useful becomes clear in the next chapter when I consider one of Avicenna's refutations of the existence of a void.

Theoretical Science and the Search for Causes: Demonstrations

A second aspect of Avicenna's theory of science concerns how causes are related to the syllogism and more specifically to the demonstrative syllogism (*burhān*), which according to Avicenna is "a syllogism constituting certainty," (*Book of Demonstration*, I.7, 31.11). As such it begins with necessary and certain premises from which is deduced not only that the conclusion is the case, but also that the conclusion cannot not be the case (ibid., I.7, 31.7–8).[19] The demonstrative syllogism, then, makes clear the necessity or inevitableness obtaining between the subject matter designated by the syllogism's major and minor terms.

Avicenna divides demonstrative knowledge itself into two categories depending upon the type of demonstration employed. Thus, he distinguishes between what came to be known in the Latin tradition as the demonstration *propter quid*, that is, the demonstration giving "the reason why" (*burhān lima*) or simply the demonstration-why, and what was known as the demonstration *quia*, that is, the demonstration giving "the fact that" (*burhān al-inna*), or simply the demonstration-that.[20] The demonstration-that is further divided into two subspecies: a demonstration-that which leads from one correlative effect to another correlative effect, called an "absolute demonstration-that" (*burhān al-inna ʿalá l-iṭlāq*), and a demonstration-that which leads from an effect to the cause, called an "indication" (*dalīl*).

Concerning the two types of demonstration-that, Avicenna suffices himself with providing definitions and examples of both. Thus, the absolute demonstration-that "accords with the existing middle term's neither being a cause nor an effect of the major's existing in the minor; rather, [the middle term] is something related to or coextensive with [the major term] in relation to its cause, where [the middle term] accidentally accompanies it or something else simultaneous with it in the nature" (ibid., I.7, 32.7–10). He gives the following syllogism as an example: Whoever exhibits cloudy viscous urine is feared to have encephalitis; this individual (who is suffering from a fever) has exhibited such symptoms; thus, this individual is feared to have encephalitis. In this case, notes Avicenna, neither the symptoms nor having encephalitis is the cause or the effect of the other; rather, they are both effects of some unstated cause, which Avicenna identifies with the motion of heated humors toward the head and their evacuation from it. What is important to note about the absolute demonstration-that is that even though the syllogism neither proceeds from nor leads to a cause, there nonetheless is a necessary, natural causal relation between the two terms, namely, they both are effects of some common cause, even if that cause is not made explicitly clear in the syllogism. Had there been no such causal relation, and the two terms had been merely coincidental accidents, then there would have been no demonstration.

The second of the two demonstrations-that, namely, an indication, "accords with [the middle term's] existing as the effect of the major's existing in the minor" (ibid., I.7, 32.10). Here Avicenna provides several examples. For instance, every recurring tertian fever is a result of bile's putrefaction; the individual has a recurring tertian fever; therefore, his fever is a result of bile's putrefaction. Similar examples are given concerning the Moon's relative position in relation to the Sun and the Moon's various phases; the Moon's being eclipsed when it passes between the Earth and the Sun; and wood's burning when put into contact with fire. What is common to all of these examples is that one starts from some effect and then concludes to the effect's cause.

Demonstration in the most proper sense according to Avicenna is the demonstration-why. This demonstration is a syllogism "that gives the cause with respect to both issues [namely, *that* such and such is the case as well as *why* such and such is the case], such that [the syllogism's] middle term is like the cause that verifies (*taṣdīq*) the major's belonging to the minor (or its denial),[21] and so it is a cause of the major's belonging to the minor (or its denial)" (ibid., I.7, 32.5–7). In his examples of the demonstration-why, Avicenna returns to his earlier examples used in clarifying an indication, but now he converts the examples such that the middle term is the cause of the effect. So, for example: Whoever suffers from a putrefaction of bile owing to the congestion of bile and the pores' being obstructed is suffering from a recurring tertian fever; this individual is suffering from such putrefaction of the bile, therefore, this individual is suffering from a recurring tertian fever. Here, the major premise should be understood as a definition of "tertian fever," namely, as a "putrefaction of bile" (genus) brought about by "a congestion and obstruction of the pores" (difference), where these are the causes of a tertian fever. In short, the demonstration-why, like the demonstration-that, inherently involves necessary, natural, causal relations. Unlike the demonstration-that, however, the demonstration-why makes clear exactly what that causal relation is.

As Avicenna's examples suggest, he believes that there is an inherent relation between demonstrations and causes; for demonstrations make clear the causes of a given phenomenon, while a knowledge of a phenomenon's causes guarantees necessary, perpetual certainty, which Avicenna takes to be the goal of scientific knowledge. In fact, argues Avicenna, this certitude is ensured only when one comes to know the causes of the phenomenon. As for defending the existence of such causal relations, in a very real sense Avicenna simply takes the reality of natural causality for granted as part of his realism. Indeed, for Avicenna to deny natural causal relations (as certain Islamic speculative theologians in fact did) would make the events in the world matters of mere happenstance and arbitrary and so would leave unexplained the manifest regular and orderly occurrence of events. In effect, for Avicenna to deny causal relations would undermine the very possibility of science understood as an investigation and explanation of the world's order, a position that Avicenna simply will not countenance.[22]

To summarize this section briefly, for Avicenna the goal of science is to obtain a type of certitude about the way the world is. One way such certitude can be reached is through demonstrations, that is, sound syllogisms, which provide necessary and eternal knowledge. In order to provide such knowledge, maintains Avicenna, the propositions used in demonstrations must mirror the actual causal relations in the world, ideally by direct causal relations, as in the case of demonstrations-why, or at the very least involving indirect causal relations, as in the two cases of demonstrations-that. In subsequent chapters (especially chapters 3 and 7), I discuss the various types of causal relations investigated in scientific research, but for now the most important ones are formal and material causation, since it is these causes that are reflected in the definitions that give the essence of a thing.

Acquiring the Definitions and First Principles of Science

As has been seen, demonstrations can provide certitude according to Avicenna because they reflect the actual causal structure of the world; however, like Aristotle before him, Avicenna denies that everything can be demonstrated (*Book of Demonstration*, II.1). That is because, argues Avicenna, who is himself following Aristotle's *Posterior Analytics*, I 3, such a position would require that in order to know anything, either one must have gone through an infinite number of demonstrations (for the principles of any demonstration would then themselves need to be demonstrated ad infinitum) or one has given a circular demonstration (for one and the same premise would have to be a principle and conclusion of itself to stop the regress). Both alternatives Avicenna complains would undermine the practice of science itself. In order to avoid either of these two outcomes, Avicenna maintains that demonstrative knowledge must proceed from prior knowledge or the so-called first principles of a science. These first principles are the existence claims and definitions of a given science and are not demonstrated within the science itself—though in some cases, although not all, they may be demonstrated in a "higher science." Instead, relative to a given science, its first principles must simply be posited by that science without demonstration (*Book of Demonstration*, I.12, 58.14–17).

Avicenna frequently states throughout the *Book of Demonstration* that a discussion of how the first principles of a science are acquired belongs properly to the science of psychology, for an account of how one acquires such principles for Avicenna ultimately involves describing the various (properfunctioning) psychological and cognitive processes involved in human thought, as well as any natural posits required to explain what we as human cognizers in fact do. Indeed, in chapters 4 and 5, I consider in some detail the psychology underlying Avicenna's theory of concept formation and the acquisition of scientific knowledge. For now, however, I merely focus on Avicenna's discussion of two possible methodologies for acquiring first principles, namely, induction, or, more specifically, certain criticisms and limitations Avicenna imposes on its use, and methodic experience.[23]

Induction

While like Aristotle before him Avicenna takes a staunchly empirical approach to the sciences (or at least the natural sciences),[24] it is on the subject of induction, which is frequently considered a cornerstone of empiricism, that Avicenna most notably parts way with Aristotle and his epistemology and philosophy of science. Here it should be noted that the conception of induction with which Avicenna takes issue is not the naïve notion of induction that simply involves making a generalization from a limited number of observations; rather, Avicenna is critiquing a technical Aristotelian notion of induction (Gk. *epagōgē*, Ar. *istiqrā'*), which I discuss more fully below. This technical Aristotelian sense of induction involves, not only generalizations, but also a formal syllogism, and is intended to establish the first principles of a science. In contrast with Aristotle, Avicenna is overall skeptical of the merit of induction as an adequate tool for scientific inquiry (at least as Aristotle presented induction in *Prior Analytics*, II 23). Avicenna describes induction in the following lackluster terms:

> When the particular instances [of the first principle] are considered inductively, they call the intellect's attention to the belief of the universal; however, the induction that proceeds from sensory perception and the particulars in no way makes belief of a universal necessary, but only draws attention to it. For example, [when] two things both touch a third thing, but not each another, they require that that [third] thing is divisible. This aforementioned claim, however, may not be something established in the soul as well as it is sensibly perceived in its particular instances, which the intellect does notice and believes. (*Book of Demonstration*, III.5, 161.14–18)

For Avicenna, induction is at most merely a pointer that draws one's attention to the pertinent facts surrounding some state of affairs. Induction, then, does not make clear what the cause of that state of affairs is or even that there must be a cause. Although Avicenna's reservations toward induction might incline one to think that he is being anti-empirical in his approach to science, such an assessment would be wrong.

Both in the *Book of Demonstration* (I.9) and the *Book of Syllogism* (IX.22), Avicenna lays out what he finds problematic about induction. Induction as described by Aristotle in his logical works has two elements: One involves the sensible content of induction, and the other the rational structure of induction, namely, the syllogism associated with induction. If Aristotelian induction is to provide one with the necessary and certain first principles of a science, then the necessity and certainty of the conclusion of an inductive syllogism must be due either to its sensory element or its rational element.

Avicenna begins his critique of induction by first noting that the purported necessity and certainty that induction is supposed to provide about causal relations cannot be known solely through induction's sensory element, for, in good empirical fashion, Avicenna recognizes that the necessity of a causal relation and the certainty about it are not direct objects of sensation. If the necessity and certainty are due to induction's rational component, continues Avicenna, the syllogism associated with induction should not be question begging. Yet, complains Avicenna, in the scientifically interesting cases of induction one of the premises of the inductive syllogism is always better known than its conclusion, and so the induction is neither informative nor capable of making clear a first principle of a science.

Let us consider Avicenna's argument for this last claim. At IX.22 in the *Book of Syllogism*, Avicenna claims that induction in fact is successful in those cases where its divisions are exhaustive, as, for example, when animal is divided into mortal and immortal, or rational and irrational. The difficulty arises when one uses some other type of division that does not involve contradictory pairs. So, to take an example from Aristotle's *Prior Analytics*, II 23, assume one divides long-lived animals into horses, oxen, humans, and the like, and then one wants to use this premise to make clear inductively the cause of these animals' longevity. Thus, one might reason (as Aristotle in fact did) as follows:

1. all horses, oxen, humans, and the like are gall-less (major premise);
2. long-lived animals are horses, oxen, humans, and the like (minor premise);
3. therefore, long-lived animals are gall-less.

Avicenna's earlier point concerning exhaustive division was that the induction works only if one can be certain that one has correctly identified all and only long-lived animals in the minor premise. One could be certain of this identification, Avicenna however maintains, only if one knew what it is about this set of animals that guarantees that they and only they are the long-lived ones, but this knowledge would simply be to know the cause of these animals' longevity, the very premise one wanted to make clear. Thus, it cannot be induction's rational element, at least in the scientifically interesting cases of induction, that explains the purported necessity and certainty of its conclusion; for, complains Avicenna, the syllogism is question begging.

The necessity and certainty required by scientific knowledge, then, cannot arise from either induction's sensory or rational elements. Again, Avicenna is not dismissing Aristotelian induction outright; it certainly has its place in science for him as a means of drawing one's attention to pertinent facts. Still, if induction is intended to establish the facts about some causal relation and so provide the first principle of a science, Avicenna contends that it simply fails.

Methodic Experience

Avicenna instead wants to replace the technical Aristotelian notion of induction with his own conception of methodic experience (*tajriba*), which like induction has both a sensory and rational, or syllogistic, component. Unlike induction, however, methodic experience does not purport to explain *why*, that is, what the causal relation is between two terms of a first principle, but only to identify *that* there is a causal relation between those terms.

> [Methodic experience] is not like induction, for induction, in chancing upon the particulars, does not occasion universal certain knowledge, even if it might be something drawing attention [to it], whereas methodic experience does. Indeed, methodic experience is like the observer and perceiver seeing and sensing that certain things belong to a single kind upon which follows the occurrence of a given action or affection. So, when that is repeated numerous times, the intellect judges that this is an essential feature belonging to this thing that is not some mere chance occurrence, since that which is by chance does not occur always. An example of this is our judgment that a magnet attracts iron, and that scammony purges bile. (*Book of Demonstration*, III.5, 161.20–162.3)

In methodic experience, there is the regular observation that two things always occur together without any falsifying evidence to the contrary. The regularity of the observation provides the basis for a hidden syllogism, claims Avicenna, namely that whenever two things always occur together without any falsifying instance there must be a cause relating those two things, and since these two things regularly occur together, there must be a cause relating them. So, for example, one always observes a magnet's attracting iron. Given the regularity of this occurrence, there must be some causal relation, maintains Avicenna, that exists between the magnet's attraction and the iron, otherwise the attraction would not always occur. Avicenna's general idea is that if there were absolutely nothing linking two regularly joined events or things to one another, then the laws of probability would dictate that the two should on occasion not occur together, which is contrary to observation. Methodic experience has not explained what this causal relation is, but it has established that there is such a relation. Thus, given the fact that propositions obtained from methodic experience must involve some causal relation between the terms, such propositions, claims Avicenna, can still be used as first principles of a science in order to explain other phenomena.

As for the knowledge acquired through methodic experience, Avicenna is quite insistent that although the knowledge so obtained is necessary, the necessity in question is only conditional necessity and applies only to the domain under which the examination was made.

> [Methodic experience] does not provide *absolute* universal syllogistic knowledge, but only *conditional* universal [knowledge], that is, this thing that is repeated to the senses adheres to its nature as an ongoing thing with respect to the domain in which it is repeated to the senses (unless there is an obstacle). Thus, [the knowledge] is universal with this condition but not absolutely universal. (*Book of Demonstration*, I.9, 46.20–23)

It is because knowledge of the first principles acquired through methodic experience is limited to the domain under which the examination took place that Avicenna further warns us that in light of new empirical data one may need to revise one's claims. For example, he considers the case of the scientist who has repeatedly observed that on administering scammony there is always an accompanying purging of bile.

> We also do not preclude that in some country a disposition and special attribute are associated with scammony not to purge (or there is absent in it a disposition and special attribute); however, it is necessary that our judgment based upon methodic experience is that the scammony commonplace to us and perceived [before us], either from its essence or from the nature in it, purges bile (unless it opposed by an obstacle). (ibid., I.9, 48.4–7)

Thus, the only thing that one can legitimately conclude from methodic experience, according to Avicenna, is that those varieties of scammony that have been tested always lead to this expected result; however, should new varieties of scammony become available that do not conform to the earlier findings, the initial hypothesis must be revised, and of course this point can be extended to all cases of knowledge acquired through methodic experience. In the end, while it is true that Avicenna was critical of the notion of induction that he inherited and wanted to replace it with his own conception of methodic experience, his conception of methodic experience is perhaps closer to our own understanding of what induction is than the earlier account of it that he wanted to replace.

To conclude this chapter, for Avicenna scientific knowledge involves two facets: conceptualization and verification. Logic treats those universal features of essences that follow upon their being conceptualized and so existing in the mind, whereas the various sciences focus on verification, namely, discovering and making clear those causal relations among essences inasmuch as they exist concretely in the world. The two most important logical tools used in the various sciences are for Avicenna definitions and demonstrations, both of which are closely related to the causes sought in the various sciences. Thus, the genus and difference that constitute a definition reflect, but are not wholly identical with, the material and formal causes of a thing's essence, while the middle term of a demonstration either expresses, or in some sense is connected with, the causal relation linking the terms of a demonstration. In his works specifically dedicated to philosophy of science, Avicenna outlines a number of methods that the scientist uses to discover these causal relations. What should be emphasized about these methods, as well as about Avicenna's general attitude toward science, are the strong empirical or naturalistic elements as opposed to so-called rational or a priori elements. In the next chapter, I consider how Avicenna uses a number of the logical points developed in his *Book of Demonstration* to tackle and to resolve problems in natural philosophy, that is, the science of physics.

3

NATURAL SCIENCE

Introduction

In the previous chapter I looked at Avicenna's division of the sciences. I observed there that for Avicenna natural philosophy includes those sciences that investigate things that are mixed with motion. Broadly, the natural sciences can be divided further into those that investigate inanimate things, as, for example, the sciences of cosmology and meteorology, and those that investigate animate things, as, for example, the sciences of biology and psychology. In subsequent chapters, I shall treat various issues proper to certain of these special physical sciences. In the present chapter, however, I focus on Avicenna's discussion of the most general principles of natural things, that is, those principles assumed by all of the special physical sciences. To this end, I begin by looking at Avicenna's enumeration and account of the principles of nature, that is, the causes required for there to be motion, regardless of whether it is the motion of something animate or inanimate. After considering the principles of nature, I turn to Avicenna's analysis of motion and certain purported necessary conditions needed if there is to be motion, such as place, void, time, and the continuum as well as Avicenna's arguments against atomism. I then quickly consider Avicenna's theory of *mayl*, or inclination, and its role in his dynamics, and conclude with his account of substantial change, the elements, and his initial introduction of a "Giver of Forms."

The Principles of Nature

At the start of Avicenna's *Physics*, he reiterates that the subject of natural science is "perceptible body from the perspective of being subject to change" (*Physics*, I.1, 7.7–8). Natural science at its most general level investigates the principles of such bodies: first those causes that account for the body's being a body, and then any additional causes (if there are any) that might be needed to explain the change or motion in those bodies.

In most general terms, a "natural body" is for Avicenna any substance in which one can posit the three dimensions length, breadth, and depth (*Physics*, I.2, 13.4–6). A natural body must have both that which explains its being susceptible to or potentially having three dimensions (as well as potentially having any subsequent specifications, attributes, or the like) and that which explains its actually having three dimensions (and again any subsequent specifications, attributes, or the like).[1] Of these two aspects of natural bodies, that is, their being susceptible to and then their actually having dimensions, Avicenna writes:

> In the view of [the natural philosopher], these most deserve to be called "principles." They are two: The first is like the wood of the bed, and the other is [like] the form and shape of bed-ness in the bed. What is like the wood of the bed is called, according to various considerations, "prime matter," "subject," "matter," "constituent," and "element," while what is like the form of the bed-ness is called "form." (*Physics*, I.2, 13.15–14.1)

Form and matter, for Avicenna, constitute the "internal principles" for the existence and subsistence of natural bodies.

Again, the general science of physics wants to analyze its concepts into the most basic terms used in explaining the physical world. Thus, form and matter here need to be analyzed in terms of the simplest accounts required for the existence of a natural body. As for the form, this is the form of corporeality, which is that form that explains the natural body's actually having dimensions. Avicenna says of the form of corporeality that it is either prior to all other generic, specific, and accidental forms that might inform matter, or it is joined with them and is not separate from them. The distinction that Avicenna is drawing here is the same one he drew in his logical works between body qua matter and body qua genus, for one can consider body either as possessing only tri-dimensionality, in which case the form of corporeality is prior to all other forms, or as encompassing all forms compatible with being a body, one of which is the form of corporeality. In either case, it is clear that whatever holds of corporeality likewise holds of natural bodies. In other places in his *Physics* and *Metaphysics*, Avicenna mentions other features that follow upon the form of corporeality, such as being divisible, localized, measurable, and even impenetrable, all of which correspondingly belong to natural bodies.

The most general account of matter employed by the natural philosopher is that of "first matter" or "prime matter" (*hayūlá*, the Arabic transliteration of the Greek *hulē*). It, as its name implies, is the first or most basic matter from which composite or more complex material things are built, or, in other words, it is what is in potency to being any of the various kinds of physical things that we see around us. Avicenna says of it, "when considered in itself without being related to anything else [prime matter] is found to be in itself devoid of these [generic, specific, or accidental] forms in actuality, while, nonetheless, having the character of receiving this [or that] form or joining with it" (*Physics*, I.1, 14.4–5). This is not to say, and Avicenna is adamant on this point, that matter is ever wholly stripped of form subsisting on its own. "It is not something actually existing except for when the form is present, in which case it exists actually through the form. If it were not the case that the form departs from it only with the arrival of another form that substitutes for it and takes its place, then matter would actually cease to be" (ibid., I.1, 14.12–14). The reason why Avicenna believes that the matter would cease to be if it lacked a form is that for him the form explains the actual existence belonging to a thing, whereas the matter explains a thing's potential existence, where "potentiality" is understood as preparedness to receive a form that is different from the form presently existing in the thing. Thus, if matter were ever wholly devoid of all forms, it would not *actually* be anything, that is, it would not exist, since any actual existence it has must come from a form. (When I consider Avicenna's account of creation in chapter 7, I consider his arguments for associating matter with potentiality more fully.)

Form and matter, then, are those internal principles that constitute a natural body. The natural body qua natural body also has additional principles inasmuch as it is subject to generation and corruption or change in general. One of these, which Avicenna acknowledges is not a "principle" in the strict sense, is privation. Avicenna's reservations about calling privation a principle almost certainly stem from his own understanding of what a principle is, namely, "anything that already has a *completed existence* in itself (whether from itself or another) and from which the existence of another thing occurs and subsists by it" (*Salvation*, "Metaphysics," I.12, 518.8–10). This understanding of what a principle is arises from his conception of science as an attempt to uncover those positive causal factors that underlie the apparent order one sees in the world. Privation as a type of negation, then, would seem incapable of mapping onto anything in the world, and so strictly speaking cannot be a cause or play any real positive role in causal processes. Still, continues Avicenna, whatever else one might think, it must be conceded that:

> privation is a condition with respect to something's being either subject to change or perfection. [That is] because if there were no privation, it would be impossible for there to be things subject to change and perfection; rather, the [same] perfection and form would always be present. Hence, to the extent that something truly is subject to change and perfection it requires a preceding privation, whereas privation, in that it is a privation, does not require the presence of change and perfection, in which case the elimination of privation necessitates the elimination of what is subject to change and perfection as such, whereas the elimination of what is subject to change and perfection does not necessitate the elimination of privation. So, in this way privation is prior and so is a principle, if a principle is whatever must exist, no matter how so, in order that some other thing exists, but not conversely. (*Physics*, I.2, 17.9–14)

Here, Avicenna, following Aristotle upon whose account of the principles of nature Avicenna's own relies heavily, explains the obvious fact that change requires a preceding privation or lack. For if something already possesses some trait, and so is not lacking it, it cannot change so as to acquire that trait. For example, if something is black, it cannot change so as to become black, since it already is black. Privation, then, is something from which change or motion proceeds, and so in that respect might be thought of as a principle of change. In the end, however, Avicenna, unlike Aristotle, prefers to think of privation not as a principle of change, but merely as something needed for change (*muḥtāj ilayhi*), which is joined to prime matter considered as potentiality. Thus, he writes the following of the privation investigated in the natural sciences:

> The form is different from the privation in that the form is in itself an essence that adds to the existence belonging to the prime matter, whereas the privation does not add to the existence that belongs to prime matter. Instead, prime matter is associated with [privation] as its state of being

correlated with this form, when [that form] does not exist, but the potentiality to receive it does. This privation is not absolute privation, but
rather a privation that has some manner of existing. It is a privation of
something concurrent with a configuration and a disposition for [that
thing] in a determinate matter. So, [for example], human does not come
out of what is wholly not-human; rather, it comes out of what is not-
human in something that is receptive to [being] human. So, generation is
by way of the form not the privation, whereas corruption is by way of the
privation not the form. (*Physics*, I.2, 18.13–17)

Thus, the privation in question is not something absolutely nonexistent, but is
a relative nonexistence correlated with the potentiality inherent in matter.

In addition to form and matter (the so-called internal principles) as well
as privation, Avicenna also includes two further natural causes that are required if a natural body is to undergo change, perfection, generation, or the
like. These are the so-called external principles, namely, the efficient and
final causes. These principles are called "external" for two reasons. First,
unlike matter and form, they need not be immediately present in the natural
body for its continued existence and subsistence, but are only required inasmuch as the natural body is undergoing some type of motion or change.
Second, although Avicenna, following Aristotle, believes that frequently the
immediate efficient and final causes reduce to the nature of the body, or,
more precisely, the natural body's formal cause, the remote or ultimate efficient and final cause refer to something external to the natural body, namely,
God, who, for Avicenna, is beyond the purview of natural philosophy.

Here Avicenna believes that a brief aside is warranted, for unlike Aristotle
who made God, or more precisely the Unmoved Mover, the apex of the
natural philosopher's investigation, Avicenna clearly believes that a discussion of God as the First Principle of all natural things must await metaphysics.
The reason that he gives for this deviation from Aristotle is that natural
philosophy investigates those things possessing natures and so subject to
change and motion. The First Principle inasmuch as it is the cause of everything possessing a nature cannot itself possess a nature; for "if the [First]
Principle were to possess a nature, it would then either be a principle of itself—which is absurd—or something other than it would be [its] efficient
principle—which is a contradiction. Given that this is the case, the natural
philosopher has no way to investigate it, since it is not in any way mixed with
natures" (*Physics*, I.2, 16.6–8). In short, the natural sciences do not investigate
every efficient and final cause, but only those possessing natures.

As for Avicenna's general characterization of the efficient and final causes, he describes them thus:

> The efficient cause is what imprinted the form belonging to bodies into their matter. So, it is through the form that the matter came to subsist, and from the two [together] there came to subsist the composite that acts through its form and is affected through its matter. The final cause is that for the sake of which these forms were imprinted into matters. (*Physics*, I.2, 15.6–9)

Later in the *Physics*, Avicenna develops his account of these causes as they apply to natural science. Thus, concerning the efficient cause he adds that "the efficient cause among natural things is said of the principle of motion in another different from it qua other,[2] where I mean by 'motion' here any emergence from a potency in the matter into act. This principle is the cause of the other's transformation and its being set into motion from potency into act" (*Physics*, I.10, 48.14–15). Avicenna further explains what he means by "in another different from it" with an example common since Aristotle, namely, of a doctor healing him or herself, for a doctor is not healed inasmuch as he or she is a doctor, but inasmuch as he or she is in need of some cure and so is a patient. As a patient, however, he or she is being considered as other than a doctor.

Avicenna's discussion of the final cause, at least in the *Physics*, is brief. Of it he says, "the final cause is the thing for the sake of which the form is present in the matter, namely, the real or supposed good, for in any production of motion that proceeds essentially and not accidentally from an agent, [that agent] desires what is a good in relation to itself—sometimes what is really [good] and sometimes what is supposedly [good], since either it is such or [at least] is supposed to be such" (*Physics*, I.10, 52.14–16).

In one sense it is obviously the case that the efficient cause causes the existence of the final cause. Still, there is for Avicenna another sense in which the final cause precedes and, in fact, is the cause of the causality of the efficient cause. Although Avicenna mentions this point in his *Physics* (I.11, 53.10–12), he says it must await its full clarification in First Philosophy. Thus, to anticipate that discussion, in the "Metaphysics" of the *Salvation*, he writes:

> The end comes to exist later than the effect, but it is prior to the rest of the causes in thingness (*shay'īya*). There is a difference between the thingness and the existence in concrete particulars, for the account [of what something is] has an existence in concrete particulars and in the

soul and is something common [to both]. That common thing, then, is the thingness. The end, insofar as it is a thing, is prior to the rest of the causes and is the cause of the causes inasmuch as they are causes, while insofar as it is something existing in concrete particulars it may come later. (*Salvation*, "Metaphysics," 519.16–520.4)

The notion of "thingness" here seems to be the idea of an essence considered in itself, or at least closely related to it, which was already encountered in the previous chapter.[3] Thus, Avicenna's point is that although the final cause, at least among natural things, is the last thing to receive a concrete existence outside of the intellect, the essence of the final cause considered in itself must be prior and then exist in the intellect so as to cause the efficient cause to produce some effect or end, since the desire for the end is what moves the efficient cause to act. In slogan form, then, the final cause is the cause of the causality of the efficient cause.

Avicenna's Analysis of Motion

Again, for Avicenna natural science is the study of perceptible bodies inasmuch as they are subject to motion. Thus, the heart of Avicenna's general physics involves a careful analysis of motion and the conditions necessary for motion. In this section, then, I consider Avicenna's conception of the form of motion, followed by his analysis of circular and rectilinear motion. In the next section, I turn to his treatment of certain conditions thought to be necessary for motion. For the most part, Avicenna follows or defends an Aristotelian account of these issues. Still, frequently he augments what Aristotle had to say in light of later criticisms that were leveled against Aristotle's positions. Also, in certain cases, most notably his analysis of motion itself, the philosophical tradition surrounding Aristotle's *Physics* played out in ways that required Avicenna to go well beyond Aristotle's own account of motion. It is primarily these innovative elements in Avicenna's natural philosophy that are the focus of the following sections.

Avicenna's General Analysis of Motion

Aristotle in his *Physics* (III 1, 201a10–11) had defined motion (Gk. *kinēsis*, Ar. *ḥaraka*) as "the *entelekheia* of what is potential insofar as it is such."

What was to become a major issue among Aristotle's Greek commentators was how to understand the enigmatic *entelekheia* in this definition of motion, a term, which it seems that Aristotle himself coined.[4] For the moment I shall leave it untranslated, and just note that it can mean either "actualizing" (progressive aspect) or "actualized" (completed aspect). As a means of clarifying this notion, these later Hellenistic commentators appealed to Aristotle's additional comments in the *De Anima* (II 1), where Aristotle distinguished between first and second *entelekheiai*.[5] The distinction is between, for example, one who knows a language, but is not currently using it—a first *entelekheia*—and one who is currently using a language—a second *entelekheia*.

With respect to motion, there was universal agreement that its second *entelekheia* refers to the final end or state of perfection reached at the termination of the motion, whereas its first *entelekheia* refers to the intermediate state of the moving thing between its initial state of potentiality and its final state of perfection, that is, its second *entelekheia*. Still, there were divergences within the commentary tradition as to how a first *entelekheia* referred to this intermediate state. Some argued that a first *entelekheia* must refer to a progression or process through the intermediary magnitude toward some end or perfection. Others argued that a first *entelekheia* must refer in some sense to the completed actuality of some partial end or perfection. In other words, the dispute in the ancient world was over whether *entelekheia* is itself a process term or not. If *entelekheia* is a process term, then it is clear how Aristotle's definition of motion—again the *entelekheia* of what is potential insofar as it is such—describes a process. Alas, it describes a process by assuming a process term in the definition, whereas Aristotle's definition of motion is intended to provide the most basic account of what a process is, and so should not presuppose a process. If *entelekheia* is not a process term, then Aristotle's definition avoids circularity, but it is no longer clear how it describes a process, since a completion or perfection is the end of a process, not a process itself.

The above roughly presents the philosophical debate surrounding Aristotle's definition of motion as it reached Avicenna. Following the Arabic translation of Aristotle's *Physics*, Avicenna defines motion as "the first perfection (*kamāl*) belonging to what is in potency inasmuch as it is in potency" (*Physics*, II.1, 83.5).[6] Clearly, the Arabic translation of *entelekheia* by "perfection" already biases an Arabic-speaking philosopher toward a non-process understanding of this term, which indeed is how Avicenna understands the definition. Thus, against the process interpretation of *entelekheia* Avicenna argues, as certain earlier commentators had, that the definition of motion is intended to provide the natural philosopher with the most basic account of what a process is. As such, one's definition of motion can not employ, either explicitly or implicitly, some other process term, for "passage," "procession," "traversal," and the like—which had been used by certain earlier philosophers to explain motion—are all synonyms for motion, complained Avicenna (*Physics*, II.1, 83.14–15). In addition, such terms refer to a particular kind of motion, namely, exchange of place, and yet for Avicenna and the entire Aristotelian tradition, there are other kinds of motion as well, such as change of quantity or change of quality. Consequently, concluded Avicenna, to define motion in terms of a process is either to give a synonym for "motion" or to define the more general in terms of the more specific (ibid., 83.15–17). In either case, the purported definition for Avicenna lacks explanatory power, and so is to be rejected as a proper scientific or philosophical definition.

Given his understanding of *entelekheia*, the issue for Avicenna was to explain how Aristotle's definition of motion in fact describes a process. Indeed, solving this problem led Avicenna to perhaps his most novel physical innovation, namely, the suggestion that there must be motion at an instant, an idea that was unheard of among Aristotle's earlier Greek commentators.[7] Avicenna argued thus: Motion's definition, following Aristotle, is the (first) perfection of what is potential as potential. The first perfection in question can refer either to the perfection of the moving thing as something extending across a continuous intermediate magnitude or to its perfection at various posited intermediate points in the magnitude. In other words, motion might refer either to the perfection of the moving thing in the whole intermediate magnitude stretching from beginning to end considered in toto or to the perfection of that moving thing in one intermediary point after another.

For Avicenna it is simply impossible that motion, as it exists in the world, should be the perfection of something extending across the whole intermediate magnitude; rather, motion understood as something extended only exists as such in the mind, not in the world. Thus, Avicenna writes:

> If by "motion" one means the continuous thing intellectually understood to belong to that which undergoes motion [stretching] from start to end, then what is being moved simply does not have that while it is between

the starting and end points. Quite the contrary, supposedly it has occurred in some way only when what is moved is at the end point, but this
continuous intelligible thing has ceased to exist there and so how can it
have some real determinate existence? The fact is that this thing is not
really something that itself subsists in concrete particulars. It leaves an
impression on the retentive imagination only because its form subsists in
the mind by reason of the moved thing's relation to two places: the place
from which it departs and the place at which it arrives. Alternatively, it
might leave an impression on the retentive imagination because the form
of what is moved, which occurs at a certain place and has a certain proximity and remoteness to bodies, has been imprinted upon it. Thereafter,
by [the moving thing's] occurring at a different place and having a different proximity and remoteness, it is sensibly perceived that another form
has followed [the first]. In that case, one becomes aware of two forms
together as a single form belonging to motion. [Motion so understood],
however, does not determinately subsist in reality as it does in the mind,
since it does not determinately exist at the two limits together and the
state that is between the two has no subsistent existence. (*Physics*, II.i,
84.i–8)

Avicenna's point becomes clearer with an example. If one considers the
motion of a ball between two spatially separated places, x and y, the ball's
motion is never fully actualized as some continuous extension that at any
moment completely stretches from x to y, in the way that the spatial distance between x and y exists as fully actual all at once. Instead, during the
motion the ball exists at one spot along the spatial interval and then ceases
to exist at that spot, only to exist in another spot, and so on. Only after the
motion is completed does an idea of the motion as extending through the
interval come to exist in the mind, but of course the motion has ceased at
that point.[8]

The first option, namely that motion refers to the perfection of the moving thing in the whole intermediate magnitude stretching from beginning
to end considered in toto, is again impossible (at least as an account of motion as it exists in the world as opposed to the mind). Thus, motion, Avicenna argues, must refer to the perfection of the moving thing in one intermediary point after another, albeit only as existing at an intermediary point
for an instant.

Avicenna, thus, understands the notion of a first *entelekheia* in Aristotle's
definition of motion as a moving body's actually being at some intermediary point along the distance covered *only for an instant*. The challenge before

Avicenna is to explain how the moving body could be actually at an inter-mediary point in such a way that its being at that point implies neither that the moving body is at rest at that point nor that the distance and time involved in the motion are atomic.

The former concern, namely that the moving body would be at rest at that point, arises from the following considerations.[9] Arriving at some point is different from leaving that point. Consequently, if a mobile actually comes to be at some intermediary point, there must be an instant at which the mobile comes to be at that point and a different instant when it leaves that point. Now, if time is continuous, that is, one can continually take smaller and smaller periods of time, as Avicenna believes, and the continu-ity of time entails that between any two instants there is a period of time (for between any two points on a continuum there is an infinity of potential points), then there must be a period of time during which the moving ob-ject would be at rest at the point, namely, the time between the instant that it arrives and then the instant that it leaves that point. The real problem arises for Avicenna since he also thinks that the space traversed is continu-ous as well. Consequently, there must be a potentially infinite number of points along the traversed space, each at which the mobile would purport-edly be at rest for some (imperceptibly) short period of time. In that case, however, traversing any finite continuous magnitude, if the mobile actually comes to be at all the intermediary points, would take an infinite period of time, which obviously is false. For infinitely many short periods of time (even imperceptibly short periods of time) add up to an infinitely long period of time.

One can avoid this conclusion if one makes space or time (or both) atomic, that is, if one holds that any finite spatial or temporal magnitude is a composite of minimal spatial or temporal units, which themselves have some positive, indivisible extension. In that case, any finite spatial or tempo-ral magnitude would be composed of only a finite number of atomic parts at which the mobile need be, and indeed certain Islamic speculative theolo-gians had done just this. Such an option, however, was not open to Avi-cenna, since, as will be seen later,[10] he vehemently opposed and argued against atomism in any form.

Avicenna addresses this apparent dilemma by observing that since spa-tial points do not have extremities, they cannot have a distinct extremity where the mobile can be said to have arrived at the spatial point and a dif-ferent one where the mobile can be said to have left that point (*Physics*, II.1,

84.10–14). Consequently, maintains Avicenna, there does not need to be a distinct temporal point corresponding with when the moving object has come to be at some intermediate spatial point and then another distinct temporal point when it has ceased to be at that spot, for again the spatial point itself has no such extremities or limits with which the temporal points must correspond. Therefore, the moving thing need not be at some spatial point for more than an instant, and so it does not remain at rest there.

It is the moving thing's being at some posited intermediate point only for an instant that Avicenna ultimately identifies with the very form of motion itself.

> This is the form of motion existing in the moved thing, namely, an intermediacy between the posited starting and end points inasmuch as at any limiting point at which it is posited it did not previously exist there nor will it exist there afterwards, unlike [its state at] the points at the two extreme limits. So, this intermediacy is the form of motion and is a single description that necessarily entails that the thing is being moved and simply does not change as long as there is something being moved. (*Physics*, II.1, 84.12–14)

Again, since any intermediary point at which the moving thing is posited to be during its motion does not itself have extremities, then a fortiori an intermediary point cannot have extremities that are reached earlier and then later, for a point simply has no extremities. Consequently, Avicenna assures us, there do not have to be distinct instants of arriving and departing that correspond with purported extremities of the intermediary point. The moving thing literally is at the intermediary point only for an instant. Clearly, however, whatever is at some point only for an instant necessarily is in motion, and it is this intermediateness that Avicenna makes the very form of motion itself. Thus, the extramental reality of motion for Avicenna comes down to there being motion at a point for only an instant.

An Analysis of Circular and Rectilinear Motion

The above is Avicenna's most general analysis of motion; however, in addition to this general analysis Avicenna also undertakes a special analysis of rotational or circular motion as opposed to rectilinear motion. Unlike Aristotle, who treated circular and rectilinear motion as two species of motion with respect to the category of place, Avicenna sees the two types of motion as generically different: Rectilinear motion belongs to the category of place, whereas circular motion belongs to the category of position. This divergence from Aristotle becomes important when I consider Avicenna's discussion of place, and so I should consider it briefly now.

Avicenna gestures at the distinction between the two kinds of motion when he considers what at first glance seems to be an issue tangential to his analysis of motion. At *Physics* II.1, Avicenna notes that every motion necessarily requires a point from which it begins, or a *terminus a quo* (*mā minhi*), and a point at which it ends, or a *terminus ad quem* (*mā ilayhi*). The *terminus a quo* is the initial state of actuality with respect to some accident, such as the place where it is, that changes with respect to the moving object. The *terminus ad quem* is the final state of actuality that is realized at the completion of the motion. For example, when the ball moves from some spot, x, to a different spot, y, x is its initial state of actuality, or its *terminus a quo*, and y is its final state of actuality, or its *terminus ad quem*.

An apparent problem arises, however, if one requires that every motion has a *terminus a quo* and *terminus ad quem*, for such a requirement would seem to preclude the continual motion of the heavens, especially if one believes, as Avicenna did, that this motion is everlasting both into the past and the future. The heavens for Avicenna simply never were actualized at some initial *terminus a quo* from which they began to move, nor will they ever come to some *terminus ad quem* at which they will realize a final state of actuality. If, however, having these two termini is a necessary condition of motion, then the heavens could not move, certainly not eternally at any rate, as Avicenna himself believed along with the majority of philosophers working within the Aristotelian tradition.

In order to resolve this puzzle, Avicenna draws on a distinction that has already been encountered, namely, between a first and second perfection or actuality, which he used in explaining Aristotle's notion of *entelekheia* in the definition of motion. Again, the "first perfection" refers to the intermediate state or states of the motion considered from its initial beginning point to its final ending point, whereas "second perfection" refers to the end of the process at which the moving object ultimately realizes its final actuality and perfection. Avicenna now uses this distinction to draw a correlative distinction between two types of potency: potency proximate to act and potency remote from act (*Physics*, II.1, 91.9–92.4). The proximate potency of a moving object during its motion is any intermediate point in the motion at which one can posit the thing's actually coming to be at that point for an instant and so not resting there. In short, it is the potentiality that is actualized by the motion's first perfection. In contrast, the remote potency of a moving thing is that final point at which it actually comes to rest, and so it is the potentiality that is actualized by the motion's second perfection. For example, in a ball's continual motion over a distance, *xyz*, a proximate potency is actualized when the ball is actually at *y*, albeit only for an instant, whereas its remote potency is actualized only when it comes to rest at *z*. In this case, *y* is not some point in the motion where the ball actually comes to rest; rather, the ball is simply posited as having actually passed over *y* at some posited instant during the motion.

In certain motions, Avicenna continues, the *termini a quo* and *ad quem* can be one and the same point, albeit they are not simultaneously *termini a quo* and *ad quem*, but only so at two distinct instants. The motion he clearly has in mind is circular motion or rotation. Thus, if one now imagines a ball's rotating in the same place instead of rolling across a distance, a complete rotation occurs when some posited point on the ball returns to where it began. Furthermore, if one imagines the ball's making several rotations, some point on the ball will return to its initial position several times, while continuing on without coming to rest at that position. The position of that posited point, then, functions as the *terminus a quo* and *terminus ad quem* in proximate potency during the ball's rotation.

Given this analysis, Avicenna explains in what sense the heavens' motion has a *terminus a quo* and *terminus ad quem*, namely, as some position, which is posited as a matter of convention, to which some point on the celestial sphere can be in proximate potency. For example, astronomers posit being directly overhead as the position by which to calculate a sidereal day, where a sidereal day is defined as the length of time between the Sun's being directly overhead and its subsequently returning to that overhead position. What is important about Avicenna's analysis is that he has made clear how the heavens can move without needing to posit spatially distinct *termini a quo* and *ad quem*, as is required by rectilinear motion.

In effect, circular motion or rotation, for Avicenna, needs to be analyzed differently from rectilinear motion. With rectilinear motion, on the one hand, an object moves from one spatially distinct place to another spatially distinct place, and so there must be a spatially distinct *terminus a quo* and *terminus ad quem*. With circular motion, on the other hand, an observer posits some point, as a matter of convention, and then the relative position of that point functions as both *termini a quo* and *ad quem*, albeit it is not si-multaneously both, but at different instants. Consequently, on Avicenna's analysis, circular motion needs no spatially distinct absolute or natural points or locations by reference to which one defines or describes the mo-tion, as is demanded by rectilinear motion. Although Avicenna's sharp dis-tinction between rectilinear and circular rotation may seem unimportant now, it will be vital later when he addresses a significant problem that arose within Aristotelian natural philosophy concerning the placement and apparent motion of the heavens.

The Conditions Necessary for Motion

In the first section of this chapter I considered the necessary principles that Avicenna believes are involved in producing motion or change in a natu-ral body. In addition to those principles of nature, Avicenna, following Aristotle, thinks that there are other necessary conditions required for motion, such as place, time, and the continuous. Strictly speaking, these are not principles of natures, but they do represent certain accounts that must be clarified if the natural philosopher is to provide a complete analysis of motion, which, again, is the proper subject of physics. Unlike Avicenna's account of the form of motion, which represents a truly creative moment in the history of science, his treatment of the conditions necessary for motion, are, for the most part, a defense and development of traditional Aristotelian natural philosophy. Yet, his defense of Aristotle frequently involves innova-tions that set Avicenna apart from his predecessors. It is with an eye to these novel elements that I now proceed.

Place

Like Aristotle before him, Avicenna defines the place (*makān*) of a thing as the innermost, unmoving limit of a containing body (*Physics*, II.9, 137.8–9). Unfortunately, there is something problematic about this account of place, which the late Neoplatonic thinker John Philoponus (ca. 490–570) would vehemently criticize. Philoponus's objection takes the form of a dilemma. Either the outermost heavens have a place or they do not.[11] On the one hand, if the outermost heavens do have a place, then, given Aristotle's definition of place in terms of a containing body, there must be a body outside of the heavens that contains them, but for Aristotle and virtually the entire Aristotelian tradition, the universe is finite beyond which there is nothing and so there is nothing outside of the heavens that could contain them. On the other hand, if the heavens do not have a place, then it seems impossible to explain their apparent diurnal or daily motion, for according to Aristotle, and accepted by the entire Greek Aristotelian tradition, there are only three kinds of motion: motion with respect to the categories of quantity, quality, and place. It seemed an observable fact, at least to the ancient and medieval astronomer, that the heavens in their daily motion do not change either quantitatively or qualitatively. Thus, given the apparent fact that the heavens do move, they must move with respect to place, but in this horn of the dilemma one assumes that they have no place, and so a fortiori they cannot move with respect to place. In short, concluded Philoponus, Aristotle's account of place as the innermost limit of a containing body is simply inadequate.

Avicenna defends Aristotle's preferred account of place in terms of an innermost limit of a containing body. Ironically, however, he does so by invoking his un-Aristotelian position that there is a generic difference between circular and rectilinear motion, which was noted earlier. More specifically, Avicenna denies that there are only three kinds of motion. Instead, he maintains that there must be four kinds: motion with respect to the categories of quantity, quality, place, and also (unlike Aristotle and the earlier Aristotelian tradition) position, with motion with respect to position defining circular motion or rotation (*Physics*, II.3, 103.8–105.13). Given Avicenna's earlier analysis of rotational motion as falling under the category of position, he can now deny that the cosmos has a place and still can explain its apparent motion, for instead of moving with respect to place, the cosmos moves with respect to position. Thus, Avicenna goes between the horns of Philoponus's dilemma.

Although Avicenna's solution to Philoponus's objection at first glance might appear to be ad hoc, one sees that on closer inspection it provides a solution to a deeper physical problem. Philoponus's specific problem was "How could the outermost celestial sphere undergo motion with respect to place if it has no place with respect to which it changes?" Avicenna realizes that this problem is endemic to any object that rotates in the same place, for how could any rotating object undergo motion with respect to place given that in rotation there is no change of place in the sense of moving from one spatially distinct place to another spatially distinct place? Circular motion or rotation for Avicenna, then, not only requires a different analysis from that of rectilinear motion, but also it requires an entirely different categorization as to what generic kind of motion it is. Thus, by introducing positional motion, Avicenna is not merely providing a solution to Philoponus's problem in order to save Aristotle's preferred account of place, but he is augmenting Aristotle's thought in a much needed way if there is to be a complete analysis of *all* types of motion.

The Void

Another issue closely associated with that of place is that of the void, for certain pre-Socratic philosophers had argued that the void must exist if there is to be motion, while certain proponents of *kalām* had maintained that there must be a void in order to provide God with an empty place in which to create. Aristotle, in some of his most technical argumentation, turned the tables on the pre-Socratic advocates of a void and claimed that far from allowing for the possibility of motion, the existence of a void would absolutely preclude motion. Like Aristotle, Avicenna too thinks that the void cannot exist; however, where Aristotle argued for this thesis solely on the basis of a series of "physical" arguments, Avicenna offered, in addition to physical arguments, a new "conceptual" proof against the existence of the void (*Physics*, II.8, 123.7–126.6), which takes advantage of a number of the logical considerations seen in the previous chapter.[12] Avicenna's argument attempts to show that it is impossible to provide an adequate and rigorous philosophical definition of what the void is. Yet, as I noted in the previous chapter, for Avicenna any natural thing that exists must have a corresponding definition framed in terms of genus and difference, otherwise it is just a vain intelligible or fictional object.

The general structure of Avicenna's conceptual argument against a void is quite simple. He takes as his major premise one of the conclusions that has already been encountered in chapter 2, namely, if something in the physical world actually exists, then one can provide a definition of that thing in terms of genus and difference. Conversely, if one cannot provide a definition for some purportedly natural phenomenon in terms of a genus and difference, then that term for Avicenna does not refer, and, in fact, the concept is simply an empty one.[13] Avicenna, then, exhaustively considers the various ways one might provide a definition of the void and argues that they are all wanting. Given the impossibility of providing a scientifically adequate definition of void, Avicenna concludes that the expression "void" does not refer to anything actually existing in the physical world.

Let me provide some of the details of his argument. Avicenna begins by noting that the name "void" cannot just mean "absolutely nothing," for if that were the case, there would be no dispute, since if void is absolutely nothing, then it does not exist. The void, should it exist, must be something. In fact, observes Avicenna, the advocates of the void assign to it certain positive properties, such as being extended and measurable. Thus, they themselves must take void to be "something."

Assuming that the void does possess extension and measurability, continues Avicenna, it does so either essentially or accidentally. If the properties of extension and measurability belong to the void essentially, then the void is essentially quantity, and indeed three-dimensional quantity. In that case, void would have the very same definition as quantity. Avicenna criticizes this suggestion by noting a point that has already been seen when discussing the principles of nature, namely that tri-dimensionality is itself the very form of corporeality, which itself initially imprints and configures matter, and so makes matter a natural body (*Physics*, I.2, 13.4–15.5, and II.7, 120.15–122.8).[14] Thus, if the very essence or nature of void were that of quantity, and so that of tri-dimensionality, then, according to Avicenna's argument, the void would necessarily imprint and configure matter and thereby produce a natural body. Clearly, however, the proponents of the void would deny that the void actively imprints the bodies that pass through it, for void is thought to be something passive, which bodies simply move through, not something that in some way constitutes or acts on bodies. Thus, the void's definition cannot for Avicenna be identified essentially with the definition of quantity.

Thus, the void must possess extension and measurability accidentally, in which case the void might either be an accident or a substance accidentally possessing extension and measurability. Avicenna does away with the suggestion that the void might be an accident accidentally possessing extension and measurability by simply observing that if the void were an accident, then it could no longer play the role for which it was intended, namely, as that which bodies enter and move through. That is because no body enters and moves through an accident, and yet, asserts Avicenna, the proponents of the void think that bodies do enter and move through the void (*Physics*, I.8, 124.4–6).[15]

Avicenna next considers the suggestion that void is a substance to which extension and measurability accidentally belong. If void falls under the genus "substance," Avicenna observes, it could have as its differences either (1) something that exists in a substrate, or (2) something that does not exist in a substrate (*Physics*, II.7, 124.7–16). The distinction Avicenna seems to be marking here is between a material substance and immaterial substances. On the one hand, if the void is a substance that exists with its substrate, which would be matter, then should the matter not exist, neither would the void exist. Of course the proponents of void think that the void exists, whether it is occupied by matter or not. On the other hand, "*not* existing in a substrate" cannot be a difference of the genus substance that would constitute the definition of void, for as noted in the previous chapter a negation cannot function as a difference in definitions.[16] Thus, for Avicenna some positive factor must function as a difference in the strict sense required by a definition, if there is to be a scientifically and philosophically adequate definition of the void. Although Avicenna suggests a number of possible candidates to which the advocates of void may try to appeal in order to provide a proper definition of void (*Physics*, II.8, 125.9–126.6), in the end all of these suggestions for Avicenna either fail to mark a difference between other substances (and so are not strict, definition-making differences) or they are negations (and so, again, fail Avicenna's criteria for definition-making differences).

Avicenna ultimately sums up his conceptual argument against the void thus: "This division between a [three-dimensional] interval in matter and an interval not in matter [that is, a void] is not a division by means of a species-making difference; rather, it is a division by means of some concomitant accidents external to the constitution of the interval as a species" (*Physics*, II.8, 126.4–6).[17] In other words, no adequate definition can be given of what a void interval, as opposed to the interval filled by a natural body, would be. Thus, given Avicenna's position that if something exists in the physical world, one can provide a definition of it in terms of genus and difference, and yet nothing can adequately function as the void's difference in such a definition, Avicenna concludes that the notion of void is, like its name, a vacuous concept. Again, this is not Avicenna's only argument against the void. Indeed, he rehearses many of Aristotle's own physical arguments, albeit frequently with his own unique flair. Still, this argument does show how Avicenna's conception of the general relation between logic and science can be used in the specific sciences.

Time

Avicenna, much along the lines of Aristotle, defined time as "a magnitude belonging to circular motion with respect to priority and posteriority" (*Salvation*, "Physics," II.9, 231). Unlike Aristotle, however, Avicenna begins his temporal account with an explicit positive proof for the reality of time. Here it is worth noting that neither Aristotle nor subsequent Aristotelians prior to Avicenna attempted explicitly to prove the existence of time. Yet given that at *Physics* IV 10 Aristotle himself had presented a number of arguments for why one might deny the reality of time and then did not follow up these criticisms with explicit responses, such a proof for the reality of time would seemingly have been a desideratum. Avicenna's proof, then, offered a much needed addition to the tradition.

Avicenna's proof assumes the reality of motion and certain empirical kinematic facts about our changing world, and then goes on to show that one could not explain these facts unless time is real.[18] Given that the subject matter of natural science is natural bodies inasmuch as they are subject to motion or change, Avicenna takes the existence of motion as a fact, while the various kinematic facts Avicenna takes as simply matters of empirical observation. The first one is that every motion involves a certain rate of fastness or slowness; one might say a rate of displacement or velocity. Given this feature of motion, the following additional facts need explaining maintains Avicenna:

1. If two moving objects have the same velocity and start and stop together (that is, simultaneously), then they traverse the same distance.
2. If two moving objects have the same velocity and both end together, yet the first begins before the second, then the second traverses less distance than the first.
3. If two moving objects have different velocities and start and stop together, then the slower moving object traverses less distance than the faster moving object.

Given these facts, two more facts become apparent. Thus, on the basis of (1) and (3), Avicenna observes that:

4. Any moving object that has some designated velocity also has a certain "possibility" (*imkān*) to traverse a certain determinate distance, where a beginning and ending can be marked off with respect to that possibility.

Also on the basis of (2), it follows that:

5. If two moving objects have the same designated velocity, and yet the first begins moving before the second, but they both end together,

then the second has less of this possibility and so traverses less
distance.

In the case of (5), the possibilities of the two moving objects to traverse a
distance are not equal in magnitude; rather, the whole of the possibility of
the second moving object is congruent or corresponds with only a part of
the possibility of the first.

Although Avicenna avoids using overtly temporal terms in his presentation of these facts, their explanation becomes clearer if one introduces
such language. So assume two people out for a stroll at a pace of 4 mph.
For Avicenna there is associated with this velocity a certain possibility to
cross four miles. This possibility is itself determined by the beginning and
ending of the motion. Thus, let one person start walking at, for example,
12:00, while the second begins at 12:15, with again both moving at a velocity of 4 mph. Now, let them both end their motions at 1:00. Clearly, the
possibility that the second person has for moving over a distance is less
than the possibility that the first has. Still, continues Avicenna, the possibility of the second is congruent with or maps onto a part of the possibility
of the first, namely, with three-fourths of the first's possibility in the example. Consequently, this possibility associated with motion can be more or
less, and as such it must be a certain magnitude or measure, which is related to the distance covered by the motion at a given velocity.[19] For example, a certain possibility, namely one hour, corresponds exactly with the
walk of a person moving uniformly at 4 mph. once he or she has covered
four miles.

Avicenna's argument thus far has shown, first, that a certain possibility
that is associated with motion (by which he clearly is intending time) must
exist if one is to explain certain kinematic phenomena about our world,
and, second, that this possibility is a certain magnitude. Avicenna now argues that this magnitude cannot be the magnitude of the moving body, that
body's velocity, or the distance over which the body moves.

> This possibility is, in fact, something divided, and whatever is divided is
> either a magnitude or possesses a magnitude. Hence, this possibility is
> not lacking a magnitude, and its magnitude must either be the magni-
> tude of the distance or some other magnitude. If it were the distance,
> things equal in distance would be equal in this possibility, but this is not
> the case, and so it is some other magnitude. Next, either it is the magni-
> tude of what is moved or it is not. It is not, however, the magnitude of

what is moved, otherwise the greater the moved thing is the greater it would be in this magnitude, but that is not the case. Therefore, it is neither the magnitude of the distance nor the magnitude of what is moved. It is also known that that magnitude is neither the very motion itself nor the velocity. [That follows] since motions, in that they are motions, agree in being motion. Also, motions [frequently] agree in velocity, while differing with respect to this magnitude. Likewise, they frequently differ with respect to velocity, while agreeing with respect to this magnitude. So, a magnitude belonging to a possibility has been established to exist, where [that possibility] occurs with motions between the prior and the posterior—the occurrence of which requires a delimited distance—that is neither the magnitude of what is moved nor the distance nor is it motion itself. (*Physics*, II.11, 156.3–11)

That the possibility in question cannot be the distance is obvious for Avicenna, since if this magnitude were the distance, then any two motions over the same distance would, by assumption, agree in the possibility required to cover the distance. In other words, two moving things would cover the same distance in the same time regardless of their velocities. That follows since the magnitude sought, which in fact is time, is by hypothesis assumed to be identical with the distance, and the ensuing result of such an identification is, observes Avicenna, clearly gainsaid by the fact that a given distance can be traversed more quickly or slowly depending upon the velocity. The magnitude in question, continues Avicenna, cannot be the bulk or magnitude of the moving object, since if they were one and the same, then the greater the (temporal) magnitude, the greater the size of the moving object, again a patently false conclusion. Clearly, the magnitude sought is not simply motion itself, for any two motions considered simply as motion agree, that is, they both are the perfection of a potentiality as such, and yet clearly the possibility in question can vary. Finally, this magnitude cannot be identified with the velocity of the moving object, says Avicenna, for if it were, then any two moving objects agreeing in velocity would always cover the same distance, which again is clearly false in the case where one moving object begins later than another, while they both stop together. The possibility or magnitude in question, Avicenna announces, is simply what people call "time" (*Physics*, II.11, 156.17). Thus, given the reality of motion and the various facts one observes about moving bodies, time must exist, which is what Avicenna wanted to prove. Not only does Avicenna's explicit proof for the reality of time make up for a deficiency in Aristotle's and other thinkers' earlier discussions of time, but also, when I turn to Avicenna's cosmology in chapter 7, his unique construal of time as a possibility becomes quite important.

Avicenna's Critique of Atomism and His Account of the Continuous

I have already mentioned that for Avicenna motion, time, and space, are continuous. In this respect, Avicenna was in direct opposition with atomic theories of motion, time, and space that were prevalent in the medieval Arabic-speaking world, particularly among Islamic speculative theologians.[20] Thus, I should consider some of his reasons for rejecting atomism as well as his defense against certain historical problems associated with the idea of a continuum.

I consider only two of Avicenna's arguments for rejecting atomism: one concerning the impossibility of explaining how an aggregate of indivisible atoms could give rise to a perceptible body, and the other arising from certain geometrical considerations.[21] The notion of an atom, which Avicenna rejects, is that of a minimal, positive extension or magnitude that is not only physically indivisible but also conceptually indivisible. Should such indivisible parts exist, Avicenna wants to know how they could be aggregated so as to result in a body such as the ones that we perceive around us. Such aggregation could take place by atoms' being either (1) in succession, (2) contiguous, (3) interpenetrating, or (4) continuous with one another. Avicenna does not believe (1), succession, is a serious contender, since if indivisible parts were only in succession there would be void spaces between them and so there would not result the seemingly continuous bodies, which one perceives and are the focus of the discussion (*Physics*, III.4, 189.13–14). One can further add that since Avicenna has shown that the notion of void space is meaningless, the suggestion that there are indivisible parts with void space between them is likewise meaningless.

As for explaining the aggregation of indivisible parts into a body by contiguity, continuity, or interpenetration, Avicenna writes:

> When [purportedly indivisible atoms] are aggregated according to either continuity or contiguity, then each one of them is divisible into what is occupied and what is unoccupied, what is being touched and what is not being touched, according to what we explained in the preceding chapters.

If they do not interpenetrate, then when one of them, x, contacts another, y, and then a third one, z, comes into contact with one of the two, [for example, y,], then necessarily z is hindered from contacting x by the intermediacy of y's contact. In that case, each one essentially confers to the contact what the other had not—this is self-explanatory. So, the intermediate object, y, is divisible. If they are in contact completely, then they interpenetrate. In that case, a magnitude is not increased by their aggregation, and so whenever they are aggregated they would be like the unit, which has neither length, nor breadth, nor depth. Since these indivisible parts do not aggregate in such a way that a body is thereby composed of them, the body is not reducible to them. Thus, the division of bodies does not terminate at parts that cannot be divided by any type of division, and the same holds for all other magnitudes (I mean surfaces and lines). (*Physics*, III.4, 189.14–190.3)

Here Avicenna has one imagine three purportedly physically and conceptually indivisible atoms, x, y, and z, aggregated so as to form a body. So one might think of something like the following.

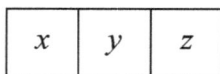

x	y	z

Avicenna observes that the atom must be at least conceptually divisible in either the case of contiguity—where, when in contact, the limits of each of the atoms remain distinct—or the case of continuity—where, when in contact, the two atoms share a common limit. That follows since if y is separating x and z, such that x and z are not in contact with each other, then y must have a limit that is in contact with x, and that limit must be distinct from its limit that is in contact with z. Consequently, y, which was purportedly conceptually indivisible, is conceptually divisible into its two limits, which, Avicenna points out, is a contradiction. Should one argue that y does not have distinct limits that separate x from z, then nothing in principle prevents x from occupying the same space as y and similarly for z. In this case there is interpenetration; however, interpenetration, insists Avicenna, is incapable of explaining how the aggregation of atoms results in a perceptible body. One could add a hundred, ten thousand, even a million such atoms, all interpenetrating, and they would only ever be the size of one imperceptible atom. Consequently, concludes Avicenna, since it is a matter of observation that perceptible bodies exist, and yet an atomic theory countenancing indivisible parts cannot explain how such bodies exist, the theory is empirically inadequate.

The second of Avicenna's arguments against atomism shows that atomism is at odds with our best mathematical theories, since it cannot even approximate the Pythagorean theorem, the most well-proven theorem in all of mathematics.

> In fact, the existence of indivisible parts would necessarily entail that there be no circles, nor right triangles, nor many other [geometrical] figures. . . . [For example] when two sides of a right triangle are each ten units, then the hypotenuse is the square root of two hundred, which [according to the present view] would either be an absurdity that does not exist, or it is true, but parts would be broken up, which [according to the present view] they are not. (*Physics*, III.4, 190.8–11)

Here, for the sake of presentation, consider a 3x3 square of space supposedly formed from indivisible atoms and then consider a right triangle constructed on that purportedly atomic space, such as the following.

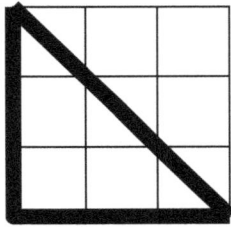

According to the Pythagorean theorem, the sum of the square of the two legs of the atomic triangle should equal the square of its hypotenuse. In the case of atomic space, however, since the number of atomic units that make up the hypotenuse is equally three atomic units like the legs, one has $3^2 + 3^2 = 3^2$, or $9 + 9 = 9$, which is patently false. Atomic space, then concludes Avicenna, cannot even approximate the Pythagorean theorem. Moreover, it does no good to say that the diagonals of the supposedly atomic units are longer than their sides, since the atom is supposedly the smallest unit possible. Thus, if the diagonal of the supposed atomic unit is greater than one of its sides, it would be greater by an amount less than the smallest possible unit, which, Avicenna notes, is absurd.

Given these arguments, and several others, Avicenna rejects atomism in favor of theories of continual motion, time, and space; however, he also recognizes that the notion of a continuum has its own share of philosophical problems that need to be addressed. Historically, perhaps the most pressing problem was Zeno's (in)famous dichotomy paradox, framed in terms of a potentially infinite number of halfway points that a continuum seems to presuppose.

Zeno had argued that in order to move from one point to another point on a continuous magnitude one must first reach the halfway point. Yet before one can reach that halfway point one must reach a point halfway to it, and so on ad infinitum. Consequently, one could never cover a continuous space, for the motion would involve traversing an infinite number of half-distances, but traversing the infinite was thought to be impossible.

Aristotle gave his solution to this paradox at *Physics*, VIII 8 in a notoriously difficult passage, but the general strategy of his response is something like this. In a continuous magnitude there is a potentially, but not actually, infinite number of points. Any of the potential infinity of points along the continuous magnitude becomes actualized only if the object moving along the magnitude stops at that potential point and so makes it actual. Consequently, although the continuous magnitude is the sort of thing that can accidentally be divided at any number of points or half-distances by the moving object's stopping at that potential point, essentially and of itself the continuous magnitude does not for Aristotle have an actually infinite number of points or half-distances in it, and so an infinite is not traversed. Thus, Zeno's paradox never arises.

Unfortunately, such a solution is not open to Avicenna, for it has been seen that on his analysis of motion the actuality mentioned in the definition of motion (where again the definition of motion is "the actuality (or perfection) of what is potential as potential") refers to a moving thing's *actually*, not merely potentially, being at the various intermediate points in the continuum during the motion, albeit only as existing at a given intermediary point for an instant. Despite the differences in their analyses of motion, Avicenna adopts a variant of Aristotle's solution to Zeno's paradox, though with a very Avicennan twist.

He begins by clarifying the notion of continuous magnitude that is at stake in Zeno's paradox, saying:

> It is like what happens when we imagine or posit that a line that is actually one has two parts, where we distinguish one [part] from the other by positing, and in that way a limit is distinguished for it, being the very same limit of the other part. . . . Each one of the two [parts], however, exists in itself only as long as there is the positing, and so when the positing ceases, there

no longer is *this* and *that* [part]; rather, there is the unified whole not actually having a division in it. Now, if what occurs through positing were to be something [really] existing in the thing itself and not by positing, then the existence of an actually infinite number of parts would be possible (as we shall explain), but this is absurd. (*Physics*, III.2, 182.6–10)

The heart of Avicenna's claim here is that, as with Aristotle's account, there never is an infinity of actualized points in a continuous magnitude; rather, a point becomes actualized in the magnitude, according to Avicenna, only by an act of positing or supposition.

Although in the present passage Avicenna speaks only of "positing" or "supposition" (*farḍ*), he adds later that pointing (*ishāra*) at a spot, or touching (*mumāssa*), or being parallel with (*muwāzāh*) the spot likewise actualize points in the magnitude (*Physics*, III.3, 184.6–16). Since, for Avicenna, the moving object actually does successively touch all of a continuum during a continuous motion, and at any instant during the motion the moving object must actually be at some point on the continuum, an actually infinite number of points must be actualized on Avicenna's view.[22] What is important, however, and what Avicenna repeatedly reminds his reader, is that the various points, which are in some way indicated or touched, do not have any actual or independent existence in the magnitude itself. Whatever actual existence they might have exists only as long as the acts or states of positing, touching, and the like are occurring, whereas the actualized existence of any point completely ceases once these various states or acts themselves cease. Thus, for Avicenna there is no time at which an actualized infinity of points simultaneously exists during a continuous motion, even though the moving object has actually, and not merely potentially, been at all the points. What is important to note is that Avicenna, unlike many of his predecessors in the Aristotelian tradition, happily allows the possibility of traversing a (potential) infinite. This concession, and his arguments for it, will become even more important when I consider Avicenna's position concerning the eternity of the world in chapter 7.

Avicenna's Dynamics: Inclination (*Mayl*)

Up to now I have focused on concepts in what might be considered the kinematics of Avicenna's natural philosophy. If one turns to his dynamics, then the key concept is certainly that of *mayl*, which one might tentatively render as "inclination."[23] With varying degrees of caution, it has been claimed that Avicenna's theory of inclination foreshadows certain salient features of Newtonian mechanics.[24] In this section, I want to look at Avicenna's notion of *mayl* and argue that in fact his theory of inclination is, like much of his natural philosophy, an extremely sophisticated and original application of Aristotelian points and not a precursor to a modern quantified dynamics.

Avicenna never rigorously and systematically analyzes *mayl* in the way he does other central concepts in his natural philosophy. Indeed, from the scattered passages concerning *mayl* one would be hard pressed to elicit a single univocal account of it. Avicenna speaks of "natural-inclination," "forced-inclination" (or "impressed-power") as well as "psychic-inclination." Moreover, under "natural-inclination" some inclinations produce circular motions, whereas others rectilinear motions. It is natural and forced inclinations as they appear in Avicenna's *Physics* that I want to consider here.

In his *Book of Definitions*, Avicenna defines "inclination" as "a quantity by which the body offers resistance to whatever prevents [the body] from moving in a given direction."[25] He develops the idea of inclination's resistance or repulsion of a body in his *Physics*, where he observes that the existence of inclination can be verified empirically by the fact that either a moving thing repels what obstructs it or what obstructs it needs to exert some power to oppose the moving thing (*Physics*, IV.8, 298.4-5). Let me give two examples of Avicenna's point, which make clear these two different sorts of inclination, namely, natural- and forced-inclination. First, if one holds a stone, one experiences the stone's exerting a certain downward force on the hand that tries to push the hand out of the way. Conversely, one is aware of exerting a certain force on the stone in order to prevent it from its downward path. Avicenna designates the force exerted by the stone's natural downward motion its "natural-inclination." In general, Avicenna envisions "natural inclination" as corresponding with Aristotle's notion that the ancient natural elements—earth, water, air, and fire—as well as the composites of these elements, naturally tend toward their proper places, namely, up, down, or to the middle.[26] Now, consider another example: Imagine the same stone's being tossed, for example, horizontally, and someone's catching it. As in the first example, at the moment one catches the stone, one again feels a force pushing against the hand as well as the need to exert a certain force to keep the stone from continuing on its trajectory; however, now the force is not experienced as vertical or downward, but as horizontal or to the side. Avicenna designates the force that is in a direction different from the stone's natural downward inclination "forced-inclination" or "impressed power," an idea most frequently associated with the Neoplatonic philosopher, John Philoponus.

Avicenna further asserts that if a body is displaced from some initial resting place and continues on to some given terminus, then there must be a cause that is continuously connected with the body during its motion to that terminus. Furthermore, this cause must depart from the initial resting place along with the body. This cause, which Avicenna identifies with inclination, is related to, or perhaps proportional with, the force needed to displace the body from some initial resting place and the force that the body has to resist or repel what opposes it (*Physics*, IV.8, 298.4–18).[27]

Avicenna further maintains that the determinate quantity of inclination in a moving body can vary at different instants during the motion.[28] It is because the inclination in the body varies at different instants during the motion that the body's motion accelerates or decelerates, where the variations in the body's inclination at different instants are a function of the body's proximity and remoteness, presumably, from either its natural place in the case of natural inclination, or its projector in the case of forced-inclination. As an object approaches its natural place, according to Avicenna, its natural inclination increases and so there is acceleration, whereas deceleration occurs in projectile motion because the forced inclination wanes the farther the object is from its projector inasmuch as the resisting power of the medium exhausts the impressed power.

Perhaps one of the most modern sounding aspects of Avicenna's theory of inclination comes when he discusses what would happen if there were projectile motion in a void, should a void exist, that is, when there is no resistance. Again, recall that Avicenna denies the existence of a void. Among his "physical" arguments against its existence is one that invokes his notion of inclination. His argument in simplest terms is that if the void were to exist, then, given the nature of forced inclination, a projectile shot in a void would continue on its trajectory without ceasing or deviating from its course, which certainly seems to anticipate some important features of the modern notion of inertia.

In the first part of his proof, Avicenna argues against the notion of impressed power or inclination developed by Philoponus. The latter had argued that inclination is self-exhausting and so during the course of a projectile's motion the impressed power or inclination would ultimately expend itself. Thus, for Philoponus, even in a void, if something were projected in it, the projectile would finally come to rest. In contrast, Avicenna argues:

> If in the void the projectile is forcibly moved as a result of some power, [the motion] must continue without ever abating or being interrupted. [That follows] because when the power is in the body, it either remains or there [comes to be] a privation of its existence (ta'damu). If it remains, then the motion would continue perpetually. If there is a privation of its existence, or it even weakens, its privation or weakening is either from a cause or owing to itself. The discussion concerning privation will provide you the way to proceed with respect to weakening. It is impossible for the privation of [the power's] existence to be owing to itself, for whatever necessarily is a privation of existence owing to itself cannot exist at any time. If its privation is by a cause, then that cause is either in the moved body or in something else. If [the cause of the privation of the motion] is in the moved body, and at the beginning of the motion it had not actually been causing that [privation], but in fact had been overpowered, and then later became a cause and dominated, then there is another cause for its being such, in which case an infinite regress results. If the cause is either external to the body or cooperates with the cause that is in the body, then the agent or co-operative cause acts either by direct contact or not. If it acts by direct contact, then it is a body that is directly contacting the projectile, but this cause would not exist in a pure void. Thus, the forced motion would neither abate nor stop in the pure void. If it does not act by direct contact but is something or other that acts at a distance, then why did it not act initially? The counterargument is just like the argument concerning the cause if it were in the body [that is, it leads to an infinite regress of causes]. It is most appropriate, instead, that the continuous succession of opposing things is what causes this power to decrease and corrupt, but, unless the motion is not in a pure void, this is impossible. (*Physics*, II.8, 133.6–134.1)

Here Avicenna argues against the suggestion that inclination or impressed power is self-expending, for if a projectile does come to rest, reasons Avicenna, then there must be some cause of its coming to rest. The cause of the cessation of the projectile's motion must be either (1) internal or (2) external to the impressed motion. On the one hand, if it is internal to the impressed motion itself, then one and the same impressed motion is both the cause of the production and the cessation of the projectile's motion. In this case, one and the same thing would be the cause of contradictory effects, which Avicenna finds to be absurd. If, on the other hand, the cause of the projectile's coming to rest is external, then either, (2a), that cause exists within the void itself or, (2b), it exists outside of the void. It cannot, (2a), exist within the void itself, argues Avicenna, for the void by definition is devoid of anything that could act as such a cause. If, (2b), the cause is external to the void (call the cause, x), then, Avicenna asks, why did x cause the cessation of the projectile's motion when it did rather than not initially preventing it? If something else, y, causes x to produce the cessation when it does, then one is on the road to an infinite regress. Given that all the possibilities for the cessation of an impressed motion in a void have been exhausted and all come up wanting, Avicenna concludes that if there is a void, then projectile motion within it must be conserved and so endure infinitely.

Such an argument certainly seems to anticipate some important features of inertia. First, it suggests that in the absence of a force, an object continues moving uninterrupted on account of its forced inclination. Second, Avicenna's same argument is applicable to deviations in the projectile's trajectory in a void, in which case the motion should continue in a rectilinear line. Third, the same argument would apply as well to the projectile's mean speed. The similarities between Avicenna's notion of inclination and Newton's notion of inertia, however, are more apparent than real, which becomes evident once Avicenna's argument is taken within its broader context and not just the immediate issue of criticizing the idea of a self-exhausting inclination.

The broader context is again Avicenna's attempt to show that there is no void, where the above argument establishes the major premise in that proof, namely, if there were a void, then a finite impressed power could produce an infinitely enduring motion. If Avicenna were to have anticipated the modern notion of inertia, then he would have needed to implicitly assume the antecedent of this conditional, namely, the (hypothetical) possibility of a void; however, the issue of the possible existence of the void is the very one at stake. Avicenna, in fact, maintains that the existence of a void is impossible precisely because the consequent is impossible, namely that motion could be perpetually conserved in a void.

His reasoning for denying the possibility of the conservation of motion in a void is that if there were a void, and given the non-self-expending nature of inclination, then if a finite agent, such as myself, were to shoot an arrow into a void, I could produce an infinite effect, namely, the infinitely enduring motion of the arrow in the void. Although Avicenna is extremely reticent about assigning determinate ratios or correspondences among mover, mobile, time, and distance, the one ratio he adamantly holds is that if one of these factors is finite, then they all must be finite (*Physics*, IV.15, 333.3–9). For Avicenna it is simply impossible that a finite agent can produce an infinite effect,[29] but such an infinite effect would be possible if a void were to exist. Thus, this argument, far from affirming some principle approaching the modern notion of inertia, once understood in its broader context, explicitly opposes the doctrine of the conservation of motion in a void.

Substantial Changes and the Elements

Most of the previous discussions concerned Avicenna's account of motion, that is, changes in the categories of quality (alterations), quantity (augmentations and diminutions), place (rectilinear motions), and position (rotations). Inasmuch as all of these changes occur with respect to some accident belonging to a substance, they may be called "accidental changes." For Avicenna, following the Aristotelian tradition, there is also a further type of change, namely, with respect to the category of substance, or what is simply called "substantial change." Substantial changes involve the coming into being of a new substance from another, whether of the same kind, as when an offspring is produced, or of a different kind, such as in elemental changes, as when water is heated and becomes steam (which to the ancient and medieval mind was tantamount to water's becoming the element air).

Unlike accidental changes, which always take a period of time to occur, substantial changes, according to Avicenna, do not take any time, but occur all at once. In other words, when a substance of kind A becomes a substance of kind B, then that change must occur at an instant. The reason that Avicenna gives for why accidental changes can occur over a period of time, while substantial changes cannot, is that in accidental changes the substance bearing the accident remains throughout the change, and so can act as the subject of the newly emerging accident (*Physics*, II.3, 98.9–100.18). In the case of substantial change, however, if some initial substance, A, were to cease to be and no new substantial form were to come and inform the prime matter that had been underlying substance A, the prime matter, as noted, would for Avicenna simply cease to exist (for it is form that is causally explanatory of any actual existence that the prime matter might have). Consequently, if substance A's transition to B were to take some time, there would not really be a change of A. That is because substance A would be corrupted, and so cease to exist, after which there would be a period of time when neither A nor B exists, and then substance B would, as it were, miraculously be generated out of nothing. Thus, if anything, substance B would have come into being from nothing, but it would not be true that it came to be from substance A. If one maintains that some other substance, C, came to be during the time that A was changing to B, then the same question can be applied to C: Does it come to be instantaneously with the cessation of A, or does it too come to be over a period of time? Since this same question can be asked ad infinitum for any further intermediary substances, and with each change some actually new substance must come to be, if substantial change were gradual, it would involve an actually infinite number of specifically different substances coming to be; however, maintains Avicenna, there is not an actual infinity of different kinds or species. Therefore, he concludes, substantial change must occur all at once.

Still, Avicenna is aware that there are cases where it appears as if the change from one kind of substance to another is gradual, such as when sperm and ovum come together and seemingly gradually become, for instance, a human. What in fact occurs in these cases, maintains Avicenna, is that a certain underlying substance undergoes certain accidental alterations, as, for example, changes in how hot or cold or wet or dry it is. These accidental changes, which again take time, are preparatory for the substantial change in that they gradually alter the underlying matter so as to make it suitable for a new substantial form that is then impressed instantaneously upon the properly disposed matter such that a new kind of substance is originated.

Here a brief discussion about the ancient and medieval understanding of the elements and elemental change up to the time of Avicenna will help explain his introduction of perhaps one of the most novel features of his natural philosophy, psychology, and even to a certain extent, his metaphysics, namely, his appeal to a Giver of Forms (*wāhib aṣ-ṣuwar*), which is an immaterial substance or Intellect that bestows substantial forms on properly prepared matter. According to Aristotelian elemental theory—and, indeed, a position extending back at least as early as the pre-Socratic philosopher Empedocles—there are four basic elements: earth, water, air, and fire.[30] Here earth, water, air, and fire should be viewed as the ancient and medieval analog to the modern elements making up our periodical table. As such, ancient and medieval scientists considered elemental earth, water, air, and fire not to be the garden variety instances of these that we experience around us—which, in fact, were thought actually to involve a mixture of all four of the ancient elements with one element preponderating—rather, elemental earth, water, air, and fire were taken to be the pure, unmixed instances of these.

The elements themselves are in turn associated with two primary qualities taken from two sets of contrary qualitative powers: hot/cold and wet/dry. Thus, the element earth is associated with the primary qualities of cold and dry; water with cold and wet; air with hot and wet; and, finally, fire with hot and dry. Each of these qualities is in turn associated with certain very basic powers: acting on in the case of hot, being acted on in the case of cold, while wet has the power to receive and dry the power to retain. At least to this point, Avicenna is in agreement; however, Aristotle, and virtually all of those working within the Aristotelian tradition up to Avicenna,[31] additionally identified an element's substantial form with the ratio of the mixture of the element's two primary qualities. Thus, the very substantial form of earthy substances, for example, is to have a predominance of the qualities cold and dry. So, the greater the extent that cold and dry dominate in something, the more earthlike that thing is, whereas earth in its ideal state would have *only* cold and *only* dry with no admixture of hot and wet tempering these primary qualities.

Given this identification of an element's substantial form with its mixture of primary qualities, Aristotle and those following him explained substantial changes among the elements with seeming ease. Inasmuch as the primary qualities inherent in an element act on other elements (for example, the element fire heats other elements), sufficient changes in one element's primary qualities can ultimately reach a point where the mixture of the effected element's primary qualities no longer has a ratio commensurate with being an element of that kind. In that case, there would be a substantial change. So, for example, if water, a cold-wet mixture, is heated to a point that hot dominates the cold, there comes to be a new mixture, namely, a hot-wet one, which again is identified with the element air, and indeed when one vigorously heats water, it becomes steam, which is like air. Similarly, on the traditional Aristotelian view, when the same water is cooled, the cooling begins to affect the element's fluidity, namely, its wet quality, and so the water becomes increasingly dryer, as it were, and thus more like a cold-dry mixture. Indeed in its frozen states, water does exhibit many of the features of the element earth: It is solid and even somewhat powdery if it is cold enough.

Despite the philosophical elegance and explanatory power of this Aristotelian account of elemental change, Avicenna believes that it was fundamentally flawed inasmuch as it identified an element's substantial form with its proportion of hot/cold and wet/dry, which, Avicenna rightly notes, are qualities and so accidents of a substance.[32] Thus, Avicenna argues:

> The commentators become confused about that because they should distinguish between [substantial] forms and accidents referring to the distinction between the natural forms belonging to those bodies and their qualities. Because they believe that either all or some qualities are certain [substantial] forms of these bodies (even though they are susceptible to intensification and diminution), their best representative advocates a system where the qualities of [the bodies] are preserved, while the force is abated, and so the bodies are potentially unmixed. (*Generation and Corruption*, 6, 127.18–128.4)

Avicenna, then, continues that what one ought to believe about the relation of qualities to the substantial forms of the elements is virtually the opposite:

> Each one of the elements has a substantial form by which it is what it is and upon which certain perfections follow from the categories of quality, quantity, and where [that is, the category of place] and from which each body can be specified by [(1)] a certain coldness and heat due to the form as well as a certain dryness and moistness due to the matter joined to the form, [(2)] a certain natural measure of quantity, and [(3)] a natural rest and motion. (*Generation and Corruption*, 6, 129.15–130.1)

The problem Avicenna is raising against the traditional Aristotelian account of elemental change is this: Qualities, contra Aristotle and many of his commentators, cannot be identified with substantial forms, because qualities are accidents, and accidents are ontologically posterior to their subjects. The simple fact, asserts Avicenna, is that the substantial form is that by which the subject subsists, and on this point Aristotle agrees. So, the substantial form is ontologically prior to the accidents that subsist in that substance as their subject. Consequently, if elemental substantial forms were identical with their primary qualities, Avicenna complains, they would be both ontologically prior and posterior to themselves, which is absurd. In other words, Aristotle has put the proverbial cart before the horse. Accidents, even primary ones, Avicenna notes, presuppose the existence of a substance, and the substance itself presupposes the existence of the substantial form. In short, the traditional Aristotelian account of the nature of elemental substantial forms, complains Avicenna, involves circular causation: Qualities purportedly causally explain the substantial forms, but the substantial forms causally explain qualities.

Avicenna's own account concerning elemental, and indeed all substantial change, is that natural efficient causes, such as the elements' own primary qualities, can affect the qualities of the matter and so prepare the matter for a new substantial form. They cannot, however, educe that form from the previously existing matter otherwise it would again make substantial forms dependent upon accidental qualities, where in fact, maintains Avicenna, just the reverse is the case. Since natural efficient causes, which affect only a natural substance's accidental features, cannot bestow a new substantial form on the prepared matter, there must be something outside of the natural order of the four elements that does so, an entity that Avicenna dubs the Giver of Forms. The Giver of Forms—which, as will be seen in chapter 5, Avicenna also identifies with the Active Intellect of his psychology—is not God, but the lowest of the immaterial Intellects in Avicenna's spiritual hierarchy of which I shall have more to say in chapter 7.

For Avicenna, the Giver of Forms acts much like a natural force. It continuously emanates the various species forms that make up our world with a regularity that is akin to a nature, albeit that emanation is still a volitional act according to Avicenna, and so is not strictly speaking the result of a nature (*Physics*, I.5, 30.6–16). These emanated species forms, then, are always present, as it were, albeit they observably manifest themselves only when there is a properly disposed material recipient. In this respect, the emanation of the Giver of Forms might be likened to radio waves that are all around us yet not heard, while the preparatory role of natural efficient causes is like tuning a radio. The radio is gradually tuned, but once it is tuned to a given station, the radio wave, as it were, instantaneously produces a sound in the radio, which on the present analogy is comparable to a new substance. What is important to note is that most of the work involved in producing a new substance, in fact, is undertaken by those terrestrial causes that prepare the matter by heating, cooling, drying, and moistening the prior substance, just as most of the work in changing the radio station involves turning the radio's knob. With the introduction of an immaterial substance, let me conclude my discussion of Avicenna's general account of natural philosophy. Avicenna returns to many of the principles and concepts presented in his general account of natural science when he turns to issues in other sciences, such as metaphysics and specific natural sciences, such as psychology, which is the subject of the next chapter.

4

PSYCHOLOGY I

Soul and the Senses

Introduction

For Avicenna, as well as most ancient and medieval philosophers, philosophical psychology is one of the special sciences of physics or natural philosophy. The reason for this classification becomes clear once one recalls that for Avicenna the proper subject of natural philosophy generally is body, inasmuch as it undergoes motion or change. As for the proper subject of psychology, Avicenna identifies it with *living* bodies, inasmuch as they undergo and perform those activities, that is, motions and changes associated with a living thing, such as self-nourishment, growth, reproduction, and in the cases of higher life forms, sensation, locomotion, and even rational thought. In short, psychology treats a subset of natural bodies, namely, animate bodies, and it is for this reason that ancient and medieval natural philosophers subsumed psychology under physics as one of its so-called subaltern sciences.

In this chapter, I first look at Avicenna's discussion of the cause of the activities associated with a living body, which he identifies with the soul, as well as those life activities themselves. After very briefly discussing Avicenna's comments on the powers of the vegetative soul, I focus on the powers of the animal soul. I begin with his discussion of perception via the external senses, namely, the well-known senses of hearing, sight, smell, touch, and taste, with a particular focus on the power of vision and the role he sees light playing in vision. I then turn to the so-called internal faculties or senses that Avicenna identifies. As a first pass, internal faculties or senses for Avicenna include, for instance, those acts of sensory perception that do not require the immediate presence of an externally sensible object for that perception, such as remembering some past event, or imagining some future one, or even dreaming of a pink elephant. Also, the internal faculties include instances of sensory acts that involve the awareness of something (perhaps) external that is not immediately perceived by the external senses, like, for example, one's awareness that time has passed (time's passing is certainly not directly seen, heard, or the like) or perceiving that some food is good to eat (it might have a particular smell or visual appearance but these are different from recognizing that it is good to eat). Here, I look at the criteria by which Avicenna deduces his list of the various kinds of internal faculties with a particular focus on the compositive imagination and cogitative faculty. An understanding of Avicenna's conception of sight and light as well as the roles of these internal senses, helps pave the way for appreciating his account of the human intellect and its proper act of cognition, as well as his account of self-awareness, which are the subjects of the next chapter.

Soul and Life

For Avicenna, as has been noted, sciences are concerned with uncovering and investigating the causes of various phenomena. Consequently, the science of psychology is primarily interested in the cause (or causes) belonging to living bodies that explains that set of activities unique to them as living. Thus, in I.1 of the *Psychology* of the *Cure*, Avicenna begins by pointing out that it is simply a matter of empirical observation that certain bodies sensibly perceive and move about voluntarily, as well as taking in nourishment, growing, and reproducing. These activities, he continues, cannot belong to them simply inasmuch as they are bodies, for otherwise all bodies would manifest these activities, which they clearly do not. A stone may be split in two or fall to the ground, but no one would say that in such cases it has reproduced or moved around of its own will. Given this difference between the natural activities of different kinds of bodies, living bodies must have some other principle or cause in addition to their mere corporeality. It is this principle for Avicenna that explains why those bodies perform these very activities that distinguish them from nonliving bodies. The cause or principle "out of which these activities issue and, in short, anything that is a principle for the performance of any activities that do not follow a uniform course devoid of volition," Avicenna concludes, "we call 'soul' (*nafs*)" (*Psychology*, I.1, 4.5–7).

While Avicenna has introduced the notion of the soul very early, it is important to note that his conception of the soul, at least as presented here, is not a metaphysically loaded one. It is merely a tag to indicate that thing or things, whatever it or they might be, that living bodies have that nonliving bodies lack and on account of which the living bodies do those activities that define them as living. Any of the religious or metaphysical biases one might have about the term "soul" need to be left behind at this point. It may turn out that, in fact, the soul (or at least some souls) can, for example, survive the death of the body, receive eternal blessing or punishment, and the like, but such positions require independent demonstrations, and cannot simply be inferred from the fact that souls, understood as animating principles, exist. For, as Avicenna insists, "for now, we have established the existence of something that is a principle only of what we have stated [namely, it is a cause of various activities associated with being alive] and [then only] in the sense that it has a particular accident" (*Psychology*, I.1, 4.10–11). The accident in question is that the soul has a certain relation to the body, since "relation" is understood as one of the traditional Aristotelian categories of accidents. In other words, the foregoing proof that souls exist tells one nothing about what Avicenna calls "the substance of the soul" and what belongs to the soul in itself, but only that it is something related to the body that explains the activities in question. In this respect, Avicenna emphasizes that he has merely established that there is a certain mover for the activities of a living body but not what that mover is (ibid., I.1, 5.2–3).

Avicenna's focus thus far, and indeed a focus that continues throughout his *Psychology*, is on the activities, motions, and changes associated with being alive. In Avicenna's time, just as today, philosophers, psychologists, and biologists alike were hesitant to give a simple definition of life. Instead, they preferred to give a list of activities or functions by which one can identify a living thing. In broad strokes, Avicenna, following Aristotle, divides this list into three general sorts of activities (*Psychology*, "preface," 1): those activities associated with the most basic life forms, namely, plants, and include the activities of self-nourishment, growth, and reproduction; those activities associated with higher life forms, namely, animals, and include, as a minimum, sensation (at least touch, which could register pleasure and pain), while in higher animals would encompass all of the senses as well as the activity of volitional motion; and finally, that activity or function that ancient and medieval natural philosophers viewed as setting humans off from brute animals, namely, understanding or intellection (*'aql*).[1] The possession of a vegetative soul, then, explains why plants are able to nourish themselves, grow, and reproduce. The possession of an animal soul not only encompasses all of the activities definitive of plant life, but also explains why animals can perform the various activities unique to them. Finally, possession of the human soul explains all of the aforementioned lower activities, plant and animal alike, as well as the proper human activity of thought.

In his smaller encyclopedic work, the *Salvation*, Avicenna explains that the soul belonging to a living thing is dependent, in large part, upon the elemental mix that makes up the natural body of the living thing (*Salvation*, "Psychology," 1, 318.2–4). As noted in the previous chapter, for Avicenna there are four basic elements: earth, water, air, and fire. The element earth, recall, was associated with the qualities of cold/dry; water with cold/wet; air with hot/wet; and finally fire with hot/dry. Each of these qualities is in turn also associated with certain very basic powers: acting on in the case of hot, being acted on in the case of cold, while wet has the power to receive and dry the power to retain. It was believed, then, that the more well balanced the elemental mixture constituting a body, the larger the range of activities that that body can potentially perform.

The elemental mix then is preparatory for the body's having the soul that it does (and thus for performing the activities that are definitive of whatever species of life to which it belongs); nonetheless, it is the soul according to Avicenna that completes and perfects the body with respect to its species. Consequently, he argues that since the soul belongs to the given body, and indeed perfects the existence of that body such that it is actually a specific plant or animal, the soul must belong to the very subsistence of that body (*Psychology*, I.1, 5.3–6). In other words, the soul must be related to the body as one of its inherent causes, namely, either that principle by which it is in potency (that is, the material principle of the body) or that principle by which the potency is made actual (that is, the formal principle of the body). Again, the elemental mixture associated with a body explains the *potential* range of activities that belong to it. So, there can be no doubt, says Avicenna, that the body is that through which the living thing is what it is potentially. Now, if the soul likewise were merely something by which a living body is what it is potentially, then the soul would not in fact complete and perfect the living thing insofar as it is plant or animal. That is because it is not merely potentially being able to perform the various activities that completes and perfects the plant or animal but actually being able to perform those activities. Hence, if the soul only explained the living body's potential capacity to perform the activities associated with life—in other words, if the soul were simply the material principle of the body—there would need to be yet another principle that explains the actual capacity to perform those activities. Yet, as has been seen, the soul is the very principle that explains the actual performance of those activities. Thus, the soul cannot be the material principle of a living body. Therefore, concludes Avicenna, the soul "is a form, or like a form, or like a perfection (*kamāl*)" (*Psychology*, I.1, 6.1).

In fact, Avicenna is hesitant to identify the soul with form, as Aristotle in fact did (*De anima*, II 1, 412a19–20). In the end, Avicenna prefers to think of the soul as a perfection of the natural body rather than a form. In part, this preference reflects Avicenna's adherence to what in fact was the canonical Aristotelian definition of the soul, which Avicenna repeats: "The soul is the first perfection of a natural body possessed of organs that performs the activities of life" (*Psychology*, I.1, 12.6–8).[2] The distinction between first and second perfection, which was already encountered when considering Avicenna's definition of motion, reappears here in his use of "first perfection" to define the soul. In this context, Avicenna writes: "The 'first perfection' is that by which the species actually becomes a species, like the shape that belongs to the sword. The 'second perfection' is whatever comes after the thing's species, such as its activities and passions, like the act of cutting that belongs to the sword" (ibid., I.1, 11.7–10). In short, the use of "first perfection" in the definition is to emphasize that the soul is what completes and perfects the body. The soul is that which gives the body the actual powers to perform those activities definitive of being alive even when the living thing is not actively performing those activities—as, for example, when the animal is asleep and so not sensing or moving—whereas the second perfection is the actual performance of those activities.

Still, there were additional philosophical and historical reasons that also influenced Avicenna's preference for taking the soul to be more properly a perfection rather than a form. For Avicenna, following certain earlier

philosophers,[3] the very essence and existence of a form is spoken of in relation to matter.[4] Form makes matter determinately exist. Hence, while it
would be wrong to say that the matter causes the existence of the form, a
form for Avicenna cannot exist independently of matter, for again the form
essentially informs matter (ibid., I.1, 7.2–6). Consequently, if the soul were
simply the form of the body, the presumption would be that it could not
exist separate from the body, yet this was a question that Avicenna wanted
at least to leave open. Moreover, there were no less than two philosophical
traditions flowing into Avicenna's own discussion of the soul: the Aristotelian
one, which views the soul as the very form of an organic body, as well as the
Platonic or Neoplatonic tradition, which sees the soul as an immaterial
substance distinct from the body that merely uses the body in the way, for
example, a charioteer uses a chariot.[5] Here again, Avicenna wants to keep
these two alternatives alive. Given these concerns, Avicenna plumps for the
use of "perfection" when defining the soul. That is because:

> While every form is a perfection, not every perfection is a form. For the
> ruler is a perfection of the city, and the captain is a perfection of the ship,
> but they are not respectively a form of the city and form of the ship. So
> whatever perfection that is itself separate is not in fact the form belong-
> ing to matter and in the matter, since the form that is in the matter is the
> from imprinted in it and subsisting through it (*Psychology*, I.1, 6.13–17).

In fact, as I note later, one of the characteristics that distinguishes Avicenna's
psychology from that of most other medieval thinkers working within the
Aristotelian tradition is his advocacy of a substance dualism in the case of
the human soul or intellect. In other words, for Avicenna the human body
and soul are two distinct substances, one material the other immaterial.
For, again humans have in Avicenna's mind a unique activity that defines
them as humans, namely, rational thought, and in book V, he will argue
that this activity can only be accounted for if the human intellect is an immaterial substance.

Despite his substance dualism in the case of humans, Avicenna is keenly
aware that even between a human's body and his or her soul there exists a
very close relationship. In fact, with the exception of the last book of his
Psychology, most of Avicenna's psychological work is dedicated to the powers of the souls with respect to bodily functions, such as the external and
internal senses, both of which absolutely require a body, and altogether
cease with the destruction of the body. As has already been seen, Avicenna

classifies these powers, or faculties (sing. *qūwa*), into three basic sorts: those associated with the vegetative soul, those associated with the animal soul, and finally those associated with the human soul.

Although I consider some of these activities in more detail later, I should at least gesture at them here to provide a general introduction to Avicenna's psychology. Again, Avicenna identifies the activities associated with the vegetative soul with self-nourishment, growth, and reproduction. The first, and most general, divisions of the powers associated with the animal soul are those powers that bring about motion and perception. Motive powers, in turn, might be such as to provide the individual with an incentive to move, whether inasmuch as the individual desires something (the appetitive faculty), or fears/is angered by something (the irascible faculty). Additionally, motive powers include the power distributed throughout the muscles and nerves that actually produces motion in the animal, and thus moves it toward the desired object in the case of appetite and causes it to flee or fight in the cases of fear and anger. The animal's power of perception is also of two sorts: external perception and internal perception. Finally, the human or rational soul, which is also called "intellect," is likewise of two sorts: the practical and the theoretical intellect. As an image to help grasp the relation between the practical and theoretical intellects, Avicenna likens them to two faces of the human soul: the one worldly, the other, as it were, other-worldly. For the practical intellect is turned downward toward the management of the body, being influenced by the body and material needs and desires, while the theoretical intellect is turned upward toward the higher principles and causes, which are the source of all knowledge and understanding (*Psychology*, I.5, 47.14–18; *Salvation*, "Psychology," 4, 332.8–13).

Despite the great diversity of powers associated with living things, Avicenna sees them all as closely interrelated, indeed even forming a hierarchy. It would be best, he says, if one thinks of each of the lower souls as being a condition for what follows. In fact, suggests Avicenna, one might take the vegetative soul as a genus for animal souls, and animal soul as a genus for the human soul (*Psychology*, I.5, 40.4–13). Moreover, there is for Avicenna a relation of "ruler and ruled" found among them. Thus, the theoretical intellect rules the practical intellect, which in turn rules the internal senses. The internal senses are served by the external senses, which provide the former with their contact and raw data about the world. These perceptive powers themselves are served by the motive or moving powers, where the inciting powers rule over the powers that produce motion. The powers of the vegetative soul are in their turn subservient to the powers of the animal soul. Finally, among the vegetative powers, the power of reproduction is followed in nobility by the power of growth, which is itself followed lastly by the power of self-nourishment.

The Vegetative Soul and
the External Senses

The Vegetative Soul

My comments concerning Avicenna's views about the vegetative soul are short because Avicenna's own account is short, consisting, in the *Cure*, of one single small chapter at the opening of his discussion of the external senses (*Psychology*, II.1). In general, Avicenna argues that one must assign plants and animals the powers or faculties of the vegetative soul because one sees them nourishing themselves, growing, and reproducing. They simply could not do these acts if they did not have the powers to do them. The three powers are seen to be distinct from one another since one observes that plants and animals may manifest one of the powers while not manifesting another (save nutrition, which, as noted when discussing the hierarchy of the soul's power, is the most basic of all life activities). Thus, for example, reproduction is different from self-nourishment, since while an infant clearly has the power to nourish itself and grow, it does not yet have the power to reproduce. Similarly, a decrepit or even fully mature plant or animal may stop growing, while not lacking the power of self-nourishment, and thus these powers must be distinct too.

In general, the nutritive power involves the taking in of food or nutriment, and then the body's breaking it down into something like itself, which is then followed by the transmission of the usable nutriment so as to replace what the body has used up. In the case of growth, the aliment has the potential to extend between two adjoining parts of the various organs, muscles, and the like and causes them to move apart and so settle between those bodily parts, in which case the size of the body expands. This expansion, says Avicenna, is not haphazard but ideally is directed toward reaching the plant or animal's perfection of growth, that is, a magnitude that falls within the proper range of size and shape relative to whatever species it is.

In the case of reproduction, Avicenna continues, that power separates off a part of the parent body, namely, the seed in the case of plants, or semen, whether male or female,[6] in the case of animals. The reproductive power, then, inheres in that part. When the matter and place are prepared to receive that part—as, for example, a fertile womb in the case of semen— and that part possessing the reproductive power comes to be present there, the power begins to perform its function. For Avicenna, the proper function of the reproductive power is strictly speaking simply to prepare the matter for the soul that will then complete and perfect the living thing with respect to its species. In other words, the reproductive power merely brings about a body whose elemental mixture is suitable for a soul of the same kind as the parent. It does not produce or educe the species soul by which there actually is an individual of that species. The actual infusion or impressing of the soul into the body comes to be, according to Avicenna, through that immaterial principle that he dubs the "Giver of Forms" (*wāhib aṣ-ṣuwar*), which was mentioned in the last chapter. I shall have more to say about the Giver of Forms, which Avicenna also identifies with the "Active Intellect," in the next chapter and again in chapter 7.

Perception and Abstraction

Like the powers of the vegetative soul, Avicenna has little to say about the various motive powers that belong to the animal. In the case of the motive power that produces motion, certainly the reason for Avicenna's rather superficial treatment of it in the *Psychology* is that it more fittingly belongs to a discussion of anatomy and physiology. As for the powers that incite motion, namely, the appetitive and irascible faculties, they are intimately wound up with the powers of perception (*idrāk*). Thus, it is perception that is for Avicenna the most significant activity of animals (and even to a certain extent of humans, for it is intellectual perception that is our proper function). Given the importance of perception to Avicenna's overall psychology, it is important for one to consider his understanding of this activity in some depth.

According to Avicenna, all perception "is nothing but taking in the form of the perceptible in one way or another" (*Psychology*, II.2, 58.2–3). More precisely, perception involves, in the case of perceiving material objects, the percipient individual's being impressed by either the form (*ṣūra*) or connotational attribute (*ma'ná*) of that object (or even the thing itself [*dhāt*] or essence in the case of intellectually perceiving, although for the moment I shall set aside such perception).

Most animal perception, then, has as its object either a form or connotational attribute, the two of which Avicenna is very careful to distinguish.

> Form is something that both the internal and external senses perceive, but the external sense perceives it first and then relays it to the internal sense. . . . The connotational attribute is something that the soul perceives from the sensible without the external senses first perceiving it (*Psychology*, I.5, 43.6–11).

The example Avicenna gives in the *Psychology* of perceiving the form is a sheep's perception of a wolf. The sheep sees the color and shape of the wolf; it smells the wolf; it hears its growling; and if it is not careful it feels the wolf's weight upon it. All of these are perceptible features that follow upon the wolf's form, and are all immediately perceived by the sheep's external senses. Via the external senses this data is then perceived by the sheep's internal senses. Thus, for instance, all the data from the external senses is fed into the internal sense of *fantasia*, the so-called common sense (*ḥiss mushtarak*). Avicenna's use of "common sense," a notion that can be traced back at least as far as Aristotle, as is much of Avicenna's discussion thus far concerning sensation, should not be confused with sound judgment or wisdom; rather, it is that internal sense faculty that brings together all the disparate pieces of sensory information into a unified sensible experience, in this case a unified wolf-perception. Should the sheep survive its encounter with the wolf, the form of this unified wolf-perception is in turn stored in the retentive imagination (*khayāl*) or form-bearing faculty (*qūwa muṣawwira*). In short, the sensible form is immediately perceived by the external senses and only then, through their intermediacy, perceived by the internal senses.

In contrast, the *connotational attribute* is perceived only by the internal senses and not at all by an external sense, despite the fact that the connotational attribute is there in the sensible object. So, returning to the sheep example, when it encounters the wolf, one of the things that it perceives is that the wolf is dangerous. Clearly, the perceived danger presented by the wolf is not some color, shape, smell, or the like belonging to the wolf, and yet there is some feature or features about the wolf that the sheep's internal senses recognize and by which it perceives the wolf as a threat. Other examples of connotational attributes given by Avicenna in such works as the

Physics are time, space, and motion. In all of these examples, the connotational attribute is some nonsensible feature (in the sense of not directly perceived by the external senses) that nonetheless belongs to and is conveyed by material things, and so insofar as it is nonsensible it must be perceived only internally.

Given Avicenna's distinction between forms and connotational attributes, it should be no surprise that he distinguishes different kinds of perception. There is perception performed by the external senses, which has just been considered, namely, seeing, hearing, tasting, smelling, and touching. There is the perception of the internal senses, such as imagining, as well as the perceptive operation of the estimative faculty, which I discuss shortly. There is likewise the intellect's perception of universal concepts or intelligibles (sing. *ma'qūl*), such as humanity as opposed to a particular human, a form of perception that is the human's proper act of understanding. While the distinction between forms and connotational attributes goes some of the way toward showing what specifically differentiates the various kinds of perception, it is the degrees of abstraction (*tajrīd*) involved in the particular perceptive acts that Avicenna explicitly uses to distinguish the different kinds of perception (*Psychology*, II.2, 58–61).

In its most general sense, abstraction for Avicenna involves extracting the form, connotational attribute, or even intelligible species from matter.[7] Avicenna also describes abstraction as peeling away the material concomitants—such as having a certain quantity, quality, or even having spatial and temporal locations—that are the hallmarks of natural bodies studied by both general physics and psychology. Indeed, as was seen in chapter 2, the essences of natural things considered in themselves—which in a very real sense are the proper objects of animal perception—are particularized by their presence in matter, and can be conceptualized only insofar as one ignores, sets aside, or in someway disregards the accidents that follow upon matter. The various degrees of abstraction simply are the various degrees of grasping essences in themselves independent of matter and their relation to matter.[8]

Thus, in sensation, the sensible object, Avicenna observes, is not wholly abstracted from the matter itself (*Psychology*, II.2, 59.11–14). This is clear from the fact that in order for one to perceive sensibly a given material object, the sensible perception requires the very presence of that object. Once the object is removed from the sensory field, the correlative sensation ceases. Thus, while in sensation there is spatial separation between the perceived material object and the sense organ, the material object must nonetheless remain within the sense organ's immediate field of operation if the perception is to continue.

Avicenna next observes that between sensation and the act of the retentive imagination there is a higher degree of abstraction, and so a different kind of perception (ibid., 59.14–60.10). In the case of imagination, the imagined object is abstracted from the very matter of the object itself and so can be perceived even in the absence of the material object. Still, the imagined object is not fully abstracted from the concomitants or accidents of matter, "since the form that is in the retentive imagination depends upon the sensible form and on a certain quantification, qualification, and position" (ibid., 60.4–6). In other words, an animal cannot produce an image or picture in the imagination that does not have some imagined size, shape, color, and position of its part, all features, as noted in chapter 2, that follow upon matter. Thus, even though imagination, unlike sensation, can operate in the absence of a material concrete particular, it still has a very decided connection with matter.

The degree of abstraction between the retentive imagination and the estimative faculty is even greater (ibid., 60.10–61.5). That is because, as has been seen, the estimative faculty for Avicenna perceives the nonsensible aspects of material things (or even the imaginable aspects, in the sense of forming a picturelike image). Examples of the objects of the estimative faculty are, again, things like the sheep's perception of danger, our perception of space, motion, and time, and here, Avicenna further adds, one's perception that certain things are good or not good.[9]

The final degree of abstraction, where all associations with matter and its accidents are removed, occurs in the case of intellectual perception, which is discussed more fully in the next chapter. To sum up before turning to Avicenna's discussion of the external senses, that activity that defines animals and humans alike is perception. Perception, as Avicenna observes, can be of different kinds that are distinguished by the degree to which the perceptible object is abstracted from matter and the concomitants of matter.

The External Senses

Again the most basic or rudimentary act of perception is sensation. In general, for Avicenna all sensation involves a certain power or faculty, which is arrayed in a corresponding sense organ, and in the act of sensation that sense organ is impressed by a sensible form proper to that power (*Salvation*, "Psychology," 3, 323.8–10). So, for example, according to Avicenna, the faculty of hearing is a power arrayed in the nerve dispersed on the surface of the ear canal, which is disposed so as to perceive "the form of what is transmitted to it from the air's oscillation between what causes [the air] to vibrate and what receives [that] vibration, [with] the air so oscillating that it produces sound" (*Psychology*, I.5, 42.1–3). When hearing occurs, the eardrum is impressed by these oscillations of the air and vibrates in harmony with them. It is this affection of the eardrum, namely, its vibrating at the same frequency as the oscillating air, that Avicenna identifies with hearing.

As for smell, Avicenna identifies it with "a faculty, [which is] arrayed in the two appendages in the anterior part of the brain resembling two nipples, that perceives what is transmitted to it by the air in the nasal passages, such as the odor present in the vapor mingled with [the air] or the odor imprinted in it through alteration by an odoriferous body" (ibid., 42.5–9). As one might expect, Avicenna locates taste on the nerves spread throughout the tongue, where the sensation of taste occurs when the chewed substance begins to dissolve and the sensible forms of tastes found in it mingle with the salivary fluids so as to effect the tongue (ibid., 42.9–11).

To this point, much of Avicenna's accounts concerning the mechanics and chemistry of the various senses should not to be too unfamiliar to modern readers. The situation changes in the case of the sensation of touch, for, whereas it is common for us to identify touch with a single sense modality, Avicenna has doubts as to whether it is a single, unified modality. He, instead, thinks that the term "touch" (*lams*) encompasses four different sorts of sensation (ibid., 42.11–43.1). These are for Avicenna the categorically different sensations of (1) hot and cold, (2) wet and dry, (3) hard and soft, and finally (4) rough and smooth. The reason that one often thinks that touch is a single faculty, argues Avicenna, is that all four of the powers come together in a single organ, namely, they are arrayed in the nerves of the skin and flesh of the entire body. Like the other sense modalities, however, the various senses of touch involve the perception of what comes into contact with the body and causes an alteration of the bodily temperament and elemental configuration, such as, for example, the hot/cold and wet/dry features that in a sense are constitutive of the body's elemental mixture.

The final faculty of sensation is vision, which I treat more fully in the next section. In summary form, however, this faculty is for Avicenna arrayed in the so-called hollow nerves—or what we would today call the "optical nerves." Vision occurs when the visible forms are impressed upon the vitreous humor in the optical nerves. More precisely, according to Avicenna, the visible forms are the sensible images of bodies possessing color that are transmitted through actually transparent bodies, such as air or water, to the surface of the eye by means of radiant light, and then from there excite the vitreous humor.

To sum up, then, for Avicenna every case of perception by one of the external senses involves some material object's transmitting a sensible form or sensible species of itself to the relevant sense organ. That sensible form, then, impresses itself on the correlative sense organ, where the corresponding act of sensation is nothing more than that organ's being so impressed. Since this manner of perception involves something's coming from without and impressing itself *into* the sense organ, Avicenna adopts what has historically been termed an "intromission model or theory of perception."

Vision

Avicenna thinks that it is obvious in the cases of taste, touch, smell, and hearing that they occur according to the intromission model of perception, again, the theory that claims that perception involves something's coming from without and entering into the perceiver and impressing itself on the sense faculty. In the case of vision, however, Avicenna observes that there have been differences of opinion: Some saying (Aristotle and Avicenna among them) that, as with the rest of the senses, vision too occurs according to the intromission model, whereas others advocated what has been called an extramission model of vision.[10]

According to the extramission model of vision, seeing takes place not by something's entering the eyes, but by something's exiting from the eyes, whether it be some sort of ray, as the mathematical models of Euclid and Ptolemy assumed, or an optical *pneuma* or spirit that purportedly alters the surrounding air so as to make it usable as a tool by the animal's visual system, as the materialistic model of the Stoics and the physician Galen required. While the extramission theory of vision might seem odd to us today, it had some apparent advantages over the intromission theory that made it a real contender in at least the ancient and early medieval periods. First, one does not have to countenance specterlike sensible forms being transmitted through the air or other medium. Second, if perception is nothing more than the reception of a sensible form, as the intromission model of perception maintains, and the intervening air or water between a given sensible object and a perceiver are also receiving the sensible form, it seems that, based upon the intromission model's own principles, the air or water should likewise perceive those forms.[11] Such a problem obviously does not arise for the extramission theory. Third, and arguably the most significant reason for adopting the extramission model, is that it allowed for an elegant mathematical explanation of a number of problems related to visual perspective, as, for example, why an object appears smaller the farther it is away from the perceiver. So, for example, Ptolemy in his *Optics*, maintained that a visual flux emanates from the eye so as to form a cone. The introduction of a cone, then, allowed Ptolemy to apply simple geometrical theorems and explanations to physical problems associated with vision, such as, again, explaining the relative size of objects seen at different distances, as well as several other such phenomena. In this instance, he simply lays it down that the smaller the angle through which an object is seen, the smaller the object appears. Thus, consider the diagram presented in figure 4.1. Let the object EF initially be seen at some distance such that it forms the angle BAC. Next, let EF be moved to a further distance and call it E′F′. In this case, E′F′ is now seen through the smaller angle DAC. Given this situation, Ptolemy simply claimed that since the angle DAC is smaller than the angle BAC when EF is further away, E′F′ (again that is EF at the farther distance) in fact appears smaller, just as we perceive it.

Despite the advantages that an extramission theory might bring, Avicenna ardently defended the intromission model of vision. In fact, so much so that he dedicates the whole of book III of his *Psychology* to developing his own version of the intromission model of vision as well as presenting and severely

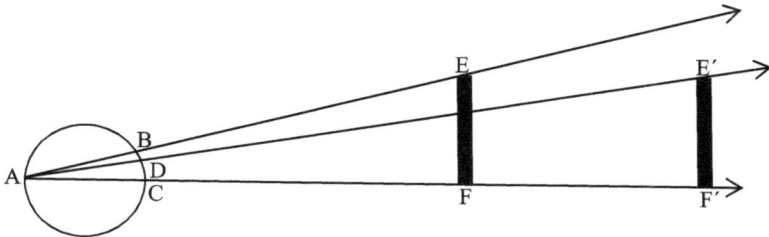

FIGURE 4.1.

criticizing opposing theories. The major proponent of the intromission theory in the ancient world was Aristotle; however, Avicenna's own adherence to that theory is not due to any slavish devotion to Aristotle, since in many respects Avicenna's theory of vision and its accompanying theory of light are radically different from Aristotle's. Indeed, Dag Hasse[12] has brought to our attention the fact that Avicenna's mature theory of light—which is closely connected with his theory of vision—is not at all the standard Aristotelian account, where light is understood as the state or affection of the medium when that medium is transparent.[13]

Avicenna, instead, has other reasons for preferring the intromission theory. First, it gives a symmetry or simplicity of explanation to his overall account of how external sensation works, and indeed, to how all the various kinds of perception work, internal sensation and intellection included. Second, Avicenna's own variety of the intromission theory represents what might be thought of as the cutting edge of optical theory of his time.[14] Third, and finally, for virtually all ancient and medieval cognitive theorists alike, human cognition is modeled on one's model of vision. A number of the innovations that Avicenna introduces in his theory of vision are in no doubt motivated by a desire to accommodate certain novel features of his own account of how intellectual perception works. Having said that, let me turn to Avicenna's optical theory.

Avicenna's Theory of Light and the Transparent

In a move that anticipates modern optical theories, Avicenna intimately joins his theory of vision with a theory of light. Thus, book III of his *Psychology* begins, "We now should discuss vision, but discussing it requires discussing light, the transparent, and color, as well as how the connection between sensation and the visible object of sensation occurs" (*Psychology*, III.1, 91.1–3). What immediately follows in the first chapter of this book is an in-depth discussion of the vocabulary of light. Avicenna begins by noting that as a matter of linguistic convention the Arabic terms *ḍaw'*, *nūr*, and *shuʿāʿ* are often used interchangeably, all roughly corresponding with "light." For the purposes of discussing vision, however, he wants to assign each term a technical meaning. In the present context Avicenna says that he is not particularly concerned with *shuʿāʿ*, a term that one can safely translate as "ray," and which I discuss more thoroughly later. Instead, here he focuses on *ḍaw'* and *nūr*. The first term, *ḍaw'*, one might render as "luminous light." Luminous light is that which is observed when one considers luminous bodies like the Sun or fire without taking into account the light's color, as, for example, its being yellow, white, or red. Such light belongs essentially to luminous bodies, and it is by that luminous light that those bodies themselves are essentially visible. He next defines *nūr* as "the thing that radiates (*yasṭa'u*) from [the body having luminous light], and is then imagined to fall upon bodies, in which case [this type of light] will appear white, black, or green" (ibid., III.1, 91.8–9). For present purposes, one can term this kind of light "radiant light."[15]

Having provided general descriptions of luminous light and radiant light, he now approaches them from a different angle, namely, the bodies to which they belong. He notes that there are two classes of bodies. On the one hand, there are those bodies that when positioned between a would-be-perceiver and a luminous body, such as fire, hinder the perceiver from seeing the luminous body behind them. They are what one might term "opaque bodies." On the other hand, there are also those bodies, like air and water, which do not hinder one from seeing a luminous body that is positioned behind them. Such bodies are, Avicenna notes, "transparent" (*shaffāf*). Opaque bodies are again of two kinds: those that are themselves luminous, and those that are not. So, for example, a wall of fire, which is a luminous body, can just as effectively prevent one from seeing some light on the opposite side of it as a brick wall. The class of bodies that are self-luminous can be seen of themselves and need nothing further to be seen except that the body between them and the perceiver be a transparent one. Nonluminous, opaque bodies, however, cannot be seen merely given a transparent medium but need something else. Avicenna identifies nonluminous, opaque bodies with "colored objects," which, if they are to be seen, need the radiant light of a luminous body in addition to a transparent medium.

Up to this point most of what Avicenna has had to say about light, while, certainly going beyond Aristotle and the Aristotelian tradition more generally, is not at odds with that tradition. Where Avicenna's position is at odds with the Aristotelian account concerns the states of potentiality and actuality of transparent and colored objects. On the traditional Aristotelian theory, color is in a sense always actualized. It is only the medium, according to Aristotle, that is sometimes potentially transparent, and so actually dark, while at other times actually transparent and so light. That is because in

Aristotle's technical sense, light simply is the state of the actually transparent medium as such. Thus, for Aristotle a colored object fails to produce sight in a properly situated perceiver, not because there is no actual color in the object, but because the tool, namely, the medium, by which color acts upon the perceiver, is not in a proper state, that is to say, the medium is not at that time actually transparent and so light. Stated another way, the potentially transparent, that is, the dark, acts as an obstacle that prevents vision. In short, on the traditional Aristotelian model, color is always actualized, whereas it is only the medium that is in either a state of potential or actual transparency.

In contrast, for Avicenna, media, such as air and water, are strictly speaking always actually transparent, whereas it is color that might either be in a state of potentiality or actuality. Thus, he writes:

> Don't suppose that white, red, and the like actually exist in the bodies in the way that they are seen but that the dark air prevents the vision of it, for the air itself is not dark. What is dark is only that which itself receives the radiant light, whereas the air itself (even if there is nothing luminous in it) does not hinder the perception of that which receives the radiant light nor does it conceal the color when it exists in something (*Psychology*, III.1, 93.6–11).

He continues that in the absence of a luminous or radiant light one simply imagines that the air is dark. In that situation, because no light, luminous or radiant, is present, there is nothing stimulating one's visual system. Thus, it is not that one is "seeing" darkness; rather, one is simply not seeing at all. Avicenna likens this case to either being blind or having one's eyelids closed. Now, while Avicenna follows the Aristotelian tradition and occasionally speaks of the "potentially transparent," he is equally clear that a medium's becoming actually transparent does not involve any alteration in the medium itself. Instead, it involves an alteration or motion in another, either by some luminous body's moving into a given place or a radiant light's falling onto a colored object.

As for the term "color" (*lawn*), in its proper sense, Avicenna continues, it refers to the phenomenal colors, white, red, green, and so on, namely, the colors as we see them. One is simply using the term "color" equivocally, says Avicenna, if "color" is meant to refer to "various dispositions that are in the bodies, which when they receive luminous light, one of them comes to be something that we see as white and another as red" (ibid., III.1, 94.10–12).

Instead, in those bodies that are not luminous, and so not visible in themselves, a radiant light coming from a luminous body must fall upon them and blend or mix with the potential color or disposition in the body. The resultant of this mingling of radiant light and potential color is for Avicenna what one, then, perceives as the actual perceptible color (*Psychology*, III.3, 103).

Sometimes Avicenna speaks of the actual color that emanates from the illuminated body—which again is the combination of radiant light and potential color—as itself "luminous light" (*ḍaw'*), but since he almost as frequently also uses the term "ray" (*shu'ā'*), I shall use this latter term in order to avoid possible confusion. Thus, at *Psychology*, III.7, he says that a ray is what connects (*ittiṣāl*) the visible form or sensible species in the perceived object—namely, actual color—with the visual system of some perceiver in order that the object "might project its sensible image (*shabaḥ*) to the [perceiver]" (*Psychology*, III.7, 142.4–5). Also at *Psychology*, III.1, where Avicenna initially discussed light terms, he there defined "ray" as "the thing that is imagined, as it were, to well-up [from colored bodies], cloak their color, and then emanate (*yufīḍu*) from them" (ibid., III.1, 91.10–12). Avicenna more frequently expresses this sense of a ray's welling up and emanating from the body by saying that light has been reflected (*in'ikās*) from the body.[16]

Refutation of the Extramission Theory

Certainly one of the more historically important aspects of Avicenna's optical theory is his thoroughgoing criticism of the extramission theory of vision, which I mentioned at the beginning of this section, a criticism, I might add, that exploits his innovative thoughts about the nature of light and rays. Thus, returning to Avicenna's understanding of visual rays, he additionally claims that when one sees some visible object, the rays, which convey the object's sensible image, form a cone, whose base is at the sensible object and whose vertex is at the back of the crystalline humor that forms part of the eye. The sensible image projecting from the visible object affects the eye at the surface of the crystalline humor, rather than at the back of it where the vertex of the visual cone has fallen. Consequently, the sensible image affects the eye at a section of this visual cone, such as, the arc AB in figure 4.2. He next asserts that, "if the angle [at which the sensible image falls upon the surface of the crystalline humor] is larger because the thing is nearer, the

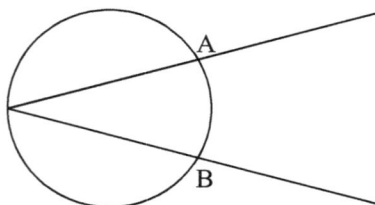

FIGURE 4.2.

section is greater and the sensible image in it is greater, whereas if the angle is smaller because the thing is farther away, the section and sensible image that is in it are smaller" (*Psychology*, III.5, 124.17–19). In effect, Avicenna's theories of light and color and the optical rays formed from their mixture allow him to appropriate what was seen as perhaps the greatest strength of the extramission theory, namely, its introduction of a visual cone that provided for the application of mathematical explanations to various problems of perspective. The real difference between Avicenna's intromission model and the earlier extramission model is that while the mathematicians had thought that the rays emanate from the eyes of the perceiver, Avicenna maintains that rays of light emanate or are reflected from the visible objects themselves and then impinge upon the visual system.

Having shown that his account has at least equal explanatory power as the extramission theory purportedly does, he goes on to argue that in fact the extramission theory cannot even take advantage of the very geometrical analysis that was thought to be its greatest strength. Avicenna argues thus: If vision involves a ray that purportedly emanates from the eyes and it comes into contact with a visible object, where the perception of that object results from the contact of that ray, then, when that ray extends to where the visible object is, one should in fact perceive the visible object according to how big the object actually is. That follows, maintains Avicenna, because the perceiver is in actual contact with the whole of the object according to its actual size via the ray emitted from the perceiver's eye. So, for instance, when there are similarly sized objects that are at different distances, the perceiver should not see them as appearing either smaller or larger just as one would not feel them as either smaller or larger even if one touched the very same object at a further distance. Moreover, if the extramission theorists claim that something comes back down the visual ray such that vision takes place in the visual system of the perceiver, then, complains Avicenna, the emanation of rays from the eyes is redundant, since one needs merely posit, as Avicenna himself has done, that rays emanate from the visible object, either owing to the object itself in the case of a luminous body, or owing to rays reflected from the object in the case of a colored object. In short, Avicenna's intromission theory is just as empirically adequate as the extramission one, while also being the simpler scientific explanation.

Certain physical absurdities, notes Avicenna, also result from the extramission theory. For example, among the things that one sees are the stars of the outermost heavens. Consequently, any animal capable of such vision, were the extramission theory correct, would need to be able to produce enough optical *pneuma* or visual flux to form a cone that extends to the outermost celestial sphere. This optical cone that is purportedly produced by the animal, Avicenna hastens to add, would at its base take in nearly one whole hemisphere of the heavens. Thus the animal, whose size when compared with that of the heavens is negligible, would be required to produce a staggering amount of optical *pneuma* or visual flux every time it peaks at the heavens. Additionally, this cone would have to be formed virtually instantaneously with the opening of the eyes. Moreover, mocks Avicenna, in the case of the Galenic account—where the optical *pneuma* alters the air so as to transform it into a tool or organ of sight—it should be that when many viewers are gathered together the amount of optical *pneuma* is of a larger quantity and so everyone's sight should be sharper, or, at the very least, those of poor eyesight should see better. Avicenna finds the consequences of the extramission model simply beyond credulity. In the end, he concludes, the purported mathematical and naturalistic explanations that initially made the extramission model seem attractive simply are not there.[17]

To finish up Avicenna's theory of vision, let me briefly consider his views concerning the physiology of vision (*Psychology*, III.8, 151–154). I have already noted that, for Avicenna, vision requires that the sensible image of a visible object be conveyed through a transparent medium via rays emanating from the visible object itself. These rays, which apparently emanate in all directions, again form a cone relative to a properly functioning visual system in a perceiver that is facing the visible object, where the vertex of that cone falls at the back of the crystalline humor, which makes up part of the eye. Once this sensible image impinges upon the eye, it stimulates or impresses itself on the crystalline humor; however, there is not vision at this point, Avicenna insists, since if there were, there would be two distinct sensible images in the two eyes, and the single visible object would be seen as two. Instead, the sensible image is transferred via a conveying *pneuma* (*rūḥ*)[18] along the optical nerves, to the optic chiasma (*ṣalīb*), at which there is then vision.

After reaching the optic chiasma, the sensible image impressed in the *pneuma* is then conveyed to the anterior ventricle of the brain where it is again impressed upon the common sense—which is one of the internal senses that I shall take up in more detail in the next section. It is in the common sense that there occurs "the perfection of vision" (*Psychology*, III.8, 152.8), as Avicenna calls it. After the sensible image appears in the common sense, it passes on to the retentive imagination, also called the form-bearing faculty, which is arrayed behind the anterior ventricle of the brain where the image is stored until it is called up by the estimative faculty. At the time that the image is needed, Avicenna writes:

> [The estimative faculty] opens up the *cerebellar vermis* (*dūda*) by removing what is between the two porous appendages (which [just] are the *cerebellar vermis*) and [the form that is in the retentive imagination] conjoins with the *pneuma* harboring the estimative faculty by means of the *pneuma* harboring the faculty of the compositive imagination (which in humans is called the cogitative [faculty]). The form that is in the retentive imagination is then imprinted onto the *pneuma* of the estimative faculty, and the faculty of the compositive imagination, which serves the estimative faculty, conveys what is in the retentive imagination to it (*Psychology*, III.8, 153.10–14).

In the next section, I consider the various internal faculties mentioned in this passage in more detail. For now, however, this should give one at least a sense of how Avicenna sees data derived from vision, and indeed the external senses in general, being internalized and then stored in the brain.

Before turning to the internal senses, let me quickly sum up the most salient points of Avicenna's optical theory. Light is of two types. There is luminous light, which belongs to certain bodies like the Sun and fire, and by which these bodies are visible in themselves. Additionally, there is radiant light, which radiates from luminous bodies and mixes with the potential colors of certain other types of bodies. Thereafter the mixture of radiant light and potential color forms a ray that is reflected from the visible object. When this ray is connected with a perceiver who is facing the visible object, a sensible image of the visible object projects toward the perceiver and is seen as actual color, and therein there is vision.

The Internal Senses

Certainly one of Avicenna's main contributions to the science of psychology is his exploration and mapping of the so-called internal sense faculties. Indeed, many of the various operations that Aristotle had previously subsumed under the single internal sense of *phantasia*, Avicenna would disambiguate in a principled way. Moreover, despite the fact that Avicenna, as will become clear, is a dualist when it comes to the human intellect and body (that it to say, he believes that the intellect is an immaterial substance wholly distinct from the material substance of the body), he, nonetheless, assigns a large portion of our daily cognitive operations to the internal senses, and even grants that the activities of certain internal senses are at least preparatory for the intellect's operation.[19]

Avicenna identifies five internal senses: (1) the common sense (*ḥiss mushtarak*), also sometimes called *fantasia*; (2) the retentive imagination (*khayāl*), which he also terms the form-bearing faculty (*qūwa muṣawwira*); (3) the compositive imagination (*mutakhayyila*), which in humans is transformed into the cogitative faculty (*qūwa mutafakkira*) when it is being used by the intellect; (4) the estimative faculty (*qūwa wahmīya*); and finally (5) memory (*dhikr*). Avicenna's identification of these five internal powers is not haphazard but is the result of three distinct principles of faculty differentiation (*Psychology*, I.5, 43.1–44.3): (1) the principle of differentiation between different cognitive objects; (2) the principle of differentiation between receptive and retentive powers; and (3) the principle of differentiation between active and passive powers.

The Principles of Faculty Differentiation

The first principle, namely that faculties are differentiated on the basis of different cognitive objects, is one with a prestigious pedigree going back at least as far as Plato.[20] Still, Avicenna's application of this principle is unique because of his distinction between forms and connotational attributes, which was seen when considering one of the ways that Avicenna distinguished external from internal senses. To repeat some of that discussion again, forms, for Avicenna, are those objects of perception that are immediately grasped by the external senses and then, through the intermediacy of the external senses, are perceived by the internal senses. Connotational attributes, in contrast, are in no way perceived by the external senses but only immediately by the internal senses, as, for example, perceiving that a wolf is dangerous, or that time has passed, or even that something is good or not good. In short, connotational attributes are nonsensible features inherent in material objects. Based on this principle of faculty differentiation Avicenna, then, distinguishes between the power of common sense (or *fantasia*), which perceives sensible forms, and that of the estimative faculty, which perceives connotational attributes.

The next principle of faculty differentiation involves the differences between receptive and retentive faculties. Avicenna bases this principle upon another one that is familiar within the Aristotelian psychological tradition, namely that a single power cannot both receive and retain its proper object. The reason for this limitation on a single power is that ultimately the internal senses are for Avicenna physiological faculties or powers harbored in the brain. In other words, they are corporeal. As such they have definite powers, qualities, and even limitations based upon the elemental makeup of that part of the brain where they are harbored. So, for example, when a given internal sense receives its proper object, that object impresses itself onto the internal sense. Being impressed, however, requires that the sense organ's compositional makeup have a certain degree of fluidity or malleability, which for the ancient and medieval scientists would be due to a predominance of elemental water existing in that organ. In contrast, what explains some impression's being retained and being stable is the qualitative dryness of the organ, which according to ancient and medieval chemistry is explained by a predominance of elemental earth in the organ. Hence, if the same organ were both to receive and to retain its proper object, it would simultaneously have to be predominantly wet and dry. Since these are contrary qualities, a single power's both receiving and retaining its proper object would involve a physical absurdity. Consequently, concludes Avicenna, different faculties must be assigned to these different functions: The common sense, as noted, receives the sensible forms, while the retentive imagination retains them, and similarly the estimative faculty receives the connotational attributes, while memory retains them.

The final principle distinguishes those faculties that are passive (and so are merely acted upon by their proper objects) and those faculties that are active (and so in some way manipulate their proper objects). To state the same point slightly differently, passive faculties merely perceive their proper objects as those objects present themselves, while an active faculty can alter what has been presented to the animal so that it has a perception of something new and/or different from what in fact was perceived. For example, my common sense can only perceive the coffee in my cup as tepid and slightly burnt, but I can imagine it as piping hot and fresh. Using this principle, Avicenna thus distinguishes the compositive imagination (which can separate and recombine the retained forms and connotational attributes into new objects of internal sensation) from the common sense and estimative faculties (both of which merely receive and are impressed by forms and connotational attributes).

The Internal Senses

Based upon the best anatomical research of his time,[21] Avicenna placed the common sense in the anterior ventricle of the brain. Its function, as has been seen, is to receive all the forms imprinted on the external senses, which are then conveyed to the common sense. It is in the common sense that the distinct sensory input of each of the external senses is unified into an integrated sensible experience. It is because of this faculty that, for example, I experience the brown-colored, warm, hot-wet, coffee aroma, and flavor with the accompanying slurping sound when I drink it, as a single, unified coffee experience.

After the forms of the external senses are unified in the common sense, the form of that integrated, sensible experience is conveyed to the retentive imagination and stored there until the compositive imagination needs it. Because the retentive imagination bears the sensible forms, it also sometimes goes by the more descriptive name, "the form-bearing faculty." This faculty, Avicenna tells us, is arrayed behind the anterior ventricle of the brain.

Avicenna locates the estimative faculty at the back of the medial ventricle.[22] Its function, as has been noted, is to perceive the connotational attributes, which again are not perceptible to the external senses, but which are nonetheless in particular sensible objects. Avicenna also thinks that the estimative faculty frequently controls the compositive imagination's function of combining and dividing sensible forms and connotational attributes, a point to which I return momentarily. In all animals, other than humans, the operation of the estimative faculty is for Avicenna that animal's highest function. Indeed, even in humans it is the estimative faculty that undertakes most of our day-to-day interactions with the world around us. Thus, as Avicenna repeats frequently in his psychological works, it is the estimative faculty that perceives things like the goodness or pleasantness of some object, as well as the harmfulness or ire-inciting properties of some experience. Thus, in all animals, humans included, it is the estimative faculty that, for example, recognizes that some ripe piece of fruit is good, or some individual is desirable as a mate. This information is in turn conveyed to the appetitive faculty that incites the motive faculty to move toward the fruit, the potential mate, and the like. Moreover, since in his *Physics* Avicenna also includes things like time and space as objects of the estimative faculty, it seems reasonable to conclude that for him this faculty aids in the animal's maneuvering toward the desired object. So, for example, I have presented Avicenna's explanation as to why the greater the distance an object is from the perceiver the smaller it appears; however, appearing as small or large on one's visual field is different from appearing as farther or nearer away, even if the latter is explanatory of the former. Yet it is knowing or estimating the distance from an object that is important for moving toward that thing. Inasmuch as the estimative faculty perceives things like spatial relations, it would seem that Avicenna envisions it as interpreting two-dimensional visual data as the three-dimensional space in which the animal actually finds itself and through which it has to move. Thus, the animal perceives that its immediate experience is not, for example, of a small berry immediately in front of it but of a medium-sized apple at a distance. In short, the estimative faculty is what sets the appetitive and irascible faculties into action, and then plays an important role in guiding the animal's motion toward or away from some given thing, which, again, for most animals are their most important animate activities.

The faculty of memory, which is arrayed in the posterior ventricle, has for Avicenna the function of retaining the insensible connotational attributes in particular objects perceived by the estimative faculty. Avicenna likens the relation between memory and the estimative faculty to the relation between the retentive imagination and the common sense.

The final faculty of animal souls is that of the compositive imagination, which, when under the control of the human intellect, goes by the name "cogitative faculty."[23] As noted, Avicenna locates this faculty in the medial ventricle of the brain at the *cerebellar vermis*. Concerning it, Avicenna writes:

> We know with certainty that it is natural for us to combine and separate parts of sensibles objects with other parts, not according to the form that we found in them externally nor even affirming that some of them exist

or do not. Thus, in us there must be some faculty by which we do that. This [faculty], when the intellect is using it, is called the "cogitative [faculty]," while when the animal faculty is using it, it is called the "compositive imagination" (*Psychology*, IV.1, 165.19–166.4).

The compositive imagination is thus characterized for Avicenna by its power "to combine and separate parts of sensible objects with other parts." While such combining and separating can give rise to such fantastical images as paisley elephants with wings, it is neither limited to such outlandish images nor even merely pictorial images. It is in fact this faculty by which the animal may see itself in the future sating some desire, whether for food, a mate, or the like. It is likewise that faculty by which one imagines how certain foods would taste together. It, moreover, gives rise to dreams, whether daydreams or sleeping dreams. Indeed, in humans it is that faculty that vocalizes the words that one hears when one is engaged in internal discourse, and, as one might guess, it also imagines certain shapes, figures, or other images that one might use when trying to solve problems in mathematics or even other practical sorts of issues.

As for the compositive imagination's activity, it sometimes acts independently, and so is not controlled by anything else, while at other times it can be brought into the service of either the estimative faculty or the human intellect. In its free state, its activity of combining and separating sensible images is random and haphazard. Indeed, one might not even be aware that one is combining and separating such images, as, for example, when one has been daydreaming and only later becomes actively conscious that his or her mind has been wandering. Deborah Black describes this faculty in its free state thus: "In its absolute and uncontrolled state, then, the compositive imagination is characterized by incessant activity. That is, by its nature [the compositive] imagination composes and divides images and intentions continually and, as one would say now, subconsciously."[24] When the estimative faculty takes control of the compositive imagination, it puts it to use in order to imagine possible courses of action that are in some way beneficial to the animal: what to use as shelter, or how to obtain some food, or how to attract a mate. It is precisely because the animal's estimative faculty takes control of the compositive imagination and has it imagine possible courses of action that Avicenna believes that the estimative faculty is the highest function of the brute animal, for imagining courses of action is the closest thing to rational thought that nonhuman animals can do.

In humans, the compositive imagination can additionally come under the control of the intellect, and when it is under the control of the intellect, it becomes the cogitative faculty.[25] To be clear, it is *not* that humans have the cogitative faculty in lieu of a compositive imagination; rather, the cogitative faculty is a special name given to the human's compositive imagination only when it is being controlled by the human intellect. The activity (or motions) of the cogitative faculty is, for Avicenna, preparatory for the operation of the intellect. For instance, if one is presented with a geometrical problem, one might imagine a diagram in one's mind's eye, or one might literally talk through a problem in the form of an internally vocalized dialogue. Whether one imagines figures that one then divides, rotates, draws line through, and the like, or one internally vocalizes the propositions of an argument that one is considering, these, and activities like them, are all operations of the compositive imagination. Indeed, they must be since they all involve sensible representations inasmuch as they are internally seen, heard, or the like, and thus have not been completely abstracted from the concomitants of matter. At the instant that one has the "aha" experience, however, that is to say, one perceives the explanation that solves the problem with which one is wrestling, then there is an activity of the intellect. The intellect and its operations, however, are the topic of the next chapter, to which I now turn.

5

PSYCHOLOGY II

Intellect

Introduction

I have noted that Avicenna's general approach in the *Psychology* is to identify different activities that characterize the various kinds of living things,
and then to consider the nature of the cause of those activities, namely, the
soul. The activity that sets humans apart from all other animals is, according to Avicenna, who is himself following a long philosophical tradition,
understanding or the possession of scientific knowledge (*'ilm*). Thus, writes
Avicenna, "The property most specific to the human is to conceptualize the
universal, intellectually understand connotational attributes completely abstracted from all matter . . ., and to arrive at a knowledge of what is unknown from what is intellectually known such that there is verification and
conceptualization (*taṣdīq wa taṣawwur*)" (*Psychology*, V.1, 206.11–13). Since
these activities are proper to the intellect, it is the possession of an
intellect that sets humans apart from all other animals. As one brief point of
clarification, while I follow Avicenna and speak of the (human) intellect,
strictly speaking the intellect is a power or faculty of the human soul. Thus,
whatever turns out to be true of the nature of this intellectual faculty is so
because it holds true of the human soul itself.

   As I mentioned in the previous chapter, Avicenna identifies two aspects
of the human intellect: the practical intellect (*'aql 'āmil*) and the theoretical

intellect (*'aql 'ālim* or *'aql naẓarī*). The practical intellect is concerned with the welfare of the body and bodily interactions that are the results of deliberation. It is what determines what is right, wrong, and permissible, and perceives the morally good and evil. As such, the practical intellect is particularly involved in the formation of moral temperaments, and for that reason I defer discussing it until chapter 8. In this chapter I concentrate mainly on Avicenna's account of the theoretical intellect, which in fact is Avicenna's own primary concern when he discusses the intellect in the final book of his *Psychology*. To this end I begin with Avicenna's account of the stages of intellectual development before turning to the nature of the human theoretical intellect. Concerning it, I focus first on Avicenna's arguments for its immateriality, then its temporal origination, and also its incorruptibility, that is, its immortality. After discussing these topics, I turn to its relation to the Active Intellect and intellectual memory. I then take up Avicenna's discussion of self-awareness (*shu'ūr bi-dh-dhāt*), and conclude by looking at his naturalistic account of prophecy.

Stages of the Intellect

In most basic terms, the theoretical intellect is something that can "be impressed by the universal forms abstracted from matter" (*Psychology*, I.5, 48.1–2). In other words, the theoretical intellect is that power that humans have that allows us to perceive the essences of things inasmuch as those essences are not particularized by material concomitants, such as quantitative, qualitative, spatial, or temporal determinations. When those essences already exist separated from matter, that is to say, they have an immaterial existence, as in the cases of the so-called Intelligences and God, they are actually intelligible in themselves. In the *Psychology*, which again is a work of natural philosophy, Avicenna is more concerned with a human's knowledge of material things, which in a sense are the primary or at least first things known by us. According to Avicenna, the essences considered in material things are only potentially intelligible, and as such they must be abstracted or stripped of the particularizing accidents that follow upon their existing in matter. Only when they are considered without any particularity, and so are taken as universals, can the intellect conceptualize the essences of material things. In a general way, which I discuss more fully in what follows, the intellect's act of perceiving the essence of a material thing involves the presence of an image in the compositive imagination. That image, when abstracted from all of its material concomitants or particularizing accidents, is illuminated by something analogous to light. Once so illuminated, the image casts an intelligible version of itself onto the theoretical intellect, which is impressed there. The abstracted intelligible's being so impressed upon the theoretical intellect is what Avicenna means by "intellectual perception."

Obviously, then, if the intellect is to perform its proper function of intellectual perception or intellecting, it must be the sort of thing that can be impressed and so receive intelligible forms. Depending upon the degree to which the intellect has received various abstracted forms, Avicenna assigns different names to it.[1] Thus, inasmuch as the human intellect is considered in absolute potentiality to any intelligible form, Avicenna, following a long tradition going back at least to Alexander of Aphrodisias, labels it the "material intellect" (*'aql hayūlānī*), although it also sometimes goes by the title "potential intellect" (*Psychology*, I.5, 48.18–49.5). The name *"material* intellect" is not applied because the intellect necessarily is material, but because it resembles prime matter, which is disposed to receiving any material form. So, in like manner the material intellect has no proper form of its own, but is disposed to receive any intelligible form.

The first intelligibles impressed upon the intellect are "the primary intelligibles" (*ma 'qūlāt ūlá*), namely, those objects of knowledge that are self-evident, as, for example, the so-called laws of thought, such as "anything is identical with itself," or "something cannot simultaneously exist and not exist in all the same respects," or "something either exists or does not exist" (ibid., 49.10–11). Avicenna himself gives as an example, "the whole is greater than the part." The intellect considered only inasmuch as it is impressed with these primary intelligibles is called a "dispositional intellect" (*'aql bi-l-malaka*) (ibid., 49.5–15). In this respect, then, the dispositional intellect might be thought of as the intellect possessed of the most basic inference rules required for rational thought or discourse, without considering any content upon which those rules might be applied. So, for example, it would be like knowing that if p implies q, and p is the case, then q is the case, without considering any actual application of that rule, as, for example, knowing that if it is raining, then the streets are wet, and since it is raining, inferring that the streets are wet.

When in addition to the primary intelligibles the human intellect possesses some substantive information and content about the world and things in it, then it is called an "actual intellect" (*'aql bi-l-fi'l*) (ibid., 49.16–50.2).

The actual intellect knows the definitions of things, and so intellectually perceives genera, differences, and species, as well as the properties and at least necessary accidents of some of the various species existing in the world. It is called "actual," because it has acquired these intelligibles and so has access to them whenever it wants.

Strictly speaking, both the dispositional intellect and the actual intellect refer to the human's mere disposition to possess certain intelligibles, but not the actual use of those intelligibles. When the intellect has the intelligibles present before it and is actually considering them, and additionally it perceives—or perhaps is aware or conscious—that it is actually perceiving these intelligibles, it is in that state of actuality called the "acquired intellect" ('aql mustafād) (ibid., 50.2–9). This intellect is called the "acquired intellect" because it must acquire, from another separate intellect, something that is like the intellectual version of acquired or luminous light, a point to which Avicenna returns in book V of his *Psychology*.

This separate intellect that actualizes human intellects is the "Active (or Agent) Intellect" ('aql fa'āl), which Avicenna seems to identify with the Giver of Forms (although never explicitly). For Avicenna, the Active Intellect is not some stage or power belonging to individual humans, but a separate substance in its own right that acts upon the human intellect to bring about intellectual perception. In fact, it is wholly unlike a human intellect in that it is not brought from a state of potentially intellecting to a state of actually intellecting; rather, from all eternity it is actually intellecting. Avicenna, following a long philosophical tradition, likens the role of the Active Intellect in cognition to that of the Sun's in vision. Before turning to the Active Intellect and the act of intellectually perceiving, however, I should first consider in some detail Avicenna's account of the nature of the human theoretical intellect.

The Immateriality of the Theoretical Intellect

Again, the theoretical intellect is for Avicenna that sort of thing that can be impressed so as to receive intelligible objects. Moreover, the essence of a material thing is intelligible, contends Avicenna, only to the extent that it has been completely abstracted from those particularizing characteristics that are the concomitants of matter, for example, having a particular shape, size, sensible color, location, and so on. Once the essence has been stripped of all the particularizing characteristics, there is a universal, and it is precisely because of the intelligible object's universality that it must be immaterial. Hence, if there is to be intellectual perception, the theoretical intellect must be something capable of receiving or being impressed by immaterial, intelligible forms, or what we might simply call "concepts." Consequently, the immediate question before Avicenna is whether the theoretical intellect could perform this function, namely, of receiving or being impressed by immaterial concepts, if it were material. He argues that it cannot, and so concludes that if the theoretical intellect is to perform its proper function, it must be an immaterial substance in its own right.

One of Avicenna's demonstrations for the intellect's immateriality (*Psychology*, V.2, 210.6–214.5), and certainly his most developed proof, starts with the assumption that the material intellect—again that part of the soul in which concepts come to reside or to inhere—is a material body. The assumption is a part of a *reductio ad absurdum* style argument, where Avicenna argues that every way of conceiving the intellect as material precludes its receiving immaterial intelligibles, and so precludes the very act that the intellect is supposed to explain. Avicenna begins thus: If the material intellect were some faculty or power of a corporeal organ, like the brain, then that corporeal organ or body must either be (1) indivisible or (2) divisible; this division exhausts all possibilities.

If the body, which is purportedly associated with the intellect, is indivisible, then it must either (1.a) have no extension (and so is a point) or (1.b) have some extension (and so is an atom). Now, a point, Avicenna tells us, is a certain termination of a divisible magnitude and as such a point has no existence independent of that magnitude (ibid., 210.7–15). In like fashion, whatever inheres in a point does so by inhering in the magnitude of which that point is a limit. So, for example, one might say that a certain color inheres in some point on a table because the surface of the table is colored, and the point is a limit of the table's surface. Therefore, if an intelligible object were to inhere in the intellect as in a point, it could do so only if it also inhered in a divisible magnitude that is limited by that point. Consequently, the answer to whether intelligibles could inhere in a point depends upon whether they could inhere in a divisible magnitude, that is, option (2) listed above, and so Avicenna defers discussion of this point until then.

Before that, however, he turns to option (1.b), namely, the suggestion that the receptacle of one's intelligible objects or concepts is an atom, that is, an indivisible yet extended magnitude. I have already noted in chapter 3 that he has a number of arguments to show that atoms, understood as conceptually indivisible minimal magnitudes, are impossible.[2] In the *Psychology* (V.2, 210.15–211.13), he briefly rehearses one of those arguments. Assume that three atoms are in contact with one another so as to form a line ABC. Either B separates A from C, such that A does not touch C, or A does touch C. If B separates A from C, such that none of A touches C, then the purportedly conceptually indivisible atom, B, can be divided into the side touching A and the side touching C, in which case what is indivisible would be divisible, which is a contradiction. If B does not separate A from C, and so A touches C, then atoms would interpenetrate one another so as to form a magnitude no greater than a single atom; however, it was assumed in this case that they formed a three-atom line, and so there is again a contradiction. Atoms, Avicenna concludes, cannot exist, and so a fortiori, the material intellect cannot be an atom. Thus, the intellect cannot be associated with an indivisible magnitude, whether that magnitude is punctiform or atomic.

Avicenna now considers option (2), which takes the receptacle of one's concepts, again, the material intellect, to be a body of some divisible magnitude. Whatever inheres in a divisible magnitude, Avicenna notes, is at least accidentally divisible as well. For example, color becomes divided accidentally when the surface of a table in which that color inheres is itself divided. If an intelligible object were localized in some divisible material organ, such as part of the brain, then should that part of the brain be divided into two parts, the intelligible object likewise would be divided accidentally into two parts. These two purported parts of the divided concept, observes Avicenna, must be either (2.a) similar or (2.b) dissimilar (ibid., 211.18–19).

The purported two parts of the intelligible object cannot be similar (2.a), argues Avicenna, because were one to recombine them so as to make a whole, the whole would be no different from the part, and yet a whole is different from a part (ibid., 211.19–212.9). One cannot say that the whole intelligible object is bulkier or larger than either of the purported similar parts; for if the combination of the parts of the intelligible object involved an increase in size, shape, or number, then the intelligible object itself would have to be something material, for size, shape, or number are concomitants of matter, but a concept is intelligible for Avicenna precisely because it is immaterial.

If (2.b), the two parts of an immaterial intelligible object are dissimilar, and that dissimilarity cannot be explained by reference to material concomitants, then these dissimilar parts must correspond with the parts of a definition, namely, genus and difference. So, for example, consider the concept of humanity. It can conceptually be divided into animal (a genus) and rational (a difference). Avicenna lists a number of absurdities that follow upon this hypothesis (ibid., 212.12–213.15). For instance, assuming that the receptacle for concepts is a divisible (nonatomic) magnitude, it would be continuous, and, as I noted in chapter 3, continuous magnitudes for Avicenna are potentially divisible infinitely.[3] Consequently, the intelligible object purportedly inhering in a continuous magnitude would have a *potentially* infinite number of genera and differences. Avicenna takes it as an established fact, however, that essential genera and differences are not infinite, but finite. In a similar vein, Avicenna argues that since merely imagining a division of the organ cannot produce new genera and species in it in the way that merely imagining and positing a point can produce a potential division in a body, all the genera and differences would need to be *actually* present in that part of the brain. Consequently, complains Avicenna, the intelligible object purportedly inhering in a continuous magnitude not only would have a potentially infinite number of genera and differences, but also an *actually* infinite number of them. Another absurdity is to assume that we initially imagined the division of the organ (and so the accidental division of the concept) as running horizontally such that, for example, the upper half corresponds with the generic aspect of the concept and the lower half with the difference. Now imagine the division as running vertically: Either there is a half-genus and half-difference (whatever that might mean), or one can make genera and differences run around in the brain at the whim of how one decides to divide the organ purportedly harboring the faculty of the theoretical intellect. Given the number of absurdities that Avicenna finds following upon the assumption that an intelligible object can be accidentally divided into dissimilar parts, he rejects this option too. Since a concept existing in a divisible magnitude must be divisible accidentally into either similar or dissimilar parts, and yet both options lead to absurdities, Avicenna concludes that the intellect cannot be associated with a divisible magnitude.

Avicenna now finishes his demonstration for the intellect's immateriality (ibid., 214.1–5): If the material intellect, that is, the receptacle of one's concepts, were associated with some bodily organ, then again that body would have been either indivisible (and so either a point or an atom) or divisible (in which case accidentally divided concepts would have either similar or dissimilar parts). All options have led to absurdities. Therefore, the assumption that the intellect is in some way associated with a material body—again the very assumption that gave rise to those absurdities—must, Avicenna contends, be rejected. Therefore, ends Avicenna, the intellect must be an immaterial substance in its own right, and as such must be really distinct from the body.[4]

The Theoretical Intellect's Temporal Origination

Although for Avicenna the human intellect is an immaterial substance in its own right, he acknowledges that it initially needs the body for two things: one, to acquire the primary intelligibles, definitions, and other intelligibles that make up the content of conceptualization and verification; and, two, to explain the soul's origination at the place and time it is originated. As for the first function that the body plays (*Psychology*, V.3, 221.14–223.10), while the human intellect is an immaterial substance, it still needs to use a body as a tool to reach its proper perfection, which is to perceive intellectually the full range of intelligible objects. As I have noted, however, intellectual perception, at least initially, requires sensibly perceiving various particulars, a mode of perception that in fact does require a material organ. Only then, through a process of abstraction, does one come to acquire the corresponding intelligible, where the acquisition of that intelligible is itself aided by the functions of the estimative faculty and compositive imagination, again faculties that require a bodily organ. Moreover, at least initially, the intellect, when engaged in cognitive activity, takes control of the compositive imagination, which provides it with images related to certain problems in order to help facilitate conceptualization. Having said this, Avicenna also hastens to add that once the intelligibles are acquired, the intellect has less and less need of the body in order to perform its proper function. In fact, the body can even become more of a distraction than an aide to the intellect's activity.

The second role that the body plays, according to Avicenna, is to act as an occasioning cause for the origination of the human soul. That is because, as I noted at the end of chapter 3, while the production of a new substance is ultimately owing to the Giver of Forms, such a production requires the initial preparation of the material so as to provide a suitable subject for the new species form. In the case of the human soul, the prepared matter's suitability is that it can be used as a tool by the intellect.

Of course the body's being the occasioning cause for the origination of a new human soul assumes that the human soul does not antedate an individual's body.[5] Avicenna is quite adamant that in fact each individual human soul is something temporally originated (*ḥādith*). He provides the following argument as proof (ibid., 223.11–227.10). Assume that a soul exists temporally prior to the body. In that case, there could either be (1) numerically many souls, or (2) one numerically single soul. Now, begins Avicenna, if souls are numerically many prior to their being in bodies, their multiplicity is due to either (1.a) their essence and form or (1.b) that which receives that essence and form, namely, the matter or body. Since the essence and form of a thing specifies what is one and the same in species—for example, rational animality in the human species—the purportedly preexisting human souls could not be many owing to their essence alone, argues Avicenna, for, again, this is one and the same for all humans. Thus, option (1.a) must be rejected. As for option (1.b), namely that what differentiates multiple human souls purportedly existing prior to their existence in a body is just the body in which they exist, is patently self-stultifying, for one is considering those souls supposedly before they exist in bodies. Thus, Avicenna concludes that if the human soul's existence precedes the existence of the body, it could not do so as numerically many souls existing prior to the body.

Alternatively, perhaps the purportedly preexisting human soul is numerically one and the same soul for each and every human. In that case, continues Avicenna, then either (2.a) two embodied souls would be two parts of numerically one and the same soul or (2.b) numerically one and the same soul would exist in two different bodies. In other words, in the first option there is some overarching "über-soul," part of which exists in my body, for example, and part of which exists in yours, whereas in the second case, this "über-soul" has no parts, but exists wholly in you and me. Now, if (2.a) two souls were two parts of numerically one and the same soul, then, argues Avicenna, the soul must be divisible into either (2.a.i) quantitative parts or (2.a.b) nonquantitative parts such as the human soul's animality and rationality, which one might call the soul's "constitutive elements." Insofar as the human soul is immaterial, as Avicenna has argued, it can have no quantitative parts, and so option (2.a.i) fails, whereas if (2.a.ii), namely, the soul is divided into its constitutive elements, then the soul of one human, would, for example, be animal but not rational, and vice versa for the other soul, a conclusion that is clearly false. Hence, concludes Avicenna, two souls cannot be two parts of numerically one and the same soul.

The assumption (2.b) that numerically one and the same soul could exist in two different bodies likewise leads to certain absurdities, says Avicenna. For instance, any particular act that belongs properly to the soul inasmuch as it is immaterial, and so cannot be explained by appeal to the body, would have to be shared by any individual humans sharing one and the same immaterial soul. So, for example, anything that one individual intellectually perceives—where intellectual perception is again the proper activity of the intellect alone, and qua intellectually perceiving takes place wholly independent of the body—would likewise have to be intellectually perceived by all who are sharing that intellect. That is because all of the intellectually perceiving individuals would share one and the same intellect on the present assumption, and so all would be impressed by the same intelligible. In other words, whatever one person knows, everybody should know, a conclusion that is obviously false, for some individuals clearly know things that others do not. The assumption that gave rise to this absurdity, namely that numerically one and the same soul could exist in two different bodies, thus, must also be rejected.

To sum up, if the human soul were to preexist the appearance of a properly disposed body, there would have to be either numerically many preexisting souls or only numerically one and the same soul—these exhaust the possible options—and yet, maintains Avicenna, both suggestions lead to absurdity. Avicenna thus concludes that each properly disposed body capable of being used as a tool by an intellect must have originated for it a human soul at the moment the matter is so prepared to receive that soul. In short, the human soul, even though it is an immaterial substance, has a temporal origination just like the individual substantial forms of all other natural things.

The Immortality of the Human Intellect

Having explained that the intellect must be an immaterial substance distinct from the body, but that, unlike other immaterial substances—such as the Intelligences and the divinity, which have existed eternally—the human soul must be temporally originated, Avicenna takes up in *Psychology*, V.4 the issue of whether the human soul is immortal in the sense of being capable of surviving the corruption of the body.[6] He begins by observing that if the corruption of one thing, x, entails the corruption of another, y, then x and y must be dependent upon (*ta'alluq*) each other in one of three ways (*Psychology*, V.4, 227.14–17): (1) x and y may be codependent or equivalent with respect to existence (*mukāfi' fī l-wujūd*) (such as in the essential relation between a concave and convex curve or the accidental relation of being "next to"); (2) x may be essentially prior to y, and so x is a cause of y; or (3) x may be essentially posterior to y, and so x is an effect of y.

Avicenna quickly dismisses the suggestion that the immaterial intellect and material body are codependent upon each other or equivalent with respect to existence except in an accidental way (ibid., 227.17–228.2). He argues thus: If they are codependent, the codependence again must be either essential or accidental. On the one hand, if the codependence were essential, then neither the soul nor the body taken alone would be a substance in its own right, but rather only together would they form a single substance. In other words, the body and human intellect, even if conceptually distinct, would have to be essentially and actually the same substance, similar to the way that a single line can be both a concave and convex line depending upon how it is considered. The body and intellect taken together, however, cannot form a single substance or be essentially and actually the same, for the intellect is essentially an immaterial substance, while the body is essentially a material one, and being immaterial is essentially opposed to being material. Thus, the human intellect and body cannot depend upon each other essentially.

On the other hand, if the codependence were merely an accidental relation, such as "being next to or in," then, although the destruction of one of the *relata* would bring about the destruction of the relation between the two, its destruction need not entail the destruction of the other *relatum*. So just as if one house is next to another and then is destroyed, it does not follow that the second house has also been destroyed, so likewise even if the intellect has an accidental codependence upon a body, it does not follow that the destruction of the body entails the destruction of the intellect.

Next Avicenna considers the suggestion that the body and soul are related such that the body is the cause of the soul (ibid., 228.3–230.4). In that case, he continues, the body must be either the human soul's (a) material, (b) efficient, (c) formal, or (d) final cause. Insofar as the human soul is an immaterial substance, it has no material cause and so option (a) cannot be the case.

Next, matter, according to Avicenna, is wholly inert and as such only acts through the form presently informing it. Thus, body qua material does not itself act, but what does not act cannot be an efficient cause, and so the body cannot be the efficient cause of the soul. Hence option (b) fails to be the case. As for the formal cause, it is that which accounts for the activities of a thing, but as has been noted repeatedly it is the soul that accounts for the human's animate activities, and as such the human soul or intellect has a better right to be a formal cause of the body than the other way around. Consequently, option (c) must be false. Similarly, the final cause is the end for which a thing functions or that for the sake of which a thing acts. As has been noted, however, the body functions strictly for the sake of the activity of the intellect, which is the human's proper end. So, again the intellect is more fittingly the final cause of the body than vice versa. Thus, Avicenna rejects option (d). Since the body cannot stand to the intellect in any of the traditional causal ways, either as matter, form, agent, or end, the body, Avicenna concludes, cannot be essentially prior to the soul.

If the soul is essentially (though not temporally) prior to the body, says Avicenna, then were it corrupted, the body would be corrupted. From that fact, however, it does not follow that if the body is corrupted, the human soul is corrupted. Still, it might turn out that the corruption of the body indicates the corruption of the human soul, especially if there is no other way to explain the corruption of the body except by the corruption of the soul (ibid., 230.5–231.2). So, consider, for example, the proverbial saying "Where there is smoke there is fire." Fire (or some other form of combustion) is essentially prior to smoke and indeed the cause of the smoke. Consequently, should one not see the fire, but sees the smoke, one is assured that a fire is present and, conversely, when one no longer sees the smoke, there is a presumption that the fire has been extinguished. Perhaps, then, the body is essentially posterior to the human soul in the way that smoke is posterior to the fire such that when the body fails to perform the activities associated with life, one can presume that the cause of those activities has also passed away.

Such an inference would be valid, maintains Avicenna, if and only if the body has no principles unique to it alone that can explain the body's own corruption. The body, so claims Avicenna, in fact does have principles unique to it that can and do explain its corruption, namely, it elemental composition and humoral mix. More exactly, as I have noted before, according to the best science of the time complex bodies are composites of the four elements, fire, air, water, and earth, which themselves form the four humors of animal bodies: blood, phlegm, yellow and black bile, all of which, in the case of animals, are combined by an innate animal heat. The nature of heat, Avicenna however notes,[7] ultimately brings about dissolution and transformation. Consequently, the human body must eventually corrupt owing to its very elemental and humoral nature. In contrast, since this elemental composition and humoral temperament follow solely upon the body's materiality, such corruptive causes cannot apply to an immaterial substance such as an intellect. Thus, while the living body must corrupt owing to its very nature, the principles that bring about its corruption, namely, possessing an innate heat, simply cannot apply to the immaterial human intellect.

Thus, concludes Avicenna by way of summary, the corruption of the body would entail the corruption of the soul only if the body exists codependently with it, or it is either a cause or essential effect of the soul. Since none of these types of dependence relations applies to the relation between body and soul, the death of the body need not entail the destruction of the human soul.[8] Consequently, Avicenna finishes, the soul can and does survive the body's death, continuing to carry on an intellectual existence wholly disassociated from the body, an existence that Avicenna identifies with true blessedness (sa'āda) and the afterlife, which I consider in chapter 8.

Although Avicenna believes that the above argument shows that the soul can survive the death of the body, it does not necessarily show that the human soul is something incorruptible in itself. In other words, while the destruction of the body need not entail the death of the human soul, perhaps there are principles unique to the human intellect itself that could explain its corruption, in which case it would not be immortal. Thus, to cut short this kind of objection, Avicenna offers a proof for the human soul's incorruptibility reminiscent of arguments found in Plato's *Phaedo* and Plotinus' *Enneads*.[9]

Avicenna's version of the argument runs as follows (ibid., 231.3–233.5): That which has both an actuality and potentiality must be a form-matter composite, for it is the form that explains x's being actually F, while the matter explains its being potentially not-F, that is, potentiality necessarily inheres in matter. Now, if something that has the actuality of persisting or enduring is potentially corruptible, then it must, while actually persisting or enduring, have the potentiality to not continue to endure but to corrupt. Consequently, if the human intellect were corruptible, then while it is actually persisting or enduring, it would have the potentiality of not persisting or enduring. In that case, however, the intellect would necessarily be something material, for inasmuch as it has a certain potentiality, that potentiality requires matter in which to inhere.[10] As has been noted, Avicenna has forcefully argued that the human intellect is not material, but immaterial. He thus concludes that the human intellect is not corruptible. Simply stated, for Avicenna, something is susceptible to corruption if and only if it is a composite of form and matter, whereas, if something is not linked to matter in any respect, then that thing is incorruptible. Once Avicenna adds this further premise concerning the nature of corruptibility, his argument for the immateriality of the soul is in effect an argument for its immortality as well.

The Active Intellect

Up to this point Avicenna has been speaking about the substance of the human intellect: What its nature must be in order to perform its proper function, its origination and, in some sense, its destiny. At book V.5 of the *Psychology* he turns to the very activity of the human intellect itself: What is required for that activity and how it occurs. More specifically, he addresses how our material intellect emerges from a state of potentially knowing certain things to a state of actually knowing those things. This emergence, Avicenna believes, requires a separate intellect that is always actual and never potential, which he identifies with the Active or Agent Intellect (*'aql fa''āl*).[11] While the whole of Avicenna's discussion and vocabulary concerning the role of the Active Intellect is reminiscent of Aristotle's own discussion in *De anima*, III 5 and that of subsequent Greek- and Arabic-speaking commentators, Avicenna's own novel understanding of many of the key concepts used to explain the Active Intellect, such as his conception of light and vision, make his view uniquely his own.

Concerning the need for the Active Intellect and its role in bringing the human intellect from a state of potentially knowing to one of actually knowing, Avicenna writes:

> The human soul is at one time potentially intellecting and thereafter comes to be intellecting actually. Now, whatever emerges from potency to act does so only by means of a cause in act that brings about its emergence. So, in the present case there is a cause that brings about our souls' emergence from potency to act with respect to the objects of intellection.

Since it is the cause providing the intellectualizing forms (*ṣuwar ʿaqlīya*), it is nothing but an actual intellect in whom the principles of the intellectualizing forms are separate (*Psychology*, V.5, 234.9-13).

The general thrust of Avicenna's argument here is that whatever goes from a state of potentiality to one of actuality requires some cause. Thus, since an individual human soul does go from a state of potentially intellecting when it does not know some particular thing to one of actually intellecting once it comes to know that thing, there must be some cause for this actualization. Avicenna identifies this cause with the Active Intellect.

More specifically, Avicenna tells us that the Active Intellect provides one with the intellectualizing forms, which one can safely assume to be wholly free of material concomitants (for being separated from matter is the hallmark of anything intellectual). Moreover, since the Active Intellect provides the intellectualizing forms separated from matter, it must of itself already possess those forms immaterially, for if it needed to abstract or separate those forms from matter, the Active Intellect itself would only possess them potentially. In that case, there would need to be yet another cause explaining the actualization of the potentially intelligibles in the Active Intellect itself. Avicenna stops the regress by maintaining that the Active Intellect is an actual intellect that already possesses all the intelligibles, primary or otherwise, not as potential but as actual (and so wholly without any trace of materiality).

Having established the need for the Active Intellect to explain human intellection, as well as suggesting what the nature of the Active Intellect is, Avicenna turns to a description of how the Active Intellect affects one so as to bring about intellectual perception. In a discussion that hearkens one back to Plato's *Republic*[12] and Aristotle's *De anima*,[13] Avicenna likens the role of the Active Intellect to sunlight and human intellection to vision.

[The Active Intellect's] relation to our souls is that of the Sun to our vision. Now, just as the Sun is actually visible in itself and through its radiant light (*nūr*) it makes actually visible what is not actually visible, so likewise is the state of this intellect vis-à-vis our souls. [That] is because when the intellectual faculty reviews the particulars that are in the retentive imagination, and the aforementioned Active Intellect radiates its light into us [and] upon them, the things separated from matter and its concomitants are altered and impressed upon the rational soul. ["Being altered" is here] not in the sense that [the particulars] themselves are transferred from the compositive imagination to our intellect, nor [is "being impressed"] in the sense

that the connotational attribute immersed in the [material] concomitants—
which in itself and with regard to its very being is separate [from matter]—
makes something like itself. Quite the contrary, ["being altered" and
"being impressed"] are in the sense that reviewing [the particulars] prepares the soul in order that the thing separate from matter [coming] from
the Active Intellect [that is, again, the intellectualizing forms] emanates
upon them. Discursive thought and selective attention are then certain
motions that prepare the soul to receive the emanation. [This] is like [how]
middle terms prepare [the soul] to receive the conclusion in the most convincing way, although the first is according to one way and the second according to another, as you will come to know. So when a certain relation to
this form falls to the rational soul by means of the Active Intellect's radiant
activity, then from [the relation] there comes to be in [the human soul]
something that in one way is of the genus of [the form] and in another way
is not. Just like when luminous light falls on colored objects, it produces
from them an impression on the visual system that is not in every way
[reduced] to their sum, so likewise the images that are potentially intelligible become actually intelligible—not themselves but what is acquired from
them. In fact, just as the impression of the sensible forms conveyed by
means of luminous light is not itself those forms, but rather something related to them that is engendered by means of the luminous light in the recipient facing [the light], so likewise when the rational soul reviews those
forms in the retentive imagination and the radiant light of the Active Intellect comes into a type of contact with them, then they are prepared so
that from the luminous light of the Active Intellect they come to be the
abstract version of those forms free from [material] taints within [the rational soul] (*Psychology*, V.5, 234.14–236.2).

Again, while the light imagery and use of vision as a model for explaining
intellectual perception are not new to Avicenna—indeed almost every philosopher up to his time had used the same language—I hope to show that
Avicenna's novel understanding of the various key concepts, which I discussed in chapter 4 concerning light and vision, make his account of intellectual perception uniquely his own.

First, and as a preliminary remark, lurking behind the above passage is
Avicenna's own theory of essences. Recall that while essences can be considered in themselves, they only ever exist either as concrete particulars, and so
possess certain accidents and forms that follow on their being in matter, or
they exist as conceptualized, and so possess certain accidents and forms that
follow on their being in the intellect.

Second, as humans, the starting point for our intellectual perception of the essences of natural things comes from first sensibly experiencing those essences as they exist in the material things around us that make up our world. Later, Avicenna says that in principle the intellect could encounter only a single individual of a given kind in order to have all it needs concerning the essential features of that kind (*Psychology*, V.5, 236.10–237.11). That is because the essence is what is common to all tokens of a given type. Consequently, there is nothing essentially different that belongs to Paul, for example, that does not also belong to Peter inasmuch as they are humans; experiencing different individuals of the same kind does not increase the number of essential features that the intellect can access. Still, even if certain rare individuals need encounter only a single individual of a kind in order to grasp what is essential to that kind, human cognition (even of this rare kind) must begin in some way with encountering material, sensible things.

Still, in this very act of perceiving the world around us by means of the external senses, there is for Avicenna already, as I have noted, a degree of abstraction from matter. Through the various stages of the abstractive process more and more of the material concomitants are stripped away from those essences. At their most abstracted state while still being sensible, those essences exist in the images that are housed in the retentive imagination and are manipulated by the compositive imagination. This image in the compositive imagination is a potential intelligible in its most proximate form to actuality. It is at this point that the human intellect can take control of the compositive imagination, turning it into the cogitative faculty. The subsequent manipulation of the image takes the form of separating and dividing the humors in the brain in which the sensible image is impressed, and it is through this activity of the compositive imagination that the human soul is prepared to receive the Active Intellect's emanation so as to turn the potentially intelligible object in the brain into an actually intelligible object impressed upon the intellect.

Third, at the final stage of abstraction, that is, when all the material concomitants are stripped from the essence, the intellect selectively attends to the essential features of the essence of the thing as that essence exists in the compositive imagination. Again, in the compositive imagination, the essence is embedded in a particular image, or, what Avicenna calls elsewhere, a "vague individual" (*shakhṣ muntashir*) that can be "thought to be of any existing individual of that genus or single species" (*Physics*, I.1,

11.5–6).[14] When the intellect abstracts the essence from the vague individual, it is simply selectively attending to that kind's essential features and so setting to one side those accidental features that belong to the essence as a result of its existence in matter.

Once the human intellect has abstracted the essence, the essence is no longer existing as a concrete particular, for all the accidents that follow upon being in matter and that particularize its existing as a concrete particular have been removed. Again, however, essences for Avicenna always and only exist either as concrete particulars or as conceptualized. Thus, when all the material accidents have been set to one side, that is, when the essence has been properly prepared, the essence must acquire those intellectualizing forms that particularize it such that it exists as conceptualized. Here, Avicenna intends by "intellectualizing forms," I contend, just those intelligible accidents that he mentioned in the *Introduction* of the *Cure*.[15] Examples of such conceptualizing accidents or intellectualizing forms would include universality and particularity in predication as well as essentiality and accidentality in predication.[16] It is because the intelligible impressed on the human intellect has acquired the intellectualizing forms that the human intellect is called at this stage the "acquired intellect."

One is now led to a fourth point: namely, how Avicenna understands the illumination and vision vocabulary used to explain intellectual perception. As one might expect, his analogy with light and vision draws heavily upon his own theory of these ideas. Here there are a number of points of similarity, and, since again Avicenna wants to model his theory of cognition on his theory of vision, it will be useful to consider some of the more important comparisons.

So to begin with the most obvious point of comparison: The Active Intellect is likened to the Sun, and just as the Sun is both luminous in itself as well as being a source of radiant light, so the Active Intellect, as one of the immaterial substances, is intelligible in itself as well as being a source of intelligibility for human intellects.[17]

Second, as with the Sun, there radiates from the Active Intellect an analogue of radiant light in the form of intellectualizing forms. The intellectualizing forms mix with the potentially, but not actually, intelligible object found in the human soul, that is, with the sensible image in the imagination abstracted from all of its material concomitants. Once the intellectualizing forms mix with the potentially intelligible essence, the essence comes to be actually intelligible. In this respect, there is a comparison between the functions of the Sun's radiant light and the Active Intellect's emanation. That is because, according to Avicenna, it is only by a radiant light's mixing with potential color that there comes to be actual color, just as it is only by the intellectualizing forms' mixing with the potentially intelligible that there comes to be something actually intelligible in the material intellect. Here, the eye—or more exactly the optic chiasma—would be the analogue of the material intellect.

A third point of comparison is the need for a certain type of alteration and preparatory motion in both cognition and vision. Again, sensible forms stored in the imagination are potentially intelligible in the way that certain bodies in the absence of a luminous body are potentially colored. In the case of the potentially colored object, the required motion is locomotion: either moving some light to where the object is, or moving the object to where the light is. In its cognitive counterpart, the motion involves the cogitative faculty's combing and dividing the forms in the retentive imagination— literally a kind of motion—either as those forms manifest themselves as images or the linguistic counterparts thereof.

Here there is now a fourth and I believe final point of comparison. The actually intelligible object—that is the abstracted essence mixed with the emanation from the Active Intellect—then impresses itself upon the material intellect. There is now intellectual perception. The point of comparison is that intellectual perception, which again is a type of being impressed, occurs in just the way that the sensible image impresses itself on the eye when there is vision. For, as Avicenna says, what comes to exist in the material intellect, while being of the same genus as the form in the retentive imagination, cannot simply be reduced to that form any more than what comes to exist in the eye, namely, the sensible image conveying a body's color, can be reduced to that body's various dispositions that are identified with potential color. The intelligible species is only efficacious when there is a mixture of the potentially intelligible and the intellectualizing forms or accidents emanating from the Active Intellect, just as color is only efficacious when there is a mixture of potential color and the radiant light of a luminous body.

In addition to Avicenna's comparison of the Active Intellect with the Sun and their respective roles in intellectual and sensible perceptions, there is also a decided likeness between the operations that Avicenna assigns to the Active Intellect and the Giver of Forms. Indeed, all evidence suggests that Avicenna saw the Active Intellect and the Giver of Forms as two names for a single entity. Thus, it should not be too surprising that the role that Avicenna assigns to the Giver of Forms in substantial generation has a psychological counterpart in the role of the Active Intellect in intellection. Thus, as I noted in chapter 3, natural efficient causes, according to Avicenna, play a preparatory role in substantial change. They do this by bringing about alterations in the hot and cold and wet and dry composition of some matter. When the material has been sufficiently prepared by these alterations, the Giver of Forms, with absolute consistency, emanates or impresses into the prepared matter a new substantial form or essence.

Similarly, when the various human sensory faculties first externally and then internally perceive the in-mattered essence, they alter the impressed essence, whether by abstraction or combining and dividing. In other words, operations occurring in various bodily organs prepare the potentially intelligible object (which again is just the in-mattered essence) for an emanation from the Active Intellect. Once the potentially intelligible object has been sufficiently prepared by these alterations, the Active Intellect, again with absolute consistency, emanates the intellectualizing forms that make the potentially intelligible actually intelligible. The actual intelligible then impresses itself onto the human intellect and there is intellectual perception. Just as qualitative changes in some matter cannot educe a new species form, so likewise bodily alterations of a material, particular, and potentially intelligible object cannot educe an immaterial, universal, and actually intelligible object. In both cases, something outside the natural order is required.

It is also because the Active Intellect doubles as the Giver of Forms that Avicenna "appears to combine two incompatible concepts in one doctrine: either the intelligible forms emanate from above or they are abstracted from the data collected by the senses, but not both."[18] Despite the seeming incompatibility, for Avicenna both claims are in fact true. That is because the intelligible object is a combination of an essence and the intellectualizing forms or accidents, both of which emanate from the Giver of Forms-*cum*-Active Intellect as a single emanation.

Let me try to provide a fuller explanation of this last point. A general principle of Avicenna's philosophical system is that whatever is received is received according to the mode of the receiver. In other words, limitations belonging to that which is being acted upon or receiving a given form restrain the forms that an agent can impose upon the recipient; for example, while a carpenter (agent) might possess the knowledge and equipment to give some suitable material (recipient) the form of a chair, he or she cannot shape water (at least not while it is in its liquid form) into a chair, while he or she can impose that form onto wood. Similarly, when the emanated intelligible essences encounter suitably disposed matter, the matter can receive only the essences themselves, not the intelligible or intellectualizing forms or accidents, which require an immaterial recipient. The intellectualizing forms or accidents, then, are not received when essences inform the matter in the generation of new substances, for again the reception of what is intelligible occurs only in the case where the recipient is immaterial.

Humans in the act of sensibly perceiving in turn receive these essences together with the accompanying material accidents and concomitants that have become associated with them through their existence in matter. It is precisely because humans do receive the essences together with the material accidents and concomitants that the process of abstraction is required. When the material accidents and concomitants are stripped away, however, the essences are then themselves prepared to re-receive the intelligible accidents that are again being emanated by the Active Intellect-*cum*-Giver of Forms. Therefore, in a very real sense human intellectual perception is for Avicenna nothing more than the reception of an emanation from the Active Intellect/ Giver of Forms, even though the reception of that emanation could not occur without sensation, abstraction, and a lot of activity in the brain.

Intellectual Memory

Not only has Avicenna been able to provide a single model of how vision and intellection occur—indeed even a single account of how all perception works—but his introduction of the Active Intellect has also provided him with a single model for explaining two seemingly disparate phenomena: substantial change and human cognition. Moreover, the introduction of the Active Intellect as a separate intellect, which is always actually intellecting, offers Avicenna a solution to another problem, namely, how to explain intellectual memory as opposed to remembering images, which can be stored in the brain.

The philosophical issue is this: If the intelligible is only actually intelligible inasmuch as it is stripped of all material concomitants, and so wholly immaterial, then once one has come to know some intelligible, where is it retained when one is not actually thinking it? On the one hand, an actual intelligible is unlike sensible forms and connotational attributes that can be stored in parts of the brain, for a material organ, as has been seen, cannot receive something immaterial so as to retain it. Thus, intelligible objects cannot be stored somewhere in the brain when they are not actually being thought. On the other hand, if they are retained in the human intellect itself, they would be impressed there, but to be impressed by an intelligible is just the intellectual perception of that intelligible. In other words, if the intelligibles were stored in the human intellect itself, one would always actually be thinking those intelligibles. Such a conclusion is clearly false, since most people reading this were probably not thinking, for example, of the concept "aardvark" but now may have gone from potentially intellecting an aardvark to actually intellecting one.

Avicenna's solution to this problem is to claim that the Active Intellect is the storehouse of the intelligibles, for it is always intellecting all the essences of things found in our world. As such it assures that they remain always actually intelligible even if no particular human is presently intellecting them.

As for accessing those intelligibles, Avicenna tells us that once one has actually come to know something (*ta'allum*) one has a perfect disposition or preparedness to conjoin with the Active Intellect in order to retrieve the intelligibles stored there.

> Coming to know something is seeking the complete disposition (*isti'dād*) for conjunction so that from it there is the intellection that is simple, and then from it the forms are emanated, being separated in the soul by means of discursive reasoning. So the disposition before coming to know something is deficient, whereas the disposition after coming to know something is complete. Consequently, it is characteristic of knowing something that when what is connected with the sought intelligible comes to mind, and the soul turns to look—where "looking" is to return to the principle that gives intellection [namely, the Active Intellect]—there is a conjunction with it. There then emanates from it the power of abstract intellection (*qūwa l-'aql al-mujarrid*) that follows the emanation that produces separation. When [one] turns away from it, [the power] recedes, in which case that form comes to be in potency, however, a potency in close proximity to act. So, initially coming to know something is like treating the eye, but then when the eye is healthy, whenever it wants it looks at something from which a given form is taken, while when it turns from that thing, that [thing] comes to be in potency proximate to act. Now, so long as the human soul taken [more] generally [than just the

intellect] is in the body it cannot receive the Active Intellect all at once, and instead its state is as we said (*Psychology*, V.6, 247.3–15).

Avicenna's general idea is relatively clear, even if perhaps his language here is not. Once, through a process of abstraction and selective attention, one has stripped away the concomitants from the potentially intelligible (where the potentially intelligible is just the vague individual in the imagination) a certain disposition or aptitude is brought to perfection in the particular human to conjoin with the Active Intellect and to see that intelligible there. The initial abstractive process would be like healing or cleansing an eye so that it can now see, where the damaged eye is analogous to the deficient disposition of the intellect. Once healed, the eye need not see some given thing, although it can potentially see it. Should the healthy eye, however, turn toward that thing (and assuming the object is illuminated), the eye actually sees it. Likewise, once an intelligible has been acquired, there exists a potential that had not existed before to perceive that intelligible, what Avicenna calls "the perfect disposition." Furthermore, analogous to someone's turning toward a visible object, when there is brought to mind something connected with some previously acquired intelligible, that intelligible is intellectually perceived.

Clearly for Avicenna, once the human soul is free of the body it is able to access the intelligibles in the Active Intellect immediately and without any intermediary image. In contrast, as long as the human soul is in an embodied state, I suspect that Avicenna thinks (although it is not clear) that one still needs some image to access the intelligibles stored in the Active Intellect. In other words, when the intellect calls up the image, it has the perfect disposition to see the essential characteristics embedded in that image—that is, the intellect, as it were, knows what to ignore and not take into account in the image—and so is able to conjoin with the Active Intellect at will. Thus, for example, when I mentioned "aardvark" earlier, one sees the word on the page and perhaps either sees an image or hears the linguistic counterpart (which again for Avicenna is an image in the imagination) and is thus carried to the corresponding intelligible stored in the Active Intellect.

There is some textual basis for my suspicion:

[T]he power really belongs to the soul by which it [can] intellect whatever it wants. So, when it wants, it conjoins [with the Active Intellect] and the intelligible form emanates into it, where that [intelligible] form is in fact the acquired intellect and the former power is the actual intellect in us inasmuch as we can [perform] the act of the intellect. The acquired intellect is the actual intellect insofar as it is perfect, *whereas the conceptualization of objects of the compositive imagination is a return of the soul to the storehouse of the sensible objects*: The first [that is, the acquired intellect] looks upward, while the later [that is, the actual intellect] looks downward. So, if it becomes free of the body and the accidents of the body, then in that case it can completely conjoin with the Active Intellect, and there it encounters intellectual beauty and eternal pleasure, as we will discuss in its place (ibid., 247.20–248.8; emphasis added).

The sense of this passage appears to be that while in the body, our actual intellect still accesses the images in the compositive imagination. Through the intermediacy of these images the actual intellect conjoins with the Active Intellect, which illuminates those images in us so as to perfect and transform the intellect into the acquired intellect.

Self-Awareness: Identification of the Act, Agent, and Object of the Intellect and "Becoming the Thing Known"

While for Avicenna virtually all of the human's initial intellectual activity begins with the perception of the essences of things that require matter for their existence, the human intellect's highest perfection comes in knowing immaterial substances, that is, essences that do not require matter for their existence. While Avicenna consistently says that immaterial substances are intelligible in themselves inasmuch as they do not require a process of abstraction in order to be made intelligible, he also recognizes that for us humans they are frequently the last things to be intellectually perceived. Indeed, many humans may never intellectually grasp them at all.

Avicenna insists that the inability to conceptualize such substances is not owing to anything about those substances in themselves, but owing to the soul's (accidental) association or connection with matter. For just as the inability to gaze upon the Sun is not owing to something about the Sun that prevents it from being seen—in fact it, more than anything else, is visible—but owing to the weakness of the material makeup of the eye, so likewise one's being associated with a body distracts one from knowing the immaterial substances (*Psychology*, V.5, 237.16–238.17).

Perhaps it is because the human soul is at the lowest wrung of the hierarchy of immaterial substances that for Avicenna one may have an easier time conceptualizing oneself as immaterial than grasping the separate Intellects and the divinity. Even then Avicenna concedes that recognizing that one is an immaterial substance is hard enough. When one perceives oneself intellectually, however, there is literally a type of intellectual perception that is different in kind from the intellectual perception of anything else. That is because in self-awareness "the soul conceptualizes itself, and in so doing makes itself the act of the intellect, an intellect, and an object of the intellect" (*Psychology*, V.6, 239.7–8). In other words, in conceptualizing oneself as an immaterial substance one is engaged in the intellect's proper act, namely, intellectual perception. Also, inasmuch as one is actively and presently intellecting, the intellect is at the level of the acquired intellect, namely, the intellect's perfect state. Finally, since the intellect has itself as its object, the intellect is thinking about itself thinking. Thus, in conceptualizing oneself as an immaterial substance there is for Avicenna a complete identification of act, agent, and object.

This identification of act, agent, and object of intellection does not occur when one intellectually perceives the essences of other things, asserts Avicenna, since in those cases the human intellect is not the very thing perceived. Moreover, he continues, in knowing other things, the intellect does not, indeed cannot, even become the thing known so as to bring about the intellectual identification of act, agent, and object. In this respect, Avicenna is expressly rejecting a tradition that has its origins in Aristotle's *De anima*,[19] although Avicenna himself points to Porphyry as its primary proponent (ibid., 240.3–6).[20] Joseph Owens, when speaking of this idea in Aristotle, sums up the position that Avicenna wants to reject nicely:

> You *are* the things perceived or known. Knower and thing known . . . become one and the same in the actuality of cognition. From the strictly epistemological standpoint, this thoroughgoing identity of knower and thing known is the most important and fundamental tenet in the Aristotelian conception of knowledge.[21]

While Owens believes that the reason most people are resistant to this doctrine is that "they do not like the idea of being a brown cow or a big bad wolf just because they are seeing those animals or thinking about them," Avicenna rejects the idea on purely philosophical grounds.[22]

His criticism, which employs intuitions that were already present in his argument for instantaneous substantial change,[23] is directed against the more general position that anything can truly be said to become another so as to become numerically identical with it. Given this general conclusion, he can quickly show that there is no meaningful sense in which the intellect becomes the thing intellected, save in self-awareness, when knower, object known, and the act of knowing are numerically identical.

The general argument begins as follows (ibid., 239.16–240.3): When an initial thing, x, changes into another thing, y, then either x (1) continues to exist after the change or (2) x ceases to exist. If (1), x continues to exist after the change, then either (1.a), y also exists, and so y exists together with x, or (2.b), y does not exist. If (1.a), x and y exist together, then they are two things, not one. Consequently, there is not an identification of intellect and object of intellection. If (1.b), y does not exist after the change, and yet x became y, x became something nonexisting, which Avicenna finds utter nonsense (for the assumption is that x has changed, not that it has been annihilated). For the same reason one does not have to consider the logically possible but equally absurd proposition that neither x nor y remains after the change.

Thus, one is left with (2): x does not continue to exist after the change but y does. There are, maintains Avicenna, two related problems that plague this suggestion: the first general, the second related to the soul specifically. First, the more general complaint is that if x has ceased to exist, then in what meaningful sense has something nonexisting *become* another? There has been a cessation of one thing and the origination of another, but not one becoming the other. One can make sense of a pot's becoming hot or some underlying matter's becoming a new substance, but in both cases there is an underlying thing that initially was the other thing potentially, and it was that underlying thing that remains throughout the change that becomes the other. On the present assumption, however, the intellect ceases to be what it is and becomes the thing known; there is no underlying thing.

Second, the concern specific to the intellect (ibid., 240.8–241.4) is that the species form or essence—which the intellect is purportedly to become—is what actualizes a substance such that it is the kind that it is. The form in itself simply is the actuality of a thing, and as such the form has no potentiality. It is the recipient or underlying thing or matter in which there is potentiality. Thus, if the intellect were to take on the species form of wolf when it intellects wolf, to use Owens's example, there would be the actuality of the wolf, and no longer any potentiality. In that case, the intellect would no longer be able to become any other form. If one maintains that the intellect somehow retains its potential to receive other forms and essences despite its being a certain actuality qua becoming a given form, then one and the same thing would be something receiving and not receiving, which, Avicenna notes, is clearly a contradiction.

In the end, Avicenna finds the whole suggestion of the soul's becoming the thing known incomprehensible, and prefers his own account of intellectual perception. Only in the case of self-awareness is there for humans any genuine identification of intellection, intellect, and what is intellected, although Avicenna intimates, in anticipation of his own account of the Necessary Existent in itself, that perhaps some other entity can know all things simply by knowing itself.

Self-Awareness: The Nexus of Conscious Experience and the "Flying Man"

In self-awareness, thinks Avicenna, one consciously reflects on oneself as an object of intellection. As such, self-awareness might be thought of as a second-order awareness: being aware of oneself as an object of awareness. Avicenna, however, also identifies a more basic or primitive form of self-awareness that he believes is essential not only to the intellect but also to the human soul more generally. This primitive self-awareness is the subconscious awareness of the *I* that accompanies all of one's actions and conscious experiences, underlying and unifying them.[24] It is for Avicenna our awareness of the very substance of our soul considered independently of its relation to the body and bodily activities. It is one's self (*dhāt*).

That there is such a nexus where all of one's conscious experiences—whether of external or internal sensibles, desires, anger, intellectual perception, or the like—come together is evidenced for Avicenna by the fact that the various faculties do affect one another. Thus, sight may bring about desire, and yet light and color—the proper objects of vision—are not what is desired. Hunger may cloud the ability to think straight, and yet the intellect has no organ such as to experience appetites. A simple daydream might distract one from esteeming some danger immediately in front of oneself, and yet sensible forms—whether externally sensed or internally imagined—are not objects of the estimative faculty but only connotational attributes are. Despite the fact that these activities are all diverse and do not share a common instrument, one meaningfully says things like "When *I* saw it, *I* knew what it was and *I* desired it, and *I* then began thinking how

I could get it." Simply stated there is some single subject of all of these disparate experiences, namely, the *I*. Moreover, for Avicenna, inasmuch as I am aware of having any experience, I am aware that *I* am the one having it; for Avicenna this level of self-awareness is the most basic.

The question that Avicenna now asks is whether this nexus of one's experiences—in a real sense one's self—is the body or some part of the body, or, as Avicenna himself believes, not a body at all. Avicenna offers three arguments to support his contention that one should not identify the self or *I* with the body. The first one is reminiscent of his argument that the animating principle of living things cannot be the body as such, otherwise all bodies would be alive (*Psychology*, V.7, 254.1–6). Analogously, he then argues that it cannot belong to the body as such to be a nexus of experiences, otherwise all bodies—whether a brain, bone, or big toe—would gather into themselves conscious experiences, a conclusion that Avicenna takes to be manifestly false. Thus, it cannot belong to the body as such to be a nexus of one's experiences; rather, being a nexus must be some perfection belonging to the body. The perfection of the body simply is, as Avicenna had argued at the very beginning of the *Psychology*, the soul.[25]

Second, this nexus is again that which receives and unifies all of one's experiences (*Psychology*, V.7, 254.6–20). Among these experiences, however, is intellectual perception. Now, as Avicenna had argued at *Psychology* V.2, the recipient of intelligibles must be immaterial. For the same reason, then, that which receives and unifies one's intellectual perceptions must be immaterial. Therefore, concludes Avicenna, the nexus of experiences is immaterial, namely, it is the soul and not the body.

At this point, Avicenna considers an objection: If immaterial intelligibles need an *immaterial* substratum to receive them, then why should those experiences associated with matter—whether as sensed, imagined, or the like—not require a *material* substratum to receive them? Avicenna's response is that while powers in an immaterial substance may spread out from it so as to use bodies as instruments, material things cannot receive immaterial things. In general, the response, which is not as developed as one might hope, seems to be that while it has been shown that intellectual perceptions can only be received in an immaterial receptacle, it has not been demonstrated that the other kinds of perceptions must be received only in a bodily organ. Assuming the unity of our conscious experience, however, the presumption is again that all of our experiences are gathered together in a single nexus. Consequently, given that it has been demonstrated that one class of experiences necessarily requires an immaterial recipient, whereas there is no demonstration that the rest cannot be gathered together there as well, the nexus of our experiences, Avicenna concludes, is immaterial. Thus, while one may not know what the mechanism is that permits mind-body interaction, the onus of proof is, contends Avicenna, on those detractors who think that such interaction cannot take place.[26]

Avicenna begins his third and final argument (*Psychology*, V.7, 255.1–257.17) that if what is most truly the *I* were a body, it would be either the whole of the body or some part of the body, such as a bodily organ like the brain or heart. Now, the *I* cannot be the whole of the body qua whole, for one can lose part of one's body, like an arm or leg, in which case that original whole no longer exists, and yet the *I* remains. (In fact, Avicenna believes that there are intuitive reasons for thinking that even if one lost the whole of one's body the *I* would still remain, a point to which I shall return shortly.)

The *I* also cannot be merely some part of the body or some organ like the brain, continues Avicenna, for while one is always aware of oneself, one only becomes aware of one's organs after some empirical investigation or being taught about those organs. In that case, before being made aware of whatever organ or bodily part one might want to identify with the self, how can one be said to be self-aware? Certainly, the newborn infant is at some primitive level aware "*I* am hungry"—and it is because he or she is aware of being hungry that he or she cries. Yet just as obviously, the infant is wholly ignorant of having organs. If one identifies the self with a bodily organ, complains Avicenna, our infant, for example, would be aware of something of which he or she is not aware, but these are two mutually exclusive states.

Clearly, this argument is the weakest of the three, for while Commissioner Gordon, for example, may be aware that the person in front of him is Bruce Wayne, he might not at all be aware that Batman is in front of him, despite the fact that Bruce Wayne is identical to Batman. Still, this last argument does provide Avicenna with another opportunity to repeat his famous "Flying Man" thought experiment.[27] He initially presented it in book I.1 of the *Psychology*, when raising the issue of what the substance of the soul might be like considered in itself and independent of the activities it produces in the body and the effects of those activities.

The setup of the thought experiment is simple enough: Imagine that a human—for example, Adam or Eve—was created all at once, not in Eden but floating in air or in a void. Moreover, our flying man's sight is veiled, the environment is totally devoid of sounds, odors, or tastes, and he is additionally splayed out so that no parts of his body are having sensory contact with other parts. Even given complete sensory deprivation, Avicenna believes that the individual would still affirm his or her existence. Thus, he concludes that one cannot identify what is most truly one's self, the *I*, with one's body.

Again as an argument for the immateriality of the self, such a thought experiment is wanting; however, Avicenna never intended it as an argument for the immateriality of the self. Instead, as he himself repeatedly says, he is merely trying to point us in the right direction or to prime our intuitions about the very nature of the self or *I* (*Psychology*, I.1, 15.19–16.2).

To see this, let me up approach Avicenna's thought experiment, as it were, backward. Instead of imagining an Adam or Eve totally unaware of any experiences except of themselves (if this is even possible), consider yourself with all your experiences, whether sensations, memories, concepts, or the like. Now imagine yourself in some "Freaky Friday" episode, where you find yourself, for example, in my body. In other words, it is your memories, thoughts, personality, or, in general, mental life, experiencing the world through a body different from the one you in fact have, namely, mine. Would you say, "*I* have your experiences!" or "*I* am in your body!". If you find yourself saying, "*I* am in your body!" then you share Avicenna's intuition at a very basic level.

Now, imagine that you can retain all of those experiences, save any sensible sensations. In effect, imagine yourself in a disembodied state and moreover unable to access the external world in any way, while still having all of your memories and concepts. Again, would you say, "*I* have no body!" or "*I* have no memories and concepts" or conversely "A ghost has my memories and concepts!" Again, if you said, "*I* have no body!" you share Avicenna's intuition.

Again, imagine that one by one your memories are removed until only your concepts or universal ideas are left. So, for example, you would still know that all humans are animals, except there is no accompanying image of a human. Again, if in such a case, you find yourself saying, "*I* have no memories!" (even if you think that this is a depleted version of yourself), you are still sharing Avicenna's intuition about the nature of the self or *I*.

Finally, imagine that one by one you are stripped of your concepts ending finally with the concepts of "thing" and then "existence" itself. At which point in this stripping process could you no longer say, "*I* am something" or "*I* exist"? For Avicenna, it is only when your very existence is removed that the *I* ceases.

Again, as Avicenna himself repeatedly says, the "flying man" thought experiment is not an argument as such to show that one should identify oneself with an immaterial soul rather than the body; he feels that he can demonstrate the immateriality of the human intellect without appealing to such fantasy-style arguments. Still, he does want to use it as a tool so that one can think rightly about what he believes that we humans are. The *I* is most truly us regardless of whether there is any bodily input—at least this is the intuition that Avicenna wants us to have.

Prophecy

I conclude this chapter with Avicenna's account of prophecy, which itself relies on many of the psychological notions put forth thus far.[28] Whereas today we tend to think of prophecy, veridical dreams, and the like as outside the scope of scientific inquiry, Avicenna did not. He, like all of those around him, took such events as factual phenomena, and as such they are for him just as open to scientific scrutiny and in need of scientific explanation as any other natural phenomenon. Indeed, far from considering prophecy and the like as supernatural or a divine gift conferred upon whomever God wills, Avicenna viewed these phenomena as natural and as such requiring a natural explanation. He found such an explanation in psychology (*Psychology*, V.6, 248.9–250.4).

For Avicenna, as has been seen, a human comes to know and to understand something when the intellect receives the intelligible object or concept of that thing. As such, the human intellect has a certain natural disposition to receive concepts, where this disposition varies between individuals: Some individuals just do not "get things," while others do, some get things faster, some slower. When this capacity or disposition to get things is strong, Avicenna terms it "insight" or "intuition" (*ḥads*) (ibid., 248.12–13).[29]

The person with insight is, with relative ease, able to make initial contact or conjunction with the Active Intellect, which again brings about intellectual perception. In fact, continues Avicenna, for some people their insight is so intense that it is as if they know everything on their own without being taught those things. Moreover, they recognize these things almost immediately. In these very few individuals with the highest level of insight—which Avicenna identifies with prophets—their insight so abounds that it overflows and deluges their compositive imaginations in the form of visions and voices.

From a modern point of view this feature may be the most arresting one about Avicenna's conception of prophecy, since he sees it is a wholly natural phenomenon. As such, it is not God who chooses the prophet (or at least not directly); rather, it is the properly prepared or disposed human soul that explains why someone has prophetic revelation. Moreover, recall that it is the elemental mix or humoral temperament that occasions the production of the soul suitable to that body. Thus, in a certain sense it is the elemental mix or humoral temperament that explains the prophet's disposition to receive the soul that he or she does, and so made possible that he or she is a prophet. This prophetic soul Avicenna also calls the "sacred intellect" ('aql qudsī).

What the sacred intellect intellectually perceives (as well as hears and sees in imaginative forms) is in fact the universal causal order (or some representation thereof), what Avicenna frequently terms "the order of the good." For Avicenna this involves the prophet's conjoining with the Active Intellect and obtaining the middle term of a syllogism, where again middle terms are the logical counterparts of the causes found in the world.[30] Thus, inasmuch as the prophet possesses the middle terms or causal explanations, he or she has genuine scientific knowledge.

Inasmuch as his or her compositive imagination is flooded with images representing this scientific knowledge, the prophet is able to convey to the masses through these images and metaphors truths about the order of the good, that is, the divine universal order, which most people would not otherwise have grasped or done so only after arduous scientific investigation. Avicenna says that the prophet "blazes with insight" (V.6, 249.19–20) and so wholly grasps the necessary causal order inherent in the world, his or her immediate place in that order, and how that causal order must inevitably play out in the future, thus suggesting how prophets can predict future events.

This causal order, now not limited to merely natural things but extending to existence as such, makes up an important part of the subject matter of the science of metaphysics as Avicenna envisions it, and it is to that subject that I now turn.

6

METAPHYSICS I

Theology

Introduction: The Subject Matter of Metaphysics

With the introduction of an immaterial intellect, Avicenna has in a very real sense moved beyond the science of physics, for again the proper subject of natural philosophy is movable body, whereas the intellect as has been noted is not a body. Instead, the investigation of immaterial substances, according to Avicenna, belongs to the science of metaphysics. Now there can be no doubt that in a very real sense Avicenna's metaphysics is in many respects the culmination and crowning achievement of his philosophical system. Avicenna himself certainly thought as much. But what is metaphysics as a science? To be more exact, what is the proper subject of the science of metaphysics?[1] The proper subject of logic, according to Avicenna, is the secondary intelligibles such as genus, difference, and species inasmuch as these can be traced back to the primary intelligibles, namely, the universals of the various kinds like horse-ness and humanity, whose individual and particular instances actually exist in the world. The proper object of natural philosophy is again material bodies insofar as they are subject to motion. The proper subject of mathematics is quantity, whether a magnitude or number, albeit quantity considered independent of any particular matter, regardless of whether the quantity in question actually exists or does not exist materially.

What then is the proper subject of metaphysics? In the end, Avicenna identifies metaphysics' proper subject matter with that which exists inasmuch as it exists—an account that readers of Aristotle's *Metaphysics* Γ will recognize, for there Aristotle says, "there is a science that studies being qua being";[2] however, before concluding as much Avicenna had to address the claims of two other candidates that had become popular contenders by his time for the title of the proper subject of metaphysics. These are that metaphysics properly studies either (1) God or, in some way or other, (2) causes more generally.

One can certainly understand why God (or, more generally, immaterial beings) may have such a claim to being the proper subject of metaphysics, for if natural philosophy treats material bodies, while mathematics treats the features of material bodies considered independent of their matter, then metaphysics, one might naturally presume, should treat things, such as God, that are actually immaterial. While Avicenna happily concedes that God and God's existence are issues treated in metaphysics, he adamantly denies that the existence of God is the proper subject of metaphysics (*Metaphysics*, I.1, 3.16–4.19).

His argument for this position presupposes a certain conception of the nature of a science. All sciences, according to Avicenna following Aristotle,[3] must begin from certain presuppositions that cannot be demonstrated in the given science, but have to be taken without demonstration. Such presuppositions must simply be posited, or, perhaps demonstrated in some higher science. These presuppositions include among other things the existence claims of the given science, namely, those things that the science has to assume to exist in order to proceed at all. The first thing posited among these existence claims is the existence of the proper subject matter of that science. So, for example, physics does not attempt to demonstrate that there are bodies subject to motion or change. It simply takes such bodies for granted, whereas it is only in a higher science, namely, metaphysics, that there is a demonstration why there are such bodies.

Given this conception of the relation between the existence claims of a given science and that science's proper subject matter, Avicenna argues that if God were the proper subject of metaphysics, then the existence of God could not be demonstrated, at least not within the science of metaphysics; rather, either it would not be demonstrable at all or it would necessarily be demonstrated in some other science. As for God's existence being indemonstrable, that would be either because the divinity's existence is self-evident or it is something that simply cannot be demonstrated. Avicenna considers it obvious that God's existence is not self-evident,[4] nor does he think that one should despair of finding a demonstration that God exists, for he believes that he himself has discovered one.[5] As for whether the existence of God can be demonstrated in another science, if so, then that science would have to be either logic, natural philosophy, mathematics, or one of the practical philosophies such as ethics or politics, but none of these, in fact, establishes that God exists, or so asserts Avicenna.

At this point, one might complain (and Averroes later would) that in Aristotle's *Physics* (VIII 5), Aristotle had proven that there is an Unmoved Mover, which certainly many philosophers had and would in the future identify with God. In fact, Avicenna himself felt like he had also demonstrated the existence of an Unmoved Mover in his own *Physics* (IV.15) using a proof much like that of Aristotle. While Avicenna was convinced that physics could demonstrate that there is indeed some first, unmoved cause of motion, he did not think that one was justified in identifying this cause with God. Avicenna himself identified this Unmoved Mover with the immaterial substance (or Intelligence) associated with the outermost sphere of the heavens, but not God. At best, this entity is the cause of the motion of our cosmos, but not of the very existence of the cosmos itself. In contrast, God (at least as Avicenna understood that term) is the very cause of all existence itself. Thus, Aristotle's Unmoved Mover fails to meet Avicenna's criteria for Godhood. What Avicenna contended was needed was not a "physical proof" for God's existence, which he believed was incapable of demonstrating that God exists, but a "metaphysics proof" for God's existence.[6] Later I consider Avicenna's metaphysical proof for the existence of God, for now, however, suffice it so say that no other science, physics included, had, to Avicenna's mind, adequately demonstrated the existence of the cause of existence itself, and so proven that there is a true divinity.

Returning to the original point, God cannot be the proper subject of metaphysics because, again, a science does not prove the existence of its proper subject matter, but merely assumes or posits it. Consequently, if God were the subject matter of metaphysics, either there would be no demonstration of God's existence (but there is) or some other science would demonstrate it (but they do not). Hence, concludes Avicenna, the only science in which the existence of God could be demonstrated is metaphysics, and so God is not the proper subject of that science, even though metaphysics does investigate the divinity and the divine attributes.

The second suggestion that Avicenna rejects is that the subject of metaphysics is causes. Avicenna identifies four ways that such a suggestion might be understood (*Metaphysics*, I.5, 5.1–6.18): the proper subject matter of metaphysics is (1) causes insofar as they exist; (2) causes considered simply inasmuch as they are causes, that is, causality as such; (3) the causality proper to each of the four so-called Aristotelian causes, namely, the material, formal, efficient, and final causes; and (4) the interrelation between the four causes, namely, the whole causal complex, such as a form-matter composite acting for some end. As for suggestion (1), namely that metaphysics' proper subject is causes insofar as they exist, Avicenna does in fact believe that metaphysics examines their existence; however, since there are other existing things as well that it considers, one should not merely limit the proper subject of metaphysics to some subset of existents, namely, causes.

In a similar vein, he has a set of arguments directed against (2), namely that the subject of metaphysics is causality as such, which equally applies to suggestions (3), the causality of the four causes, and (4), the interrelation between the four causes. First, included among the topics that metaphysics treats are such notions as the universal and particular, actuality and potentiality, as well as necessity and possibility, but these notions are not proper to causes alone but equally apply to whatever exists. Thus, the subject of metaphysics is broader than causality simply understood.

Second, at best empirical observations show that there are constant conjunctions (*muwāfaqa*) between events, such as when one touches fire to cotton, which is then followed by the cotton's burning. Sensation, however, neither does nor can establish that some actual causal relation or causality exists between two things; rather, it is the metaphysician who demonstrates the existence of causality. Thus, for the same reason that God could not be the subject matter of metaphysics, neither can causality be the unique subject matter of metaphysics, argues Avicenna, for again a science cannot demonstrate the existence of its own proper subject. Thus, inasmuch as causality understood in most general terms cannot be the subject matter of metaphysics, neither can the specific causes and a fortiori the causal complexes composed of the specific causes be the subject matter of this science.

As for determining metaphysics' proper subject matter, Avicenna begins by listing the various topics and issues treated within metaphysics, and then asks what all of these things share in common (*Metaphysics*, I.2). That common factor will then be the subject of metaphysics. Thus, included among the particular issues that metaphysics investigates is, as has been noted, God and causes more generally (however construed). Additionally, the science of metaphysics establishes various principles assumed by the other lower sciences. Moreover, metaphysics treats substances whether, material or immaterial, as well as the so-called accidents enumerated in Aristotle's *Categories*, inasmuch as the ten categories indicate, as it were, various kinds or modes of existence. Furthermore, metaphysics determines the status of mathematical objects: Do they exist in physical bodies, or only in the mind, or is there a Platonic realm of mathematical Forms where they exist? Also, metaphysics again considers the universal and particular, actuality and potentiality, as well as necessity and possibility. Inasmuch as one or the other of these notions happens to apply to a given existent, and inasmuch as an existent happens to be described by one of these notions, these notions indicate what might be thought of as akin to proper accidents of existence.

When one considers this summary of some of the topics falling within the domain of metaphysics, Avicenna believes that it becomes clear that the only thing that they all share in common, and so is the subject matter of metaphysics, is that they are existents. Thus, concludes Avicenna, "it is the existent qua existent that is the primary subject of this science" (*Metaphysics*, I.2, 10.2).

To try to treat Avicenna's detailed and rich discussions of all of these topics, and others as well, in one, or even two chapters, would be impossible. Instead, let me begin with a very brief outline of how the *Metaphysics* from Avicenna's monumental work the *Cure* holds together overall. Then, in the remainder of this chapter and the next, I shall focus on two central metaphysical topics that bring together a number of points from throughout Avicenna's metaphysical system, as well as his philosophical system more generally. These two issues are God (or, to be more exact, Avicenna's Necessary Existent) and Creation (or, again to be more exact, possible existents).

To begin, Avicenna's general project in the *Metaphysics* is to recast the text of Aristotle's own *Metaphysics* in such a way as to fulfill the canons of a demonstrative science as set forth both by Aristotle in the *Posterior Analytics* and Avicenna himself in his *Book of Demonstration*.[7] To this end, book I of Avicenna's *Metaphysics*, as has been seen, lays out his conception of metaphysics as a science whose proper subject matter is existence qua existence. As such, existence is investigated first with respect to the kinds or divisions of existence, which Avicenna identifies with Aristotle's ten categories (roughly books II–III of Avicenna's *Metaphysics*). Second, metaphysics inquires into the proper accidents of existence—that is, those states that may or may not apply to existence—which again include such states as priority, posteriority, potentiality, actuality, universals, particulars, cause, and effect (books IV–VII). Third, the first causes—and most specifically the Necessary Existent—represent the high point of metaphysical inquiry (books VIII–IX). Additionally, since, as Aristotle had noted,[8] "one" is said in as many ways as "being," Avicenna considers a subclass of ontology, which has been rightly termed "henology" (after the Greek *hen* "one" and *logos* "account").[9] This study of unity and plurality, that is, henology, parallels the above-mentioned three areas of metaphysical investigation but now from the perspective of the "one" and the "many." Thus, the divisions and kinds of one and many are considered intermingled throughout Avicenna's discussion in books II–III, whereas the proper accidents of the one and many receive an independent treatment in book VII. The studies of existence qua existence and unity then come back together in books VIII–IX, where Avicenna treats the pure unity, God. Finally, the last book (book X, and the last chapter of book IX) discusses the "hereafter" and a human's ultimate end as well as "God's commandments" by which humans should live while here on Earth.

Again it would be impossible to cover all of these issues in any substantive way.[10] Instead, in the remainder of this chapter and the next one, I consider two closely related topics: Avicenna's theology and cosmology. In order to appreciate Avicenna's contribution to these two subjects, however, one must briefly consider the history of how philosophers had viewed God's relation to the cosmos, for this issue raises a cluster of core philosophical problems that Avicenna's metaphysical system attempts to address.[11] This brief history is then followed by a look at Avicenna's modal ontology, and a closer investigation of the Necessary Existent and the divine attributes. In the next chapter, I concentrate on possible existents and the created order.

A Brief History of the First Cause's Relation to the Cosmos

Certainly as early as Plato, if not before, Greek philosophers were discussing the issue of God's causal relation to an eternal effect, namely, an eternal cosmos. In the *Timaeus*, a self-avowedly mythical account of the origin and makeup of the cosmos, Plato says that initially the material that would make up the world as we now know it was in a state of chaos lacking any order or structure. The demiurge (loosely, Plato's equivalent to the Creator), out of its own goodness, wanted to make this chaotic matter good like itself. So looking to the paradigms, which might be identified with the Platonic realm of the Forms, the demiurge imposed form upon matter and so produced order.

Two things should be noted about Plato's account. First, inasmuch as the demiurge imposes form onto matter, one can consider it an efficient cause of the cosmos' current existence. Second, taken literally the *Timaeus* account implies that there was a time when there was chaos after which the demiurge imposes form on matter. Consequently, one can understand Plato to mean that the world as we know it with its present structure and order came to exist at some definite moment in the finite past before which this cosmos, informed as it currently is, did not exist.

This literal interpretation of Plato's *Timaeus*, however, was already being challenged as early as the time of Speusippus and Xenocrates, Plato's immediate successors at the Academy, for they argued that the demiurge stood in a causal, rather than temporal, relation to the cosmos. Consequently, on their interpretation of Plato, the cosmos is generated in the sense of being dependent upon the demiurge as upon an efficient cause, and yet the cosmos is eternal.

In response to Speusippus and Xenocrates, Aristotle seriously challenged the view that anything could be both generated, that is, the effect of an efficient cause, and eternal. Thus, at *De Caelo*, I 11–12, he distinguished various senses of "generable/ungenerable" (Gk. *genēton/agenēton*) and "imperishable/perishable" (*phtharton/aphtharton*), with the most basic senses understood in terms of "possibility" and "impossibility" (*dunaton/ adunaton*), for only if something is possible is it capable of generation. Aristotle next appealed to what are sometimes called temporal frequencies or a statistical model in order to explain the modal terms "necessity," "possibility," and "impossibility." More specifically, according to Aristotle, at least in the *De Caelo*, if something exists for *all time*, it is necessary; if it exists at *some time*, but not at another time, it is possible; and if it exists at *no time* ever, it is impossible.[12]

Aristotle, then, argued against the thesis that something is generable and yet eternal based upon this analysis of possible and impossible. The details need not bother us, since his general move is relatively straightforward: If something is generable, and so causally dependent upon another as its efficient cause, then its existence must be possible; however, if it is possible, then, given the temporal frequency account of possibility just sketched, there is a time when it does not exist. Clearly, if there is a time when it does not exist, then it is not eternal. Therefore, concludes Aristotle, whatever is generated, and so dependent upon an efficient cause, cannot be eternal. If Plato had maintained that the cosmos is both the effect of an efficient cause and eternal, as Speusippus and Xenocrates suggested, then, according to Aristotle's argument, Plato's thesis is simply incoherent.

In contrast, Aristotle's God (or more exactly his Unmoved Mover) is not an efficient cause of the cosmos' existence at all, but only a final cause that explains why the cosmos is eternally changing and always undergoing motion. In more detail, as a corollary of his *De Caelo* argument as well as on the basis of other arguments, Aristotle held that the existence of the cosmos itself, understood as a form-matter composite, must be necessary and as such it does not need an efficient cause for its existence. In other words, for Aristotle, there never has been some time when the forms and matter that make up our cosmos did not exist. Thus, they, and the composite of them, namely, the cosmos, do not need some efficient cause to explain their existence. Instead, what needs to be explained, at least according to Aristotle, is what causes the motion found in our independently existing cosmos, which he did by appealing to his Unmoved Mover qua ultimate object of desire. To this end, he claimed that the heavens desire to imitate or to be like (to the extent that that is possible) the wholly actual and eternal Unmoved Mover. They do this by perpetually rotating in place, which is as close as a moving thing, like the heavens, can come to being like the wholly actual, unchanging, and eternal Unmoved Mover. Let me repeat: Aristotle's Unmoved Mover is not an efficient cause of either the universe's existence or its motion. It is only a final cause inasmuch as it is the object of desire that an eternally existing universe through its perpetual motion strives to imitate (to the extent that that is possible).[13]

Quickly, to sum up the situation as Aristotle understood it, if the existence of the cosmos is eternal and so necessary, God can stand to it only as its final cause. Conversely, if God is the efficient cause of its existence, the cosmos must have had a temporal beginning at some time in the finite past. The question then is whether the cosmos had a temporal beginning or has existed eternally. In *Physics* VIII, Aristotle himself provided a number of arguments that the world must be eternal based upon his analysis of such physical notions as motion and time.

For example, time, as Aristotle defined it, is the measure of motion insofar as the motion is marked off into before and after (*Physics*, IV 10, 219b1–2). So, for example, time stands to motion analogously to the way that spatial measurements, such as a meter or foot, stand to distance, space, or length. Thus, on Aristotle's account of time, there can no more be a time without a motion than there could be some spatial measurement without there being some distance that is able to be measured. Neither spatial measurements, such as one meter, nor temporal measurements, such as one year, can exist independently of the thing that is being measured. Consequently, if one assumes that there had ever been a time when there was no motion, one would have committed oneself to the position that there is a motion, which time is measuring, when there is no motion, an obvious contradiction. If motion exists, however, then there must exist what is undergoing motion, namely, a body, which is nothing more than a form-matter composite. Therefore, Aristotle concludes, there has never been a time that a form-matter composite, namely, the cosmos, has not existed, to assume otherwise leads to contradiction.

In addition to Aristotle's physical proofs, later philosophers such as the Neoplatonist Proclus (412–485 CE)—who, unlike Aristotle, thought that God was both the final and efficient cause of the existence of the cosmos—offered further arguments for the cosmos' eternity, not based upon physical notions, but upon the divine nature. For example, Proclus argued that if God changed from not creating the world to creating it, this would make God subject to change.[14] Proclus, as well as thinkers before him, found a number of reasons why ascribing change to God is undesirable either from a philosophical or theological perspective. First, it was maintained that whenever something changes, there must be some cause of that change. Consequently, if God began to create after not having created, there would be something acting upon God that caused God to change from not creating to creating. God, however, is thought to be the First Cause, that is, the Cause of causes, and so, should God change, there would be a cause before the First Cause, which is a contradiction.

Second, according to Proclus, it is solely on account of divine goodness that God causes the existence of the cosmos. Hence, if the cosmos had a temporal creation in the finite past, then either there was a time when God was not good and so did not create, or a time when God was impotent and could not create what his goodness demanded. Either option is sacrilegious. In short, God seemingly cannot change. Consequently, if God creates (that is, if God is the cosmos' efficient cause), then he must create as long as he exists, but God exists eternally, and so God's creation, namely, the cosmos, must exist eternally.

Arguments such as these for the cosmos' eternity coupled with Aristotle's analysis of the relation between the existence of the cosmos and the nature of God's causality, gave rise to perhaps one of the most significant challenges for most subsequent philosophers working in both the classical Greek- and medieval Arabic-speaking worlds. The challenge was that most of these thinkers not only found the arguments for the eternity of the world convincing, but also maintained that God is *both* final and efficient cause of the cosmos. Yet again these two theses run afoul of Aristotle's *De Caelo* argument. That argument again in its simplest form is this: Whatever exists through an efficient cause is possible, and if something is possible, then, according to the temporal frequency model of modalities, there is a time when it does not exists. If there is a time when something does not exist, however, it cannot be eternal. Consequently, if the cosmos were dependent upon God as its efficient cause, it apparently could not be eternal. It would seem that these later philosophers wanted to eat their proverbial cake and have it too.

Moreover, there was a further difficulty facing those philosophers who wanted to make God both efficient cause and final cause of the cosmos. All of them affirmed God's absolute simplicity and unity, and yet it is not immediately clear how an absolutely simple being can be the source of two distinct and different forms of causality, final and efficient. In other words, for these thinkers, there is absolutely no composition in God. Thus, for example, God cannot be material, since matter can be divided into parts from which the whole is composed. Similarly, attributes such God's power, wisdom, love, and the like could not refer to different aspects of God, for then there would need to be some cause that explains how these different attributes come together to form the single entity that is God. Yet, as has been argued, God is the First Cause and so nothing causally acts upon the divinity. Now being a final cause seems to be quite distinct from being an efficient cause. So, for example, the desire to have a child, which is a final cause, is distinct from the act of procreation, which is the efficient cause (even if the two causes act together and complement each other in generating a child). Thus, the question that arose was, "How should one reconcile absolute divine simplicity with God's being both a final and efficient cause of the cosmos' existence, again given that the final and efficient causes involve distinct forms of causality?"

So, here is a brief history of perhaps the most pressing set of problems for late Greek- and early Arabic-speaking metaphysicians. First, most of these thinkers wanted to affirm that God is the efficient cause of the cosmos and that the cosmos is eternal. Yet, if the cosmos is eternal, then it has existed for all time, and according to the preferred account for explaining modalities, if something has existed for all time, it is necessary. What is necessary, however, does not need an efficient cause. In short, how can one make God the efficient cause of an eternal effect in light of the temporal frequency model for explaining modalities like possibility and necessity? Second, even if one can show how God is the efficient cause of an eternal effect, one needs also to show how an absolutely simple God, who is one in every respect, is both the efficient and final cause of the cosmos, for efficient and final causality appear to require distinct factors in the divinity to explain them. In short, what single factor could account for God's being both final and efficient cause of the cosmos' existence?

Avicenna's Modal Ontology

Perhaps the easiest way to diffuse the first challenge—namely, to explain how God can be the efficient cause of an eternal effect in light of the temporal frequency model of modalities—is simply to jettison the temporal frequency model itself. Still, the model had a decided allure for many, if not most, of the philosophers working during the pre-Avicennan time of the Islamic classical period.[15]

This was due in no small part to the fact that most early Arabic-speaking philosophers were logicians, and from the point of view of logic temporal frequencies are attractive, since they provide a semantics for the otherwise uninterpreted modal logic of Aristotle's *Prior Analytics*. So, just as today certain logicians find "possible world" talk attractive since they can explain the modal operators necessary, possible, and impossible in terms of true in all possible worlds, some possible world, and no possible worlds respectively,[16] so these medieval logicians explained these notions respectively in terms of existing at all time (and so necessary), at some time while not at another time (and so possible), and at no time (and so impossible). In short, identifying modalities with temporal frequencies allowed the medieval logician to treat modal operators as metalinguistic quantifiers.

Moreover, the temporal frequency model was not only attractive to early Arabic-speaking logicians but also to natural philosophers and metaphysicians, since it allowed them to reduce the rather opaque notions of natural necessity, possibility, and impossibility to the relatively transparent notion of time. Although we today might not find the notion of time any clearer than modalities, this was certainly not the case for the ancient and medieval philosophers. Aristotle in his *Physics* (IV 11) had provided a careful analysis of time and ultimately identified it, as already has been noted, with a certain measure of motion. Moreover, Aristotle had submitted motion to an equally rigorous analysis and identified it with the actuality of potential as such (*Physics*, III 1), where "actuality" and "potentiality" were considered perhaps the two most basic notions within Aristotle's entire system. In short, reducing modalities to temporal frequencies explained what ultimately grounds them in the physical world, namely, the act/potency relations inherent in the world. Thus, while simply divorcing the temporal frequency model from one's metaphysics might be the simplest way to address the initial challenge, it apparently comes at the cost of explanatory power with respect to one's account of modalities. What was needed was a thorough rethinking of the nature of modalities. This is precisely what Avicenna provides.

As one might expect from Avicenna's understanding of the subject matter of metaphysics, he begins his metaphysical investigation at book I.5 of the *Metaphysics* of the *Cure* with an indication that something exists (*mawjūd*) and what the divisions of existence (*wujūd*) are. (Here, I should note that Avicenna takes *mawjūd* and *wujūd* in their most general connotation, that is, Avicenna is not concerned with a particular existing thing, such as humans, or even a specific mode of existence, such as being a substance; rather, in metaphysics he again is concerned only with existence as such.)

That something exists and that there is existence, he begins, is the first thing impressed upon the soul and simply cannot be doubted (*Metaphysics*, I.5, 22.11–12; and *Salvation*, "Metaphysics," I.4, 396).[17] Trying to demonstrate that there is existence or that something exists, he argues, is a fool's errand, since all demonstrations proceed from things better known than and prior to the conclusion (ibid., 23.1–15). Thus, if one assumed that there were anything better known than and prior to existence itself, one would be committed to the existence of that thing itself, and so would have to assume its existence, but existence is the very thing that one was attempting to demonstrate. In short, for Avicenna, any proof that there is existence is inherently circular. Similar remarks hold for the notion of "thing" (*shay'*).

He next identifies the necessary (*wājib*) and the possible (*mumkin*) with the primary conceptual divisions of existence itself (*wujūd*) (ibid., 27.18–28.15).[18]

In other words, insofar as anything exists for Avicenna, it exists either necessarily or possibly. Consequently, since the necessary and the possible are ways of considering existence, then just as there is nothing more primitive by which one could define or prove the existence of existence itself, so likewise there is nothing more primitive by which one could define necessary and possible existence. Thus, he writes:

> Virtually everything that has reached you from the ancients concerning how to explain [the "necessary," "possible," and "impossible"] requires [you to do so] circularly. That is because . . . when you want to define the possible, you take either the necessary or the impossible in its definition, and there is no other way but that. [Similarly] when you want to define the necessary you take either the possible or impossible in its definition (*Metaphysics*, I.5, 27.19–28.3).

The notions of necessity, possibility, and impossibility, then, must be properly basic, that is, they do not depend upon any other notions to explain them, and so can only be defined in terms of one another.

As a brief aside, while in the *Metaphysics* Avicenna does not mention the temporal frequency model for analyzing modalities, which seemingly makes time more basic than the modalities themselves, this omission is undoubtedly because Avicenna had in his *Physics*, as I noted,[19] analyzed time in terms of possibility: Time is a certain possibility corresponding with the possibility of the moving object to cover a given distance when moving at a given speed. Thus possibility is for Avicenna more basic than time, and so it is ultimately possibility that explains time and temporal frequencies, not the other way around.

To help sharpen the distinction between necessity and possibility, Avicenna introduces the language of "through itself" (*bi-dhātihi*, sometimes also translated "in itself") and "through another" (*bi-ghayrihi*) (*Metaphysics*, I.6). At least one reason for introducing the "through itself" and "through another" vocabulary is that it provides Avicenna a way to distinguish different nuances of necessity. For there is a difference between saying that something is necessary in the sense that it simply cannot not exist—as, for instance, the existence of God is supposed to be—and saying that something is necessary on a certain condition—as, for example, given that two sets of two apples exist, then necessarily there exist four apples, although it is certainly possible that one or both of the sets of apples had not existed, in which case the four apples would not have existed.

Not only does Avicenna use the "through itself" and "through another" vocabulary to draw this distinction, but also to show how and why these two conceptions of necessity, again absolute versus conditional necessity, are opposed, if not outright contradictory, as well as filling out what it means to be a possible existent (ibid., 30.11–19). So, for example, if something, x, were necessary though itself but also necessary through another, y, then should, owing to y's nonexistence, x not exist, something purportedly necessary through itself, namely x, would not in fact be necessary through itself, an obvious contradiction. Alternatively, continues Avicenna, if y could fail to exist and yet x, which again is also purportedly necessary through y, continued to exist, then the existence of that which is necessary through another is not, in fact, at all necessary through that other, which Avicenna notes is a patent contradiction.

Moreover, for Avicenna, what is necessary through another, as opposed to necessary through itself, is in fact that which is possible through itself (ibid., 31.1–12). He argues thus: Should that other not exist (let it be y), then the existence of what is necessary through the other (and let it be x) would be impossible through itself, necessary through itself, or possible in itself, which exhausts the various ways one might consider x in or through itself. If, on the one hand, x's existence is impossible in itself, then, since what is impossible in itself cannot exist, whether the other exists or not, x, which is by assumption necessary through another, simply could not exist. Again, however, it was assumed that it does exist through another, namely, y. Hence, there is a contradiction. If, on the other hand, when y did not exist, x's existence were necessary through itself, then x would not be necessary through y, since x exists without y; however, it is assumed that x is necessary through y. So again there is a contradiction just like the one noted when considering why something cannot be both necessary through itself and through another. It remains then that what is necessary through another must be something possible in itself.

Despite the fact that Avicenna takes both necessity and possibility as primitive when it comes to defining the other, there is a sense, Avicenna notes, that necessity is in a way prior, namely, inasmuch as necessity indicates an emphasis on existence, whereas possibility has some association with nonexistence inasmuch as what is possible might not exist (*Metaphysics*, I.5, 28.16–18). Thus, inasmuch as nonexistence in no way enters the concept of necessity, and existence is better known than nonexistence, necessity has a certain conceptual priority. Thus, argues Avicenna, whenever something

actually exists or is presently occurring it is in some way or another necessary (although perhaps not necessary through itself).

His argument for this thesis begins by considering the state of existence
when something is merely possible and then the state when it is actual (*Salvation*, "Metaphysics," II.3, 548). When that thing is merely possible, it is in
a state of possible existence. When, however, that possibility has been actualized, there is a change in that thing's state of existence: What was once not
actual now exists as actual. Now, begins Avicenna, the existence of that new
(actual) state might be one of impossible existence, possible existence, or
necessary existence. This exhausts the ways something might be said to exist. Clearly, the new state is not one of impossible existence, since the existence is now actualized. As for possible existence, inasmuch as the possible
existence is itself what has changed the new state cannot also be one of possible existence. For in that case, there would have been no change in the
state of existence, and yet that is exactly what did change. Thus, it remains,
concludes Avicenna, that when anything possible in itself actually exists,
the state of its existence is necessary, albeit necessary through another.

So, for example, I presently have a library pallor, and so any tan I might
presently be said to have exists only possibly; however, should I spend my
summer vacation at the beach, my possible tan would become an actual tan.
Now, the existence of that tan cannot be impossible, since I will actually
have a tan. Furthermore, it cannot remain existing as only a possible tan,
because that would be for the tan to exist as it did before I went to the beach.
Thus, inasmuch as the actualized tan exists, and that actual existence cannot be impossible or possible, it must be necessary. Whatever actually exists,
concludes Avicenna, is necessary in some sense, whether necessary through
itself or necessary through another.

Thus, existence, according to Avicenna, can be thought of in three conceptually distinct ways: (1) that whose existence is necessary through itself,
(2) that whose existence is possible through itself, and (3) that whose existence is possible through itself, but necessary through another (that is, whatever is contingent but presently existing).

The Necessary Existent in Itself

The next step in Avicenna's analysis of the modal structure of existence is to
provide an in-depth investigation of both necessity and possibility, starting

with the notion of the necessary through itself. Before considering his analysis, I should say that I find nothing like an Anselmian ontological-style argument for the existence of God in Avicenna.[20] Consequently, I think that the question of whether there is anything necessary through itself is for Avicenna a genuinely open one. At this point of his inquiry, he is merely considering the various conceptual divisions of existence, and it could turn out that one of those conceptual divisions, such as the necessary through itself, is empty.

Having said that, if something necessary through itself should exist, then, according to Avicenna there could be only one such existent (*Metaphysics*, I.7; *Salvation*, "Metaphysics," II.4). The general argument for his claim is that if there were two necessary existents, there would be that aspect that they share in common, namely, necessary existence, and that aspect by which they differ (for if there truly were more than one, then there must be something that distinguishes *this* one from *that* one). Thus, if there were two necessary existents, each would be a whole composed of conceptually distinct parts. Now, a whole subsists through its parts, and the parts are other than the whole. Consequently, were the necessary through itself composed of conceptually distinct parts it would be necessary through another, namely, its parts. Since, as has been noted, it is a contradiction to be necessary through itself and necessary through another, Avicenna concludes, the assumption that there could be two necessary existents is false. If there is a necessary existent, then there can be only one.

Similarly, it cannot be the case that two things possible through themselves jointly become something necessary through itself (*Metaphysics*, I.6, 32.4–34.6). In other words, it cannot be the case that one thing, x, is the cause of another thing, y, where y is in turn the cause of x such that, while x and y are both possible in themselves, $\Re_{xy}$ is necessary in itself. The reason that Avicenna gives is that inasmuch as x is the cause of y, x must be essentially (even though not necessarily temporally) prior to y, and conversely, y inasmuch as it is the effect of x is posterior to x. Consequently, if x is both cause and effect of y, x must be both prior and posterior to y. Avicenna tells us, however, that it is a contradiction for a given thing to be both prior and posterior to one and the same thing, for to be prior to that thing is not to be posterior to it. Thus, that which exists necessarily through itself cannot be a composite of two subsisting entities.

Neither can the necessary through itself be some composite of internal constitutive principles, such as form and matter, or genus and difference, or the like (*Metaphysics*, I.7; *Salvation*, "Metaphysics," II.5). That is because, as has already been seen, wholes or composites exist through their parts, but again parts are other than the whole. From this conclusion it is also obvious, argues Avicenna, that something necessary through itself must be wholly immaterial, for, as I noted in chapter 3, matter requires form, but the necessary through itself cannot be a form-matter composite. In short, concludes Avicenna, if there is something that is necessary through itself, it must be absolutely unique, utterly simple, and wholly devoid of any composition.

Avicenna's project thus far has been to analyze existence into its most basic modal structure, namely, the conceptual categories of necessary existence and possible existence. Now, inasmuch as the world exists, it cannot be that both of these conceptual categories are empty, for something clearly exists. Instead, the question is whether there really are existents corresponding with both categories of existence.

It is fairly obvious that there are things that are possible through themselves while necessary through another, for all of us are in some way, for example, dependent upon the organs and limbs that constitute us, the presence of oxygen, and the like. The more pressing question is whether the category of necessary existence through itself is an empty one. In order to address this question, Avicenna develops an argument, which appeals almost exclusively to his modal metaphysics just outlined. The demonstration, which is a form of the cosmological argument, is in fact a wholly new proof for, in effect, the existence of God and God's relation to whatever is possible in itself (*Salvation*, "Metaphysics," II.12, 566–568).[21]

The argument begins with the obvious fact that something exists. Given that for Avicenna existence's basic conceptual divisions are the necessary through itself and the possible in itself, if what exists is necessary through itself, there exists something necessary through itself, and the argument is done.

If the existing thing is possible in itself, then Avicenna has us consider it along with every other actually existing thing that is possible in itself, whether there be a finite or infinite number of such things. In other words, consider the mereological sum or whole (*jumla*) of all and only actually existing things that are possible in themselves. Since this whole is itself an existing thing, then, given Avicenna's ontology, it either must exist necessarily through itself or possibly through itself. The whole of all things possible through themselves, argues Avicenna, cannot be something existing necessarily through itself, for that which is necessary through itself does not exist through another. Yet, as has already been seen, wholes exist through their parts. Thus, if the whole of all things possible through themselves were necessary through itself, then something necessary through itself would be necessary through another, which Avicenna points out is a contradiction.

So this whole must be something possible through itself, but since this whole actually exists, then, given Avicenna's analysis of actual existence, it must be necessary through another. Now, continues Avicenna, this other can be either internal or external to the whole. If it is internal, and so is a part of the whole, then that part itself must exist either necessarily through itself or possibly in itself. Whatever is internal to the whole of all and only things possible in themselves could not exist necessarily through itself, since, again, only things possible in themselves are included within the whole. Thus, something would be both necessary through itself and possible in itself, which is a contradiction. If this part were possible in itself, then since the existence of the whole itself is through that part, and so all the parts within that whole are through it, that part's existence would be through itself. In that case the part would be necessary through itself, but this part was assumed to be possible in itself, and so there is again a contradiction. Thus, the existence of the whole of all things possible in themselves must be through something external to that whole, but all possible existents are included within the whole, and so this external thing cannot be possible in itself. The only other division of existence, concludes Avicenna, is that which exists necessarily through itself, and therefore, something necessary through itself exists.[22]

There are a few things to note about this argument. The first thing is that if one sets aside the modal metaphysics underlying it, then the argument is extremely modest in the premises it requires. Avicenna assumes something about sets or mereological sums, namely that they subsist through their members, but such a claim seems to be almost true by definition. Thus, the argument's most ontologically or physically robust claim is simply that something exists.

Second, Avicenna goes on to end his argument by pointing out a subsidiary conclusion, namely that there cannot be an infinite number of actually existing simultaneous causes. He argues thus:

> Things existing possibly terminate in a cause existing necessarily, in which case not every [effect] that exists as something possible has

simultaneously with it a cause that exists as something possible. Hence an infinite number of causes existing at a single time is impossible (*Salvation*, "Metaphysics," II.12, 568.12–13).

In other words, the proof shows that a causal chain whose members are all simultaneously actual must terminate at its two ends, namely, the possible effect on the one side, and the Necessary Existent on the other.

There are two points of interest about this subsidiary conclusion. One is that unlike other cosmological proofs for the existence of God, Avicenna's argument nowhere requires as a premise that an actual infinite is impossible; rather, Avicenna's version in fact proves this claim. The other point is that inasmuch as one identifies the cosmos with the sum of all actually existing possible things assumed in the argument, Avicenna's Necessary Existent turns out to be the efficient cause of the cosmos' existence, for it is the Necessary Existent itself that ultimately explains why everything else exists. Thus, in addition to providing an argument for the existence of something necessary in itself, which might be identified with the divinity, Avicenna has also shown that the Necessary Existent is the efficient cause of the cosmos. Moreover, since Avicenna takes possibility as properly basic, and not explained in terms of temporal frequencies, he has successfully blocked Aristotle's *De Caelo* argument. Whether the cosmos is eternal is an issue I take up in the next chapter, but for now just note that Avicenna has successfully countered the initial objection, namely that whatever is possible, and so requires an efficient cause to exist, cannot exist eternally, for that objection rested squarely on a temporal frequency analysis of modalities, which is absent in Avicenna's metaphysics.

Third, since in Avicenna's modal ontology there is only necessary existence and possible existence, and since something actually exists only if it is necessary, then the final end or perfection of all things existing possibly in themselves is to exist as necessary. In other words, what everything desires is actual existence or, to be more precise, the proper perfection of its existence. As noted, however, whatever actually exists is necessary according to Avicenna's ontology. Thus, within Avicenna's framework, what everything desires is necessary existence. Therefore, inasmuch as Avicenna's Necessary Existent is that which is necessary through or in itself, it is the ultimate object of desire for all things possible in themselves. In Aristotelian terms, Avicenna's Necessary Existent is that which all other existents want to imitate. Still, since things possible through themselves cannot be necessary through themselves, they achieve their final perfection by imitating the necessary through itself the only way that they can, namely, by being necessary through another. Whatever else one might think about this argument today, it would have satisfied the ancient and medieval mind in showing that, and how Avicenna's Necessary Existent is a final cause for the existence of the cosmos.

Finally, when considering Avicenna's conceptual analysis of the necessary through itself, it was seen that what exists through itself had to be one and wholly simple. One now sees that Avicenna's Necessary Existent through itself is an efficient and final cause for the cosmos' existence solely in virtue of the single factor of being necessary through itself. There is no need to refer to conceptually distinct factors within it to explain its apparently different modes of causation. Thus, Avicenna has successfully safeguarded the Necessary Existent's absolute simplicity.

The Divine Attributes

Avicenna identifies the Necessary Existent's primary attribute (*ṣifa*) with its necessary existence. Besides the fact of the Necessary Existent's existing necessarily, Avicenna believes that all other attributes by which it is described, in fact, indicate either certain negations of imperfections or relations that created things have to the Necessary Existent. Why Avicenna holds such a position is relatively clear if one remembers that one of the most pressing philosophical issues for Avicenna and his philosophical theology is to preserve divine simplicity. Negations do not require multiple positive factors existing in the divinity, while one and the same simple thing might be described in numerous ways relative to other things. In short, the divinity could have multiple negative and relative attributes and yet still remain wholly simple.

The Necessary Existent's Primary Attribute

Before turning to these negative and relational attributes, let me consider the primary attribute of necessary existence, and particularly in what sense this attribute might be said to "essentially" belong to the Necessary Existent. In the *Metaphysics* (VIII.4), Avicenna wavers between saying that the essence of the Necessary Existent is its (necessary) existence and simply denying that the Necessary Existent has any essence at all.

The reason for this is that, as I noted in chapter 2,[23] an essence can be considered in isolation from any given mode of existence. In other words, it can be considered without reference to the particular mode of existence in which it exists, whether in a concrete particular or in conceptualization, or as a particular or a universal, or the like. In fact, Avicenna tells us in the *Metaphysics* that an essence considered in itself, as, for example, horse-ness or equinity, is:

> nothing at all save horse-ness. Indeed in itself it is neither one nor many, nor something existing in either concrete particulars or in the soul, nor is it in any of that either potentially or actually such that [that] would enter into horse-ness. [The essence of horse-ness considered in itself] is in fact nothing but horse-ness (*Metaphysics*, V.1, 149.11–14).

When one considers this notion of essence as applied to the Necessary Existent, it then becomes clear why Avicenna is not happy with identifying the Necessary Existent's essence with its existence. Essences are considered in abstraction from any determinate existence, and yet the Necessary Existent simply cannot be considered independent of existence. Thus, on the one hand, one is able to consider horse-ness without thinking of it either as existing in some particular horse or as some intellectual depiction of the logical genus "animal" and the logical difference "neighing." On the other hand, in contrast, to consider the Necessary Existent independent of its particular mode of existence, namely, necessary existence through itself, is simply not to consider the Necessary Existent at all. In short, one cannot consider the Necessary Existent independent of its existence, whereas the essence of a given thing can be considered independent of that thing's mode of existence. Therefore, in a very real sense the Necessary Existent cannot have an essence.

Still, one can also understand why Avicenna is sometimes tempted to identify the Necessary Existent's essence with its necessary existence, for in that case it becomes obvious why the Necessary Existent is a self-explaining entity. To make this last point, let me briefly step out of Avicenna's own system of modal metaphysics, and instead speak in contemporary terms of a "possible-world" ontology. According to possible-world semantics, something is possible just in case it exists in at least one possible world, whereas it is necessary if it exists in all possible worlds. Now consider the mere possibility that a necessary being exists. If such a being is in fact possible, then there is one world in which a being that exists in all possible worlds exists; for to be a necessary being is, according to a possible-world ontology, to be a being that exists in all possible worlds. In that case, however, if it is even possible that a necessary being exists, it necessarily exists, for it exists in all possible worlds, which is just to be necessary. So, what explains a necessary being's actual existence in this world is that there is simply no possible world, of which the actual world is one, in which a necessary being does not exist.

Analogously, for Avicenna, should one understand the Necessary Existent's essence as identical with its existence, it turns out that it exists simply on account of what it is. That it exists is not merely some brute fact about the world but something fully self-explaining given the very essence of this entity.[24] So, for example, consider someone, like Aristotle, who takes the existence of the forms and matter that make up the cosmos as a brute fact that cannot be explained (even if their undergoing motion can). Avicenna can argue that his system is preferable to Aristotle's, since his can explain something that Aristotle's cannot, namely, why forms and matter exist at all, for, as has been seen, inasmuch as they exist possibly in themselves they depend upon the Necessary Existent as their efficient cause. If Aristotle were to complain that this is just to replace one unexplained thing's existence, such as the forms and matter that make up the cosmos, with another unexplained thing's existence, namely, the Necessary Existent, Avicenna can say, "No. The Necessary Existent is self-explaining in a way that the cosmos is not, for the Necessary Existent is the sort of thing that cannot not exist, whereas the cosmos considered in itself is something that could possibly not exist."

This is not special pleading on Avicenna's part. That is because while existence is not included within the essence of those possible things that make up the cosmos—there is nothing about horse-ness that requires that the cosmos be populated by that species of thing—existence is necessarily included in the "essence" of the Necessary Existent, for what it is to be such a thing is to exist necessarily through itself. Thus, in a very real sense Avicenna's system has a greater explanatory power than that of Aristotle's. To sum up, whereas for Avicenna the Necessary Existent cannot strictly speaking have an essence (for an essence can be considered independent of existence), loosely speaking it does inasmuch as its "essence" is its necessary existence.

The Necessary Existent's Other Attributes

At *Metaphysics*, VIII.6, Avicenna considers the attribute of perfection (*kamāl*). The perfection of a thing, as Avicenna and most medieval thinkers understood that term, refers to whatever completes (*tāmm*) that thing with respect to its existence. So, for example, the perfection of an acorn is that it comes to exist as an oak tree, and the perfection of a human is that one actualizes one's intellect. In the case of the Necessary Existent, since it lacks nothing of its existence or the perfection of its existence (for otherwise it would not be necessary through itself in every way), it must be absolutely perfect. In fact, not only is it perfect since it has all the existence that can belong to it, it is, argued Avicenna, above perfection (*fawqa t-tamām*), since it has such a superabundance of existence that all other existing things have their existence from it (*Metaphysics*, VIII.6, 283.10–14).

Also, the Necessary Existent is the pure good (*khayr maḥḍ*), for, in general, the good is whatever is desired (ibid., 283.15–18).[25] As noted, however, everything desires its own existence or the perfection of the existence proper to it, and in Avicenna's system the existence in question is necessary existence. Thus, since everything desires necessary existence, there is a real sense in which the Necessary Existent is that which everything desires and so it is the highest good. Furthermore, good is said of that which provides a thing with its existence, perfection, and good qualities (ibid., 284.8–11). Thus, since the Necessary Existent is the ultimate source of all necessary existence, perfection, and good, it is again the truest good.

In addition to these attributes, which in fact are all just different ways of considering the Necessary Existent's primary attribute of necessary existence, it has certain negative and relational attributes. The most obvious one is that it is incorporeal, which follows from Avicenna's earlier analysis of necessary existence in itself. That is because if the Necessary Existent were material, it would also require a form to actualize that matter, and thus it would be a composite of form and matter. Yet, as Avicenna has strenuously argued, the Necessary Existent is absolutely simple.

Given the immateriality of the Necessary Existent, Avicenna goes on to argue that it must be an intelligible, an intellect, and indeed the very act of intellecting (*ma'qūl*, *'aql*, *'āqil*) (ibid., 284.17–287.2). While at first glance one might think that these attributes are distinct from mere necessary existence, Avicenna argues that they not. They are in fact entailed by the Necessary Existent's immateriality, which again followed from its necessary existence.

Avicenna's argument begins by drawing upon a thesis that he had defended in the science of psychology.[26] There Avicenna had argued that what prevents a thing's being an actual intelligible object is its association with matter and the concomitants of matter. Consequently, the more abstracted or separated from matter something is, the more intelligible that thing becomes; for it is the concomitants of matter that restrict the object to being sensible, imaginable, and the like, and prevent its being impressed upon the intellect, and so being actually intelligible. Thus, whatever through itself is separate from matter is essentially intelligible, that is, it is an object of the intellect. Now, the Necessary Existent is essentially immaterial, and so separate from matter. Thus, the existence of the Necessary Existent is something essentially intelligible.

Avicenna next identifies intellect with that thing that has something essentially intelligible. In other words, only intellects are the sort of things that have intelligible objects. Since, as has been seen, the Necessary Existent has its existence essentially, and, as just noted, its existence is something essentially intelligible, the Necessary Existent essentially has something essentially intelligible, and as such must be an intellect.

As for its being its very act of intellection, Avicenna observed in his *Psychology*[27] that for an intellect to have an intelligible object is simply identical with the act of intellection. So, it follows that the Necessary Existent is essentially its act of intellection. It is worth noting that the Necessary Existent is essentially the act of intellecting, the intellect, and what is intellected. In the Necessary Existent these three are numerically one and the same; there is absolutely no multiplicity in the Necessary Existent. That is because all of these are essentially the same and ultimately reduce to its existing necessarily through itself.

Other (relational) attributes describing the Necessary Existent, such as power, volition, munificence, and being a creator, I shall consider in the next chapter when discussing the possible existence and the created order.

The Necessary Existent's Knowledge of Particulars

The question of to what extent, if at all, the divinity, however understood, knows particular individuals such as you or me, goes back at least as far as Aristotle, who had argued that the only object suitable and worthy of the

Unmoved Mover's contemplation, is the Unmoved Mover itself.[28] As for what is below it, it neither is concerned with them nor even knows them. Unlike Aristotle, Avicenna accepts that in a very special sense the Necessary Existent does know particular individuals within the created order; however, its knowledge of these particulars, and indeed its knowledge generally, is wholly unlike and incomparable with the way that possible existents know things (ibid., 287.3–290.17; *Salvation*, "Metaphysics," II.18–19).[29] So, for instance, we only know things as a result of those things acting upon us so as to produce intellectual perception. In stark contrast, for Avicenna, it is the Necessary Existent's very knowledge of things that produces those things themselves.

To make this point, Avicenna, as part of *reductio ad absurdum* style argument, has us assume that the Necessary Existent intellectually perceives things through things in the way that we do. In that case, either the Necessary Existent's intellectual act is accidental to it or is essentially identical with it. If the Necessary Existent intellects accidentally, it is not necessary in every way, for what is accidental to a thing is not something necessary. The Necessary Existent, however, is necessary in every way. So, the Necessary Existent must be essentially identical with its act of intellecting. Now, if something intellectually perceives on account of things, that is, if it intellects things by being impressed by them, then those things stand to the intellectual act as causes of it. Nothing, however, stands to the Necessary Existent as its cause, for then the Necessary Existent would not be necessary through itself, but that is exactly what it is. Therefore, concludes Avicenna, the Necessary Existent cannot intellectually perceive things through things as we do.

As for its knowledge of particulars or individuals, for Avicenna, strictly speaking, the Necessary Existent only knows itself. Still, inasmuch as it knows itself it knows that it is the principle of all existing things right down to the individuals. Thus, the Necessary Existent knows individuals inasmuch as it knows that to which its causal efficacy extends. In general, Avicenna argues as follows (*Metaphysics*, VIII.6, 288.5–13): The Necessary Existent knows itself completely and so knows itself as the principle or cause of all that exists. If, however, one completely knows a cause, one must also know all the effects of that cause. Therefore, inasmuch as the Necessary Existent is the ultimate cause of all things and completely knows itself as such, it must know all things, whether they be the causes that interact with one another or the effects that ultimately result from those interactions, which would include the individuals that come to exist actually.

Be that as it may, Avicenna also believes that there are a number of ways in which it is simply false to say that the Necessary Existent knows particulars. First, the Necessary Existent is wholly outside of the temporal order, for time, according to Avicenna, is a certain possibility measuring the motion of a changing thing, whereas no possibility or change belongs to the Necessary Existent. Inasmuch as the Necessary Existent is outside the temporal order, it does not know particulars as temporal phenomena or events, that is, as things that are currently present, or past, or future to him; rather, it knows particulars simply as (eternally) present (ibid., 287.10–14).

In other words, the Necessary Existent cannot know particulars that are changing through time as they are changing. That is because if one knows some changing thing as it is changing, one must first know that thing as possessing one nonexistent state and then as possessing some existing state. Now, if at one moment the Necessary Existent knows that something possesses a nonexistent state, and then at another moment knows that it possesses some existing state, it must have undergone some form of change, for to know something as existing is the contradictory of knowing it as nonexisting. In other words, the Necessary Existent cannot simultaneously know that one and same thing both possesses some existing state while not possessing that very same state. Hence if the Necessary Existent knew changing things as they are changing, there necessarily would have been a change in it, namely, the change from knowing that some state does not exist in the thing to now knowing that that state does exist. The Necessary Existent, however, does not undergo change, for a thing changes for some end, which is a good that perfects it. Yet, as has already been seen, the Necessary Existent is absolutely perfect and even above perfection. Thus, concludes Avicenna, the Necessary Existent cannot know changing things as they are changing; rather, it knows them in one eternal act of knowing itself as their cause.

Similarly, the Necessary Existent does not know particulars insofar as they are corruptible or undergoing corruption. Here Avicenna observes that if something is perceived as corruptible, then it must be perceived as joined to matter, for Avicenna explained in the science of physics[30] that something undergoes corruption only insofar as it is material. As he explained in his psychology,[31] however, if something is perceived as joined to matter, then it is perceived either through sensation or imagination but not by the intellect. Sensation and imagination, however, require a material organ, for example, eyes and other suitable sensory apparatuses, as well as a brain. Consequently, if the Necessary Existent perceived something as corruptible, that is, it sensibly perceived it, it would require a material organ to do so. Again, though, the Necessary Existent is wholly immaterial, and so has no material organs. Therefore, Avicenna concludes, the Necessary Existent does not perceive anything as undergoing corruption.

After considering the ways that the Necessary Existent cannot be said to know particulars, one might feel that Avicenna has sorely limited the Necessary Existent (which in many ways Avicenna wanted to identify with the God of Islam), for surely we humans can and do know things in these ways. Thus, the complaint goes: If we have the power to do certain things, shouldn't the Necessary Existent also have the power to do those things? Avicenna's response is that our need to perceive particulars as temporal and changing rather than in a simple and eternally present intellectual perception is not owing to some perfection belonging to us, but owing to certain privations inherent in us. Since the Necessary Existent has no privation, it does not need to know particulars in the various ways mentioned. In fact, it could only know them in the lesser way that we do, if it were to cease being necessary through itself, which it cannot. To put Avicenna's point crassly but vividly, we can defecate, whereas the divinity cannot; however, no one considers this "inability" a limitation on the part of God. In the same way, for Avicenna, that the Necessary Existent does not know particulars as temporal and changing is not a limitation on its knowledge; it does not know them in that way precisely because it is above needing such base processes.

Instead, argues Avicenna, the Necessary Existent knows particulars in two ways (ibid., 288.14–290.17). First, it knows those particulars that are alone in their species, as many medieval philosophers and theologians believed was true of the Sun, all the planets, as well as the Intelligences or angels. In other words, some species, call them "terrestrial species" such as humanity and horse-ness, are said of a number of individuals all of whom make up the concrete instantiation of that species at any given time, and at different times different individuals are the concrete instances of that species. Other species, call them "celestial species" such as the host of angels, always have at any given time one and the same individual as the concrete instantiation of their species. The reason for this is that for entities that have absolutely no association with matter, only the form can distinguish them (for again they have no matter that could individuate them). Thus, immaterial things can only be individuated by different species forms, each species of which has only one member. In this case then, inasmuch as the Necessary Existent knows itself to be the cause of all the various species, it knows the one and only individual falling under one of the celestial species.

Second, the Necessary Existent knows individuals among the terrestrial species inasmuch as the individuals are a result of universal causal laws. Avicenna's preferred example of such knowledge is knowledge of an eclipse, for once one knows what an eclipse is, as well as the speed and position of the planets, one can predict and so know every individual eclipse. So, for example, imagine some hapless but brilliant astronomer, who from birth was locked away in a windowless tower without clock or calendar and was never allowed to leave. Instead, our astronomer spent all of his time studying star charts and calculating the various theoretical motions of the Sun, Moon, and planets. Such an individual may well know the number of eclipses that occur in a given period of time, where they would be seen on Earth as well as the time between them, and yet, since he does not know what time or day it is, he would not be aware whether any eclipse is or is not presently occurring now. In a certain respect, the Necessary Existent's knowledge of corruptible and temporal events is like our poor astronomer's, although whereas the astronomer's knowledge, given that he is human, is impoverished, the Necessary Existent's knowledge, as I have mentioned, is not, but instead is absolutely complete.

In many respects, the image that Avicenna has in mind of the way that the Necessary Existent knows temporal and corruptible things without knowing them as such is like that of Laplace's so-called demon. In fact, Laplace's observation is germane here. He wrote:

> We may regard the present state of the universe as the effect of its past and the cause of its future. An intellect which at a certain moment would know all forces that set nature in motion, and all positions of all items of which nature is composed, if this intellect were also vast enough to submit these data to analysis, it would embrace in a single formula the movements of the greatest bodies of the universe and those of the tiniest atom, for such an intellect nothing would be uncertain and the future just like the past would be present before its eyes.[32]

Laplace's sentiment echoes one that Avicenna himself made some 800 years earlier: "The Necessary Existent intellects everything only universally; nevertheless, no individual thing escapes its notice, 'not even the weight of an atom, whether in the heavens or on Earth, escapes his notice' (*Qur'ān* 10:61)"

(*Metaphysics*, VIII.8, 288.2–3). Since the Necessary Existent knows itself, it knows itself as the ultimate cause of all that exists, and thus knows the causal order of all possible things. Consequently, the Necessary Existent knows the entire order of all possible things and their relationships vis-à-vis one another, not as unfolding, as it were, but all at once. In the next chapter, I shall consider in more detail the order of things possible in themselves, as well as the reasons Avicenna believes that this order has proceeded eternally from the Necessary Existent, and thus why he believes that the world has existed eternally.

METAPHYSICS II

Cosmology

Introduction: The
Historical Background

In the last chapter I presented a complex of problems that faced ancient and medieval philosophers concerning God's relation to the world. Of this complex of issues, the primary one treated in the last chapter involved showing Avicenna's solution to the problem of how God could be both the final and efficient cause of the world and still be simple. Additionally, many (though by no means all) of these philosophers also wanted to show that the cosmos was eternal. I noted two classical arguments for why one might hold this position. One was that of Proclus, who maintained that if, in the finite past, there were some first moment of creation, then there would be a time when God was not creating (and so would not have been a creator) and then a time when God was creating (and so becomes a creator). This change in God—which it was argued results from affirming a temporal creation—undermines divine immutability, a position that most philosophers and theologians did not want to give up. Similarly, I gave one of Aristotle's physical proofs based upon his analysis of time and motion. That argument ran thus: If there were some first moment in the finite past when the cosmos began moving, nothing moving prior to that moment, then there would be a time when there was no motion. Time, however, is just the measure of motion. Thus, to say there is a time when there is no motion is tantamount to saying there was a measured motion when there was no motion at all, a patent contradiction.

A premise common to both of these arguments is that if there were a first moment of creation, there would be a preceding time, either during which God is not creating or during which there is no motion. At least by the late classical period, however, this premise was called into question. The main line of objection for certain Christian and Muslim defenders of a temporal creation was that the sense of such seemingly temporal terms as "before" and the use of the past tense "was," both prominent features that these arguments exploit, need not indicate a preexisting time at all. Instead, argued these later critics, time is itself part of the created order. As such, it could not have temporally preexisted creation, and instead is created along with the cosmos.

These critics then maintained that Aristotle and Proclus's proofs simply beg the question when they assert that the sense of "before" in the phrase "before creation" must refer to a temporal "before." Such language, it was argued, merely means that God is ontologically prior to the world in the way that a cause might be ontologically prior though not temporally prior to an effect. So, for example, while waving a hand is clearly not temporally prior to the movement of a ring on the hand, the hand's motion is causally prior to the ring's motion inasmuch as it is the hand's motion that causes the ring to move and not vice versa. At the very least one sees such thinkers as Augustine[1] and Philoponus[2] in the West and al-Ghazālī[3] in the East raise this sort of objection. In fact, even Avicenna himself, who defends the cosmos' eternity, mentions this as a serious objection worthy of consideration.[4]

Still, there were other arguments that did not seem to require the questionable premise that there must be a time before creation. Aristotle again provides one such argument based upon his own careful investigation of coming to be and generation (*genesis*). So, for example, at *Physics* I.7, Aristotle famously analyzed coming to be in terms of three principles: (1) an underlying thing (*hupokeimenon*), namely, matter, (2) a certain privation in that underlying thing corresponding with the absence or privation of some form, and finally (3) the new form that comes to be as a result of the generation.[5] So, for example, if a quantity of water comes to be hot, there must be the water, which is the underlying thing that undergoes the change, an initial privation or absence of heat (for if the water were already hot it could not qua hot become hot), and finally the form, that is to say, the heat that comes to be in the water.

Using this analysis of coming to be as his starting point, Aristotle then argued for the eternal existence of forms and matter as follows:[6] The cosmos itself is a composite of matter and forms. Thus, if God were to generate the existence of the world, he would have to generate matter and forms; however, as has already been seen, for Aristotle every instance of coming to be or generation requires an underlying thing that undergoes the change, namely, the matter, as well as the forms that come to be and pass away. Hence, in order for there to be the generation of matter and forms, matter and forms would already have had to exist, which is clearly a contradiction. Thus, the initial assumption, namely that the form-matter composite that is the cosmos was generated at some finite time ago must be false. Therefore, concludes Aristotle, the cosmos has existed eternally.

The response to such an argument is simply to distinguish between the sort of temporal coming to be implicit in Aristotle's theory of generation, where the generation comes to be from some preexisting stuff, and "genuine creation" in which God creates ex nihilo, and thus nothing other than God is ontologically prior to creation such that it would exist or subsist independently of God's creative act. Interestingly, such a distinction, while quickly disarming Aristotle's generation argument for the eternity of the world, was not only favored by those who believed that the cosmos had a temporal creation in the finite past, but also virtually all of those thinkers who maintained that the divinity stood to the cosmos as its efficient cause, regardless of whether they thought that the cosmos had existed eternally or not. Thus, another argument in the eternalist's arsenal seems to lack the demonstrative nature that both ancient and medieval philosophers and scientists sought.

Proponents of the cosmos' temporal creation were not merely on the defense, but also actively argued that the idea of an eternally existing cosmos ran afoul of certain entrenched doctrines concerning the infinite. Perhaps the staunchest critique of Aristotle and the doctrine of the world's eternity was the Christian Neoplatonist, John Philoponus (ca. 490–570).[7] Philoponus's critique of this Aristotelian position ironically used Aristotle's own principles concerning the infinite against him. The principles Philoponus used are the seemingly self-evident claims that an actual infinite[8] is impossible, an infinite cannot be traversed, and nothing is beyond or greater than an infinite.[9] Philoponus had two main lines of objection: One, an eternal world would entail that an actual infinite has come to exist and so an infinite has been traversed, and, two, there would be sets of infinities of different sizes, and so there would be sets larger than that beyond which there is nothing more.[10]

The first of Philoponus's arguments takes the following form: If the world were eternal, as Aristotle and others believed, then it would entail that there has been an infinite number of past days. Now, if during this infinity of days, one human per day, for example, were born, then an actually infinite number of humans would have come to exist. It does not matter that they do not all exist right now, continued Philoponus, since the *number* of humans who have existed must be actually infinite. Aristotle himself, however, had said that not even number considered separately could be infinite.[11] Moreover, criticized Philoponus, the cosmos' past eternity is incompatible with the dictum that an infinite cannot be traversed, for an eternally existing cosmos would have gone through an infinity of days (as well as things generated during those days), but again traversing the infinite is impossible absolutely according to Aristotle and others.

Philoponus's second complaint was that if the cosmos were eternal, there would be varying sizes of infinities. Indeed the infinite would be susceptible to increase. For example, if the cosmos' existence were extended infinitely into the past, then the Sun, Moon, and all the planets would have orbited the Earth an infinite number of times (at least based on ancient and medieval cosmology, which has the Earth at the center of the universe). Saturn, however, makes an apparent rotation around the Earth once approximately ever thirty solar years; Jupiter once every twelve solar years; Mars once every two solar years, and the Sun, of course, once every year. Consequently, the Sun, for example, must have made thirty times as many apparent rotations around the Earth as Saturn has. Thus, asks Philoponus, "If it is not possible to traverse the infinite once, then how is it not beyond all absurdity to assume ten thousand times the infinite, or rather the infinite an infinite number of times?"[12] The challenge that this paradox presents, then, is to explain how one is to make sense of different "sizes" of infinities.

Despite the ferocity of Philoponus's polemics, many of those medieval philosophers writing in Arabic, such as Avicenna, still held that the cosmos was eternal. Thus, at least one major project for these medieval thinkers was either to revise or to reinvent arguments for the world's eternity that could address the objections to the proofs for the world's eternity as well as responding to the criticisms that it is impossible that the world's eternity be consistent with long-held beliefs about infinity.

In both his physics and metaphysics, Avicenna undertakes this project. In many respects Avicenna's "new" arguments for the world's eternity are variants of the classical proofs for that thesis, except that Avicenna adds new modal premises that allow him to address the objections mentioned head-on. To appreciate these new arguments, I need first to present in some depth Avicenna's conception of possibility and what exists possibly in itself, as well as considering how Avicenna envisions the most basic modes of possible existence, namely, substances and accidents, with a particular emphasis on forms and matter. The reason for emphasizing forms and matter is that in Avicenna's ontology, like Aristotle's before him, substances are prior to accidents. Moreover, the conceptually most basic kinds of substances, from which particular substances, like earth, oaks, humans, and so forth are composed, are forms and matter. After discussing the formal and material causes, I then turn to Avicenna's notion of causality generally. Upon completing this investigation of the makeup of the realm of possible existence, one will be in a position to appreciate Avicenna's new modal arguments for the world's eternity and his response to the criticism against that thesis. This chapter, then, concludes with a section on the Necessary Existent's relation to possible existence as exemplified in Avicenna's unique twist on the Neoplatonic theory of emanation.

Creation and Possible Existence in Itself

As I have noted in the previous chapter, for Avicenna all things possible in themselves ultimately depend upon the Necessary Existent for their own actual existence, or, as Avicenna would have it, their own necessary existence, albeit an existence necessary only through another. So, in a real sense all things possible in themselves when actualized are ultimately the creation of the Necessary Existent. Avicenna, however, distinguishes two forms of creation: what one might call "atemporal creation" (*ibdā*'), or creation absolutely, and "temporal creation" (*ḥudūth*), or coming to be.[13] In atemporal or absolute creation nothing precedes the creative act except the being of the Creator, who is only ontologically, not temporally, prior to the creation. Avicenna's notion of atemporal creation is one of genuine creation ex nihilo, and so is unlike Aristotle's notion of generation, which required preexisting forms and matter. In this respect, Avicenna's notion of atemporal creation is sensitive to the complaint of the temporal creationists when they say that the world's being created after not existing need not imply that there was a time before creation. Still, there is also nothing about Avicenna's notion of absolute or atemporal creation that precludes the Creator from creating eternally. Hence, there is nothing that requires that there be some first moment in the finite past when the Creator began creating. As for temporal creation or, more exactly, coming to be, it involves some sort of motion, or change, and the coming to be at some time of something after it was not. So, for example, virtually all the events that we experience around us involve coming to be—I came to exist after not existing; you are reading this sentence after not having read it, and the like. Thus, our world (or at least the world of sublunar physics in Avicenna's mind) inherently involves coming to be.

In order to answer the question of whether the cosmos in general has existed eternally or had a temporal beginning in the finite past, Avicenna undertakes an analysis of the possible existents that make up the cosmos, an analysis, I might add, that was arguably the most thoroughgoing investigation of possibility in the ancient and medieval world.[14] The primary focus of Avicenna's analysis is on the possibility of those things involving coming to be, and with a particular eye to whether forms and matter, considered absolutely, as well as motion and time, must be eternal or could have had a temporal beginning. Still, much of what he has to say about the nature of possibility equally applies to the possibility of atemporally created things, such as for Avicenna the immaterial Intelligences.

In book II.1 of his *Metaphysics*, Avicenna begins by considering two divisions of existence found among the things that are possible in themselves though necessary through another (*Metaphysics*, II.1, 45.9–13). The first division includes those things that exist in another—call that other the "subject" (*mawḍūʿ*)—and cannot exist separate from that subject, even though they are not themselves (material or formal) parts of the subject. The second includes those things that do not exist in another in this way. The first class consists of the so-called accidents—namely, quantity, quality, position, relation, when, where, possession, action, and passion—while the second class is that of substances.

Assuming this simple division, Avicenna has us consider the possible existence (*mumkin al-wujūd* or *jāʾiz al-wujūd*) in itself considered merely as possible, and thus considered independent of any necessary existence it might have derived from another. He then asks whether possible existence in itself is either something subsisting in itself, and so a substance in its own right, or something inhering in a subject or substrate (*Physics*, III.11; *Metaphysics*, IV.2).

Avicenna denies that possibility is a substance in its own right on the basis that substances do not essentially involve relations (*ghayr muḍāf*)—nothing else is needed to complete, perfect, or understand them as substances—whereas possibilities are always correlative and so always require something else if they are to be intellectually understood—for at least two related things are needed to complete one's understanding of any relation (*Physics*, III.11, 233.4–5; *Metaphysics*, IV.2, 136.16–17). Avicenna makes this point about relation clearly at *Metaphysics*, III.10, where he explains that a relation (*iḍāfa*) is some essence, such as fatherhood, or being a sibling, that belongs to a given thing and can be intellectually perceived only by reference to (*bil-qiyās ilá*) something else.[15] So, for example, a father, according to Avicenna, really has some aspect, fatherhood, that belongs to him, where the notion of fatherhood is relational inasmuch as it can be understood only by reference to having an offspring.

Thus, when one says, "*x* has the possibility of coming to be F" or even some blanket statement like "possibility exists," one understands it only by reference to understanding what F is (or some necessary, that is, actual existence) and then recognizing the absence of F (or that necessary existence) in *x* (*Physics*, III.11, 233.5–6). Now, the argument continues, if possibility in itself were a substance, then it would have all the traits of a substance, and so substance and possibility would either both involve relations or both would not, but clearly that is not the case. So, for example, if one takes substances, such as humans, horses, oak trees, and the like, nothing more is needed to complete or perfect what this substance is or what is understood by it. To say, "*This* (pointing to a particular tree) is an oak (or more generally, a substance)" is a complete thought. In contrast, possibility is understood always and only relative to something; to say, "*This* (pointing to an acorn) is a possibility" is incomplete without some further reference, whether implicitly or explicitly, to that for or of which it is a possibility, namely an oak (or, for that matter, lunch for a squirrel, or ammunition for a slingshot, and so on). That is because an acorn is not possibly a human, a horse, or the like, but only possibly an oak. More generally, there is nothing that is just *a possibility* in the way there can be just a substance; rather, it is always *a possibility for* . . . whatever.

Moreover, continues Avicenna, possibility cannot be the substance-*cum*-relation, that is, the substance-relation complex. That is because possibility,

Avicenna insists, is simply the relative absence of some necessary existence. In other words, possibility is the privation or absence of some presently and actually existing thing. In contrast, the substance-relation complex is precisely something presently and actually existing. Thus, Avicenna concludes, possibility is not a substance in its own right, and consequently it must exist in a substrate.

In a very real sense, the core of Avicenna's analysis of possibility in itself is contained in his notion of possibility's being a certain privation or absence (*'adam*) relative to some necessary or actual existence, and so I should linger over it. Again, Avicenna has strenuously argued that there can only be one thing whose existence is necessary through itself, namely, the Necessary Existent. Everything else when it actually exists, though necessary through another, is merely possible in itself. Now, what distinguishes possible existents from the Necessary Existent could be either that they possess some positive aspect, which would then be some form of necessary existence that the Necessary Existent lacks, or they lack some necessary existence that the Necessary Existent possesses.

Clearly, no possible existent can possess some necessary existence that the Necessary Existent lacks, since the Necessary Existent of itself is that which lacks no necessary existence. In other words, it lacks nothing that would perfect its existence. Thus, that by which possible existents are distinct from the Necessary Existent is their absence or privation of some necessary existence, for any necessary existence that they have is in imitation of the Necessary Existent. Perhaps one model, then, by which to understand Avicenna's point about possibility—one, however, that Avicenna himself does not use—is to think of a "chain of being"[16] extending from the Necessary Existent to absolute and genuine nonexistence (*lā wujūd*) with varying degrees of privation or absence of some necessary existence in between. In this case, to be some species of possible existence in itself, then, is simply to lack some necessary existence and so to fall somewhere below the Necessary Existent on the chain of being while not being absolutely nonexistent.

As for why such and such a degree of privation should correspond with such and such a species of possible existence—such as being an Intelligence like the Active Intellect, or being a human, or being an oak tree—Avicenna is adamant that there can be no cause that explains this (*Metaphysics*, VI.1, 197.9–198.7). Certainly, there is a cause for why such a possible existent has whatever degree of necessary existence it has when it actually exists, namely, the Necessary Existent and any intermediary causes between it and the

Necessary Existent. Also, those things that come to be after not having existed for some time have causes for both their coming to be necessary when they do and not existing before that time, namely, the prior absence and then presence of the cause or causes of their necessary existence. Still, none of these are a cause for the privation or absence of the necessary existence that makes some possible existent the very kind that it is.

Does such a position mean that Avicenna thinks that possible existence stands alongside of necessary existence as a principle of creation? No. Avicenna constantly emphasizes, as I noted in both chapters 2 and 3,[17] that a principle is some positive causal factor that actively plays a role in the creation or change of a thing. A privation or absence of existence is nothing positive or active. It is merely something required if there is to be creation or change.[18] So, for example, it is impossible for x to change into F if it already is F, and so the privation of F is required for that particular change. That privation, however, is not some coprinciple acting alongside of the efficient cause to bring about the effect.

Similarly, it is impossible for the Necessary Existent to create something that is of itself necessary through itself (for something created, and so necessary through another, cannot become necessary through itself). Thus, whatever is created must lack some necessary existence inasmuch as it is part of the created order, and as such the privation or absence of existence, reasons Avicenna, is required by any act of creation. Is privation something in some sense? Yes. But it is not some existing thing that is a coprinciple alongside of the Necessary Existent acting to bring about the created order. At the end of this chapter, I shall return to this point. For now, however, it is enough to note that for Avicenna whatever exists possibly through itself, whether it is created atemporally or temporally, has through and of itself only the privation or absence of some necessary existence. Whatever necessary existence it has, it ultimately has through the Necessary Existent.

Still, one might object that Avicenna's analysis of possibility makes possibility too independent of the deity. Indeed, according to certain Islamic speculative theologians, the grounds for and explanation of possibility (*istiṭā'a*) is in fact the power (*qudra*) of an agent, for a thing is possible, so they maintained, only if the agent has the power to do or create it.[19] To clarify this suggestion more I should note that most Islamic speculative theologians were occasionalists and as such reserved all causal efficacy or agency for God alone.[20] Thus, the position of many Islamic theologians was that something is possible just in case God could do it.

Avicenna's response is to observe that God's power does not extend to what is impossible, but only to what is possible (*Physics*, III.11, 233.10–234.1; *Metaphysics*, IV.2, 139.13–140.6). Consequently, it does not speak ill of the divine power that God cannot make something that, for instance, involves a contradiction. Power, rather, is always referred to what is possible in itself.

Given that power has as its proper scope the possible in itself, Avicenna argues against explaining possibility in terms of power thus: If, as the theologians maintained, something is possible just in case God has the power to do that thing, then when one says that God is omnipotent and so has the power to do everything that is possible (a seemingly meaningful statement), all one is really saying is that God has the power to do everything that God has the power to do (a trivially true and thus vacuous statement). In a similar vein, if possibility is identical with the power of an agent, Avicenna continues, then a manifestly false statement, such as "I (Jon) have the power to do whatever is possible" turns out to be in fact a true statement, for I (Jon) do have the power to do whatever I have the power to do. In short, complains Avicenna, if possibility can be reduced to the power of an agent, one should be able to replace one term, whether "power" or "possibility," with the other *salva veritate*, and so preserve the truth value of any statement in which one or the other term appears, but in fact one cannot. In effect, ends Avicenna, without some independent notion of possibility, God's omnipotence itself becomes vacuous, since everything has the power to do whatever it has the power to do.

In then end, Avicenna maintains that possibility is merely the relative absence of some necessary existence. Whatever necessary existence a created thing has, it ultimately has from the Necessary Existent; whatever it lacks with respect to necessary existence it has through itself. Thus, in a very real sense when the Necessary Existent causes what is possible in itself to be necessary, it is creating ex nihilo, if by ex nihilo one means creating from no actually existing prior thing.

The Possibility of What Comes
to Be, Matter, and Forms

The Possibility of Coming to Be

In the preceding section, I considered Avicenna's general analysis of possibility as it applies to both what is atemporally and temporally created. Now,

I turn specifically to Avicenna's analysis of the possibility belonging to what is temporally created, that is, the creation of things that come to be after not having existed (*Physics*, III.11, 232.15–233.3; *Metaphysics*, IV.2, 136.9–138.8; *Salvation*, "Metaphysics," I.17, 536). Avicenna notes that whatever comes to be (*ḥādith*) must be either temporally or ontologically preceded by the possibility of its coming to be, for if there were no possibility for its coming to be, argues Avicenna, then its coming to exist as actual would be impossible. From the preceding section, one has seen Avicenna's arguments for why the possibility of coming to be could not be a substance in its own right. Thus, this prior possibility for coming to be must, according to Avicenna, inhere in a substrate.

This substrate can be either immaterial—whether uncreated, namely, the Necessary Existent, or a created immaterial being such as an Intellect— or material. I have already noted one of Avicenna's reasons for denying that the possible in itself is related to the Necessary Existent as its power, for such a suggestion, argued Avicenna, renders the notion of omnipotence vacuous. Sprinkled throughout Avicenna's corpus, one finds further reasons as well. For example, the Necessary Existent can in no way be a substrate or subject of something that is distinct from its very being. That is because the simplicity of the Necessary Existent would then be jeopardized, for there would be the Necessary Existent qua substrate and that thing that purportedly inheres in the Necessary Existent. Consequently, given that possible existence is clearly distinct from necessary existence, the Necessary Existent cannot both be absolutely simple, which Avicenna has argued that it is, and the substrate of possible existence.

It remains then that if possibility in itself inheres in an immaterial substrate, it would have to be one that is created and so possible in itself, such as a human intellect, or the Active Intellect, or the like. If that intellect is something that comes to be, like the human intellect, then the possibility of its coming to be must precede its actually coming to be. In that case, one finds oneself faced with the initial question: In what does the possibility of that intellect that comes to be inhere?

Avicenna next considers whether the possibility of coming to be could inhere in an intellect that is atemporally created, such as the Giver of Forms or Active Intellect (*Metaphysics*, IV.2, 138.4–139.1).[21] Avicenna grants that such an intellect does have the potential (*qūwa*) to produce the species forms of things that come to be after not having existed. So, for example, the Giver of Forms bestows the species forms that make up the various natural kinds here in the sublunar world. Still, continues Avicenna, the

Giver of Forms must either be producing these forms always or producing them at some times and not at others. If, on the one hand, it comes to produce them at some time after not having produced them, then one again has a case of something coming to be, namely, its producing some forms after not having produced them. In that case, the possibility of that production preceded its coming to be, and one again finds oneself at the beginning: In what does the possibility of producing some form after not producing it inhere? On the other hand, if the Giver of Forms is always producing the forms that make up the various kinds of thing in the sublunar world, then its influence is constant, and there is no explanation of why a given thing that came to be (call it x) had not previously existed, given that the Giver of Forms was producing x's form even when x was not existing. In short, there has to be yet some other factor than merely the production of forms to explain x's coming to be after not having existed.

To sum up quickly: Since the possibility of what comes to be is not a substance, Avicenna argues that it must inhere in some substrate. That substrate could be either immaterial or material. It has already been noted why an immaterial intellect alone is not enough to explain the possibility of something's coming to be after not having been. Given that such possibility exists, and that it is not self-subsistent, but subsists in a substrate, and that this substrate cannot solely be something immaterial, Avicenna concludes:

> We ourselves call the possibility of existence the potentiality of existence, and we call that which underlies the potentiality of existence in which there is the potentiality of the existence of the thing a "subject," "prime matter," "matter," and the like, on account of many different considerations.[22] Thus, matter precedes whatever comes to be (*Metaphysics*, IV.2, 140.15–17).[23]

When considering possibility in itself, it was seen that it is a certain relative notion, namely, the privation or absence of some necessary existence. It was also seen that it requires some substrate. While in the case of things that are atemporally (or eternally) created that substrate might be an immaterial intellect, in the case of those things that change from not having actually existed to actually existing, namely, those things that make up the sublunar realm in which we find ourselves, the substrate of their possibility is for Avicenna matter.[24] Thus, a full understanding of possibility, at least as Avicenna understands it, requires an analysis of the matter in which the possibility of temporally coming to be inheres.

Matter and Form

I have already noted that for Avicenna there is among possible existents a division between those things that never exist separate from a subject, even though they are not themselves (material or formal) parts of the subject, namely, accidents, and those things that do not exist in a subject, namely, substances. Of these two classes, Avicenna argues, substances are ontologically prior. He reasons thus (*Metaphysics*, II.1, 45.9–13): Inasmuch as some accident exists in a subject, that subject too must be either an accident or a substance. Since Avicenna believes that it is impossible that some determinate thing, such as a wren, a robin, or the like, should have an infinite number of subjects presently existing in it, the series must terminate with that which itself is not in a subject. As has been seen, for Avicenna it is substance that is not in a subject. Consequently, the series of accidents terminates at a substance, which is the ultimate grounds for the rest of those things in the series, and so substance is causally prior to accidents.

Again, then, a substance is that which does not exist inseparably from a subject and is not a part of the subject; however, Avicenna also distinguishes between a subject (*mawḍūʿ*) and a substrate or locus or receptacle (all various translations of the Arabic *maḥall*) (*Metaphysics*, II.1, 46.18–47.10). A subject, on the one hand, he tells us, is that which subsists in itself inasmuch as it has been specified to some determinate species, and as such is a cause for the subsistence of those things inhering in the particular instance of that species. A substrate, on the other hand, is anything in which something inheres or is established, and, through that thing, the substrate comes to be in some state. In this respect, then, a substrate, locus, or receptacle is more general than a subject, since while things may inhere in either a subject or a substrate, a subject must already subsist as some species of thing, such as a human or a horse, while such a specified existence need not be the case with respect to a substrate.

Bearing this distinction in mind, Avicenna claims that both matter and forms—in the strict sense of species forms,[25] such as the form of humanity or equinity (and so not accidental forms, such as the form of heat)—are both substances. Matter clearly is a substance on the present definition since it is not in another, as in a subject, but is the ultimate substrate of all material forms. Equally clear is that the immaterial forms of the Intelligences are not in a subject and so are substances. As for the various material species forms that are in a substrate, namely, species forms such as those of human, horse, oak tree, and the like, they are not strictly speaking in a subject, since the matter only exists as specified, and so as a subject, owing to the presence of that very species form existing in it. As for the composites of matter and some species form, for Avicenna they too are substances, since they are the subjects of the various accidents or accidental forms that exist in that composite.

Although material species forms require matter as that in which they inhere, matter also requires species forms in order to subsist. In fact, argues Avicenna, matter can never be completely devoid of some form or other, a thesis we saw him merely assert in his *Physics*, but now he demonstrates. While at *Metaphysics*, II.3 he provides a number of arguments for this thesis, the general move is this: If matter—again understood as the most basic substrate underlying all forms—were ever completely stripped of every form, then it would be something completely devoid of any magnitude; for magnitude is an accidental form belonging to a substance. Moreover, matter could not occupy any space, or be continuous and divisible, since all of these states follow upon some quantitative or positional form. While an existence separate from these quantitative and positional states might be fitting for an *immaterial* substance, they would, in effect, render matter as a substance nil. In the end, argues Avicenna, if matter is to subsist at all, it requires some species form qua species form (*Physics*, I.2, 14.1–15.5; *Metaphysics*, II.4). In other words, the subsistence of matter does not depend upon any particular species form, such as that for dolphins, orangutans, or maples; it just needs some species form or other. Consequently, inasmuch as matter depends upon forms, forms are the cause of matter's subsistence.

As for the subsistence of the forms themselves, clearly the cause of their subsistence cannot be the matter, argues Avicenna, for such a state of affairs would involve circular causation. That is because the actual existence or subsistence of matter is, as has just been seen, the effect of a form, and an effect that subsists through some cause cannot be the cause of its own cause's subsistence (*Metaphysics*, II.4, 70.11–16). The cause of the forms' subsistence is instead for Avicenna that entity that bestows the various species forms onto the properly prepared or disposed matter, namely, the Giver of Forms. Finally, with respect to the subsistence of composite substances, such as this particular human or that particular dog, it is the form and matter together that are the causes for its existence.

Quickly to recapitulate, the possibility of something's coming to be after not having been is for Avicenna a relational notion: It refers to the relative absence of some necessary existence. Inasmuch as this possibility is relational, it requires some substrate in which to inhere. Avicenna identifies this substrate, at least in the case of things that come to be after not having been, with matter. Matter, again, is a substance (for it is the substrate of all species forms), and so can function as a substrate for the possibility of what comes to be. Still, it is a substance whose existence is tenuous and requires some species form to make it subsist. Without some form or other matter would fall into nonexistence along with the possibility inherent in it.

Causality

Before turning to Avicenna's arguments for the eternity of the cosmos, I still need to consider the notion of causality at work in his philosophical system, for not only will such a discussion round out Avicenna's understanding of the cosmos, but certain features of his notion of causality are also central to one of his arguments for the world's eternity.

In addition to form and matter, Avicenna, following a long Aristotelian tradition, identifies two further causes: efficient cause (or the agent) and final cause (or the end) (*Metaphysics*, VI.1; *Salvation*, "Metaphysics," I.12). Avicenna again defines the formal cause as that part of a subsisting thing by which that thing actually is what it is, while the material cause is that part of a subsisting thing by which that thing potentially is what it is and in which the potentiality of its existence resides.[26] The final cause or end is that for the sake of which the existence of something distinct from the cause is realized. As for the efficient cause or agent, Avicenna defines it as that which provides or bestows some existence essentially distinct from its own.[27]

Avicenna additionally distinguishes between the "natural efficient cause," and what might be termed the "metaphysical efficient cause." The natural efficient cause merely produces motion, whether with respect to the category of quantity (as in the case of augmentation or diminution such as growing or deteriorating in size), or quality (as in alteration such as heating and cooling), or place (such as locomotion), or position (such as rotating in place). In contrast, the metaphysical efficient cause produces existence or being itself, either by producing existence absolutely (as in the case of the Necessary Existent) or producing the various species forms that give a specific existence to matter (as in the case of the Giver of Forms). Natural efficient causes then are efficient causes in the sense that they bring about the existence of certain motions or changes in some material subject or substrate. As such, natural efficient causes play the role of preparatory causes that dispose and prepare the matter by either moving it to some suitable place or altering certain qualitative features of the matter, rendering it receptive to the influence of a metaphysical efficient cause, which in its turn bestows the species form by which the substance is the kind that it is.

According to Avicenna's conception of causation, when the entire causal complex actually exists, that is, there actually is suitably disposed matter and a metaphysical efficient cause imparting a given form for some good, the effect of this causal complex cannot but occur. In other words, for Avicenna there can be no temporal gaps between so-called essentially ordered causes and their effects. Here, an "essentially ordered cause" is any cause that the particular effect essentially depends upon right now in order to exist, as, for example, I depend upon the form of humanity informing matter right now if I am to exist at this moment as a human. In this respect, my dependence upon form and matter for my existence is, for Avicenna, different from my dependence upon my so-called temporally ordered causes, like, for example, my dependence upon my father and mother for my existence. Essentially ordered causes must exist simultaneously with their effect, whereas temporally ordered causes need not.

One argument that Avicenna gives in his smaller encyclopedic work, the *Salvation*, for this thesis (namely that essentially ordered or metaphysical causes must exist simultaneously with their effects) comes from his notion of necessity (*Salvation*, "Metaphysics," II.1). One characteristic of necessity is that its opposite implies a contradiction. Thus, assume a certain proposition. If that assumed proposition entails a contradiction, then the initial proposition's opposite must be necessary. Such a situation holds for all modes of necessity, including what is necessary through another at the time that it actually exists. That is because one cannot, without contradiction, assume that something, when it is necessary through another, does not actually exist, since this is to assume that something, when it actually exists, does not actually exist.

In like fashion, argues Avicenna, to assume that causes do *not* necessitate their effects leads to an explicit contradiction. Here, an example will make the point. From repeated observations, Avicenna believes that one can infer that fire has the active causal power to burn, and that cotton has the passive power to be burned. So, let fire, and all the active causal powers required for burning, be put in contact with cotton along with all the passive causal powers required for being burned. Now assume that the expected effect, the burning of the cotton, does not occur. In this case either one of two things could explain why the cotton is not burning. Either that which has the active causal power to burn, namely, the whole complex of requisite active causal powers, does not have the active causal power to burn, which is clearly a contradiction—for all of the requisite active causal powers cannot simultaneously have and not have the active power to burn. Or, *mutatis mutandis*, that which has the passive causal power to be burned, namely, the whole complex of requisite passive causal powers, does not have the passive causal power to be burned, and there again is a contradiction. In general terms, then, the assumption that the effect is not necessitated by its causes when all the causes are present leads to an explicit contradiction; however, in that case, concludes Avicenna, its opposite must be necessary, and so causes must necessitate their effects.

In a similar vein, Avicenna also believes that the efficient cause of a thing's existence must exist simultaneously with its effect and must continue to exist as an efficient cause as long as the effect exists. Now, it is common to think that the efficient cause is only required to bring something into existence. Thus, one might believe that once a given thing comes to exist it no longer needs an efficient cause but can subsist on its own—as, for example, the parents are efficient causes of their offspring, and yet the offspring, once born, continue to exist even should the parents pass away.

Avicenna in contrast argues that such a conception of the efficient cause is misguided. He reasons thus (*Metaphysics*, VI.1, 198.8–9.16): After something, x, comes to be (*ḥudūth*), it exists, and, according to Avicenna's modal ontology, that continued existence is either one of (I) possible existence (and so is necessary through another) or (II) necessary existence. As for (I)— again that x's continued existence after coming to be is merely possible existence—prior to x's coming to exist the only thing that one could really or truthfully say about x is that x does not exist. In other words, x considered prior to its coming to be is nothing more than the absence or privation of some necessary or actual existence, which again is just what it means to exist possibly in itself. Consequently, if x's existence after it comes to be remains mere possible existence in itself, there has been no change in the mode of existence attributed to x; it still remains as only possibly existing. Yet the mode of x's existence is exactly what changes when x comes to be after not having been. Moreover, inasmuch as possible existence is related to nonexistence, possible existence cannot be the cause of x's continued existence after x comes to be, for nonexistence, even relative nonexistence, cannot, for Avicenna, cause anything.

If, (II), x's continued existence is necessary, then it is either (II.a) necessary through itself or (II.b) necessary through another. Obviously, x's continued existence, which came to be after not having been, is not (II.a) necessary through itself, for inasmuch as it came to exist after not existing, x is something whose existence is possible in itself. Nothing for Avicenna can simultaneously be necessary in itself and possible in itself, nor, as was argued in the previous chapter, can something be a necessary existent through itself and through another.[28] Hence, if x's continued existence is necessary, it must be (II.b) necessary through another. That other, Avicenna goes on, might be (II.b.1) the very act of coming to be, (II.b.2) some attribute belonging to the essence of x, or (II.b.3) something distinct from x. The very act of coming to be (II.b.1) cannot be that other that is presently causing x's continued necessary existence, since the very act of x's coming to be ceased once x actually comes to exist. What does not exist, which in this case is the coming to be of x, cannot presently exist as the cause of x's continued necessary existence.

If that other by which x continues to exist is some attribute of x's own essence (II.b.2), then that attribute, inasmuch as it exists, is (according to Avicenna modal ontology) either (II.b.2.i) necessary in itself or (II.b.2.ii) necessary through another. Now, if (II.b.2.i) one of the attributes of x's essence is that it is necessary in itself, then x's existence would be necessary in itself (for it would have necessary existence essentially). Again, however, x is something existing possibly in itself but is necessary through another. If (II.b.2.ii), the attribute comes to exist together with the coming to be of x, then the initial question can be asked of the attribute, "Is that attribute's continued existence one of necessary or possible existence?" and one finds oneself in an explanatory circle. Thus, (II.b.3), x's subsistence, that is, its continued existence once it comes to exist after having not existed, must be due to some cause distinct from x. For Avicenna, then, the proximate (metaphysical) efficient cause for the subsistence of species forms—namely, those forms that make up the simple and composite substances of the sublunar realm—is the Giver of Forms, whereas the remote and ultimate cause sustaining the existence of the entire universe of things possible in themselves is the Necessary Existent. One now has all the elements to understand Avicenna's arguments for the eternity of the world, and in fact why he thinks it is irreligious to think otherwise.

Avicenna's Modal Arguments for
the Eternity of the World

Avicenna presents various arguments for the eternity of the world both in his *Physics* (III.11) and his *Metaphysics* (IX.1). In general, all of his arguments are variations on proofs that had been formulated in the Greek world, except all are now given a uniquely Avicennan stamp. Thus, the first of his arguments that I consider is based upon Aristotle's argument that generation requires matter and forms, except now Avicenna begins with his analysis of possibility that has been discussed. Avicenna's second argument draws upon Aristotle's proof from the nature of time, but now exploiting Avicenna's own analysis of time in terms of possibility. Finally, the last argument is a version of Proclus's argument drawn from the nature of the creator, but in this case Avicenna appeals to his own conception of causality, which, as has just been seen, is heavily imbued with his modal ontology.

The Modal Proof from the Nature
of Temporally Created Things

Avicenna's first argument is a *reductio*-style argument (*Physics*, III.11, 232.14–230.12; *Metaphysics*, IX.1, 300.7–302.10; *Salvation*, "Metaphysics," II.22, 604–608). Here he assumes that the cosmos came to exist at some finite time in the past "before" which there was only God. (He leaves open the possibility that "before" here might be taken in a nontemporal sense.) Still, before the cosmos came to exist, its existence, which includes the sublunar realm of material species forms and matter, had to be possible in itself. If the existence of the cosmos were not possible in itself, then it would have to be either necessary in itself or impossible in itself. Inasmuch as the cosmos has purportedly come to be after not having been, it cannot be necessary in itself. Also, it cannot be impossible in itself, since what is impossible never exists, and the cosmos clearly exists.

Thus, since the existence of the cosmos—understood as a composite of both immaterial and material forms as well as the matter in which material forms inhere—is something possible in itself, that possibility, asserts Avicenna, must precede the coming to be of the cosmos. Moreover, when considering the possibility of existents that temporally come to be after having not existed, such as individual animals, plants, and the like, it was noted that possibility is not a substance in its own right, but requires some substrate. It was further noted that matter must be that substrate for those existents that temporally come to be. Consequently, assuming that the cosmos—again understood as the composite of forms and matter—were temporally created in the finite past, matter, Avicenna observes, would have existed prior to its own creation, which is absurd.

Moreover, matter, as Avicenna has argued, cannot subsist considered merely as the indeterminate substrate of what might possibly exist; rather, matter needs some species form through which it subsists, the cause of which is ultimately traced back to the Necessary Existent. Thus, should the cosmos have been created in the finite past, forms also would have had to have existed prior to their creation, which, again, is absurd. In short, the possibility to create the world exists only as long as the matter exists, and the matter actually exists only when it is being in-formed. The possibility of the cosmos' existence, however, maintains Avicenna, has eternally existed. Thus, the form-matter composite, which is the cosmos itself, has eternally existed, albeit eternally dependent upon the Necessary Existent as its ultimate (metaphysical) efficient cause. What is important to note about Avicenna's version of Aristotle's argument is that while it makes the forms and matter that make up our cosmos everlasting, and so the cosmos has always existed, unlike Aristotle's earlier argument it also makes the forms and matter of the cosmos eternally dependent upon the Necessary Existent as their efficient cause.

The Modal Proof from the Nature of Time

Avicenna's second modal proof for the eternity of the world is derived from the nature of time (*Physics*, III.11, 238.15–39.8; *Metaphysics*, IX.1, 304.8–307.6; *Salvation*, "Physics," II.9, 228–230). Time for Avicenna, as I noted when considering his temporal theory,[29] corresponds with the possibility to traverse longer distances or a greater number of rotations when two things move at the same rate of speed. Now, again as part of a *reductio*-style argument, Avicenna assumes that the universe is temporally finite—for example, it was created 10,000 years ago (where a "year" corresponds with a single apparent solar rotation as we would measure it now). In this case, it still would have been possible, maintains Avicenna, for the Necessary Existent to have created a greater number of solar rotations than it purportedly did, for example, 20,000 rotations. (Since Avicenna identifies the Necessary

Existent with God he thinks it would be sacrilege to deny otherwise.) Moreover, continues Avicenna, it could have been possible for the Necessary Existent to create the extra 10,000 possible rotations such that 20,000 solar rotations would have elapsed up to the present day. Simply put, there is the possibility for the universe to have undergone a longer motion in the past than it purportedly has.

If, however, there is a possibility for the Necessary Existent to have created a greater number of solar rotations than it purportedly did, there must have been a time when the Necessary Existent was not creating the world. For again on Avicenna's analysis of time, time is just the possibility for uniformly moving objects to cover greater distances or more rotations. In other words, assuming that Avicenna's analysis of time is correct, simply affirming the existence of some possibility for certain earlier rotations, and so the possibility of a longer motion, is to affirm the existence of time. There is no illicit modal shift here. Inasmuch as one is a modal realist and believes that possibilities exist as real features of the world, and time corresponds with a certain possibility itself—a premise that, as was seen in chapter 3, followed from certain basic kinematic facts—then the inference from the existence of this real possibility, to time's real existence is a valid one. Consequently, within Avicenna's framework, he is completely justified in arguing that given the mere possibility that the cosmos could have undergone changes and motion longer than it purportedly has, and that the possible length of these changes could be indefinitely large, then time must have always existed reaching into the infinite past and will always exist reaching into the infinite future inasmuch as time corresponds and in fact is for Avicenna identical with the very possibility for these indefinitely long motions.

Given this conclusion, Avicenna can now repeat Aristotle's proof for the eternity of the world from time but again with his modal twist. That argument was that if there were a first moment in the finite past when the cosmos either began to move or was created, there would have been a time before that purported first moment. Whereas Aristotle simply took this premise as some undemonstrated first principle, Avicenna has provided an independent proof for it from his modal analysis of time. Avicenna then observes that when there is a time, there must also be a motion, for motion is the very subject in which time inheres and has its existence. If there is motion, however, there must be something undergoing the motion, namely, a form-matter composite, which again Avicenna identifies with the cosmos itself. Consequently, if one assumes that the cosmos—again a composite of forms and matter—were created at some moment in the finite past, one would be committed to the existence of forms and matter, when forms and matter purportedly did not exist. The conclusion is absurd, so the assumption that gave rise to it, namely that the cosmos was created in the finite past, concludes Avicenna, must likewise be absurd. Avicenna concludes that even though it is true that the cosmos is causally dependent upon the Necessary Existent, and so the Necessary Existent is the creator of the universe, the divinity has from all eternity been creating it.

Proof from the Nature of Causation and the Necessary Existent

Again Avicenna's third argument is a variant of Proclus's proof, namely that, since the divinity creates from its eternal goodness and that goodness never changes, it has been eternally creating (*Metaphysics*, XI.1, 302.11– 304.6; *Salvation*, "Metaphysics," II.23, 609–612). Recall that by the time of the medieval Islamic period, thinkers on both sides—whether for or against an eternal creation—wanted to make God both the final and efficient cause of the cosmos' existence. Again, however, on Avicenna's analysis of causation, the effect must be necessitated simultaneously with the existence of the effect's complete cause. For Avicenna there simply are no temporal gaps between a complete complex of essentially ordered, or metaphysical, causes and its effect. Thus, if the Necessary Existent exists, whatever proceeds from it as its effect must also exist. Were it the case, then, that the Necessary Existent were to exist and yet the cosmos were not to exist, the Necessary Existent could not be the complete efficient cause of the cosmos given Avicenna's account of causality.

In that case, continues Avicenna, something else, x, which completes the causal complex, must have come to exist that previously had not existed, as, for example, a will to create. Whatever x might be, it either comes to be in the Necessary Existent itself or not. If it does not come to be in the Necessary Existent itself, then the question concerning the cause of x's coming to be still stands, for the Necessary Existent is assumed to be the complete cause of all things, and x supposedly came to be after not having been. If x, whatever it is, comes to be in the Necessary Existent, then the Necessary Existent has changed, and has come to have some existence that it did not previously have. The Necessary Existent, as Avicenna has argued frequently, exists necessarily in every respect, so it cannot change in any way. Thus, this option is false. Simply put, inasmuch as the Necessary Existent is the eternally unchanging complete cause of the cosmos' own necessary existence, and since effects must exist simultaneously and together with their complete causes, the cosmos, maintains Avicenna, must exist eternally as something necessary through the Necessary Existent.

With these three arguments, one sees Avicenna rehabilitating certain classical arguments for the eternity of the world, however, doing so in such a way as to avoid the objections raised against their classical predecessors. Thus, none of Avicenna's arguments presupposes that there was a time before creation. In fact, Avicenna's second argument, far from presupposing that there has always been time, provides a proof for that claim. Similarly, unlike Aristotle's argument based upon his analysis of generation, and the assumption that generation presupposes forms and matter, Avicenna's variant starts from the even more basic notion of the very possibility of there being generation and coming to be. Similarly, Avicenna's final argument draws heavily upon his modal ontology for its conception of both causality and the divine nature.

Infinity and the Possibility of an Eternal World

Despite Avicenna's Herculean efforts, until he can counter the absurdities that Philoponus raised against the notion of an infinitely extended past, the temporal and eternal creationists' positions are, at best, at a standstill. Again, the objections that Philoponus presented followed upon certain strongly held intuitions about infinity, such as it cannot be traversed and that there cannot be an actual infinity. Philoponus, as I noted, had two lines of criticism: One, an eternal world would entail that an actual infinite has come to exist and so an infinite has been traversed and; two, there would be sets of infinities of different sizes, and so sets larger than that beyond which there is nothing more.

Philoponus, like many others, took it as simply self-evident that an infinite could not be traversed. In stark contrast, Avicenna, as far as I am aware, nowhere outright denies that an infinite can be traversed absolutely.[30] Instead, when Avicenna mentions the impossibility of traversing the infinite at all, it is always in a qualified way: An infinite cannot be traversed *in a finite period of time.*[31] Without this qualification, Avicenna sees no problem with traversing an infinite, again provided that there is an infinite amount of time to do so. In fact, in his *Metaphysics* as part of a response to Philoponus, he quite explicitly maintains that not only is it possible to traverse an infinite temporal causal chain, but, in fact, it is necessary.

> We do not preclude an infinite [number of] ancillary and preparatory causes, one [temporally] preceding the other. In fact, that must necessarily be the case, since each temporally created thing has become necessary after not having been necessary because of the necessity of its cause at that moment . . . and its cause also having become necessary. So with respect to particular things, there must be an infinity of antecedent things by which the actually existing causes necessarily come to be certain actual causes of [the particulars] (*Metaphysics*, VI.2, 202.7–10).

In this passage Avicenna is explaining why a given temporal event or thing comes to be at the time that it does and not earlier, where the reason is that the matter was only prepared to take on a new form at that time.[32] As such, there must have been temporally prior causes that prepared the matter, but of course those temporally prior causes are also temporal events or things, which themselves need temporally prior causes, and so on ad infinitum. Thus, according to Avicenna, an infinite number of temporally prior preparatory causes must have been traversed.

While for all intents and purposes Avicenna's claim here is nothing more than a restatement of Philoponus's original objection that an eternal past would entail the traversal of an infinite, the onus of proof has changed. Since Avicenna believes that he has demonstrated that the cosmos is eternal, and so an infinite has been traversed (albeit it has had all the infinite time in the past to do so), he is now challenging Philoponus and those of like mind to demonstrate that the traversal of an infinite is impossible. If they cannot, and one, like Avicenna himself, is willing to accept that in an infinite amount of time an infinite can be traversed, then one of Philoponus's objections collapses.

Recall, however, that Philoponus had a follow-up objection, namely that the traversal of an infinite, even if all the members are not currently present, still entails that an actually infinite number has been realized, and an actual infinite, no matter how construed, is impossible, or at least Philoponus would have one believe. In the *Physics* (II.11, 238.3–15), Avicenna responds, complaining that Philoponus fails to appreciate the distinction between "each one" (*kull wāḥid*) and "whole" (*kull*). So, for example, while it is true that each one of the parts of a thing is a part, it is false that the whole of that thing is a part. Similarly, contends Avicenna, while it is possible that each one of an actual infinite has existed, it need not be possible for the whole of that infinite to exist as a whole.

In fact, using the each one/whole distinction, Avicenna argues that the whole of all past events is not, as it were, collected together into an actually existing set (*jumla*) (ibid., 237.13–238.2).[33] At best, he observes, they have been collected together in some intellectual depiction (*waṣf al-ʿaql*). A collection in an intellectual depiction, however, is only equivocally like a collection existing in reality or extramentally, which is a genuine set, for the collection of all animals as a logical notion existing in the intellect, Avicenna points out, is "decidedly not the set of them [existing extramentally]" (ibid., 238.2). Of course, if something does not exist, then it is inappropriate to say that it is actually any thing, at least in any proper sense of "actual." Thus, concludes Avicenna, it is simply unforgivable to speak of the set of past events as actually infinite, for no such set exists.

Using the same strategy, Avicenna further addresses Philoponus's objection about the rotations of the planets and greater and smaller infinities (ibid., 236.14–237.12). Again, there is no actually existing infinite set of rotations; rather, Avicenna reminds us that they are said to be infinite in that "whatever number our estimative faculty imagines to belong to the motions, we find a number that was before it" (ibid., 237.2). As for the whole set of rotations, that does not exist. Now, continues Avicenna, notions such as "more" and "less" as well as "finite" and "infinite" either apply or do not apply to nonexistent things. If they do not apply to nonexistent things, then the objection disappears, whereas if such terms do apply, then, chides Avicenna, they must equally apply to the infinity of future rotations that will occur. Since most defenders of the world's past temporal creation, in fact, conceded that future time will be infinite, they find themselves, as it were, hoisted on their own petard.

In the end, Avicenna believes that all the arguments against the eternity of the world, based upon certain presumed absurdities following on the notion of infinity, depend upon undemonstrated intuitions that we have about the infinite.[34] Since Avicenna believes that he has truly demonstrated the eternity of the world, he is willing to set aside all of these undemonstrated assumptions about the infinite. In this respect, Avicenna, like Cantor centuries later, should be praised for recognizing that deeply entrenched intuitions about infinity can be demonstrated to be simply wrong.

The Emanation of the Cosmos

In this chapter and the preceding one I have considered how Avicenna envisions the Necessary Existent in itself as both the final and efficient cause of the existence of an eternally enduring cosmos. Before turning to the emanation schema that Avicenna develops to explain the "causal mechanism" by which the Necessary Existent creates the cosmos, I should briefly mention how he (and indeed virtually all thinkers working during the ancient and medieval period) envisioned the topography of the cosmos.

Emanation and the Cosmos

For those working within the classical physics and astronomy of Aristotle and Ptolemy respectively, the Earth is roughly at the center of the universe.[35] The sublunar realm includes the four elements earth, water, air, and fire, where these elements are understood in terms of their various rectilinear motions. So, for example, the element earth tends down toward the center, while the element fire tends up toward the sphere of the Moon, with water and air moving in a straight line toward places intermediate between those of earth and fire.

Since the Moon, Sun, planets, and stars were believed to move not rectilinearly but circularly, it was thought that they involved some yet different material or element, the so-called quintessence or ether. These celestial spheres (sing. *falak*) were in their turn thought to rotate approximately around the Earth. The number of celestial spheres is finite, since most medieval thinkers argued that the space of the cosmos is itself finite, ending with the outermost celestial sphere. The number of spheres included that of the Moon, those of the two inner planets, Venus and Mercury, the Sun, and the rest of the observable, outer planets, Mars, Jupiter, and Saturn. In addition to the planets there was the sphere of the fixed stars and the outermost sphere, which was needed to account for the procession of the equinox. Further spheres were postulated as needed in order to account for such phenomena as retrograde motion.[36]

Now, just as in the sublunar realm, the circular motion of these celestial bodies does not belong to them qua (ethereal) body. Instead, each celestial sphere needs some proximate mover, which, Avicenna concludes, after a lengthy discussion (*Metaphysics*, IX.2), cannot be merely the nature or form of the celestial body but must be a soul. In addition, Avicenna argued that associated with each of the celestial sphere-soul composites there is also a completely immaterial Intellect or Intelligence that is the cause of the soul and the celestial body. Any given Intellect is itself produced by whatever Intellect is causally above it, with all the Intellects forming a causal chain that terminates with the Necessary Existent as the ultimate cause of everything below it.

As for how the Necessary Existent causes the existence of what is under it, Avicenna appeals to the Greek Neoplatonic theory of emanation or overflowing (*fayaḍān*). According to the emanationist schema, there overflows from whatever is perfect a certain secondary activity. For example, light emanates from the Sun, and heat emanates from fire; light and heat are not identical with the Sun and fire but are the effects of the Sun and fire given what the Sun and fire are. Unfortunately, the analogy is not exact: All of these examples are of natural or physical processes, which occur as a matter of natural necessity, whereas emanation in the case of the Necessary Existent proceeds, according to Avicenna, and as I shall explain soon, voluntarily. Thus, in the case of the Necessary Existent, since for Avicenna it is not merely perfect but above perfection, necessary existence itself proceeds from it, albeit voluntarily.

Since the Necessary Existent is absolutely simple, however, Avicenna does not think that it can be the direct or immediate cause of the necessary existence belonging to all the various Intellects and different kinds of possible existents below it (*Metaphysics*, IX.4, 328.5–330.4). That is because inasmuch as these possible existents represent different kinds of created things there would have to be different causal facets in the Necessary Existent to explain the multiplicity of diverse things proceeding from it, were it the direct and immediate rather than ultimate cause of all of the various existents below it. Instead, argues Avicenna, from something absolutely one only one thing comes. Still, all the complexity that is in the cosmos is in the Necessary Existent but again in a unified and noncomposite way. So, while the following analogy is far from exact, the noncomposite complexity of the Necessary Existent might be likened to the kernel of an acorn that, although it is homogenous throughout, nonetheless contains all the complexity and information that manifests itself in the various and diverse aspects of the mature oak tree.

Still, the problem of explaining how the Necessary Existent can be the ultimate cause of the apparent multiplicity in the cosmos remains. For if the first Intellect that proceeds from the Necessary Existent is one, then, given Avicenna's principle, what proceeds from it should also be one. The emanationist schema, then, seemingly cannot explain how it is that from one emanated Intellect there can emanate three things: the Intellect below it, as well as its own associated soul, and the celestial sphere (for such an emanation appears to violate the dictum that from one only one proceeds). The situation only becomes that much graver when one tries to explain how the multiplicity of the sublunar realm came to be.

Avicenna's modal ontology yet again provides him with a neat solution to this problem of medieval cosmology. From the Necessary Existent there emanates for Avicenna the Intellect associated with the outermost celestial sphere. This Intellect must itself already be composite, for it is something possible in itself but necessary through another. Now, continues Avicenna, when this Intellect contemplates the Necessary Existent, there emanates from that first Intellect another Intellect—let this second Intellect be the one associated with the fixed stars. In addition to contemplating the Necessary Existent, the first Intellect also contemplates itself, but, as has already been seen, it is something composite consisting of its own possible existence and the necessary existence it has from another. Thus, according to Avicenna's own unique emanative scheme, when the first Intellect contemplates itself as something merely possible in itself, there emanates from it a certain celestial body, whereas when it contemplates itself as necessary through another, it emanates that celestial body's soul. This process continues at the level of the second Intellect. Now, however, the second Intellect contemplates its relation to the first Intellect and the Necessary Existent. This emanative process continues cascading downward with new Intellects, souls, and celestial bodies being produced until it reaches the Active Intellect or Giver of Forms, which is the Intellect that produces the Moon and lunar soul.

At this level, the Active Intellect or Giver of Forms, with its associated degree of possible existence and so privation, is simply incapable of emanating a single unified existent. Instead, a multiplicity of forms overflows from it that are incapable of subsisting on their own as the immaterial intellects do, and so these forms require matter in the way discussed earlier. That such a multiplicity should result is almost entailed by Avicenna's analysis of possibility in terms of the absence or privation of necessary existence, and the close association that the Neoplatonizing Aristotelian tradition finds between existence and unity. For as there is a greater and greater falling away from or absence of necessary existence so there would be for ancient and medieval thinkers a greater and greater loss of unity. Still, as for why the loss of unity should lead to multiplicity where it does, there can be for Avicenna no causal explanation. That is because at this point one reaches the possible existents that are forever coming to be, and, as we have seen Avicenna argue, there is no cause for why a certain degree of privation should correspond with the possible existent with which it does.

Emanation and the Necessary Existent

As for why the Necessary Existent should create the cosmos, Avicenna is adamant that it simply cannot be because of some cause other than the Necessary Existent itself. Thus, at book IX.4 of the *Metaphysics* of the *Cure* Avicenna states:

> It is impossible that [the Necessary Existent in itself] should in any way have some principle or cause—whether [the cause be] that from which, concerning which, by which, or for the sake of which—such that it would exist on account of a certain given thing. Because of this, it is impossible that the being of the cosmos should result from [the Necessary Existent in itself] in a way that there would be some intention (*qaṣd*)—like our intention—for its generating the cosmos and for [the cosmos'] existence such that [the Necessary Existent in itself] intends [its generation] for the sake of something other than itself (*Metaphysics*, IX.4, 326.10–13).

The reason why Avicenna believes that the Necessary existent cannot intend the creation of the cosmos is because it would introduce multiplicity into the divinity, a pitfall, as has been noted, that Avicenna goes to great lengths to avoid. He enumerates the multiplicity that intention would entail thus (ibid., 326.14–16): First, there will be something in the Necessary Existent that is the cause of its intending, namely, its knowledge that the intention is necessary, desirable, or there is some good in it; second, there would be the act by which the intention is acquired; third, and finally, there would be that which is acquired by acting for that intention. All of this Avicenna believes is simply absurd, given that the Necessary Existent is absolutely simple.

Thus, Avicenna concludes that the Necessary Existent does not intend (*qaṣd*) the existence of the world, but he is also quick to add that neither does that which proceeds from the Necessary Existent proceed by nature, that is, by necessity. Avicenna's general argument at this point is to assert that there are two conditions that guarantee that a given act is *not* by nature: One is that there is a recognition (*ma'rifa*) on the part of the agent that it is performing that act, and the other is that the act involves the consent (*riḍā*) of the agent.

First, argues Avicenna, the Necessary Existent obviously recognizes that the existence of the cosmos emanates from it, since it exists as a pure intellect intellecting itself, as seen in the last chapter. Thus, there is nothing about its existence that it does not know or recognize. Second, continues Avicenna, the created order emanates from the Necessary Existent with its consent because consent, according to Avicenna, occurs (1) when one knows what proceeds from oneself, and (2) when there is nothing that hinders or interferes with that procession. Consequently, since, as has been seen, the Necessary Existent knows what proceeds from itself, and nothing causally acts on it so as to interfere with what proceeds from it, emanation, that is, divine efficient causality, must for Avicenna be at the consent of the Necessary Existent. Consequently, he concludes, the emanation of existence from the Necessary Existent is not by nature but through divine will or volition (*irāda*).

While there is certainly something paradoxical in saying that while the Necessary Existent does not intend the creation of the cosmos, it nonetheless wills it, the paradox, at least for Avicenna, is merely one of semantics. For Avicenna, there is a distinction between intention (*qaṣd*) and volition (*irāda*), namely, the contrast between the way that humans will or intend something because we need some good other than ourselves, and the way that the Necessary Existent wills something, where nothing is willed or wanted except for the good that is the very existence of the Necessary Existent.[37] To elaborate this point, Avicenna insists that the good that the Necessary Existent knows and wills in its emanative act is nothing other than its very self or very being, in Arabic its *dhāt*. In other words, it knows itself as the Necessary through itself; it knows that it is good; and knowing that it is good, it wills its existence. Here, Avicenna is just reiterating in a different way the claim that I noted in the previous chapter: The Necessary Existent is a self-explaining entity.

Now, according to Avicenna, in knowing itself the Necessary Existent knows, in one simple intellectual perception, the order of the good with respect to existence (*niẓām al-khayr fī l-wujūd*) (ibid., 377.9). Moreover, to know this good is for the Necessary Existent to will this good, for again to will is for Avicenna just to act knowingly and not be hindered from so acting. Indeed, it is this knowledge of itself as the pure good that is the cause of the existence of whatever it knows. Finally, the existence of what it knows in no way completes, perfects, or benefits the Necessary Existent; rather, maintains Avicenna, it is only the created existence, which results from the Necessary Existent's knowing itself, that is completed, perfected, and benefited. In the human act of intending or willing, in contrast, there is always (1) some external good willed or intended, (2) willing so as to act for that good, and (3) the benefit or enhancement for oneself acquired from that good. In the divine act of willing, however, there is no external good that the Necessary Existent wills for its own sake. There is no separate act of willing the good that is distinct from knowing that good. Finally, there is no benefit that the Necessary Existent acquires as a result of its emanating the existence of the cosmos. The created order alone is the sole recipient of any acquired good. Creating the cosmos thus in no way makes the Necessary Existent better. Its creative act is for Avicenna a purely (indeed the only truly) altruistic act.

As for the order of the good as it manifests itself here on Earth, whether through divine providence or how we interact with others, or even our individual ultimate good or end, these are all issues for the next chapter.

8

VALUE THEORY

Introduction

Unlike such theoretical sciences as physics and metaphysics about which
Avicenna has much to say, he has relatively little to say explicitly about such
practical sciences as ethics and politics. In fact, in his monumental philosophical encyclopedia, the *Cure*, he dedicates no independent volume to
issues in value theory, and instead contents himself with six chapters at the
end of his *Metaphysics*. In those chapters, mixing elements from Plato,
Aristotle, and Islam itself, Avicenna deals with the proper good of the human
understood in terms of the hereafter, discusses the virtuous city, developing
it against the backdrop of his own emanative scheme, gives an account of
the philosopher-prophet that is reminiscent of Plato's philosopher-king,
and then finally provides what might be thought of as a philosophical interpretation of the religious dictates of Islam. In his psychological works he
additionally treats in a passing fashion the formation of morals, and there
are other bits and pieces concerned with issues in value theory sprinkled
throughout the corpus of his work as well. Thus, providing a systematic
account of Avicenna's conception of practical philosophy presents something of a challenge for his interpreters.

The scarcity of explicit writings on practical philosophy in Avicenna's
system, however, is not due to any lack of interest on his part for this area of

thought. Instead, I contend, it is owing to his conception of the human good, both at the individual level (ethics) and at the level of human interactions (politics). Like many ancient and medieval thinkers, Avicenna's primary philosophical concern, when it came to ethical and political issues, was with what a flourishing or happy life (*sa'āda*, which translates the Greek *eudaimonia*) is, and how to achieve such a life, where such a life would, of course, be the good life. Avicenna says about the good (*khayr*) that in general it "is that which everything desires, and what everything desires is either existence or the perfection of existence as such" (*Metaphysics*, VIII.6, 283.15–16). He immediately follows up this unrestricted claim, following Aristotle,[1] with the caveat that "the good is what everything desires *with respect to the definition of* [*its kind*] and by which its existence is completed" (ibid., 284.1, emphasis added). Thus, for Avicenna a proper understanding of what the human good is depends upon what the proper perfection or existence of the kind human is.

In his *Psychology*, it was noted that the highest and most perfect activity of a human is that of the intellect. Avicenna further differentiated the human intellect into the practical intellect and the theoretical intellect, the activity of the practical intellect being subordinate to that of the theoretical intellect. Consequently, by Avicenna's lights the proper good of the human is to perform that function or operation that is the human's most complete or perfect activity, namely, to theorize and to contemplate, and particularly to contemplate the best and most noble thing, namely, the Necessary Existent.

Given that Avicenna believes that the proper perfection of humans is to theorize, he would have seen his various works on the theoretical sciences as providing his reader, or at least the intellectually gifted reader, with the wherewithal to attain his or her proper end or good qua human. Baldly stated, it would seem that Avicenna views the practical life as part and parcel of the theoretical one, or, to be more exact, the contemplative life simply is the perfection and completion of the life aimed at in the practical philosophies. Still, the full fruition of the contemplative life does not come to be in the here and now according to Avicenna, but in the hereafter. In a very real sense then, ethical theory, understood as the philosophical investigation of the proper end or good of humans, is for Avicenna a continuation of metaphysics; for humans only find their highest good once free from the distractions of the body such that in that state they are able to contemplate fully and completely the divinity.

To help explain Avicenna's position concerning our ultimate destiny and the role of practical philosophy in achieving that end, I again in this chapter return to Avicenna's distinction between the theoretical and practical intellect, now paying special attention to the formation of our moral temperaments and their role in helping us to achieve our proper perfection. Since Avicenna believes that the proper formation of these temperaments and the life of the human species require communal association, I also consider what might be thought of as Avicenna's political theory, which at its core has the Avicennan counterpart to the Platonic "Philosopher-King," namely, Avicenna's "Prophet-Lawgiver." Once completing this background, I turn to Avicenna's conception of the return or afterlife (ma'ād) and the pleasures and pains that one might expect to experience there depending upon the life one has lived here. I then conclude with Avicenna's account of providence and his general theodicy, that is, his account of why evil exists in a world created by a wholly good God.

The Practical Intellect and Moral Temperaments

In chapter 5,[2] I noted that for Avicenna the true nature of the human self cannot be identified with the human body. The self is in fact for him immaterial. Still, the human self has close ties to the body, for the appearance of a suitable body occasions the Giver of Forms to produce a human soul whenever it does. Moreover, Avicenna is insistent that the intellect initially needs the body in order to acquire those potential intelligibles that allow it to perform its proper activity and so perfect itself. Thus, while we should not identify ourselves with our body, our initial dependence and indeed ultimate management of the body are crucial to our flourishing as humans (*Psychology*, IV.5, 221.12–223.10). In fact, Avicenna contends, humans, or more exactly human souls, possess a unique position in the cosmos because of this relation. The human soul, Avicenna tells us, is, as it were, Janus-faced, looking both toward the immaterial realm of intelligibles and the material realm of the body:

> The human soul, though one substance, has a relation and reference to two sides, one below it and one above it, and for each side there is a faculty through which the connection between it and that side is ordered. The practical faculty, then, is the one that the soul possesses for the

connection with the side below it, that is, the body and its maintenance. The theoretical faculty is the one that the soul possesses for the connection to the side above it, to be affected by it, learn from it, and receive from it. So, it is as though our soul has two faces, one directed to the body—and this is the one that must not endure any effect of a type entailed by the body's nature—and another one directed to the lofty principles—and this is the one that must always be receptive to and affected by what is there. It is from the lower side that the moral dispositions (akhlāq) are produced, whereas it is from the higher side that the sciences are produced (Psychology, I.5, 47.8–18).

What Avicenna here terms "the lower side" is in fact the practical intellect, which manages and directs the activities of the body required by our bodily existence and interactions with the physical world.

The appropriate ethical actions and social interactions are in turn "determined by reflecting on what is required by customary opinions specific to [those activities]" (ibid., 45.20). These bodily activities, Avicenna continues, might be relative to our appetitive faculty, the compositive imagination, and the estimative faculty,[3] or even the intellect itself. In relation to the appetitive faculty, the practical intellect gives rise to various socially appropriate human emotions, such as shame or modesty as well as laughter and weeping relative to given situation, whereas when the practical intellect is joined with the compositive imagination or estimative faculty it gives rise to a knowledge of those arts, crafts, and occupations (such as medicine, carpentry, farming, and the like) by which we manage and control the ever-changing world in which we live (ibid., 46.3–8).

It is with respect to itself together with the theoretical intellect that for Avicenna the practical intellect touches on the truly ethical; for the practical and theoretical intellect acting in unison give rise to the beliefs associated with practical actions that are the widespread common opinions, as, for example, lying and oppression are bad, and the application of those widespread common opinions to particular situations (ibid., 46.9–15). While Avicenna is quick to remark that such moral dicta are not at the level of first principles, he does think it important to note that they arise as a result of the theoretical intellect's reflecting upon the widespread mores and conventions of a society, mores and conventions, as will be seen, that are initially imposed by a lawmaker-prophet. Thus, the moral judgments can and do function like general rules by which one might flourish in a society. The practical intellect in turn takes these general moral claims and applies them to the particular day-to-day cases with which we find ourselves confronted in order to determine whether to proceed or to avoid some particular line of action, whether the action is beneficial or harmful, as well as whether the particular action is morally good or bad (*Psychology*, V.1, 206.11–209.13).

In fact, claims Avicenna, the formation of one's moral temperaments (sing. *khulq*) is based upon whether the practical intellect does or does not successfully act in accordance with these moral judgments in a particular case when there are bodily desires opposing those judgments (*Psychology*, I.5, 46.15–47.7; *Salvation*, "Psychology," 3, 330–332). Vices then result when the bodily passions dominate the practical intellect, and one ignores the course dictated by reason, whereas moral virtues occur when bodily desires are subordinated to the practical intellect and reason. Thus, for example, one has the vice of dishonesty when one regularly ignores the dictum "lying is bad" because one has some desire to acquire some apparent bodily good or avoid some possible harm, whereas one has the virtue of honesty when one avoids lying regardless of the personal loss or affliction caused by following that dictum. For Avicenna, then, vice is a decided deficiency of the proper human perfection, namely, the activity of the intellect, for in acting viciously one rejects the conclusions of the human intellect in preference for irrational bodily desires.

As for the nature of the moral temperaments, Avicenna begins his own analysis by initially following the position of Aristotle as presented at *Nicomachean Ethics*, II 1–6. Thus, Avicenna identifies moral temperament with "a disposition [or habit (*malaka*)] by which certain actions readily originate from the soul without prior deliberation" (*Metaphysics*, IX, 7, 354.7). In similar Aristotelian fashion, Avicenna also asserts that one should act upon the mean (*tawassuṭ*) between two contrary moral temperaments (namely, between an excess and deficiency), not simply to do moderate actions without acquiring a moderate disposition, but precisely in order to acquire a moderate disposition. Now, like Aristotle before him, Avicenna holds that excesses and deficiencies are in fact vices; however, he additionally maintains that they are the necessary results of our animal faculties, and thus of our being in a body. Consequently, the reason one should want to acquire a moderate disposition, maintains Avicenna, is in order that one might "transcend the conditions that tie [us to the body] and preserve the proper state of the rational soul, while so preparing [the rational soul] to go beyond and transcend [the body]" (ibid., 354.16–17).

In this respect, Avicenna is less like Aristotle and more like Plato's Socrates of the *Phaedo* (64a): One lives the virtuous or moderate life as a practice for death and dying, where "death" is understood as the separation of the soul from the body. Also like Plato before him, Avicenna justifies this position by appealing to what should be our proper desire, namely, the perfection or completion of ourselves as humans, where again for Avicenna that perfection is the act of our rational faculty, namely, intellectual activity. It is precisely because the body constantly distracts one and pulls one away from this activity that Avicenna sees bodily desires and needs as vices: They prevent one from achieving his or her full perfection as a human. Therefore, to the extent that a moderate disposition trains us to ignore or at least not to give into bodily desires, such a life prepares one for the separation of the soul from the body. It is only in the disembodied state for Avicenna that the properly prepared soul is able to perform its proper perfection most fully, and only then truly flourish and be ultimately happy.

The "Philosopher-Prophet" and Laws

Avicenna is aware that there is a decided tension between the proper perfection of the human, which involves the soul's disassociating itself from the body so as to contemplate completely the Necessary Existent, and the soul's function of managing the body as well as its reliance on the body in order to acquire the potential intelligibles needed for its proper perfection. It is perhaps because of this tension that humans differ from other animals in that humans can only truly live well and flourish within a community, where all members work together for one another's mutual benefit. While other animals too may live a communal life, what marks human communities off from those others species is for Avicenna the specialization of tasks among its members. Thus, not all humans perform the same jobs in their communities, but one grows vegetables, another bakes, one sews, and yet another makes the tools, and so on (*Metaphysics*, X.2, 364.7–12). The fact that humans do perform specialized tasks rather than everyone performing every task, made the formation of cities necessary, argues Avicenna in a sentiment echoing Plato before him, for the various individuals performing their specialized tasks needed to congregate in well-defined areas where they could enjoy the benefits of one another's labor.[4]

Since the existence and survival of humans requires working together for their mutual benefit and engaging in business transactions (*muʿāmala*), just laws governing such transactions are, maintains Avicenna, essential (ibid., 364.16–365.12). He moreover believes that in order for these laws to be just and fair for all, they cannot merely be the result of private opinions (for there is the risk that individuals will disagree and prefer their own good to the communal good). Since laws governing human associations and interactions aid in the existence and survival of the human species as well as being necessary for the individual human in order that he or she reaches his or her proper perfection, these laws make up part of the overall order of the good that exists in the cosmos. As such Avicenna thinks it is simply impossible that divine providence (*ʿināya ūlá*), properly understood as the Necessary Existent's willing itself and so willing the order of the good,[5] would not provide the very basis of these laws necessary for human existence and survival, namely, by providing divine lawgivers in the form of prophets.

In chapter 5, I gave Avicenna's account of prophecy and how the prophet, owing to the perfect state of his or her soul, almost immediately and, as it were, without being taught recognizes the order of the good, namely, the divine causal order. Moreover, the prophet also sees this order in the form of images that he or she then uses to convey the divine will to others.

At the very heart of prophetic law are, Avicenna tells us, certain beliefs about the Necessary Existent or God. Thus, for example, we must believe that God exists and has created us; that God is absolutely one (that is, that "there is no god but God"); that God is all powerful and all knowing; that we must obey God; and that God has prepared for us an afterlife, heaven for those who obey, hell for those who do not (*Metaphysics*, X.2, 365.13–17). Beyond this relatively simple set of religious beliefs, the prophet does not speak, says Avicenna, since those of weaker intellects may not be able to grasp the various doctrinal issues associated with the true nature of God, such as God's immateriality and the like (ibid., 365.18–366.8).

Since individuals with a prophetic soul are few and far between, continues Avicenna, the prophet must also impose certain obligations upon the people that are to be performed regularly in order to help the people remember what the prophet has demanded that they believe. These obligations in part take the form of acts of worship (*Metaphysics*, X.3, 367–370). The first such act of worship, which is to be performed daily and indeed several times a day, says Avicenna, is prayer to God. Such prayer focuses the mind on God and the afterlife, the contemplation of which is the proper perfection of humans. Moreover, to help us break the ties that bind us to our bodies and hinder our proper function, the prophet imposes further acts of worship, such as fasting, giving of one's own material goods to those less fortunate, as well as undertaking the difficulties of pilgrimage. All of these acts of worship not only help us remember the laws given by the prophet, but also, continues Avicenna, they better prepare us to disassociate ourselves from the distractions of our body and so focus our full attention on God. Here it is certainly worth noting that Avicenna has in effect reproduced and validated the five so-called Pillars of Islam: the *Shahāda* or Muslim profession of faith ("there is no god but God"), prayer, alms, fasting (during Ramadan), and the *Ḥajj*, that is, pilgrimage to Mecca.

In fact, Avicenna warns us, unless these actions are accompanied by knowledge of, and indeed a desire for greater knowledge of, God, the mere nonreflective performance of them becomes nothing more than a tawdry business transaction (*mu'āmala*) (*Pointers and Reminders*, namaṭ 9, 199). Thus, for example, religious asceticism that is unaccompanied by contemplation of God, complains Avicenna, is actually a form of hedonism, since the ascetic is merely foregoing the pleasures of this life in hope of greater pleasures in the next. Similarly, merely performing prayers, pilgrimage, and the like without these acts being accompanied by contemplation reduces their performer to a lowly wage earner, working in this life in order to earn material gain or goods in the next. Those who truly benefit from worship are only those individuals who perform these actions in the full knowledge that they do them, not for the sake of physical pleasures in the next world, but in order to acquire a greater understanding of God, which only reaches its full perfection in the hereafter.

In addition to the doctrinal creed and acts of worship, the prophet also sets laws for the social interactions of the community. To this end, Avicenna, in a division reminiscent of Plato's *Republic*, has the prophet-lawgiver mark off three groups within the city: the rulers, craftsmen, and guardians (*Metaphysics*, X.4, 370.8–9). This ranking, he believes, helps ensure that every member of the society is assigned some place and role in the city lest anyone be idle, for the laws must preclude unemployment and idleness, which Avicenna believes to be among the greatest evils for the city. In like fashion, the lawmaker prohibits those professions, such as gambling and usury, in which property is transferred without a mutual exchange of benefit, for Avicenna sees in such professions a type of idleness in that they do not involve honest toil (ibid., 371.9–18).

The lawmaker must also prescribe laws concerning marriage, which Avicenna sees as one of the most important social institutions (ibid., 372.1–374.5). So, for example, marriage almost always results in the progeny that perpetuate the species, which is part of the order of the good. Moreover, children are more properly brought up, continues Avicenna, when both parents are involved. Similarly, whereas the lawmaker must allow for divorces, divorces should not be easily obtained, argues Avicenna, because "of the things tied to the public good, love is the most significant, and the bonds of love occur only through affection, and affection occurs only through long association" (ibid., 372.11–13). In general, Avicenna reproduces, commends, and validates much of the law set down by Muḥammad in the Qurʾān, as providing the proper religious creed, acts of worship, and the laws governing social interactions required to maximize the odds and numbers of individuals realizing their proper perfection as humans through the contemplation of God.

The Afterlife (*Maʿād*)

I have briefly considered Avicenna's account of the practical intellect and moral temperaments, which might be seen as constituting his ethical theory, followed by his view of the lawgiver-prophet and laws, which might be seen as constituting his political theory. While discussing these issues I have regularly made reference to Avicenna's position that the human's ultimate perfection, namely, the contemplation of the Necessary Existent or God, only completely occurs in a disembodied state in the afterlife. Thus, I should now turn to Avicenna's conception of the afterlife and the pleasures and pains therein.

In the *Psychology*, Avicenna had argued that not only is the human intellect essentially immaterial and so capable of existing separate from the body, but also that only in a disembodied state can the intellect fully and completely perform that action most proper to it—namely, contemplation and particularly contemplation of the Necessary Existent. In this respect there is a very real sense in which humans are natural things, but ones with a supernatural end. Avicenna is also equally aware that few would find a life devoid of any bodily pleasures—during which one everlastingly contemplates the order of the good as it emanates from the Necessary Existent—as a desirable end. To put it bluntly, for most people copulating certainly appears more desirable than contemplating.

Avicenna is quite aware of the discrepancies between what he thinks he can demonstrate about a human's highest good and the way that things might appear now. Thus, in order to justify his conclusion he provides an analysis of pleasure in the hope of convincing us that the intellectual pleasures of the afterlife are simply unimaginable to the embodied mind, in just the same way that an eunuch cannot truly imagine sexual pleasures, or the child cannot imagine why adults do not prefer to spend their hours in juvenile games (*Metaphysics*, IX.7, 349.1–6).

Pleasure (*ladhdha*) is according to Avicenna "a perception and attainment vis-à-vis the perceiver of a certain perfection and good as such" (*Pointers and Reminders*, namaṭ, 8, 191). Now, what perceives is the animal's various perceptive faculties. Thus, there are pleasures associated with each of the various external and internal senses as well as the appetitive and irascible powers or faculties. So, for example, there are the pleasures associated with a caress (touch), good food (taste), a fragrant odor (smell), a beautiful sound or sight (hearing and seeing), but there are also the pleasures of daydreaming (imagination or the estimative faculty), satisfying a hunger or need (appetitive faculty), or vanquishing a foe (irascible faculty). Avicenna makes similar comments about pain (*alam*), which parallel pleasure: "Pain is a perception and attainment vis-à-vis the perceiver of a certain imperfection and evil" (ibid.). Since all of the perceptive faculties have a corresponding pleasure and pain, reasons Avicenna, the human's faculty of intellectual perception must also have corresponding intellectual pleasures and pains.

Despite the fact that all the various pleasures share a certain formal similarity as given in the definition, they nonetheless, continues Avicenna, differ in how they are related to one another. Some pleasures are for him of a higher order than others. In other words, not all pleasures are alike; some are more pleasant than others. To help us consider how to rank the various pleasures, Avicenna provides a list of criteria for measuring them (*Metaphysics*, IX.7, 348.15–18). These criteria are of two types: those that involve the pleasures associated with perfection, and those involving the pleasure itself.

Thus, in the first category one criterion is that the more complete and excellent the associated perfection, the more pleasant the related pleasure. So, for example, while a piece of bread may take the edge off the appetite of a starving teenager and so be judged a pleasure, a full pizza that sates both his or her stomach and pallet is more pleasurable. Second, the greater the number of associated perfections, the greater the pleasure; for instance, a dinner consisting of a single dish may be pleasant, but a banquet consisting of numerous delicacies is even more so. Third, the more enduring the associated perfection, the greater it is. Thus, while a short-lived fling may be pleasant, a long-lasting loving relation is certainly more so. Fourth, the more fully one reaches and is absorbed by the perfection, the more pleasant it is. So, an example might be like the differing degrees of pleasure one takes in two books, one being merely amusing, while the other is truly enthralling.[6] As for those criteria related to the pleasure itself rather than its correlative perfection, Avicenna begins with the perfection and excellence of a given action. So, for example, while one who is playing chess may take pleasure in winning, even if dishonestly, all things being equal it would be more pleasant to win fairly. Second, and finally, the more intensely a pleasure is perceived the more pleasurable it is, which seems to go without saying.

Armed with this set of criteria, Avicenna then undertakes a comparison between bodily pleasures in toto and the intellectual pleasure to be experienced in the afterlife (ibid., 350.8–351.6). He begins by describing what this state is like:

> The perfection proper to the rational soul is to become an intelligible universe.[7] [In other words] there is impressed into [the rational soul] the form of the cosmos, the cosmos' intelligible order, and the good emanated upon it starting from the Cause of the cosmos followed by the high ranking absolutely immaterial substances and then the immaterial substances associated with bodies through the celestial bodies, their configurations, and powers until the entire configuration of existence is completely contained within [the soul] itself (*Metaphysics*, IX.7, 350.8–11).

Inasmuch as this perfection takes in the whole of existence and particularly the cause of all existence, namely, the Necessary Existent or God, there could be no perfection that is more complete and excellent. In similar fashion, continues Avicenna, since the whole of existence is going to encompass all perfections, the number of perfections associated with intellectual pleasure is going to be greater. Also, the afterlife is everlasting, and so the duration of pleasure in our disembodied state is incomparable with the short-lived pleasures experienced during our bodily existence. As for being absorbed by the perfection, the intellect, its act, and its object all become one, whereas the superficial pleasures of the body involve contact and so involve some form of duality. Avicenna goes on and notes that since the intellect is the most perfect and excellent faculty of the human, the pleasures associated with it are going to be the most perfect and excellent ones as well. Finally, with respect to the intensity of intellectual pleasure, Avicenna provides a description of it that is simply replete with double entendre. "It will get a complete feel of the object of perception, stripping it totally of the accessories that are only accidentally included in its account, and then penetrating the very ins and outs of the object of perception" (ibid., 351.3–5). Under every criterion laid down for judging between pleasures, Avicenna assures us that intellectual pleasures come out on top. The only reason that we do not recognize intellectual pleasure here and now, or at best only get a hint of it, is because either our body impedes or distracts us from it, or we are steeped in vice and immoderation, which again is owing to our embodied state (ibid., 351.7–13).

Such a state of happiness, Avicenna reminds us, is reserved for those capable of intellectual and rational activity who have actively striven to understand God and God's creation as completely as they could. In contrast, he continues, hell and misery await those who, while capable of such intellectual activity, have chosen not to strive after such knowledge or have opposed such knowledge, either simply denying the existence of God and the order of the good outright, or dogmatically clinging to opinions that oppose the truth (ibid., 353.7–9). Again, recall that for Avicenna pain is a perception and attainment of a certain imperfection and evil. When these irreligious souls are separated from the body they will perceive that they do not have that perfection proper to humans as intellectual beings. Hence, they perceive in themselves an imperfection and lack of a proper good, but to perceive an imperfection and lack of a proper good is just for Avicenna to be in pain. For the damned, the pain will be directly proportional to the pleasure that the blessed experience. "That then is the misery and punishment with which a fire that tears [you] apart and a blistering cold that freezes [you to your] marrow pale in comparison" (ibid., 352.6–7).

As for the souls of simpletons and those who never understood what their proper perfection as humans is, Avicenna believes that if they have lived moderate lives, lives presumably following the dictates set down by the prophet, then the separation of their souls from their bodies will be relatively easy (ibid., 356.1–18). Since they have been habituated to set aside the passions of the body, Avicenna thinks that through God's mercy they will come to a state of comfort and rest, not feeling the intense pleasures of the truly blessed but also feeling no pain. As for those simple-minded souls who behaved viciously in this life and gave themselves over to excess and deficiency, they will find themselves still tied to bodily desires. Since they have no body to satisfy these desires, they will remain forever unfulfilled and so these souls will be pained in the hereafter.

Avicenna additionally suggests that what he has heard from certain other scholars might be true (ibid.), and if so it would allow for bodily pleasures and pains of a certain sort in the afterlife despite the separation of body and soul. The suggestion is that these separated souls may in some way be able to take celestial material as the subject of certain soul-activities that require a body like the activities of imagining and dreaming. The idea is that the simple-minded soul, vicariously using a celestial body, will imagine that it has a body, and, through such an imagined body, it will experience all the pleasures or torments that the individual learned about from the Qur'ān or other sacred scriptures. In other words, it would seem that Avicenna is imagining a Cartesian demonlike scenario, where there is produced in the souls of simpletons the phenomenal experiences of a physical heaven or hell replete with bodily pains or pleasures even though there are no extramental places corresponding with these experiences.

Providence and Evil

At *Metaphysics*, IX.6, Avicenna begins his account of divine providence (*'ināya*) with the observation that the Necessary Existent does not create the cosmos for our sake or, for that matter, for the sake of any created thing. The reason he gives for his position—the details of which he had provided earlier at *Metaphysics*, IX.3—is, in quite general terms, that when some agent acts for the sake of a given thing, x, then x stands to the agent as a final cause, which is a certain good that improves or completes the agent. Consequently, if the Necessary Existent were to create the cosmos for the sake of created things, then its creating the cosmos would make the Necessary Existent better or more complete than it would have been should it not have created. Of course, as Avicenna never grows weary of reminding us, there is no good proper to the Necessary Existent that it does not have of itself or essentially. Therefore, it can neither create the cosmos for the sake of, nor be concerned about, the created ordered (*Metaphysics*, IX.6, 339.4–6).

Still, Avicenna hastens to add, the obvious manifestations of order and design in both the heavens and here on Earth are clear indications of the presence of a divine providence. For providence, he tells us, is "the First [Cause's] knowing through itself that according to which the order of the good exists and that [the First] is essentially the cause of the good and perfection commensurate with possible [existence] and that [the First] consents to it in the way noted earlier" (ibid., 339.8–10).[8] In other words, in that the Necessary Existent wills itself, it wills the order of the good. In that we are part of that order, all that we need for our good and perfection is contained within the order of the good emanating from the Necessary Existent. Simply put, all created things are amply provided for by the Necessary Existent's emanative or creative act even though that act is not for the sake of anything other than the Necessary Existent itself.

Avicenna begins addressing the issue of the presence of evil in our world, and so its presence in the order of the good itself, by making a number of observations about evil. First, "evil" (*sharr*), he points out, is said in many ways (ibid., 339.13–40.17).[9] For instance, one refers to a deficiency or imperfection in a thing as an evil, such as ignorance or physical deformity. Such evil might be thought of as internal to the thing. Evil might also refer to something external to the thing, where the evil consists in one's being aware or perceiving either the presence or absence of a cause that inflicts the evil. Thus, for example, one who is freezing perceives the absence of a fire (or other suitable heat source) as an evil, while one trapped in a burning house perceives the presence of fire as an evil.

Second, following in a long line of Neoplatonic thinkers, Avicenna sees evil as having no positive existence or reality of its own. Instead, evil is properly an absence or privation of some good or existence. Third, and closely related to the last point, Avicenna adds that not just any privation or absence is an evil, but only a privation of some perfection required by the nature of the thing, where the perfections in question are grounded in the very species and nature of the thing (ibid., 340.11–12). Thus, there is nothing evil about the fact that a rock cannot see. Only in something of which sight is one of the perfections and goods of that kind of thing is the absence of sight and blindness an evil.

Fourth, and as a corollary of the last point, there is for Avicenna nothing that is simply absolute, pure evil; rather, like the notion of good, evil is always either relative to the kind of thing suffering the evil, or relative to some particular situation. In fact, to the extent that evil is understood as a privation of some good or perfection, and being or existence itself is a perfection or good, absolute privation could only refer to absolute nonexistence.

Consequently, since Avicenna's analysis of the Necessary Existent entails that it is not even possible that the Necessary Existent not exist, and so necessarily something must exist, absolute evil itself has to be impossible.

This point leads Avicenna to a fifth observation: Anything whose existence is at its ultimate perfection, and so has no potency in it, cannot be touched by evil. Now, as seen in chapter 7,[10] Avicenna believes that potency requires matter as its bearer or subject. Thus, none of the higher Intelligences can suffer any evil according to Avicenna, for they are wholly immaterial. Only the material things found in the sublunar realm can experience evil, and they suffer evil precisely because they are things that temporally come to be and change. In other words, things here in the sublunar world are not the sorts of things that come to be, fully realizing their proper perfection. Instead, they acquire their perfection through a process of change. Thus, evil, understood as a privation of some good or perfection proper to the kind, may befall temporally changing things precisely because of the kind of things that they are, namely, things that temporally come to be and possess a potentiality for some good or perfection.

Given Avicenna's third observation—namely that any particular evil is always relative to a certain kind and that evil is confined to natural kinds, namely, things that undergo change—Avicenna can go part of the way toward explaining why natural evil appears in the order of the good emanating from the Necessary Existent or God. (Natural evil, which also goes by the name "surd evil" is like, for example, a fire started by lightening. It is to be contrasted with an evil that is the result of willful agent, as, for example, the evil associated with a fire started by arson.) In the case of external, natural things that are apprehended as causes of evil, the explanation is fairly straightforward (ibid., 340.18–343.14). When something x causes some perceived harm in y or prevents y from receiving some good, x can be considered either in itself or relative to its effect on y.

When x is considered merely in itself or essentially as the kind of thing that it is, then its performing the functions characteristic of its kind is a good or perfection of x. So, for example, when fire burns, it is being a good instance of its kind. Likewise, when it rains or snows and a fire is put out, the water is being a good instance of its kind. That things should be good instances of their kinds in fact contributes to the order of the good. Therefore, natural things considered in themselves or essentially are not evil but good.

When, however, x is considered relative to y, and x either prevents y from obtaining some good or removes some good from y, then x is considered an evil relative to or accidentally to y. Thus, when someone is burned by a fire, the fire is perceived as a cause of evil relative to the one burned, for certainly if that same person were freezing the fire would be perceived as a good. Conversely, if rain were to prevent a freezing person from starting a fire, the impediment to and absence of the fire would be perceived as an evil. Inasmuch as x is considered relative to y, and relations are accidental, x's being a cause of some evil for y is accidental. In short, what Avicenna wants us to recognize is that none of the various things that make up the natural order is essentially a cause of evil or an evil cause. Considered in themselves and essentially, they are all good. Natural or surd evil resulting from external causes, then, is an accidental consequence of natural things performing their necessary and proper activities. Thus, it cannot be said that the Necessary Existent or God creates evil essentially or *per se*, but only as a necessary consequence of creating good.

As for the existence of the so-called internal evils, such as physical deformity, Avicenna returns to the principles of causation discussed in both his *Physics* and *Metaphysics* (ibid., 344.14–347.12). Again, there are two orders of causes for things that come to be temporally: one, the natural, accidental causes that prepare the material to receive a given species forms, as, for example, changing the qualities of hot/cold and wet/dry in a thing, and, two, a metaphysical, essential cause of that species form itself, namely, the Giver of Forms.

Now, as a matter of purely natural causation, two causal chains may intersect such that one interferes with another that is preparing the matter, and so adversely affect the matter such that it does not properly or completely receive the species form when it is bestowed. So, for example, Avicenna believes that within the mother's womb the mixture of male and female semen is warmed and so prepared for the reception of a given form. Moreover, if during this period the mother, as a result of a natural causal chain, came down with a fever, the excess heat could very well adversely affect fetal development. In that case, the naturally affected matter may not completely receive the species form. As a result the child would be deformed. Nothing is essentially the cause of the deformity; rather, it is only the accidental conjunction of two causal series that produced the evil. Again, one sees that the Necessary Existent or God does not create evil essentially or *per se*; rather, it results as a necessary consequence of its creating good.

Unfortunately, Avicenna says very little about moral evils, that is, willful acts of harm or evil. He does say, however, that such evils arise only when some individual has personally decided upon such a line of action (ibid., 341.17–342.3). The individual, however, has personally decided upon that line of action, not because he or she is a human or a soul, but because the individual has been habituated and has a moral temperament disposing him or her to desire some apparent good that is expected to result from that act. Such faulty judgment, as noted, results when the practical intellect does not overcome its state of being in matter but succumbs to the body's natural desires. Thus, insofar as the Necessary Existent is the ultimate cause for the existence of the human species, and it is not in virtue of being human that moral evils exist but owing to immoral personal decisions on the part of individual humans, the Necessary Existent is not for Avicenna the cause of moral evil. In this respect, then, it seems that Avicenna must adopt some form of compatibilism, for, as just noted, he believes that we are moral agents and we are responsible for our actions, and yet he also maintains that this moral responsibility can be reconciled with the type of causal determinism he endorses.

Still, one might complain that it is the very fact that the Necessary Existent created a world in which there exist things that can inflict and be subject to evil that there is any evil at all. Certainly it seems possible that God or the Necessary Existent could have created a world better than this one by creating a world free of evil. While Avicenna concedes that the Necessary Existent could have created a world free of evil, he denies that it would be a better world (ibid., 343.1–8). His argument for this conclusion is that no world like the present one, in which there are temporal, changing, physical things, can be free from the kind of accidental evils already mentioned. These again are the necessary results of there being things that exist in time, are material, and need to undergo change in order to perfect themselves.

As for why such species are subject to evil, when discussing Avicenna's conception of possibility, I noted that he adamantly denies that there can be a cause for why a given degree of privation along the chain of perfection or necessary existence should correspond with whatever species of possible existence that it does. In other words, there neither is nor can be a cause for why the members of certain species come to exist only after having not existed, and thus require matter for their coming to be. There is no cause for why these members do not eternally exist at their ultimate perfection, and thus must undergo change to realize their proper perfection. As a corollary, for Avicenna there simply can be no cause of the fact that certain species of possible existents are subject to evil, for that is just to ask what is the cause of their being subject to time, change, and the limitations of matter.

Consequently, since for Avicenna it is impossible for the species of individuals that make up the sublunar realm to exist without evil's existing, the Necessary Existent could create a world free of evil only if it created a world devoid of all the species subject to time, change, and the limitations of matter. While such a world would indeed have no evil in it, it would, Avicenna notes, also lack all the goods and perfections that only exist in temporally changing things. Now, if by a "better" world one means a world with a greater amount of good realized in a greater number of species, then, for Avicenna, a world in which evil can exist is, ironically, better than a world where it cannot. Thus, while as far as I can see Avicenna never commits himself to this world's being "the best of all possible worlds," it is better than a world in which evil is rendered impossible.

Again, in general Avicenna has little to say explicitly about issues in value theory. Still, I hope to have shown that it is also false to say he was not concerned at all with political and ethical issues. Instead, I believe, he saw himself as so integrating these issues into every aspect of his philosophical system that a volume or two explicitly dedicated to them was perhaps superfluous. Moreover, since much of his discussion related to political and ethical issues involves providing a theoretical framework for understanding and justifying Islamic religious practices, he may well have seen the Qur'ān and the traditions of the prophet Muḥammad as providing the practical application of his own ethical and political theories.

9

MEDICINE AND THE LIFE SCIENCES

Introduction

As well as being one of the greatest Muslim philosophers of the medieval period, Avicenna was also known as the "Prince of Physicians." His *Canon of Medicine* was the standard medical textbook in Europe well into the seventeenth century (and even beyond) and still remains a source of authority among groups of traditional healers in the Middle East. In outline, the work consists of five books, including a general discussion of the scientific background to medicine and anatomy, an account of the therapeutic properties of substances used in medicine, a book devoted to specific or localized ailments, and another book to more general diseases, such as fever, that affect the whole body, and finally a treatise on pharmacology. In general, Avicenna derives his system of medicine from that of the Graeco-Roman physician Galen (129–200 CE)—who himself took Hippocratic medicine as his starting point. Avicenna additionally augments his Greek medical and anatomical sources with developments made by physicians in Islamic lands, such as those of Abū Bakr ar-Rāzī (the Latin Rhazes; 865–925 or 932) and ʿAlī ibn al-ʿAbbās al-Majūsī (the Latin Haly Abbas; d. ca. 990). Still, when it comes to the philosophical underpinnings of medicine, Avicenna is more apt to defer to Aristotle than to the physicians themselves when there is disagreement.

While it is true that Avicenna's system of medicine in the main is derivative, namely, an amalgamation of Aristotle, Galen, and others, it would be wrong on that account to dismiss it as not being of historical, philosophical, and scientific interest and importance in its own right. First, Galen's own medical and philosophical corpus extends to twenty volumes in its modern edition, which itself does not include some treatises that are only extant in Arabic translation.[1] Consequently, given the extent of his writings, mastering Galen's corpus was a tedious and painstaking enterprise for the medieval physician. Moreover, since few physicians would be able to possess the complete Galenic opera, they were often without any practical reference work of medicine. Thus, Avicenna's comparatively short five-volume *Canon of Medicine* was a godsend for later physicians, whether as an introductory textbook for those just beginning to study the art of medicine or as a relatively concise and easily manageable handbook of the best medicine at the time for the seasoned doctor.

A second point of importance about Avicenna's medical writing is that when Galen himself was writing, the Neoplatonized Aristotelianism that would emerge in Alexandria as the dominant philosophical system during the Middle Ages in the Islamic world had not yet been developed. Indeed, Aristotelianism at Galen's time was in genuine competition with such philosophical schools as Skepticism, Stoicism, and Middle Platonism. Galen himself in fact preferred Stoic materialism as the underlying physics for his medical theory, a theory, one might add, that viewed the human soul as a subtle material substance and so was diametrically opposed to the immaterialist view that Avicenna espoused in his psychology. As a consequence, in Avicenna's day there was something of a scientific crisis at least for philosophers, for the best medicine of the time was based on a materialism that was at odds with what was believed to be the best physical and psychological theories of the time. It is thus no wonder that a continuing theme in Avicenna's medical writing was to retain as much of Galen's humoral medical theory as was possible, while protecting Avicenna's own preferred doctrine of an immaterial human intellect from Galenic subversion.[2]

A third important aspect of Avicenna's medical theory, which is closely related to the last point, becomes obvious to anyone who reads Avicenna's *Canon*, for one cannot but be impressed with how well-integrated Avicennan medicine is within the overall scientific and philosophical system that he developed. Time and time again, Avicenna easily resolves thorny technical issues in medicine simply by referring the reader to his philosophical discussions in his works on physics, biology, and even metaphysics. The importance, then, of the *Canon*, and indeed Avicenna's medical writings more generally, is that it formed an integral part of a medieval worldview that incorporated and explained virtually every area of human intellectual pursuit.

In the next few sections, I consider, first, where Avicenna envisions medicine within his general classification of the sciences. Next, I present the general principles of the humoral medicine that Avicenna adopts, and then discuss Avicenna's views about health and the causes of disease or malady more generally. I conclude by considering a concrete issue of a medical-philosophical nature treated in Avicenna's writings, namely, a problem associated with embryonic development and specifically whether it occurs gradually, as observation seems to suggest, or in stages, as theory seems to dictate. This problem was itself entwined with another: the ancient and medieval medical debate over the status of female semen—namely, the issue of what the female contributes to the physical makeup of the offspring.

The Classification of Medicine
as a Science

In chapter 1[3] I considered the ancient and medieval course curriculum that Avicenna would have inherited from his Greek predecessors. While this course curriculum—which at least for the natural sciences closely paralleled the physical writings of Aristotle—initially provided merely a pedagogical classification of the sciences, later thinkers viewed it as pointing to a much deeper reality. Not only was the course curriculum of Aristotle's texts viewed as a classification of all the sciences, but also that classification was more importantly thought to represent the very structure of the cosmos itself.[4] So, for example, it was thought that the sciences are divided into those whose purpose is to produce some action (the so-called practical sciences) and those whose goal is knowledge for knowledge's sake without regard for action (the so-called theoretical sciences); such a division would seem to cut reality at its joints. Similarly, it was thought that there could be only three basic kinds of theoretical sciences—physics, mathematics, and metaphysics—precisely because beings or existents came either as immaterial (the purported subject of metaphysics at least in the later Hellenistic period) or as material, where the material ones can be further considered either independently of their material conditions (the objects of mathematics) or they cannot be so considered (the objects of physics or natural philosophy); again, an apparently clean and exhaustive division of what exists. Of course, under these theoretical sciences there are also further subaltern sciences as they were termed. So, for example, psychology, which treats the subclass of living physical things falls under physics, and under psychology there is zoology, which treats the subclass of living things that are animals (as opposed to plants).

The science of medicine presents a unique problem: While it is clearly concerned with action, namely, the production of health and the curing of disease, and so one might think of it as a practical science, it just as obviously has a strong theoretical aspect that seems suited to its being one of the subaltern sciences falling under a physical science such as biology.

It is certainly to Avicenna's credit that instead of turning a blind eye to the classification of medicine, and indeed its ontological status, he attempted to fit it into his overall scientific schema. At the opening of his *Canon*, Avicenna defines medicine as "the science from which one comes to recognize the states of the human body on the part of health and the loss thereof in order to preserve the health as something realized as well as recovering it when lost" (*Canon*, "Volume One," I.1.i, 29.6–7). As such, medicine is for Avicenna one of the mixed sciences—like, for example, engineering, which mixes both the science of geometry and the art of building—and thus medicine has both a theoretical and practical component.

As for medicine's practical element, Avicenna does not, in fact, identify it with the actual treatment of the patient; rather, it is "the division of the science of medicine in which the training provides an opinion (*ra'y*), where that opinion is associated with an explanation of how to treat [the patient]" (ibid., I.1.i, 29.9–20). In other words, Avicenna sees medicine inasmuch as it is a practical science as involving the construction of practical syllogisms that lead to opinion and not certainty or necessary knowledge. Still, such syllogisms must rest on certain theoretical definitions, propositions, and the like, and it is medicine's theoretical division that provides at least some of these starting points.

Avicenna identifies medicine's theoretical component with one of the subsidiary branches (*far'ī*) of the science of physics ("On the Divisions of the Theoretical Science," 87–88). Other such subsidiary physical sciences include astrology, physiognomy, dream interpretation, talisman making, the art of incantations, and alchemy. While today we might find the inclusion of medicine alongside of so many pseudosciences odd, if not outright belittling, it is important to note that Avicenna would not have viewed any of the aforementioned sciences as necessarily pseudosciences. Take astrology, for example.[5] Avicenna believed that the movements and position of the heavens (the subject of the science of astronomy), directly affect the elemental composition and temperamental makeup of things in the sublunar realm, a position articulated as early as Aristotle and held by virtually every philosopher in the ancient and medieval world up to and through the time of Avicenna. Moreover, inasmuch as the heavenly motions purportedly influence one's temperamental makeup, they would also determine one's overall psychological disposition, which in its turn affects the choices that one makes and ways one acts. In short, according to Avicenna's own view of physics and psychology, and indeed the best science at the time, the motions of the heavens do influence our life and actions. Consequently, Avicenna could and did happily accept that in principle there could be a science of astrology that is a subsidiary of physics; however, he also adds the caveat that in practice there is no such science, at least not in the proper sense of "science" as Avicenna understood it.

His reason for this caveat is that the notion of science that he adopts essentially involves having necessary knowledge. In the case of astrology, there simply are too many factors and precision calculations that need to be made in order to attain the required necessity. Consequently, for Avicenna, the astrologer can at best have only probable and approximate knowledge, which, to Avicenna's mind, would not have been science properly speaking. It is probably for the same reason that Avicenna relegated medicine to a subsidiary science of physics; for since so many factors come to play in human health (let alone the specific factors of any given individual), at best all the physician can hope to achieve is probability and approximation. Still, in principle medicine could impart necessary knowledge, even if not in practice, and consequently for Avicenna it is one of the branches of theoretical physics.

Inasmuch as medicine is for Avicenna a subsidiary science falling under physics, it merely posits and does not attempt to prove those scientific propositions demonstrated in the sciences that stand above it. In fact, Avicenna chastises physicians such as Galen and others, with their materialist basis for medicine, who dabbled in higher natural sciences and yet were unqualified to do so. Thus, maintains Avicenna, the physician must simply take as first principles the number and nature of the elements, what the most basic natural causes are, and the like. Still, it is up to the doctor to determine and investigate all the claims proper to medicine itself, such as what health and disease are; to identify the various so-called humors and vital spirits or *pneumas*; to determine the kinds of diseases and their nature; and so on. In the next sections I shall consider some of these points in more detail.

The Theoretical Basis of Medicine

Since theoretical medicine is a science for Avicenna, and all sciences aim to uncover the underlying causes of their proper subject, medicine seeks to understand the causes of health and disease (*Canon*, "Volume One," I.1.ii, 30–32). Moreover, since medicine is a physical science, the physician seeks the same causes as those sought by the natural philosopher, namely, the material, efficient, formal, and final causes, and particularly for medicine, those that are conducive to health or disease. The most immediate material causes are the human body and the various organs and *pneumas* or vital spirits that make it up; next are the humors, which I shall discuss shortly; and then ultimately the elements. The formal causes that medicine seeks are bodily temperaments (*mizāj*), powers or faculties (*qūwa*) of the body, and bodily structures or compositions (*tarkīb*). Efficient causes in medicine are anything that produces changes in or preserves the states of the human body, which can range from food and drink, to sleep or lack thereof, climate, place of residence, and the like. Finally, the final cause of medicine is to recognize the actions, the powers or faculties required for those actions, and the *pneumas* or vital spirits that harbor those powers. The physician additionally posits as first principles, albeit ones demonstrated in higher physical sciences, that elements, temperaments, humors, powers or faculties, and *pneumas* exist as well as what their numbers are, and perhaps where they are localized. In the rest of this section, I shall consider these principles individually in more detail.

As for the elements (sing. *rukn*), I have noted that following a long tradition Avicenna recognizes four: earth, water, air, and fire (ibid., I.2, 33–34). Avicenna, again following Aristotle, likewise associated with each element two primary qualities, one of which is active, the other passive, namely, hot/cold (active qualities) and wet/dry (passive qualities). In general, hot was thought to diffuse and separate, while cold draws things together, whereas the quality of wetness is what receives impressions, while dry preserves impressions. Through natural causal interactions, including the motion of heavenly bodies, these four simple elements mix together in varying proportions that give rise to composite bodies of various temperaments (or mixtures).

Temperaments (sing. *mizāj*)—again the mixtures of varying proportions of the four elements and their accompanying qualities—can either be well balanced, such that the various primary qualities nearly balance each other off, or not well balanced (ibid., I.3.i, 35–40). From among all the various natural kinds, maintains Avicenna, the temperament associated with the human species is the closest one to a near perfect balance. By this, Avicenna does not mean that the human temperament in a fully developed human is some homogeneous state throughout (even if it initially started out as a homogeneous mix). In fact, as Avicenna will claim, the various organs that make up the fully developed human body are of very different temperaments, as, for example, the brain is predominately cool, while the heart is hot, the liver wet, and bones dry (ibid., I.3.ii, 41–42). Also, some of the various humors are hotter and others cooler, some drier while others wetter. Thus, when Avicenna speaks of the human temperament as being the most well balanced, he means that in the fully developed human the quite different qualities of all of these organs, humors, and the like average each other out as it were.

Additionally, he notes that a natural kind's temperament should not be imagined as some exact point on a scale; rather, the temperament associated with a certain natural kind involves a fixed range of hot/cold and wet/dry combinations that are conducive to that natural kind and only beyond which that temperament and its associated kind cease. Within this range, which Avicenna seems to envision as a continuum, there is a potentially infinite number of varieties, and Avicenna warns the physician that, "he must recognize that each individual [human] requires a temperament proper and unique to him or her that no one [else] can have in common" (ibid., I.3.i, 37.23–24). This is probably one of the reasons why Avicenna feels that medicine can only lead to opinion rather than certainty, for it can only provide knowledge of what generally holds for the range of temperaments associated with being the kind human rather than the individual and exact temperament of a particular patient.

The individual temperaments come to be when the male and so-called female semen (we would now think of it in terms of an ovum) come together, where the various qualities associated with the individual temperament might be affected by such factors as the initial qualities of the individual parents' semen, the temperature of the womb and menstrual blood, which now becomes nutriment for the embryo, even the qualities produced by the motion of the heavens at the time that the two semen mix. In very general terms, Avicenna likens the initial stages of embryonic development to that of cheese making (ibid., I.5.ii, 63.11–64.11). The semen first begins churning until it gives rise to a drop of blood. That blood then clots forming what might be thought of as the zygote. From that blood clot there then comes to be the heart, which Avicenna, following Aristotle in opposition to Galen, identifies with the primary organ.

After the initial blood forms in the heart, continues Avicenna, there is the differentiation of the remaining humors, followed by the organs, and then the rest of the limbs, and the vital spirits or *pneumas*, all differing with respect to their particular temperaments. In all, Avicenna, following the accepted medical tradition, recognizes four humors (sing. *khilt*): blood, phlegm, yellow bile, and so-called black bile (ibid., I.4.i, 47–53). Like the elements from which they ultimately derive, the humors too are typified by the predominance of the two sets of primary active and passive qualities. Thus, as already noted, blood, the first humor formed, is hot and wet. Phlegm, which Avicenna considered to be imperfectly matured blood, is prominently a cold/wet mixture. Yellow bile is of a hot/dry temperament and is formed from the froth or foam of the blood as it is heated in the heart, while cold and dry characterize black bile, which Avicenna identifies with the sediment of normal blood.

Once there are the various humors, the organs and vital spirits or *pneumas* come to be (ibid., I.3–4, 35-57; "Cures of the Heart," §§ 1–2, 172–175). In general, Avicenna thinks that all of the humors consist of both finer attenuated parts, which are associated with hot and dry qualities inherent in the various humors, and those cold/dry parts that are coarser and "earthy." The coarser parts become differentiated into the various bodily organs, while the finer portions become the vital spirits that animate those organs. So, for example, the heart was believed to be a hot/dry organ, and, indeed, the ultimate source of all the innate heat in the body, and so it is the ultimate source of the *pneumas*. The liver is of a hot/wet temperament, and as such it is that from which all the remaining organs originate. The brain is a cold/wet organ in which the external and internal senses are arrayed as I have already explained in chapter 4. The nerves, which are the conduits of the vital spirits or *pneumas*, are cold and dry in makeup. The remaining organs, tissues, muscles, ligaments, skin, bone, hair, and the rest are as well all formed from those mixtures or combinations of the primary qualities proper to each specific one.

Vital spirits or *pneumas* (sing. *rūḥ*) function in ancient and medieval medicine much in the way that neural firings operate in modern physiology, whether it be transferring information from the sense organs to the brain, bringing about muscle movement, or the like. According to Avicenna, just like the heart is the first organ from which all the other organs ultimately spring (albeit through the intermediacy of the liver), there is initially one (primary) *pneuma* that is the origin of three further types of *pneumas*: the vegetative, reproductive, and animal spirits. In more detail, Avicenna believes that vital spirit or *pneuma* has its initial origin in the heart, and then from the heart it is dispersed to the liver, where it takes on a hepatic temperament and so can perform the vegetative functions of self-nourishment and growth; to the generative organs, where it acquires their temperament in order to perform the actions required for reproduction; or to the brain, where it is cooled and moistened, allowing it to bring about those activities proper to animals, namely, sensation and motion.

Hopefully the foregoing provides a very general background to the underlying theory of Avicennan medicine and the technical tools at the disposal of its practitioner.

Health and Malady

I have already noted that for Avicenna "medicine is the science from which one comes to recognize the states of the human body *on the part of health* and the loss thereof in order to preserve the health as something realized as well as recovering it when lost" (*Canon*, "Volume One," I.1.i, 29.6–7, my emphasis). Thus, now I should consider how Avicenna understands health (*ṣiḥḥa*) and, its opposite, malady (*maraḍ*). "Health," Avicenna says mimicking Galen, "is the disposition of the human body with respect to its temperament and structure such that all of [its] actions [or functions; Ar. *afʿāl*] proceed from it in a sound and unimpaired way," (ibid., II.1.ii, 142.10–11). Malady, in contrast, is the unnatural state or disposition opposite of health that "essentially impairs [the human body's] action [or function] necessarily and primarily, whether it be an unnatural temperament or unnatural structure [or composition]" (ibid., II.1.i, 141.8–9).

While there is in effect only one way to be healthy, namely, to be functioning naturally and properly, there are several ways, observes Avicenna, in which one's actions or functions can be impaired such that one is said to have a malady (ibid., II.1.ii, 142–143). In very general terms, however, Avicenna classifies maladies as either simple or composite, where a malady is simple just in case only a single temperament or structure is impaired, while it is composite when two or more such impairments come together to give rise to a single condition, which Avicenna seems to associate most commonly with swellings or tumors (*waram*). The simple maladies Avicenna divides further into three kinds: disorders of the temperaments, which run to some sixteen different sorts; disorders of structure or composition, such as deformities, obesity, additional fingers, and such; and finally, injuries, such as cuts, broken bones, or, in general, some loss of continuity in the organs, limbs, tissues, and such.

Drawing heavily upon Galen's etiology and causal language, Avicenna introduces three causes of health and malady broadly construed: antecedent causes, external causes (Gk. *prokatarktic*, Ar. *bādiya*), and internal, or connected, causes (Gk. *proegoumenic*, Ar. *wāṣila*). Of these three Avicenna has the following to say:

> Antecedent and internal [causes] are alike in that they are both corporeal factors (I mean, either humoral, temperamental, or structural), whereas the external causes are factors outside of the substance of the body, whether due to outside bodies—for example, what comes from blows, heating the ambient air, or taking in hot or cold foods—or from the soul (for the soul is something else other than the body)—for example, what comes from anger, fear, and the like. The antecedent and external causes are alike in that sometimes there is some intermediary between them and the states [of health and malady], whereas the external and internal causes are alike in that sometimes there is not an intermediary between them and the aforementioned state. The antecedent causes are distinct from the internal causes in that the state does not immediately follow upon the antecedent causes, but instead between the two there are other causes closer to the state than the antecedent [causes]. The antecedent causes are distinct from the external [causes] in that they are bodily. Moreover, between the antecedent causes and the state [of health or malady] there inevitably is an intermediary, while that is not necessarily the case with respect to external causes. There is absolutely no intermediary

between the internal causes and the state, whereas that is not necessarily the case with respect to the external causes and in fact both are possible with respect to them. The antecedent causes are corporeal causes (I mean, humoral, or temperamental, or structural) necessitating the state in a non-primary way, I mean, they necessitate it through an intermediary. The internal causes are [also] corporeal causes that necessitate certain bodily states in a primary way, that is, without an intermediary. The external causes are non-corporeal causes that necessitate corporeal states in a primary as well as non-primary way (*Canon*, "Volume One," II.2.i, 152.8–153.4).[6]

Avicenna then concludes his general comments on the causes of health and malady by identifying the six most important ones that the patient should consider in preserving his or her health, or the physician must take into account in returning the patient to a state of health. These are (1) the ambient air, (2) the food and drink one takes in, (3) proper physical activity (*ḥaraka*) and rest, (4) psychological activities, (5) getting enough sleep as well as not sleeping too much, and finally (6) evacuation and retention.

These last six factors are what later Galenists would term the "non naturals," all of which affect a human's temperament by moderating or altering in some way the primary qualities of hot, cold, wet, and dry. Thus, when one breathes in air, it cools the humors in the heart, and consequently, if the ambient air is excessively cold or hot, it may reduce the natural hot quality of the vital spirits too much or not enough. Moreover, the air might be excessively moist and dry, thus affecting one's temperamental balance.

Physical activity or resting from physical activity clearly increases the vital heat that is the hallmark of life, but, ironically, this same vital heat breaks down the body and ultimately leads to its corruption, making an adequate amount of rest, which ultimately cools the body, also necessary. Sleep and wakefulness, which closely resemble rest and physical activity, also affect the body's level of hot or cold: sleep cooling the body, wakefulness heating it.

Psychological activity can also influence one's temperament, argues Avicenna, particularly when the psychological activity involves remembering some past incidence or imaging some future one, especially when these mental images precipitate some emotional state. Thus, one might remember some particularly embarrassing or acrimonious event in one's life and feel flushed or hot under the collar, or imagine some frightening scenario such that one's "blood runs cold."

Food and drink, Avicenna observes, might have some initial effect when they are first taken in while having an opposite (or at least a different) effect once fully digested. So, for example, wine, inasmuch as it is a liquid, initially cools one who drinks it, but once it becomes digested it actually heats the blood, at least according the pharmacological theory at Avicenna's time. Finally, proper retention followed by evacuation ensures that food and drugs that are ingested remain in the body long enough to be fully and properly digested so that the aliment can perform its function as well as seeing that waste material does not adversely affect the flow of the humors and functioning of the organs.

In general, today we do not recognize the underlying causal explanations that ancient and medieval physicians associated with the various necessary factors or causes of health and disease. Despite that, one can still appreciate the overall goal (and frequently the efficacy) of these factors or causes in maintaining health. Indeed, living in a healthy climate, getting proper amounts of sleep, accompanied by a regimen of exercise and a well-balanced diet, as well as positive thinking and the like, are considered even today (or at least by my doctor) some of the most important factors in a healthy and well-balanced life.

Between Physics and Medicine: The Case of Embryonic Development

When discussing the classification of medicine as a science, I noted that it was one of the subsidiary sciences falling under physics. As such, medicine for Avicenna needs merely to posit those claims demonstrated in a higher physical science without trying to prove them or suggesting alternative principles. The question thus arises, "What should the physician do when medical or anatomical observation contravenes physical theory?" This was a serious issue, and all the more so since the undisputed authority in medicine, Galen, in places explicitly challenged Aristotle, the undisputed authority of physics (at least within the *falsafa* tradition in which Avicenna was firmly rooted).

So, for example, Aristotle in his biological works had argued that the heart is the primary organ in that it is first formed and is the ultimate source and origin of the undifferentiated blood from which the remaining primary organs—the liver and brain—and humors emerge. In stark contrast,

Galen maintained that there is, in fact, no organ that is primary and first in a hierarchy; rather, the heart, liver, and brain are all on equal footing. Moreover, Galen contended that the liver, not the heart as Aristotle claimed, is the source of blood.

While Avicenna ultimately sides with Aristotle, it is not because of a blind appeal to authority, but owing to a reasoned appeal to both theory and observation. Thus, he first presents Galen's position and the theoretical justification Galen gave for it, and shows how based upon theory the Galenic account is not necessary. Having shown that Galen's position is not theoretically necessary, Avicenna simply defers to the "accomplished anatomists" (aṣḥāb at-tashrīḥ al-muḥaṣṣilūn) who observe that in embryonic development "the heart is the first thing generated" (Book of Animals, III.1, 44.12–13).

Avicenna's appeal to embryonic development ironically produces philosophical difficulties for him later; for, in chapter 3, I noted that for Avicenna substantial changes do not occur gradually, but rather happen all at once.[7] Now when one considers the case of embryonic development, there is initially the semen (male and female for Avicenna), which, while potentially human, is not in fact substantially human. Consequently, when the human does come to be from the semen, there is a case of substantial change; however, on the basis of anatomical observation, it would seem that this transformation is gradual. Avicenna himself sets the empirical case against his position: "Since it is seen that the semen develops into an animal gradually and that the seed develops into a plant gradually, it is imagined on account of these [observations] that there is motion [that is, there is gradual substantial change]" (Physics, II.3, 101.1).

For Avicenna, just as Galen's purely theoretical criticism of the primacy of the heart was not alone sufficient to undermine Aristotle's anatomical observations, neither can a naïve empiricism trump one's best scientific theory. Instead, before observation can convict a theory, maintains Avicenna, one must carefully examine, test, and analyze the data. One must investigate whether there are any factors not immediately perceptible that might be contributing to the observation. In short, one must approach the observations as a scientist and not merely as a layperson. Consequently, if the observation of the apparently gradual transformation of semen into an animal truly is to count against Avicenna's thesis concerning substantial change, then this observation must be confirmed by the science of embryology.

Since Avicenna was not only an outstanding philosopher but also an accomplished physician and biologist, it should come as no surprise that in his major biological work, *The Book of Animals (Kitāb al-Ḥayawān)*, he dedicates an entire section (IX.5) to embryology.[8] The proper account of embryonic development, claims Avicenna, is one of punctuated equilibrium. Once the observations about the semen's development have been properly and scientifically scrutinized, Avicenna argues that they actually confirm rather than falsify his thesis about substantial change. This claim is subsequently borne out in *The Book of Animals*:

> Concerning an analysis of the alterations of the matter of the fetus (*janīn*) up to its completion, the first state is the churning (*zabadīya*) of the semen, which is the actuality of the formal power. The next state is the manifestation of the drop of blood in the uterine wall [or endometrium], and its continued dilation in the uterine wall. The third state is the alteration of the semen into a blood clot and after [this alteration], its alteration into the embryo (*muḍgha*).[9] Afterwards is its alteration leading to the generation of the heart and primary organs, as well as its blood vessels, which is followed by the generation of the extremities [or limbs]. For each alteration, or two together, there is a period of time where [the developing thing] remains at rest in [that state] (*The Book of Animals*, IX.5, 172.3–8).

Although it would be difficult to map Avicenna's descriptive account of embryonic development point for point against our current knowledge of it, his observations do roughly approximate what modern embryologists now believe, especially if one limits oneself to naked-eye observations. So, setting aside the details, what is significant for the present purpose is the stages of the development that Avicenna observes. First, there is the initial substance, the semen (*minā*), which remains for a while, and then all at once a new substance appears, namely, the blood clot (perhaps like our notion of a zygote). Similarly again, after a while the blood clot or zygote is replaced by a new substance that comes to be all at once, in this case, the embryo. This state is followed by the generation of the various organs and limbs. Finally, the perfected animal itself comes to be, which is yet a different substance. The change from semen to animal, thus, according to Avicenna, takes place through a series of discrete substantial changes, not a continuously gradual process.

Unfortunately, Avicenna's language in this passage can be misleading. He speaks of "alteration" (*istiḥāla*), which is the standard Arabic term for change with respect to quality, and thus implies gradual change. Indeed, as I shall point out later, Avicenna does believe that during each state there are a number of gradual (natural) qualitative changes; nevertheless, the transformation from state to state is not gradual, but punctuated. Later in *The Book of Animals* he states explicitly that the transformation from state to state involves discrete "leaps," which I shall also discuss more fully shortly.

The passage where he clarifies this point is made within the context of addressing another hotly debated question in the ancient and medieval world: "Do females produce an equivalent to male semen, and if so, what role does female semen play in procreation?" Aristotle had argued that the female's role in procreation was wholly passive. The female according to Aristotle merely provides the matter for procreation, namely, the nutritive menstrual blood, which is tantamount to saying that the female makes no active contribution to the makeup of the offspring. Avicenna in opposition to Aristotle follows Galen, albeit with certain important modifications, and maintains that females do produce semen. (It should be noted that Avicenna's agreement with Galen was facilitated by the fact that Avicenna drew upon the pseudonymous book X of Aristotle's *History of Animals* in which there is mention of female semen.)

According to Avicenna, then, females do produce something akin to semen; however, he continues, the female semen does not possess a generative power in the way that male semen does. Instead, it possesses a power by which it affects the menstrual blood's receptivity to the formative power of the male semen. The female semen imparts to the matter, that is, the menstrual blood, varying degrees of determinateness, which the male semen in turn structures or organizes, and so gives an even greater degree of determinateness. The stronger the female semen's influence is on the matter, however, the greater is the degree of the matter's determinateness. Under such conditions, the male semen has less of an opportunity to structure or organize the matter, and, vice versa, when the power of the female semen is lesser, the male semen has more of an opportunity.

Let me suggest an example that, although not found in Avicenna, hopefully will clarify his point. Clay is receptive to a number of different shapes or forms that the craftsman can impose upon it; however, if the clay is exposed to the Sun, then, to the degree that the Sun affects the clay and so hardens it, the clay becomes less pliable and so becomes less receptive to the number of forms that the craftsman can impose upon it. In our example, the clay would correspond with the menstrual blood or matter; the craftsman and the forms he or she imposes upon the clay correspond with the male semen and its formative power; and the Sun's power to dry clay corresponds with the female semen's power to affect or determine the menstrual blood. It should be noted that the Sun does not actively structure or impose form upon the clay, although it does positively affect the clay. Similarly, for Avicenna, neither does the female semen actively inform or structure the menstrual blood, although it does actively affect it.

This lengthy prelude is necessary to understand Avicenna's next point, which is directly relevant to the issue of whether embryonic development involves discrete, nongradual transformations as Avicenna's own physical theory requires. Here, Avicenna is concerned with the interplay of the male and female semen on the matter and particularly the various stages where the matter either resists or is inclined toward the structuring or organizing of the male semen's formative power.

> These individual resistances and inclinations [of the matter] are not unmixed [that is, they are not gradual], but are punctuated (*ikhtilājīya*, literally "jerky"), as if each one of them were composed of motions; however, they are completed only together with a number of convulsions [or jerks]. Indeed, it is perceived that after each group of convulsions there is a certain [period of] rest (*The Book of Animals*, 176.17–19).

Avicenna's point here is that the matter undergoes several stages of preparation such that it comes to be in varying degrees of receptivity to a form. These are in fact the natural (as opposed to metaphysical) qualitative changes that I have noted in previous chapters. The transformation from one stage to the next, however, does not according to Avicenna occur gradually but in discrete or punctuated leaps (*ikhtilājāt*). In fact, although Avicenna does not mention it here, he is anticipating the metaphysical changes that occur through the emanation of the Giver of Forms once the matter has been properly prepared to receive a new substantial form.

Indeed, this reading is confirmed if one returns to the passage in the *Physics* where Avicenna first considered the purported empirical refutation of his theory of nongradual substantial change.

> What one must know is that up to the point that the semen develops into an animal, other developments happen to it and between [these other developments] there are continuous alterations with respect to quality and quantity. Thus, the semen continues to be altered gradually, though it remains semen up to the point that the seminal form is displaced and

it becomes a blood clot. [The blood clot's] state up to the point that it is altered into an embryo is the same, and after it bones, a nervous system, veins, and other things that we shall not mention [come to be]. [The development continues] like this up to the point that [the developing thing] receives the form of life. Thereupon, it is altered and changed like this [that is, in stages] until it becomes viable and then is separated [from the parent]. Someone perceiving the transformation, however, imagines that this is a single process from one substantial form to another substantial form, and from that supposes that there is a motion with respect to the substance. That is not the case, and instead there are many motions and rests (*Physics*, II.3, 101.2–7).

At each stage in embryonic development there are for Avicenna numerous accidental changes that only occur gradually. For instance, there may be changes in the bulk or shape of the substance. Similarly, there may be changes in the hotness, coolness, and dryness, or wetness of the substance. All of these changes, as has been noted, prepare or ready the matter of the currently existing substance. Once a sufficient number of gradual accidental changes have occurred in the matter, the matter is capable of receiving a new substantial form all at once as an emanation from the Giver of Forms. The stages continue in this stepwise fashion until the developing thing receives its ultimate substantial form. Thus, far from undermining Avicenna's philosophical thesis, the development of the embryo, when carefully examined and understood in its proper scientific context, actually supports it.

While the above does not even scratch the surface of Avicenna's medical and biological works, hopefully it provides one with a very general framework for thinking about how Avicenna envisions medicine and its relation to the life sciences specifically and physics more generally, as well as giving one a sense of how Avicenna juggled the needs for empirical adequacy and theoretical consistency in the sciences.

THE AVICENNAN HERITAGE

Introduction

It would be difficult to overestimate the impact of Avicenna's system of thought on the subsequent history and development of philosophy in both the East and the West. Avicenna, in an intellectual *tour de force*, combined the Neoplatonizing tendencies favored by al-Kindī and his circle with the Aristotelianism of al-Fārābī and the Baghdad Peripatetics in a way that infused philosophy with new life, saving it from the intellectual pedantry from which it was becoming moribund. Additionally, Avicenna saw to it that his system accommodated, if not even explained, many of the primary religious phenomena and concerns of the Islamic society in which he lived, ensuring that his thought remained an influence (both as a source of inspiration and target of criticism) for Muslim scholars in multiple intellectual spheres even to this day. Moreover, it is not too much of an exaggeration to say that Avicenna's synthesis of Graeco-Arabic philosophy, with concerns central to all three of the Abrahamic religions, helped facilitate and prepare Latin Europe for the reintroduction of the Aristotelian scientific tradition. As such, Avicenna's thought played an important role in the reinvigoration of philosophy in Europe, as well as the formulation of Christian theology by such notaries as Thomas Aquinas and others. In the next few pages, I want, ever so briefly, to consider some of the more notable instances of

Avicenna's influence both on Judeo-Islamic philosophical theology and Christian scholasticism.

Avicenna's Heritage in the Judeo-Islamic World

If the ability to incite careful and intense analysis and criticism is one of the signs of the significance and substance of an idea, the animate discussions that Avicenna produced throughout all levels of Muslim intellectual life in the generations immediately following him is ample testimony to his importance. Legally conservative Ḥanbalites felt the need to renounce him; aspiring new philosophers could only make a name for themselves if they first could show elements wanting within his system; Muslim theologians were at odds with whether to embrace or excommunicate him; but whoever you were, you read Avicenna. While a full and complete study of Avicenna's influence on the subsequent development of philosophy done in Islamic lands has yet to be written—and consequently much of my ensuing discussion is of necessity impressionistic—there can simply be no doubt that his influence was extensive.[1] In order to provide at least some taste of that pervasiveness, I focus in this section on three later thinkers active in the Muslim and Jewish medieval world—al-Ghazālī, as-Suhrawardī, and Moses Maimonides—whose own thought Avicenna influenced in various ways. In the next section I shall consider Avicenna's influence in the Christian West.

While numerous Muslim theologians wrote "refutations" of key points of Avicenna's philosophy, perhaps none is better known, certainly not in the West, than that of the Ash'arite theologian and mystic Abū Ḥāmid al-Ghazālī (1058–1111) and his *The Incoherence of the Philosophers* (*Tahāfut al-falāsifa*). What is less well known is that before writing the *Incoherence*, al-Ghazālī felt compelled to establish his philosophical credentials, which he did by writing *The Intentions of the Philosophers* (*Maqāṣid al-falāsifa*). *The Intentions*, far from being an original work by al-Ghazālī, turns out to be an Arabic translation of Avicenna's own Persian *Book of Science for 'Alā' ad-Dawla*.[2] The importance of this point is that already by the time of al-Ghazālī, those active within the *madrasa*s, or religious "colleges" in the medieval Islamic world were frequently identifying Avicenna's philosophical system with philosophy plain and simple: To understand Avicenna was to understand philosophy. In fact, it is not impossible that al-Ghazālī wrote the *Incoherence* because he feared that Avicenna's system might come to supplant Ashʿarī's synthesis as the dominant philosophico-theological interpretation of Islam.

Whatever the reason, al-Ghazālī clearly perceived certain Avicennan doctrines as a threat. Thus, in the *Incoherence*, he presents twenty philosophical theses that, argues al-Ghazālī, the philosophers falsely claim to have demonstrated when they have not. Of these twenty theses, however, he finds only three truly heretical: the assertion of the eternity of the world, the denial that God knows particular, changing, and temporally bound things (as, for example, your reading this sentence right now), and the rejection of a bodily resurrection. Interestingly, as noted, Avicenna goes to some pains in the *Cure* to explain how there might be at least something akin to a bodily resurrection; and his view about God's knowledge of particulars shares many features in common with al-Ghazālī's own position (even if there is a significant difference of emphasis). Thus, the real disagreement between Avicenna and al-Ghazālī(or at least those issues for which the latter reserves the most bile) comes over the question of the world's past eternity: Avicenna holding that the cosmos' existence must extend infinitely into the past, while al-Ghazālī maintaining that there must be a first moment of creation in the finite past.

As for the theses beyond these three, al-Ghazālī can often be quite forgiving if not even conciliatory. So, for instance, al-Ghazālī happily accepts most of what Avicenna's has to say about the nature of the soul; he merely denies that Avicenna and others have demonstrated that the human soul is immortal. Here, as with other theses, al-Ghazālī is not so insistent on rejecting Avicenna's conclusions as he is on rejecting the idea that there is no need for revelation to establish those conclusions. In fact, there is a growing body of scholarship that strongly suggests that al-Ghazālī drew more heavily upon the philosophical system of Avicenna than he may have been willing to confess.[3] Instead of taking Avicennan ideas over unconditionally, however, al-Ghazālī significantly modified them to meet the needs of his own interpretation of Islam. Such modifications frequently took the form of the obvious removal of those Avicennan doctrines that were clearly irreconcilable with a more traditional interpretation of Islam, such as Avicenna's denial that the cosmos was temporally created. It also involved replacing the purely philosophical vocabulary of Avicenna's system with Qurʾānic and theological vocabulary and applying Avicennan concepts to issues unique to the Ash'arite system within which al-Ghazālī himself worked. The overall effect of al-Ghazālī's efforts was to incorporate a fair amount of *falsafa*, as articulated by Avicenna, into *kalām*, while retaining Ash'arite *kalām*'s genuinely traditional Islamic stance.

Similarly, Avicenna's philosophy was to exert considerable influence on the thought of as-Suhrawardī (1154–1191), the founder of Illuminationist philosophy (*ḥikmat al-ishrāq*). At least three elements set off Illuminationist philosophy from other forms of *falsafa*: knowledge by presence, the so-called "primacy of essence" (*aṣālat al-māhīya*), and the acceptance of Platonic Forms. Knowledge by presence is the doctrine that knowledge must ultimately be had immediately by direct (intellectual) contact, in some way, with the object of knowledge rather than through some intermediary mechanism. A central element in as-Suhrawardī's argument for knowledge by presence is his rejection of Aristotelian essential definitions given in terms of genus and difference; for, as-Suhrawardī argued in his logic, ultimately any knowledge of such definitions is circular. It is worth nothing that Avicenna in his own logic maintains that the essential features of a thing cannot be established either by demonstration or induction precisely because such proofs are inherently circular.[4] As-Suhrawardī, then, is extending Avicenna's general argument concerning the acquisition of scientific first principles to the specific case of genus and difference in scientific definitions.

As-Suhrawardī's thought is also characterized by his preference for "the primacy of essence" as opposed to the "primacy of existence" (*aṣālat al-wujūd*), which the Persian philosopher Mullā Ṣadrā (ca. 1571–1640) would defend some four hundred years later.[5] The essence-existence distinction, however, is one of the cornerstones of Avicenna's own philosophy, certainly as he presents it in the *Cure*. Even if the distinction is already present in al-Fārābī's thought, it was Avicenna who thoroughly explored and developed it. In Avicenna's philosophy, as I have suggested, essence and existence become the same in God (at least to the extent that God can be said to have an essence), namely, God's essence—literally what it is to be God—is to be necessary existence. In things other than God, essence and existence, according to Avicenna, are distinct in that nothing other than God simply exists in virtue of what it is; rather, everything else other than God requires a cause in order to exist. Still, within Avicenna's system neither existence nor essence has primacy save that everything is ultimately dependent for its existence upon the Necessary Existent. What as-Suhrawardī, and Mullā

Ṣadrā after him, have done is to emphasize basic elements already present, and prominently so, in Avicenna's own system.

Finally, while as-Suhrawardī expressly avows Platonic Forms in a way that Avicenna never did or would do, the difference between the two thinkers, at least in one important respect, is more one of semantics than content. As-Suhrawardī preferred to think of the Platonic Forms not as epistemological entities but as immaterial substances, the so-called Intelligences of ancient and medieval thought.[6] This, Avicenna himself had already virtually achieved when he argued that there must be a Giver of Forms in which the forms making up our earthly world reside as paradigms and from which they come to inform the sensible objects here on Earth.

While this parallel has been noticed, it has also been claimed that as-Suhrawardī's position differed from Avicenna's in that the latter only accepted ten such immaterial intellects.[7] In fact, Avicenna only conceded that there are ten immaterial intellects in the simplest cosmological model and that actually there are as many as required by one's best astronomy. Where in fact the two thinkers differ is simply that as-Suhrawardī allows for there to be different immaterial substances of the same species only accidentally differing, a status that Avicenna reserves for immaterial human intellects alone, whereas all other immaterial Intelligences, he maintains, differ only according to species.

None of my comments here are intended to suggest that Avicenna and as-Suhrawardī's philosophical systems are the same. They are not. I merely want to emphasize as-Suhrawardī's debt to Avicenna. In fact, Avicenna also owes a debt of sorts to as-Suhrawardī, for as-Suhrawardī, analogous to al-Ghazālī before him, recast many of Avicenna's philosophical concepts and terminology into light metaphors and the mystical language of the Sufis. The result was that Avicenna's philosophy could be incorporated into another aspect of Islamic spiritualism, namely, Sufi mysticism. In fact, the incorporation was so complete that certain twentieth-century scholars, such as Henri Corbin and his school, have argued that there was already a mystical element in Avicenna's thought, albeit only explicitly presented in Avicenna's work *The Easterners*, which is no longer extant in full.[8] Whatever the case, there can be little doubt that Avicenna's philosophy duly modified became ever more engrained in the philosophical framework of Muslim intellectual and spiritual thought.

Avicenna likewise influenced the articulation of Jewish philosophical theology. While arguably the most important philosophical element in

Avicenna's thought among later Muslim theologians was the distinction between essence and existence, a theme that runs throughout the *Cure*, among medieval Jewish theologians it appears to be Avicenna's distinction between necessary existence and possible existence, which features prominently within the *Salvation*. The distinction was in fact taken over by no less a Jewish luminary than Moses ben Maimon, that is, Maimonides (ca. 1135–1204).[9] So, for example, Maimonides' third proof for the existence of God in the *Guide for the Perplexed* (II 1), which he erroneously attributes to Aristotle, is in fact a variation of Avicenna's proof from possible and necessary existence. Moreover, in that same proof Maimonides, using the same distinction, rehearses Avicenna's own arguments for the uniqueness of the divinity and for God's incorporeality and simplicity.

More important, and in certain respects more interesting, is Maimonides' use of Avicenna's distinction in articulating to what extent God can be said to have attributes beyond necessary existence (*Guide for the Perplexed*, I 52). Avicenna's own position, one may recall, was that one could positively affirm that God was the Necessary Existent. Other than this single positive attribute, all other attributes, maintained Avicenna, have to be either negative, such as "*in*corporeal," or relational, such as "(ontologically or temporally) prior to." Maimonides' own distinctive negative theology is best seen as a give and take between himself and Avicenna, agreeing that, with the exception of the attribute of being God (that is, the Necessary Existent), one should attribute negative attributes of the divinity, while disagreeing with Avicenna that one could attribute relational ones to the divinity.

Thus, according to Maimonides, other than the attributes of action—which in fact flow from and are identical with God's necessary existence—the divinity can be described only in negative terms. In contrast with Avicenna, however, Maimonides disagreed that relational attributes should be ascribed to God, and does so, ironically, for purely Avicennan reasons. For Avicenna, there is no single category "existence," of which necessary existence and possible existence are its species; rather, both are categorically different, only sharing the name "existence" in an equivocal sense. Maimonides merely observed that in order for two things to stand in any meaningful relation they need to be at least categorically alike. To say of a lime, for instance, that the green (category of quality) is brighter, or sourer, or larger, or the like than its size (category of quantity) is just nonsense. The nonsense becomes even more exacerbated the further removed the categories involved in the purported relation are; however, between necessary existence and possible existence not even existence is shared in common but is said equivocally. Thus, nothing of the created order, according to Maimonides, can stand in any relation to God such as to give rise to a relational attribute: Strictly speaking, for Maimonides, God is not before us, in us, with us, nor can any other relational attribute be assigned to God.

In addition to drawing upon and adapting Avicenna's necessary-possible existence distinction, Maimonides also took over, albeit in a qualified way, Avicenna's account of prophecy. According to Avicenna, as noted, prophecy is not a supernatural phenomenon but a natural one, and as such is in need of a natural explanation. Within the framework of his psychology and particularly his accounts of insight (*ḥads*) and the internal sense faculty of the compositive imagination, Avicenna found just such an explanation. Avicenna's prophet far from being individually chosen by God to be a vehicle of divine inspiration is merely a human who has insight to the superlative degree so as to be able fully and properly to grasp the inherent causal structure and order of the good found in the world. The prophet in turn can then imagine and explain this order in ways that capture the imagination of others. Maimonides, in fact, accepted this natural explanation of prophecy, while also finding a place in it for God (*Guide for the Perplexed*, I 32). For, according to Maimonides, God can prevent one whose psychological disposition is otherwise of such an excellent degree so as to qualify to be a prophet from in fact becoming a prophet. Again, let me repeat, my claim is not that Maimonides' views are just those of Avicenna's—they are not—rather, I merely want to emphasize the influence that Avicenna had on the formation of Maimonides' own unique thought.

Avicenna's Heritage in the Christian World

As with the Arabic East, so with the Latin West, Avicenna's thought was a source of inspiration, particularly at the onset of the High Middle Ages. At that time there began a movement to translate Greek and Arabic scientific works into Latin that equaled the earlier Arabic translation movement in its breadth.[10] At least one indication of the high regard in which early philosophers and translators in Europe, such as Dominicus Gundissalinus (fl. 1150–1190) and his Jewish collaborator Ibn Daud (ca. 1110–1180), held Avicenna is seen in that his works were some of the first translated into Latin.

Among the works of Avicenna translated were a fair bit of the *Cure*—including a little of the logic, about two-thirds of the general physics, and complete translations of other more specific works on natural philosophy, as well as the whole of the psychology and the metaphysics—the metaphysics of the *Salvation*, and, of course, *The Canon*.[11] Avicenna's *Canon*, with its handy compendium format, proved to be immensely popular in Europe, and continued to be a medical textbook at universities into the eighteenth century. It was his philosophy, however, that would have the most enduring effect, for it would influence (sometimes negatively, other times positively) some of the great Catholic theologians and philosophers of that time, such as Albert the Great, Thomas Aquinas, and Duns Scotus.

So, for example, the foremost issue in scholastic natural philosophy involved the concept of motion, concerning which the question of in which Aristotelian category does it belong was of first most importance. Albert the Great (c. 1200–1280) gave the question the form in which it was most frequently dealt throughout medieval Europe: Is motion a flowing form (*forma fluens*) or the form of a flow (*fluxus formae*)? While the language is Albert's own, he found the statement of the problem, as he himself says, in the *Physics* of Avicenna's *Cure*. Unfortunately, owing to a faulty Latin translation of a key passage—where Avicenna in fact articulated his theory of motion at an instant and then went on and developed his notion of a limit—and Albert's own commentary on that passage, Avicenna's own contribution to this issue was not appreciated at least in the Latin West.[12] Still, it was Avicenna who raised the question that would stimulate so much discussion among Latin natural philosophers about the proper way to characterize motion.

Moreover, the psychological work of Avicenna's *Cure*, was second only to Aristotle's in influencing Albert's own psychological works. Thus, as a notable example, in Albert's *De homine*, he cited Aristotle 280 times with Avicenna coming in close behind with some 230 citations.[13] In fact, it would seem that Albert preferred the way that Avicenna structured the science of psychology over that of Aristotle, as well as giving Avicenna pride of place when discussing the vegetative soul—that is, the principle associated with the functions of self-nourishment, growth, and reproduction—as well as the internal senses, such as imagination and memory.

Perhaps of more importance in the long run was Avicenna's influence on Thomas Aquinas (1225–1274), whose system of thought still makes up much of the philosophical theology of the Catholic Church and Christian apologetics more generally. Here it is important to note that in Thomas's earlier works, he is much more willing to reference Avicenna by name in a positive way, whereas in his more mature works, such as the *Summa Theologiae* and commentaries on Aristotle, he prefers to mention Avicenna by name only when he is in disagreement with him. Such a seeming turn of opinion, I believe, is not so much because, as Thomas grew older, he came to reject the Avicennan elements that impressed him in his youth, but because by then he had so thoroughly incorporated those elements into his own system of thought that they genuinely became his own.

The most obvious case of such an appropriation is the real distinction between being (*ens*)—Avicenna would say existence—and essence (*essentia*). In fact, Thomas names one of his earlier *opuscula*, *On Being and Essence* (*De ente et essentia*), after the famous Avicennan distinction. In this work, if one sets aside the final chapter that discusses accidents, Avicenna is positively referenced more than any other philosopher, including Aristotle. Even if one includes the final chapter, where nearly half of the Aristotle references occur, Avicenna still ties Aristotle for the overall number of explicit positive references, thirteen in all. Even in Thomas's later works where the Aristotelian actuality-potentiality distinction comes to predominate, he never fully discards Avicenna's essence-existence distinction, as is clearly witnessed in Thomas's account of divine simplicity and divine perfection at *Summa Theologiae*, part I, question 3 and 4, respectively.

Even when Thomas is clearly at odds with Avicenna, such as on the subject of the cosmos' past eternity, the former very much respects and even positively draws on his Muslim predecessor. Avicenna's own position on this ever so delicate issue was that one can, in fact, demonstrate that God has been eternally creating the universe. Consequently, Avicenna believes that one can demonstrate that the world was not created at some first moment in the finite past. In contrast, Thomas denied that the cosmos' eternity could be demonstrated, but he equally denied that its temporal creation could be demonstrated. According to Thomas, one knows that the cosmos has existed for a finite period of time solely on the basis of revelation. Thus, Thomas's project was to show that purported demonstrations—whether for the eternal or temporal creation of the world—were not in fact demonstrative.

Thus, on the one hand, in a very positive way, Thomas consistently draws upon Avicenna when considering so-called demonstrations for the world's temporal createdness in order to criticize those proofs.[14] On the other hand, when he considered the arguments for the world's eternity, Avicenna's proof from necessity and possibility always appeared in Thomas's catalogue of arguments. In fact, Avicenna's proof is the premier argument for that thesis considered by Thomas in the *Summa Theologiae* (part I, question 46), as well as framing the topic in his *On the Eternity of the World* (*De Aeternitate mundi*), which, as the title indicates is dedicated to this issue. While further examples of Avicennan influence on Thomas could certainly be multiplied, these instances at least suggest the role that Avicenna played in the development of two of the more distinctive doctrines in Aquinas's thought.

Similarly, the place of Avicenna in the thought of that most subtle of scholastic thinkers, John Duns Scotus (1265/66–1308), is also beyond question. As early as 1927, the great historian of medieval philosophy, Étienne Gilson, recognized Scotus's predilection for Avicenna, and enumerated three points where Duns Scotus takes Avicenna as his point of departure: (1) his understanding of what the proper object of the science of metaphysics is; (2) his conception of being; and (3) his closely related theory of common natures.[15] Concerning the first issue, as discussed in some detail, historically there was a problem of identifying the proper object of metaphysics: is it being qua being or God (or immaterial beings more generally)? I have already noted that for Avicenna it is *existence* as such; however, the thesis that God or immaterial beings represent the proper object of metaphysical inquiry was defended by the Muslim philosopher, Averroes (1126–1198), whose influence on Latin scholasticism through his Aristotelian commentaries was no less, and perhaps greater, than Avicenna's own. Again Scotus followed Avicenna on this point, and indeed on this point Avicenna's understanding came to be the predominate one among most metaphysicians up until today.

Gilson's points (2) and (3) can be treated together, given the close connection between essences and existence in Avicenna's system and being and common natures in Scotus's. Here at least one point of influence is Avicenna's insistence that a proper understanding of God can only be attained though a careful analysis of existence itself, and, in like fashion, as Gilson notes, the whole of Scotus's metaphysics is centered on the idea of being, since there is no other idea by which one could reach God.[16] Even more evidence of the place of Avicenna in Scotus's thought is the latter's conception of common natures, where he explicitly and approvingly appeals to Avicenna's remarks about essences in book V of the metaphysics of the *Cure*, namely, they simply are what they are. In other words, for example, the essence of a horse is just horse-ness, and as such it is neither one nor many, neither universal nor particular, a point that Avicenna makes repeatedly.

Finally, more recently it has been observed that the theory of causality that lies at the heart of Scotus's proof for the existence of God, particularly with its division of physical and metaphysical causation—is as close to Avicenna's as a Christian philosopher of that time could be.[17] As with the other philosophers I have considered, let me emphasize that Scotus's thought is highly original and innovative while all the while being deeply indebted to many of the philosophical insights of his Persian predecessor.

While this chapter on Avicenna's subsequent influence is short (even shamefully so), hopefully it has provided the reader with some sense of the pervasiveness and far-reaching importance of Avicenna on later philosophers and theologians as well as the important place he holds in the development of both Eastern and Western worldviews.

APPENDIX I

Immateriality of the Intellect

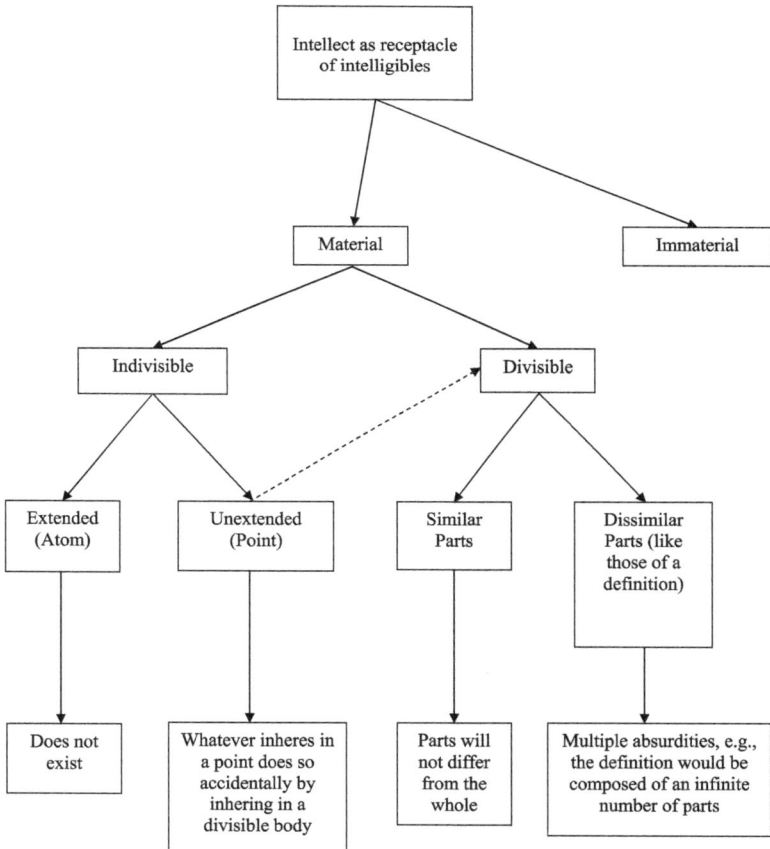

```
                    ┌─────────────────────┐
                    │ Intellect as receptacle │
                    │   of intelligibles   │
                    └─────────────────────┘
                       /              \
              ┌──────────┐          ┌──────────┐
              │ Material │          │ Immaterial │
              └──────────┘          └──────────┘
               /        \
      ┌────────────┐    ┌──────────┐
      │ Indivisible │    │ Divisible │
      └────────────┘    └──────────┘
        /      \  - - - - ->  /    \
```

Extended (Atom)	Unextended (Point)	Similar Parts	Dissimilar Parts (like those of a definition)
Does not exist	Whatever inheres in a point does so accidentally by inhering in a divisible body	Parts will not differ from the whole	Multiple absurdities, e.g., the definition would be composed of an infinite number of parts

APPENDIX 2

Incorruptibility of the Intellect

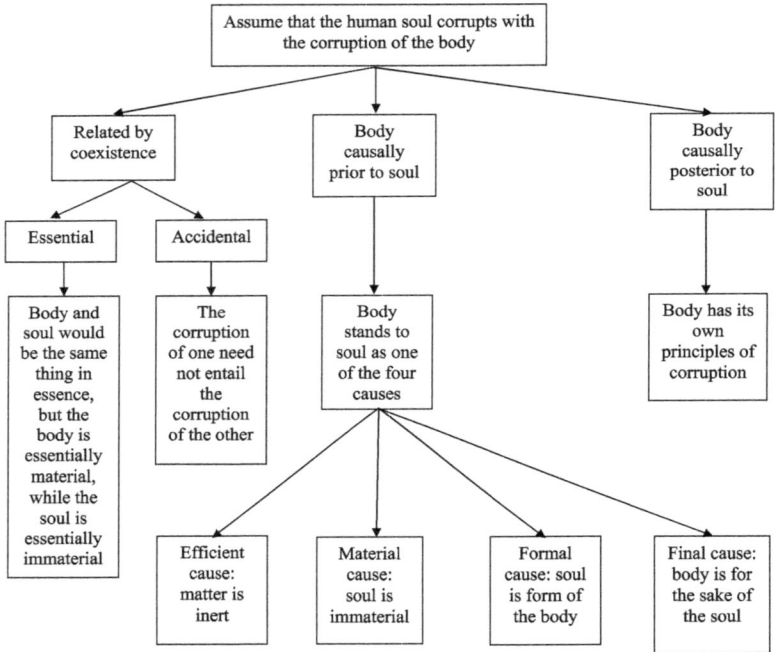

```
┌─────────────────────────────────────┐
│ Assume that the human soul corrupts  │
│ with the corruption of the body      │
└─────────────────────────────────────┘
```

Related by coexistence

Body causally prior to soul

Body causally posterior to soul

Essential

Accidental

Body and soul would be the same thing in essence, but the body is essentially material, while the soul is essentially immaterial

The corruption of one need not entail the corruption of the other

Body stands to soul as one of the four causes

Body has its own principles of corruption

Efficient cause: matter is inert

Material cause: soul is immaterial

Formal cause: soul is form of the body

Final cause: body is for the sake of the soul

APPENDIX 3

Proof for a Necessary Existent

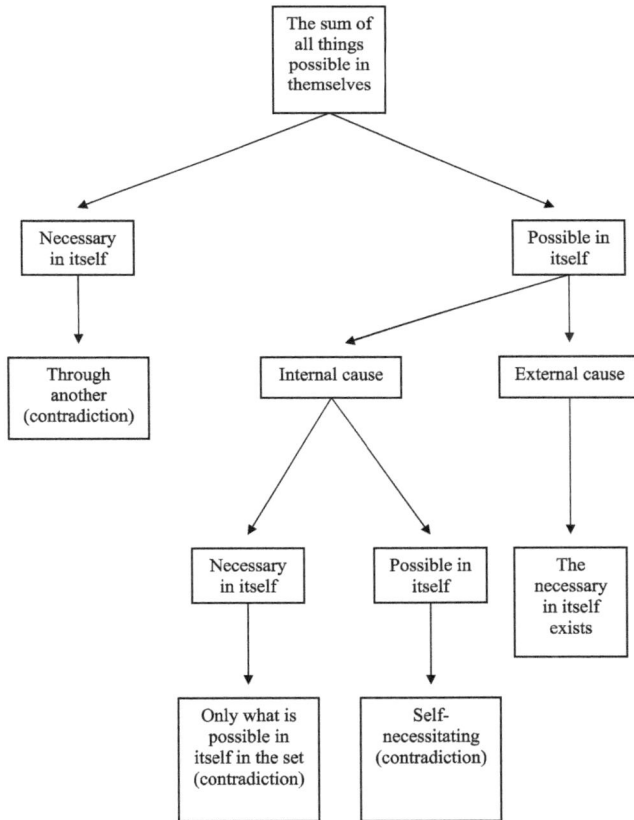

```
                    ┌──────────────┐
                    │  The sum of  │
                    │  all things  │
                    │ possible in  │
                    │  themselves  │
                    └──────────────┘
            ┌──────────────┐        ┌──────────────┐
            │  Necessary   │        │  Possible in │
            │   in itself  │        │    itself    │
            └──────────────┘        └──────────────┘
```

Through another (contradiction)	Internal cause	External cause

Necessary in itself	Possible in itself	The necessary in itself exists

Only what is possible in itself in the set (contradiction)	Self-necessitating (contradiction)

257

APPENDIX 4

Proof for a Material Subject of Possibility

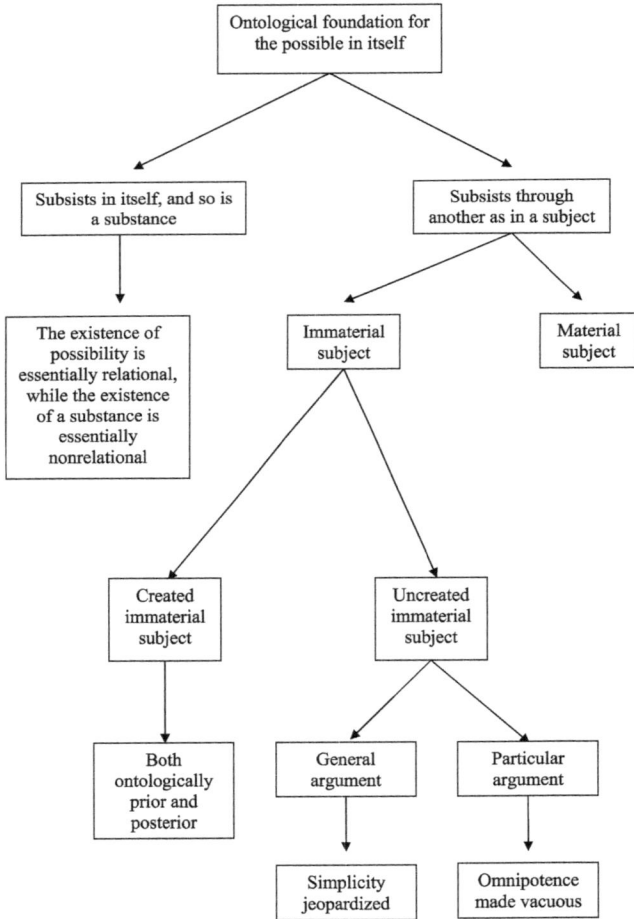

Ontological foundation for the possible in itself

- Subsists in itself, and so is a substance
  - The existence of possibility is essentially relational, while the existence of a substance is essentially nonrelational
- Subsists through another as in a subject
  - Immaterial subject
    - Created immaterial subject
      - Both ontologically prior and posterior
    - Uncreated immaterial subject
      - General argument
        - Simplicity jeopardized
      - Particular argument
        - Omnipotence made vacuous
  - Material subject

NOTES

1. Two excellent surveys of both the philosophical and historical background to Avicenna's life are Afnan (1958), especially chapters 1–2, and Goodman (2006). Also see Avicenna (1974) for Avicenna's own autobiography.

2. Still, the best study of Avicenna's indebtedness to the Aristotelian philosophical tradition is Gutas (1988).

3. While in the present introductory essay I focus more on the ancient course curriculum itself rather than the substantive philosophical and scientific issues treated by ancient thinkers, an overview of the content of some of those issues can be found in the Introduction to McGinnis and Reisman (2007).

4. For a discussion of the later Greek course curriculum see D'Ancona (2005).

5. See chapter 6, **150–53**.

6. For discussions of the fates and fortunes of Plotinus and Proclus, see respectively Adamson (2002) and Endress (1973).

7. See Aristotle, *Nicomachean Ethics*, I 1–2.

8. For a detailed study of the movement see Gutas (1998).

9. For the life and thought of al-Kindī see Adamson (2007).

10. Nestorian and Jacobite Christianity are best understood by reference to Chalcedonian Christology. The Chalcedonian formula is that within Jesus Christ there are two natures (one divine, one human), which are united into one person. In contrast, Nestorians maintain that Jesus Christ exists as two

persons: Jesus the man and Christ the Son of God, whereas Jacobites, who are a sect within Monophysitism, claim that Christ has only one nature, which is divine.

11. A complete translation of *The Perfect State* is available in al-Fārābī (1985); the first half of *The Principles of Existing Things* is available in translation in McGinnis and Reisman (2007), and most of the second half, Fauzi Najjar has translated in al-Fārābī (1963).

12. For a number of studies on *kalām* see *The Cambridge Companion to Classical Islamic Theology*, ed. Winter (2008).

13. The issue is not about a physical manifestation of the Qur'ān in the form of a book that might be in front of someone, but of the Qur'ān understood as a recitation of the very word of God. While there is some danger in comparing the Qur'ān, literally "recitation," with the *logos* ("word") found at the beginning of John's Gospel in the Christian Bible—"In the beginning was the word, and the word was with God, and the word was God" (John 1:1)—the comparison may help make the present debate more intelligible to contemporary readers. For just as certain Christological debates arose within Christianity about the relation of God to the "word," understood as Christ, so analogous debates arose within Islam about the relation of Allāh to the Qur'ān: Mu'tazilites taking the Qur'ān to be part of the created order, while others took it to be part of the divine order, and even part of the very being of God.

14. For one account of an "encounter" between Avicenna and 'Abd al-Jabbār see Dhanani (2003).

15. See R. Rashed (1984).

16. See Avicenna (1974).

17. For a translation of this work see either Bertolacci (2002), ch. 3 or McGinnis and Reisman (2007).

18. A dirham was a coin usually between 10–13 g made up of an alloy of silver (70 percent) and copper, and so worth around $2 US. Thus, Avicenna would have paid between $5.50 and $8.00 for the book.

19. See Avicenna (1974), 124–125, fn. 43.

20. See Mez (1995), 202 and 204.

21. For this dating see Gutas (1988), 103–104.

22. See Avicenna (1974), 132–133, fn. 89.

23. See Goodman (2006), 38–39.

24. See Gutas (1988), 140–141 for the later dating, and for the earlier dating see Michot (1997), 158–163.

CHAPTER 2

1. For those interested in the technical aspects of Avicenna's logic, the following English translations of some of his logical works are available: Avicenna

(1971), (1973), and (1984). An excellent overview of Avicenna's syllogistic can be found in Street (2002); and for his modal logic specifically, see Thom (2003), "Avicenna."

2. Street (2002), 132.

3. For this seminal distinction in Arabic logic and theory of knowledge, see Black (1990), 71–78.

4. Although Avicenna's use of the Arabic *ṭābaqa, yuṭābiqu, muṭābaqa* in his account of verification or truth-making can be translated "to correspond," it should not necessarily be equated with a modern "correspondence theory of truth," although it may have certain similarities.

5. Cf. *Metaphysics*, I.2, 7. See Sabra (1980) for a complete discussion of the proper object or subject matter of logic.

6. For a more complete discussion of Avicenna's theory of universal, and to which my exposition here is much indebted, see Marmura (1979) and (1992).

7. Superficially, this question appears to be the problem of the external world and the issue of whether it is even possible to have knowledge of the external world. For if what is immediately known to us is only mental objects, what justification is there that extramental objects correspond with our mental objects, or even more strongly, what justifies that there is anything except the mental? In general, Avicenna seems to have very little patience for skeptical questions such as this one; for Avicenna, we simply do have knowledge of the external world. Thus, the important question for him is not whether knowledge of the external world is possible, but what is the explanation of the fact that we do have such knowledge.

8. As will be seen later (50–51), for Avicenna the necessary certainty is, ideally, absolute necessary certainty; however, he also allows, and counts as genuinely scientific knowledge, conditional necessary certainty. See McGinnis (2003a), 323–324.

9. For now I set aside the class of immaterial intellects, which Avicenna countenances. For clearly in the case of immaterial things, such as angels or what Avicenna prefers to call simply Intellects, what particularizes them cannot be matter. Instead, for Avicenna they are individuated by the fact that each one is the unique and only instance of its kind or species. Consequently, for Avicenna no two immaterial beings can be specifically the same. Instead, each constitutes its own species, and so they differ from one another in the way, for example, man, chimpanzee, horse, and the like differ specifically from one another.

10. Again, the predicables are genus, difference, species, property, and accident.

11. For a more thorough discussion of Avicenna's division of the sciences, see Marmura (1980a) and Gutas (2003). For a general discussion of medieval theories of the division of the sciences, see Weisheipl (1978).

12. See Avicenna (1966), I.1, 3–6 and I.7, 30–31. For a general discussion of certainty in medieval Arabic philosophy, and particularly in the thought of Avicenna's immediate predecessor, al-Fārābī, see Black (2006).

13. A "necessary accident" is something that, while not making up the essence of the thing, nonetheless always accompanies that thing, as, for example, how being capable of laughter belongs to humans, and, perhaps, being extended belongs to color.

14. This claim is not exactly correct, since Avicenna does recognize two cases where a negative term might function as a strict difference: one, where the negative difference establishes one single species exactly mirroring (*nawʿ muḥaṣṣil bi-izāʾi*) the species constituted by the positive difference, as, for example, when the genus of rational numbers is divided into numbers that are divisible into two equal parts, namely, the "even," and numbers that are not divisible into two equal parts, namely, the "odd"; and, two, when in a given language there is no positive term, word, or expression corresponding with the positive causal factor constituting the species, as, for example, if one is defining "plant," which is a vegetative, living substance, but in the language there happens to be no term for "vegetative," and so one would define plant as an *in*sensate, living substance (Avicenna [1953], I.13. 78.15–79.10). Barring these two rare cases, the constitutive elements of a definition cannot be negative terms.

15. Cf. Porphyry (1975), 44–45 (*Isagoge*, 10, 9–19); here Porphyry claims that such negative differences as "*im*mortal: and "*in*sensate" are constitutive elements in the definitions of "god" and "plants" respectively.

16. Avicenna's treatment of negative terms is similar in certain salient ways to Quine's analysis of them in Quine (1953), 7–9. Quine's analysis is framed in terms of "descriptions," whereas Avicenna's is framed in terms of "positive accounts"; yet both would agree that the proper analysis of "*x* is not" is "each thing failed either to meet a certain description or to have a certain positive account."

17. A parallel discussion is found in Avicenna's *Metaphysics* of the *Cure*, V.3. Also compare Thomas Aquinas, *On Being and Essence*, ch. 3.

18. The "middle term" is the term that two premises forming a syllogism share in common, and that links the subject and predicate terms of the syllogism's conclusion together. So, for example, in the syllogism: "Whatever is material is mortal, and all humans are material; therefore, all humans are mortal," "material" is the middle term, since it is through it that one arrives at the conclusion, "humans are mortal."

19. Avicenna is quite insistent that the certainty, and thus the necessity, in question in a demonstration is not merely the certainty or necessity of the conclusion, for that the conclusion follows of necessity or with certainty is true of

every valid syllogism, whether it is a demonstration or not. For Avicenna, the relevant certainty or necessity concerns the premises, and the certainty or necessity of the conclusion is in turn derived from the premises' certainty or necessity. See Avicenna (1966), I.7, 31.11–18.

20. Aristotle suggests this distinction at *Posterior Analytics*, I 13, where he discusses the difference between understanding "the fact that" (*to hoti*) and "the reason why" (*to dioti*).

21. The "major term" and "minor term" refer respectively to the predicate and subject terms of the conclusion of a syllogism. So, for example, in the syllogism: "Whatever is material is mortal, and all humans are material; therefore, all humans are mortal," "mortal" is the major term, while "humans" is the minor term; for "human" is the subject of the conclusion, while "mortal" is the predicate.

22. I shall consider Avicenna's account of causes in chapters 3 and 7. Additional studies of his theory of causation include: Marmura (1984b), Bertolacci (2002), and Wisnovsky (2002). For a discussion of causality's role in relation to medieval Arabic metaphysics in general, see Druart (2005).

23. For a detailed discussion of Avicenna on induction and methodic experience, see McGinnis (2003a). (It should be noted that there I translated *tajriba* as "experimentation," whereas I now believe that "methodic experience" might be more appropriate.) Also see Janssens (2004), which in important ways supplements and corrects my earlier work.

24. For a discussion of Avicenna's general empirical methodology, and, more specifically, medieval Arabic physicians' empirical attitude in relation to medicine, see Gutas (2003) and McGinnis (2008). Similar ground is covered, albeit with the intent of showing that Avicenna was a skeptic, in Nuseibeh (1981).

CHAPTER 3

1. Avicenna argues for this point at length at *Metaphysics*, II.2.

2. For example, while a doctor might be the efficient cause of health in him or herself, he or she is so, not qua doctor but qua patient, and so other.

3. Also see Wisnovsky (2000) and (2003), ch. 8.

4. For a discussion of the commentary tradition surrounding this issue and the historical context it provides for Avicenna's own analysis of motion, see Wisnovsky (2003), part I.

5. Aristotle, *De anima*, II 1, 412a22–28.

6. The Arabic translation of Aristotle's definition is "motion is the perfection of what is in potency in what is such."

7. For a translation and commentary of Avicenna's analysis of motion, see Hasnawi (2001) and McGinnis (2006a). For a discussion Avicenna' s view of motion at an instant in his dynamics, see M. Rashed (2005), 295–302.

8. For a detailed discussion of Avicenna's distinction between motion as it exists in the intellect and as it exists in the world, as well as an initial introduction to Avicenna's conception of a motion at an instant, see Hasnawi (2001).

9. Aristotle himself first raised this problem in a notoriously difficult passage in *Physics*, VIII 8, 262a19–263a3, which I shall consider again at 78–79.

10. See 75–77.

11. See Philoponus (1888), 565, 1–567, 7.

12. Prior to Avicenna, al-Kindī had provided a conceptual, as opposed to physical, argument against the void as well. See al-Kindī (1950–1953), 109 and (1974), 63. Whereas al-Kindī's remarks are given almost in passing, Avicenna provides a detailed and sustained argument.

13. For a brief discussion of Avicenna's account of vain intelligibles see 269–70, fn. 16. For further studies of Avicenna's position concerning nonexistent forms or "fictional beings," see Michot (1984–1985) and (1987), and Black (1997).

14. For a detailed analysis of Avicenna's argument for this claim, see McGinnis (2006c).

15. In fact, Avicenna has a more elaborate discussion than suggested here of why void cannot fall under the genus "accident" either as a constitutive accident or a nonconstitutive accident.

16. As I noted (262, fn. 14), Avicenna does countenance the use of a negative difference in certain very limited cases, namely, in those cases where the use of a negative difference produces two and only two parallel species. If "*not* existing in a substrate" were such a negative difference, then there should be only one species of substance not existing in a subject, namely, void; however, for Avicenna and virtually the whole Arabic-speaking philosophical community, all the Intelligences are considered to be substances not existing in a subject. (Although the difference for separate Intellects is often identified with the negative term, "incorporeal" or "immaterial," there is also a common positive difference applied to them by medieval Arabic thinkers, namely, being "spiritual" (*rūḥānī*).) Therefore, "not existing in a substrate" taken alone fails to meet the necessary requirement for being a difference.

17. It might be worth noting that Avicenna's language here is the same language that he used to explain negative terms in his *Introduction*, where again one should recall that for Avicenna negations simply cannot function as differences constitutive of a definition.

18. For translations of Avicenna's chapters on time and on the now as found in the *Cure*, see Shayegan (1999) and McGinnis (1999) and (2009).

19. Cf. Aristotle, *Physics*, IV 11, 219a10–30; Avicenna, *Physics*, II.11, 157.4–7.

20. For a detailed discussion of atomism in the medieval Arabic world, see Pines (1997), Dhanani (1994), and Sabra (2006). For atomic theories of time specifically and Avicenna's criticisms of them, see McGinnis (2003b).

21. For a complete translation of Avicenna's discussion of atomism from the *Cure*, see Lettinck (1999).

22. Avicenna makes this point explicitly about continuous alterations in *at-Taʿlīqāt*, Avicenna (2000), 43–44: "When the white [thing] undergoes alteration into a black [thing], the alterations are infinite; however, they are not actual and those alteration do not exist simultaneously. Instead they are by way of being delimited (*taḥaddud*) like the situation concerning motion." The text's *taḥaddud* might alternatively be emended to *tajaddud*, in which case the text would read, "Instead they are by way of being renewed like the situation concerning motion."

23. To speak of "Avicenna's dynamics" is a bit of an anachronism, since it was not until the late seventeenth century that dynamics came to be considered as a distinct field of study, and Avicenna, like most ancient and medieval natural philosophers, indiscriminately mixed dynamic and kinematic concepts within his physics.

24. The most outspoken in this respect is Sayılı (1984); with much more reservation is Hasnawi (1984). Despite certain disagreements that I have with these authors, both articles are rich sources for understanding Avicenna's theory of inclination.

25. See Avicenna (1963), #45, 34.

26. See Aristotle, *Physics*, VIII 4, 255b15.

27. It is unclear here whether Avicenna means that the resistive force resists whatever obstructs its path or it resists being displaced, although the context seems to favor the former.

28. The following comes from *Mubāḥathāt*, Avicenna (1995), §677.

29. That is not to say that for Avicenna a temporally infinite series of finite agents extending into the future could not produce a temporally infinite effect; for example, according to Avicenna, humans have been procreating humans infinitely into the past and will continue to do so infinitely into the future. In this case, however, the infinite effect, namely, the infinite number of humans that has and will come to be, is due, not to a finite agent as such, but to the infinitely extended series of such agents, albeit that there exists such an infinite series is for Avicenna ultimately due to an infinite agent, God.

30. That natural bodies consist of only four elements is true as far as terrestrial physics was concerned, that is, the world extending from the center of the Earth up to the sphere of the Moon. The sphere of the Moon and what is beyond, however, were thought to be composed of a fifth element, the so-called "ether."

According to Avicenna what distinguished ether from the elements associated with terrestrial physics is that the latter are defined by their inclination to move in a straight line, either upward or downward, whereas ether moves circularly rather than rectilinearly.

31. There is some evidence that perhaps al-Fārābī anticipated some of the key points of Avicenna's position, namely, that something outside the natural order of forms and matter is needed to explain substantial changes; see McGinnis (forthcoming [a]).

32. For an excellent discussion of the history of the problem that Avicenna is treating here and his own solution to it, see Stone (2008).

CHAPTER 4

1. As one brief point of clarification, in this chapter and the next when I speak of "animals," I am referring specifically to the sublunar species and not those life forms that medieval philosophers associated with the so-called celestial spheres, which were thought to be animals inasmuch as they were believed to be animate. Hence, the act of the intellect is unique to the human animal so understood.

2. Cf. Aristotle, "the soul is the first *entelekheia* of a natural organic body" (*De anima*, II 1, 412b4–6). Here the English "perfection" translates the Arabic *kamāl*, which either it or the hendiadys *kamāl wa-fiʿl* ("perfection and act"), was Avicenna's preferred locution for Aristotle's *entelekheia*.

3. Cf. al-Fārābī (2007b), 84–85.

4. In this respect al-Fārābī and Avicenna differ from certain other philosophers, such as Aquinas in the Latin tradition; for Aquinas countenances subsistent immaterial forms, which he identifies with angels and perhaps even God, whereas al-Fārābī and Avicenna prefer to call such beings (depending upon various considerations), souls, intellects, and even perfections.

5. Cf. Plato, *Phaedrus*, 246a–254e.

6. The issue of "female semen" will be discussed more at 241–42; also see Musallam (1989) and (1990).

7. The traditional account of abstraction emphasizes the role of the Active Intellect as opposed to the roles played by the individual human's own intellect and sensory faculties of perception; for traditional accounts of abstraction, see Davidson (1992), ch. 4; Jabre (1984); and Nuseibeh (1989). For more recent accounts of abstraction, which emphasize the role of the human intellect in abstraction, see Hasse (2001) and McGinnis (2007b).

8. Also see Sebti (2005), who observes that essences in themselves are common to the representations in the powers of sensation, imagination, and estimation.

9. The Arabic *khayr wa-sharr*, which I have rendered "good or not good," may also be understood as "good and evil." It is not totally clear to me, however,

whether "evil," in the sense of a negative moral judgment, is what Avicenna has in mind here. For perceiving that such moral judgments, as gratuitous violence is wrong, in fact seems to be for him a more appropriate activity for the practical intellect (see, for instance, *Salvation*, "Physics," VI.3, 331.3–7). Perhaps, then, his example of the intellect's grasping good and not good is meant to grasp examples such as one's perceiving that ripe food is good to eat, while decaying meat is not good to eat.

10. For a full account of the extramission and intromission theories of vision, see Lindberg (1976), esp. chs. 1–4 (passim).

11. See Pasnau (1997), 49–60.

12. See Hasse (2000), 108–119.

13. For Aristotle's account of vision, light, and the transparent, see his *De anima*, II 7 and *De sensu*, 2–3.

14. Indeed Avicenna's optical theory, as will be seen, is in many salient ways like that of Avicenna's contemporary Ibn al-Haytham (965–1039), the Alhazen of Latin fame. For an introduction to the theory of Ibn al-Haytham, see Lindberg (1976), ch. "Alhazen and the New Intromission Theory of Vision," and the translation and commentary of Ibn al-Haytham's *Optics* by Sabra in Ibn al-Haytham (1989). The Latin translation of Ibn al-Haytham's *Optics, De aspectibus*, is in places markedly different from the Arabic; for a translation and commentary of the Latin see Smith (2001).

15. It is certainly worth noting that Ibn al-Haytham also distinguished two types of light nearly corresponding with Avicenna's division here: lights that radiate from self-luminous bodies and accidental lights that are acquired by bodies that are not self-luminous; see Ibn al-Haytham (1983) and (1989), Book I, ch. 3, esp. sections 21 and 87–88. The similarities between the two great thinkers become even greater when one compares their theories about rays radiating *from* the illuminated object (not the eye as the intromission theorists had it) so as to form a visual cone that falls upon the eye and projects a sensible image of the visible object to the visual system of the perceiver.

16. Hasse criticizes John Blund's interpretation of Avicenna on the grounds that Blund makes Avicenna's rays "somehow participate in the formation of an image in the eye by traveling themselves" (Hasse [2000], 124). According to Hasse, the sensible images "are transmitted instantaneously by the translucent medium" (ibid). To me it seems that Hasse is forcing an Aristotelian understanding onto Avicenna, and that Blund's understanding is quite possibly the correct one.

17. For a more thorough presentation of Avicenna's refutation of not only mathematically inspired extramission theories of vision, but also the Galenic extramission theory, see Lindberg (1976), 43–52.

18. *Rūḥ*, translated here as "pneuma," but which might also be rendered as "(vital) spirit," is discussed more fully in the chapter on Medicine (234–35). For now suffice it to say that it is a very fine material substance that is the immediate or proximate cause of the various animal activities, such as motion and perception. Pneuma—and it comes in different varieties—functions like the ancient and medieval analogue of electrical impulses and neural firings, whether in the brain, muscles, or elsewhere.

19. Much of this section is indebted to Black (forthcoming [b]) and Kaukua (2007).

20. See, for instance, Plato's *Republic*, 477B–478D.

21. For the sources and limits of Avicenna's anatomical knowledge, particularly brain anatomy, see Hall (2004), §II.

22. For in-depth studies of the estimative faculty in Avicenna, see Black (1993); Hasse (2000), §II.4; Hall (2006); and Kaukua (2007), ch. 3.

23. For detailed studies of Avicenna's account of the cogitative faculty, see Black (forthcoming [b]) and Gutas (2001).

24. Black (forthcoming [b]), §2, "Imagination without Reason" (second paragraph).

25. For a study of Avicenna's account of discursive thought, which is the action of the cogitative faculty, see Adamson (2004a).

CHAPTER 5

1. See Davidson (1992), 83–94 for an extended discussion of the following stages, and Druart (2000), 174–189.

2. See 75–76 for Avicenna's detailed version of the following argument.

3. See 77–79.

4. For a flowchart presentation of Avicenna's demonstration see Appendix 1.

5. See Druart (2000), 261–264.

6. See Davidson (1992), 103–116, and Druart (2000), 267–273.

7. See, for instance, *Physics*, I.14, 73.1–7.

8. For a flowchart presentation of Avicenna's demonstration see Appendix 2.

9. See Plato, *Phaedo*, 102D–106D and Plotinus, *Enneads*, IV.7.

10. I must confess that I am not certain whether Avicenna can help himself to this premise, for, as we have seen, according to him the material intellect has the potential to be impressed with intelligibles and it does so precisely because it is an immaterial substratum for concepts.

11. For discussions of the Active Intellect, see Davidson (1992), 87–94 and Acar (2003).

12. See Plato, *Republic*, VI, 507C–509C.

13. See Aristotle, *De anima*, III 5.

14. Avicenna's discussion at *Physics*, I.1, 10.8–11.9 in Avicenna (2009)—during which he introduces the notion of a "vague individual" existing in the compositive imagination—is a rich supplemental source to the present discussion.

15. See 31–32.

16. The traditional reading of Avicenna maintains that the Active Intellect emanates a complete intelligible and not just intellectualizing forms or accidents when it brings about human understanding; see Davidson (1992), 83–94. In other words, on the traditional interpretation, when we know the concept "horse-ness," for example, the universal form of horse-ness flows from the Active Intellect into the human intellect, not simply the accident(s) by which the abstracted image in the human brain is changed into a universal. Davidson himself, however, admits that this account does not fit with the analogy between the Active Intellect and the Sun (Davidson [1992], 93).

Some evidence that only intellectualizing forms (rather than a complete intelligible) are emanated from the Active Intellect in the case of cognition can be found in Avicenna's small treatise "On the Soul" ("Fī n-Nafs") in which he discusses the status of vain intelligibles or fictional objects, like a phoenix. According to Avicenna there is no essence of a phoenix within the Active Intellect; for if there were, the Active Intellect *cum* Giver of Forms would have emanated the form of phoenix-ness down upon matter, and there would have existed a concrete particular instance of such a creature in the physical world. That is because for Avicenna every possible kind of thing that can exist does exist. This conclusion follows for him since every existing thing ultimately is the result of God's goodness, where the divine goodness reaches the Earth, via the intermediacy of a series of (Active) Intellects, through a cascading process of emanations—which are certain actions that necessarily (although perhaps voluntarily) ensue (*lawāzim*) from God and these Intellects; see chapters 6 and 7 of the present volume for a further discussion. Thus, if a certain kind of thing fails to exist, it is because either God willed not to extend his goodness to it (which is at odds with God's omnibenevolence) or something about that kind is not compossible with the order of the good (even if it is not immediately obvious why such a kind is impossible). In Avicenna's own words: "Every thing that necessarily ensues from something existing in act must also exist in act. So if something impossible necessarily ensues from the Active Intellects, it must exist in act, but the conclusion is impossible. Thus, it remains that nothing impossible necessarily ensues from them nor do they intellectualize them" ("On the Soul," 156).

Thus, returning to the point of intellectualizing forms, since for Avicenna we can form a concept of a phoenix, and yet there is no essence of a phoenix in the Active Intellect (otherwise, again, there would actually exist concrete instances of them), we cannot receive from the Active Intellect the complete intelligible, phoenix-ness. Instead, or so I contend, we receive only those universalizing forms that make the potentially intelligible image of the phoenix existing in our compositive imagination into something actually intelligible in our intellect. See Avicenna (1987) for the edition and a French translation by Michot of Avicenna's treatise "On the Soul," and Michot (1984–1985) for an English translation; for an excellent study of Avicenna's account of fictional objects or vain intelligibles, with an alternative interpretation of them, see Black (1997).

17. This is a point at which I have gestured earlier. It was a standard position among most medieval philosophers (at least those working within the Neoplatonizing Aristotelian tradition) that since matter is what prevents intelligibility, anything immaterial must be intelligible in itself. Thus, in his *Book of Demonstration*, III.5, 160, Avicenna writes: "Existing things are divided into two classes: beings intelligible in existence and beings perceptible in existence. Beings intelligible in existence are those that have neither matter nor any consequential accidents of matter. They are intelligible in themselves precisely because no operation is needed to make them intelligible, and because they cannot be perceived by the senses in any way." Hence the fact that the Active Intellect is completely separate from matter guarantees for Avicenna that it is intelligible in itself.

18. Hasse (2001), 39, which is an excellent survey of both the secondary literature on this problem and the primary Avicennan texts.

19. See, for instance, *De anima*, III 4, 429a16; III 5, 430a14; III 7, 431a1 and 431b 15–17.

20. Avicenna specifically mentions Porphyry's *On the Intellect and the Intelligibles* and *On the Soul*. For a brief discussion of these works see Adamson (2008), Appendix I.

21. Owens (1991), 114.

22. Ibid.

23. See 84–85.

24. For studies of Avicenna's theory of self-awareness, see Black (forthcoming [a]) and Kaukua (2007).

25. See 90–94.

26. For a discussion of Avicenna and the mind-body problem, see Druart (1988).

27. For secondary literature on Avicenna's "flying man," see Marmura (1986) and Hasse (2000), 80–92.

28. For more in-depth treatments, see the studies of Marmura (1964); Davidson (1992), 116–123; Hasse (2000), 154–174; and Gutas (2006a).

29. For a discussion of *ḥads*, see Gutas (1988), 159–176 and (2001).

30. See 44–46.

CHAPTER 6

1. For a detailed discussion of this issue, see Bertolacci (2007), esp. §2, "Avicenna."

2. Aristotle, *Metaphysic*, IV (Γ), 1003a21–22.

3. Aristotle, *Posterior Analytics*, I 1; Avicenna, *Book of Demonstration*, I.3.

4. In this respect Avicenna does not have anything like a traditional onto-logical proof for the existence of God, although, as I shall suggest (**169–70**), he does believe that God's existence is self-explaining.

5. See **165–68**.

6. See, for example, *Commentary on Lambda*, Avicenna (1947), 23–24; *Ta'līqāt*, Avicenna (2000), 62; and the distinction was implied, though not ex-plicitly made, at *Pointers and Reminders*, Avicenna (1892), *namaṭ* 4, *faṣl* 29, 146–147. For a discussion of the historical context to this distinction, see Davidson (1987), 184–288 and Gutas (1988), 261–265.

7. The following outline is drawn from Bertolacci (2006), which is a rich source for understanding the context and composition of Avicenna's *Metaphysics*.

8. Aristotle, *Metaphysics*, IV (Γ) 2, 1003b22–34 and VII (Z), 1040b16–19.

9. Bertolacci (2006), 164.

10. Excellent monograph-length studies of Avicenna's *Metaphysics* include Wisnovsky (2003); Acar (2005); and Bertolacci (2006).

11. Robert Wisnovsky suggests an alternative set of historical issues, rooted in the Islamic intellectual milieu, that were at work in Avicenna's metaphysical system building. I do not believe that the account presented below and Wis-novsky's are incompatible; rather, they complement each other. See Wisnovsky (2003), especially Part II.

12. As a brief historical aside, most scholars consider Aristotle's *De Caelo* a very early work and it is not clear whether Aristotle later in his career was com-mitted to the strict identification of temporal and alethic modalities, for he seems aware of two-sided possibilities in the modal logic of his *Prior Analytics*, and moreover, temporal frequencies are virtually absent from his accounts of modalities in the *Metaphysics*. Be that as it may, the identification of modalities with temporal frequency would take on a life of its own in both the late classical and early Islamic worlds.

13. See Aristotle, *Metaphysics*, XII (Λ) 7, 1072a19ff.

14. See, for instance, Proclus (2001), especially argument 1, from which the following discussion is drawn.

15. For instance, Yaḥyá ibn 'Adī (1989), esp. 79–80; a partial English trans-lation can be found in McGinnis and Reisman (2007). Still, al-Fārābī at least suggested that modalities might be properly basic and intrinsic to the nature of things themselves, in which case they could not be analyzed into temporal

frequencies, albeit he did not elaborate on and develop this point; see al-Fārābī (1960), 98.25–100.25 and (1981), 92–96, as well as Adamson (2006), esp., 180–186.

16. See, for instance, Kripke (1963) and Plantinga (1974).

17. For a discussion of Avicenna on the primacy of existence, see Marmura (1984a).

18. See Bertolacci (2008).

19. See 72–75.

20. Having said this, I should note that some scholars do find at least an ontological style component to Avicenna's argument. The strongest supporter of the ontological reading is Morewedge (1979). Others who see both an ontological and cosmological element are Johnson (1984) and Mayer (2001). My own view is that strictly speaking Avicenna's argument is not an ontological one, even if it demonstrates that there is a self-explaining being. The hallmark of ontological-style arguments is that they assume only a priori premises, and so have no recourse to empirical experience. Now although Avicenna thinks that existence is one of the primary intelligibles, and so one would never remember a time when one did not know existence, it does not follow that such a conception is innate or a priori; rather, for Avicenna, existence is the very first thing that we experience and so the very first thing that is impressed on the intellect. Thus, it seems to me that the argument is not strictly speaking an ontological type argument at all, since nothing is taken as a priori. Of course, if one means by "ontological" merely that Avicenna's argument refers solely to existence or being as such without making reference to any physical facts about existence beyond the claim that something exists, then in this qualified sense his argument is an ontological one.

21. For the version of this proof in the *Cure*, see Marmura (1980b). Also see Davidson (1987), ch. IX.

22. See Appendix 3 for a flowchart presentation of Avicenna's argument.

23. See 33–34.

24. I am grateful to Eleonore Stump for this point.

25. Avicenna here is following a long tradition of philosophers that goes back at least as far as Plato. The view is that even should one desire something bad, one does not desire it insofar as the thing is bad, harmful, or the like, but inasmuch as it appears good. Thus, what is always desired is some perceived good; for what makes the thing desirable is that it will be pleasant, useful, satisfy some need, or the like, all of which belong to the desired object in virtue of its being good in some way. Avicenna's account of good and evil will be discussed more fully in chapter 8.

26. See chapter 4, 97–100.

27. See 140–43.

28. Aristotle, *Metaphysics*, XII (Λ) 9.

29. For discussions of Avicenna's theory of the Necessary Existent's knowledge of particulars see Marmura (1962), Acar (2004), and Adamson (2004b).

30. See **55–57**.

31. See **99–100**.

32. See Laplace (1951), 4.

CHAPTER 7

1. See Augustine, *The Confessions*, book XI, chapters 10–28.

2. See Philoponus (1963), 103–119; English translation in Philoponus (2005), 78–87.

3. Cf. al-Ghazālī (1997), *Incoherence of the Philosophers*, Discussion 1, second proof, 30–36.

4. See *Physics*, II.12, 160–161, where he discusses the suggestion that "before" and "after" need not be temporal particles, and *Salvation*, "Physics," II.9, 230, where he discusses the suggestion that the locution "it *was* not" need not be taken in a tensed sense.

5. See 190a13ff.

6. Aristotle, *Physics*, VIII 1, 251a8–b10, where the argument is in terms of *that which is capable of undergoing motion*, namely, matter. Also see Aristotle, *Metaphysics*, VII (Z) 7–8.

7. For an overview of many of Philoponus's anti-Aristotelian theses, see Sorabji, ed. (1987).

8. An actual infinity, very loosely, involves some definite or complete infinite quantity or number, all parts or members of which exist at the same time; although also see Bowin (2007) for a more complete discussion of Aristotelian infinity.

9. For a discussion and summary of Philoponus's specific uses of the Aristotelian doctrines of infinity against Aristotle, see Sorabji (1987), 170.

10. Philoponus usually presents both arguments together as a couplet. See Philoponus (1963), I 3, 8.27–11.21 and XVIII 3, 619.3–620.19, as well as Philoponus (1987), fragment 132.

11. Cf. Aristotle, *Physics*, III 5, 204b.

12. Philoponus (1987), 146.

13. See Janssens (1997) for a discussion of Avicenna's conception of creation and his vocabulary concerning this topic.

14. See Avicenna, *Physics*, III.11, and *Metaphysics*, IV.2.

15. *Metaphysics*, III.10, 121.17–18; also see Marmura (1975) for a detailed discussion of Avicenna's account of the relative.

16. For a general discussion of the notion of a "Great Chain of Being," see the now classic Lovejoy (1933), although Lovejoy does not mention Avicenna.

17. See 40–41, 56.

18. Interestingly, I believe that Avicenna would accept the claim that if the Necessary Existent had not created, there would be no privation or absence in Avicenna's relative sense, and so no possibility. Consequently, if the Necessary Existent had not created the world, the creation of the world would have been impossible. Still, for Avicenna this counterintuitive, if not absurd, conclusion results not because of his analysis of possibility, but because the antecedent—"if the Necessary Existent had not created"—is impossible, and from an impossible assumption anything follows. For as will be seen later in this chapter (206–8), according to Avicenna, while the Necessary Existent creates voluntarily, it does so only on account of its excess of goodness. Thus, only if the Necessary Existent were good in some way other than (maybe even lesser than) it is, could it will not to create, and it is precisely this assumption that Avicenna takes to be impossible.

19. For a discussion of their argument, see McGinnis (2006b), "Historical Background."

20. For now, see Fakhry (1958) for a study of Islamic occasionalism.

21. Avicenna does not explicitly mention the Giver of Forms, but instead speaks of something separate (*mufāriq*), namely, separate from matter and so some Intelligence or other.

22. At *Physics*, I.2, 14.14–15.5 Avicenna lists the various considerations: "This matter, inasmuch as it potentially receives a form or forms, is called its 'prime matter'; and, inasmuch as it is actually bearing a form, it is called in this [book] its 'subject.' (The sense of 'subject' here is not the sense of subject we used in logic, namely, as part of the description of substance, for prime matter is not a subject in that sense at all.) Next, inasmuch as it is common to all forms, it is called 'matter' and 'stuff' [lit. 'clay']. It is also called an 'element' because it is resolved into [elements] through a process of analysis, and so it is the simple part receptive of the form as part of the whole composite, and likewise for whatever is analogous. It is also called a 'constituent' because the composition begins from it in this very sense, and likewise for whatever is analogous. It is as though when one begins from it, it is called a 'constituent,' whereas when one begins from the composite and ends at it, then it is called an 'element,' since the element is the simplest part of the composite."

23. See also *Salvation*, "Metaphysics," I.17, 536.

24. For a flowchart presentation of Avicenna's demonstration see Appendix 4.

25. In Avicenna's technical vocabulary, the Arabic *ṣūra* ("form") specifically identifies that form that makes some particular thing the specific species that it is, whereas the term *hayʾa* (also "form," "configuration," or perhaps even

"exterior appearance") is used for the formal factor that explains a given accidental state of a particular thing.

26. For a fuller discussion, see Bertolacci (2002).

27. *Metaphysics*, VI.1, 194. See Wisnovsky (2002) and Richardson (2008), ch. 1.

28. See **162**.

29. See **73–74**.

30. It is worth nothing that in the whole of the *Physics* of the *Cure* Avicenna mentions the traversal of an infinite only (as far as I can see) three times: once with the qualification that the infinite cannot be traversed *in a finite period of time* (III.4), once when presenting the argument and position of Aristotle (III.8), and then again in the same place to distance himself from the proposition that an infinite cannot be traversed.

31. Even this seemingly self-evident claim Avicenna felt compelled to prove rather than to take as self-evident. He did so by considering the proportional ratios of a number of different interrelated factors associated with motion, such as the force impressed by the mover, the weight of and resistance to the moved object, as well as the time, distance, and speed of the motion. His general strategy was then to show that if any one of these variables is set at ∞, then the others would either likewise go to ∞ or to 0. Thus, an infinite distance's being traversed in some (positive) finite period of time contradicts the proportionalities that Avicenna felt that he had demonstrated to exist between the various arguments of the functions that he has considered. See, for example, the *Physics* of the *Cure*, III.10 and IV.15.

32. Avicenna provides the details at *Physics*, III.11, which are only implicit in the quotation cited from the *Metaphysics*.

33. Aristotle (*Physics*, III 8, 208a20–21) seems to hint at Avicenna's response, which also has some similarities with Simplicius's response, even though it does not seem as if Simplicius's commentary on the *Physics* was available in Arabic. See Simplicius (1882), 494.14–495.5.

34. See Marmura (1960) and McGinnis (forthcoming [b]).

35. Aristotle had placed the Earth exactly in the center, whereas Ptolemy had placed it slightly off center to help bring theoretical calculations in line with the observed phenomena.

36. For a more thorough discussion of the Ptolemaic astronomical model that informed most medieval thinkers, see Kuhn (1957), "Ptolemaic Astronomy," 64–72.

37. See *Taʿlīqāt*, Avicenna (2000), 16–17.

CHAPTER 8

1. Cf. Aristotle, *Nicomachean Ethics*, I 6.

2. See **144–47**.

3. For a discussion of these various faculties see chapter 4, **95, 113–16**.

4. Cf. Plato, *Republic*, II, 369B–372B.

5. See chapter 7, **207–8**.

6. The Arabic gives the superlative of the verbs for "to reach" and "to obtain" (*awṣal* and *aḥṣal*). Marmura in his translation of the *Metaphysics* (Avicenna [2005]) renders the criterion in question thus, "that whose perfection is *more accessible* to it and *more readily realized* for it" (*Metaphysics*, IX.7, 348). I have preferred to understand this somewhat oblique criterion in terms of being absorbed by the pleasure only because this seems to be the sense in which Avicenna understands it when he returns to it during his analysis of intellectual pleasure (*Metaphysics*, IX.7, 350–51).

7. While the Arabic could be read as "an intellectual knower," Avicenna is probably drawing on the so-called *Theology of Aristotle*, which in fact is a redaction of parts of Plotinus's *Enneads*, where the notion of intelligible universe or world is used; see, for example, *Enneads*, IV.7.vi.

8. See **207** for Avicenna's understanding of "consent" in this context.

9. For a study of Avicenna's theory of evil see Belo (2007), 38–51.

10. See **187–89**.

CHAPTER 9

1. See Galen (1821–33); for a list of titles by Galen at least known in the medieval Islamic world, see Meyerhof (1926).

2. See Hall (2004), §II.

3. See **4–9**.

4. See Gutas (2003), 146.

5. For Avicenna's developed thoughts on astrology, see Avicenna (2006).

6. While there is an English translation of book I of the *Canon of Medicine* (Avicenna [1999]), it should be used with due care since it was made from the Latin, which does not always follow the Arabic.

7. See **84–85**.

8. Also see Kruk (2002), §5, where she touches on the chapter discussed below, and Musallam (1990), 33–34.

9. Or, perhaps, Avicenna has in mind the *neurula* stage of the embryo.

CHAPTER 10

1. To date the best general survey, of which I am aware, of Avicenna's subsequent influence in the East is Gutas (2002) in *Avicenna and His Heritage* (Janssens and De Smet, eds. [2002]). In fact, this collection contains numerous articles relevant to situating Avicenna within the broader history of philosophy. For a general discussion of Avicenna influence on the East and West, also see Janssens (2006a).

2. See Janssens (1986).

3. See, for example, Frank (1992), Griffel (2006), and al-Akiti (2004) for Avicenna's influence on al-Ghazālī.

4. Cf. **49**.

5. For an excellent survey of Mullā Ṣadrā's philosophy, see Rahman (1975).

6. See as-Suhrawardī (1999), "Translators' Introduction," xxi.

7. See as-Suhrawardī (1999), "Translators' Introduction," xxvii.

8. See Corbin (1960) and Nasr (1996). For a criticism of their position, see Gutas (2000).

9. For an excellent survey of Maimonides' place in philosophy within the Islamic world, see Broadie (1996), and for a cautious study of Avicenna's influence on Maimonides, see Dobbs-Weinstein (2002).

10. For a general discussion of this movement, see Lindberg (1978).

11. For a complete list of Avicenna's works available in Latin translation, see the introduction to D'Alverny (1994).

12. See McGinnis (2006a).

13. See Hasse (2000), 62. Hasse's survey is also an excellent source for the overall reception and influence of the psychological part of Avicenna's *Cure* in Europe.

14. Here see McGinnis (2007a) and Gossiaux (2007).

15. See Gilson (1927).

16. Ibid., section II, especially, 100–101.

17. See Druart (2002).

BIBLIOGRAPHY

Acar, Rahim. (2003). "Intellect versus Active Intellect: Plotinus and Avicenna."
In Reisman, *Before and After Avicenna*, 69–87.

———. (2004). "Reconsidering Avicenna's Position on God's Knowledge of
Particulars." In McGinnis, *Interpreting Avicenna*, 142–156.

———. (2005). *Talking about God and Talking about Creation: Avicenna's and
Thomas Aquinas' Position*. Leiden, E. J. Brill.

Adamson, Peter. (2002). *The Arabic Plotinus: A Philosophical Study of the "Theology
of Aristotle."* London: Gerald Duckworth & Co.

———. (2004a). "Non-Discursive Thought in Avicenna's Commentary on the
Theology of Aristotle." In McGinnis, *Interpreting Avicenna*, 87–111.

———. (2004b). "On knowledge of particulars." *Proceedings of the Aristotelian
Society* 105: 257–278.

———. (2006). "The Arabic Sea Battle: al-Fārābī on the Problem of Future
Contingents." *Archiv für Geschichte der Philosophie* 88: 163–188.

———. (2007). *Al-Kindī*. Great Medieval Thinkers Series. Oxford: Oxford
University Press.

———. (2008). "*Porphyrius Arabus* on Nature and Art: 463F Smith in Context." In *Studies on Porphyry*, ed. George Karamanolis and Anne Sheppard.
London: Institute of Classical Studies.

Adamson, Peter and Richard. C. Taylor, eds. (2005). *The Cambridge Companion
to Arabic Philosophy*. Cambridge, England: Cambridge University Press,
Cambridge.

Afnan, Soheil. (1958). *Avicenna, His life and Works*. London: George Allen & Unwin.

Al-Akiti, M. Afifi. (2004). "The Three Properties of Prophethood in Certain Works of Avicenna and al-Ghazālī." In McGinnis, *Interpreting Avicenna*, 189–212.

Aquinas, Thomas. (1968). *On Being and Essence*, 2nd, rev. ed. Translated by Armand Maurer. Medieval Sources in Translation, v. 1. Toronto: Pontifical Institute of Medieval Studies.

Avicenna. (1892). *Al-Ishārāt wa-t-tanbīhāt (Pointers and Reminders)*. Edited by J. Forget. Leiden: E. J. Brill.

————. (1947). *Commentary on Lambda*. In *Arisṭū ʿinda l-ʿArab*, ed. ʿAbd ar-Raḥman Badawī. Cairo: Maktabat an-Nahḍa al-Miṣrīya.

————. (1951). *Avicenna on Theology*. Translated by Arthur J. Arberry. The Wisdom of the East series. Westport, CT: Hyperion Press.

————. (1952). *Shifāʾ, al-Manṭiq, Kitāb al-Qiyās (Book of Syllogism)*. Edited by S. Zāyed and I. Madkūr. Cairo: The General Egyptian Book Organization.

————. (1953). *Shifāʾ, al-Manṭiq, Madkhal (Introduction)*. Edited by I. Madkūr. Cairo: The General Egyptian Book Organization.

————. (1959). *Shifāʾ, aṭ-Ṭabīʿiyāt, Kitāb an-Nafs (Psychology)*. In *Avicenna's De Anima (Arabic Text): Being the Psychological Part of Kitāb al-Shifāʾ*. Edited by Fazlur Rahman. London: Oxford University Press.

————. (1963). *Kitāb al-Ḥudūd*. In *Livre des Définitions*. Edited and translated by A. M. Goichon. Cairo: Publication de l'Institut Français d'Archéologie Orientale du Caire.

————. (1966). *Shifāʾ, Kitāb al-Burhān (Book of Demonstration)*. Edited by ʿAbd ar-Raḥman Badawī, 2 ed. Cairo: Association of Authorship, Translation & Publication Press.

————. (1969). *Shifāʾ, aṭ-Ṭabīʿiyāt, al-Kawn wa-l-fasād (Generation and Corruption)*. Edited by Maḥmud Qasim. Cairo: The General Egyptian Book Organization.

————. (1970). *Shifāʾ, aṭ-Ṭabīʿiyāt, al-Ḥayawān (Book of Animals)*. Edited by ʿAbd al-Ḥalīm Muntaṣir, Saʿīd Zāyed, and ʿAbdallāh Ismāʿīl. Cairo: The General Egyptian Book Organization.

————. (1971). *Avicenna's Treatise on Logic: Part One of Danesh-Name Alai*. Translated by F. Zabeeh. The Hague: Matinus Nijhoff.

————. (1973). *The Propositional Logic of Avicenna: a Translation from* al-Shifāʾ: al-Qiyās, *with Introduction, Commentary and Glossary*. Translated by Nabil Shehaby. Dordrecht and Boston: D. Reidel Publishing Co.

————. (1974). *The Life of Ibn Sina, A Critical Edition and Annotated Translation*. Edited and translated by William Gohlman. Albany, NY: State University of New York Press.

————. (1983a). *Avicenna's Tract on Cardiac Drugs*. Translated by Hakeem Abdul Hameed. Karachi: Hamdard Foundation Press.

————. (1983b). *Shifā', aṭ-Ṭabīʿīyāt, as-Samāʿ aṭ-ṭabīʿī (Physics)*. Edited by S. Zāyed. Cairo: The General Egyptian Book Organization.

————. (1984). *Remarks and Admonitions, Part One: Logic*. Translated by Shams Inati. Wetteren: Universa Press.

————. (1985). *Najāt (Salvation)*. Edited by M. T. Dānishpazhūh. Tehran: Dānishgāh-yi Tihrān.

————. (1986). "Fī aqsām al-ʿulūm al-ʿaqlīya" ("Divisions of the Theoretical Sciences"). In *Tisʿ rasāʾil fī l-ḥikma wa-aṭ-ṭabīʿīyāt*, ed. Ḥasan ʿ Āṣī, 83–94. Beirut: Dār al-Qābis.

————. (1987). "Risāla fī n-Nafs" ("Treatise on the Soul"). Edited and French translation by J. (Y.) Michot. In "L'Épître sur la disparition des formes intelligibles vaines après la mort" d'Avicenne," *Bulletin de Philosophie Médiévale* 29: 152–170.

————. (1995). *Mubāḥathāt (Discussions)*. Edited by M. Bīdārfar. Qum: Intishārāt-i Bīdār.

————. (1996). "Al-Adwiya l-qalbīya" ("Cures of the Heart"). In *al-Mabdaʾ wa-l-maʿād, Miʿrājnama, al-Adwiya l-qalbīya*. Council for publishing the precious works in the Central Library and Documentation Center of Astan Quds Razavi, publication nos.: 1–3. Mashhad, Iran: Astan Quds Razavi.

————. (1999). *The Canon of Medicine*. Adapted by Laleh Bakhtiar from the translations of O. Cameron Gruner and Mazar H. Shah. Great Books of the Islamic World. Chicago, IL: KAZI Publications.

————. (2000). *At-Taʿlīqāt (Glosses)*. Edited by ʿAbd ar-Raḥman Badawī. Qum: Markaz-i Intishārāt-i Daftar-i Tablīghāt-i Islāmī-i Ḥawzah-i ʿIlmīyah-i Qum.

————. (2002). *Al-Qānūn fī ṭ-Ṭibb*. Edited by Saʿīd al-Ḥusām. Beirut: Dār al-Fikr.

————. (2005). *Shifāʾ, Kitāb Ilāhīyāt (Metaphysics of the Healing)*. Translated by Michael E. Marmura with Arabic edition. Provo, UT: Brigham Young University Press.

————. (2006). *Réfutation de l'astrologie*. Edited and translated by Yahya Michot. Beirut: Les editions Albouraq.

————. (2009). *Shifāʾ, aṭ-Ṭabīʿīyāt, as-Samāʿ aṭ-ṭabīʿī (Physics of the Healing)*. Translated by Jon McGinnis with Arabic edition. Provo, UT: Brigham Young University Press.

Belo, Catarina. (2007). *Chance and Determinism in Avicenna and Averroes*. Islamic philosophy, theology and science, v. 69. Leiden: E. J. Brill.

Bertolacci, Amos. (2002). "The Doctrine of Material and Formal Causality in the *Ilāhiyyāt* of Avicenna's *Kitāb Šifāʾ*." *Quaestio* 2: 125–154.

————. (2006). *The Reception of Aristotle's Metaphysics in Avicenna's* Kitāb al-Šifāʾ: *A Milestone of Western Metaphysical Thought*. Leiden: E. J. Brill.

————. (2007). "Avicenna and Averroes on the Proof of God's Existence and the Subject Matter of Metaphysics." *Medioevo* 32: 61–97.

————. (2008). "'Necessary' as Primary Concept in Avicenna's Metaphysics." In *Conoscenza e contingenza: nella tradizione aristotelica medievale*, ed. Stefano Perfetti, 31–50. Pisa: ETS.

Black, Deborah L. (1990). *Logic and Aristotle's 'Rhetoric' and 'Poetics' in Medieval Arabic Philosophy*. Leiden: E. J. Brill.

————. (1993). "Estimation (*Wahm*) in Avicenna, The Logical and Psychological Dimensions." *Dialogue* 32: 219–258.

————. (1997). "Avicenna on the Ontological and Epistemic Status of Fictional Beings." *Documenti e Studi sulla Tradizione Filosofica Medievale* 8: 425–453.

————. (2006). "Knowledge (*ʿilm*) and Certitude (*yaqīn*) in al-Fārābī's Epistemology." *Arabic Sciences and Philosophy* 16: 11–45.

————. (forthcoming [a]). "Avicenna on Individuation, Self-Awareness, and God's Knowledge of Particulars." In *Philosophical and Theological Explorations in the Abrahamic Traditions*, eds. R. Taylor, I. Omar, D. Twetten. Milwaukee, WI: Marquette University Press.

————. (forthcoming [b]). "Rational Imagination: Avicenna on the Cogitative Power." In the proceedings of the conference on Philosophical Psychology in Arabic and Latin Aristotelianism, Universidad Panamericana, Mexico City, May 2008. Leiden: E. J. Brill.

Bowin, John. (2007). "Aristotelian Infinity." *Oxford Studies in Ancient Philosophy* 32: 233–250.

Broadie, Alexander. (1996). "Maimonides." In Nasr and Leaman, *History of Islamic Philosophy*, 725–738.

Corbin, Henry. (1960). *Avicenna and the Visionary Recital*. Translated by Willard R. Trask. Bollingen Series, v. 66. Princeton, NJ: Princeton University Press.

D'Alverny, Marie-Thérèse. (1994). *Avicenna Latinus, Codices*. Louvain-la-Neuve and Leiden: E. Peeters and E. J. Brill.

D'Ancona, Cristina. (2005). "Greek into Arabic: Neoplatonism in translation." In Adamson and Taylor, *The Cambridge Companion to Arabic Philosophy*, 10–31.

Davidson, Herbert. (1987). *Proofs for Eternity, Creation and the Existence of God in Medieval Islamic and Jewish Philosophy*. New York and Oxford: Oxford University Press.

————. (1992). *Alfarabi, Avicenna, and Averroes, on Intellect*. New York and Oxford: Oxford University Press.

Dhanani, Alnoor. (1994). *The Physical Theory of Kalām: Atoms, Space, and Void in Basrian Muʿtazilī Cosmology*. Leiden: E. J. Brill.

————. (2003). "Rock in the Heavens?! The Encounter between ʿAbd al-Jabbār and Ibn Sīnā." In Reisman, *Before and After Avicenna*, 127–144.

Dobbs-Weinstein, Idit. (2002). "Maimonides' Reticence toward Ibn Sīnā." In Janssens and De Smet, *Avicenna and his Heritage*, 281–296.

Druart, Thérèse-Anne. (1988). "The Soul and Body Problem: Avicenna and Descartes." In *Arabic Philosophy and the West*, ed. Thérèse-Anne Druart, 27–49. Washington, DC: Center for Contemporary Arab Studies, Georgetown University.

————. (2000). "The human soul's individuation and its survival after the body's death: Avicenna on the causal relation between body and soul." *Arabic Sciences and Philosophy* 10: 259–273.

————. (2002). "Avicenna's Influence on Duns Scotus' Proof for the Existence of God in the *Lectura*." In Janssens and De Smet, *Avicenna and his Heritage*, 253–266.

————. (2005). "Metaphysics." In Adamson and Taylor, *The Cambridge Companion to Arabic Philosophy*, 327–348.

Endress, Gerhard. (1973). *Proclus Arabus, Zwanzig Abschnitte aus der* Institutio Theologica *in arabischer Übersetzung*. Beirut and Wiesbaden: Steiner Verlag.

Fakhry, Majid. (1958). *Islamic Occasionalism, and Its Critique by Averroës and Aquinas*. London: Allen and Unwin.

Al-Fārābī. (1960) *Alfarabi's Commentary on Aristotle's* Περι Ηερμηνειας. Edited by Wilhelm Kutsch and Stanley Marrow. Beirut: Imprimerie Catholique.

————. (1963). *The Principles of Existing Things* [most of Part 2, under the title "The Political Regime"]. Translated by Fauzi Najjar. In *Medieval Political Philosophy, A Sourcebook*, ed. Ralph Lerner and Muhsin Mahdi. Ithaca, NY: Cornell University Press.

————. (1981). *Al-Farabi's Commentary and Short Treatise on Aristotle's* De Interpretatione. Translated by F. W. Zimmermann. Oxford: Oxford University Press (for The British Academy).

————. (1985). *The Principles of the Opinions of the Inhabitants of the Perfect State*. Edited and translated by Richard Walzer. Oxford, UK: Oxford University Press; reprinted, Great Books of the Islamic World, 1998.

————. (2006). *The Aims of Aristotle's* Metaphysics. Translated by Amos Bertolacci. In Bertolacci, *The Reception of Aristotle's Metaphysics in Avicenna's* Kitāb al-Šifāʾ, ch. 3.

————. (2007a). *The Aims of Aristotle's* Metaphysics. Translated by Jon McGinnis and David C. Reisman. In McGinnis and Reisman, *Classical Arabic Philosophy*.

————. (2007b). *The Principles of Existing Things* [Part 1]. Translated by Jon McGinnis and David C. Reisman. In McGinnis and Reisman, *Classical Arabic Philosophy*.

Frank, Richard M. (1992). *Creation and the Cosmic System: Al-Ghazâlî and Avicenna*. Abhandlungen der Heidelberger Akademie der Wissenschaften. Heidelberg: Carl Winter, Universitätsverlag.

Galen. (1821–33). *Claudii Galeni Opera omnia*. Edited by C. G. Kühn. Leipzig: Repographischer Nachdruck der Ausgabe.

Al-Ghazālī. (1997). *The Incoherence of the Philosophers*. Translated by Michael E. Marmura with Arabic edition. Islamic Translation Series. Provo, UT: Brigham Young University Press.

Gilson, Étienne. (1927). "Avicenne et le point de départ de Duns Scot." *Archives d' Histoire doctrinale et Littéraire du Moyen Âge* 2: 89–149.

Goichon, Amélie Marie. (1937). *La Distinction de l'Essence et de l'Existence d'après Ibn Sīnā (Avicenne)*. Paris: Desclée de Brouwer.

———. (1938). *Lexique de la Langue Philosophique D'Ibn Sīnā (Avicenne)*. Paris: Desclée de Brouwer.

———. (1939). *Vocabulaires Comparés D'Aristote et D'Ibn Sīnā: Supplément au Lexique de la Langue Philosophique D'Ibn Sīnā (Avicenne)*. Paris: Desclée de Brouwer.

Goodman, Lenn. (2006). *Avicenna*, updated edition. Ithaca, NY: Cornell University Press.

Gossiaux, Mark D. (2007). "Thomas Aquinas on Infinite Multitudes and the Eternity of the World: A Reply to Massey." *Divinatio* 26: 205–228.

Griffel, Frank. (2006). "The Introduction of Avicennian Psychology into the Muslim Theological Discourse: The Case of al-Ghazālī (d. 1111)." In Pacheco and Meirinhos, *Intellect et Imagination dans la Philosophie Médiévale*, 571–582.

———. (2009). *Al-Ghazālī's Philosophical Theology*. Oxford: Oxford University Press.

Gutas, Dimitri. (1988). *Avicenna and the Aristotelian Tradition: Introduction to Reading Avicenna's Philosophical Works*. Leiden: E. J. Brill.

———. (1998). *Greek Thought, Arabic Culture: The Graeco-Arabic Translation Movement in Baghdad and Early 'Abbāsid Society (2nd–4th/8th–10th centuries)*. London and New York: Routledge.

———. (2000). "Avicenna's Eastern ('Oriental') Philosophy, Nature, Contents, Transmission." *Arabic Sciences and Philosophy* 10: 159–180.

———. (2001). "Intuition and Thinking: The Evolving Structure of Avicenna's Epistemology." In Wisnovsky, *Aspects of Avicenna*, 1–38.

———. (2002). "The Heritage of Avicenna: The Golden Age of Arabic Philosophy, 1000–ca. 1350." In Janssens and De Smet, *Avicenna and his Heritage*, 81–97.

———. (2003). "Medical Theory and Scientific Method in the Age of Avicenna." In Reisman, *Before and After Avicenna*, 145–162.

————. (2006a). "Imagination and Transcendental Knowledge in Avicenna." In Montgomery, *Arabic Theology, Arabic Philosophy*, 337–354.

————. (2006b). "Intellect without Limits: The Absence of Mysticism in Avicenna." In Pacheco and Meirinhos, *Intellect et Imagination dans la Philosophie Médiévale*, 351–372.

Hall, Robert E. (2004). "Intellect, Soul and Body in Ibn Sīnā: Systematic Synthesis and Development of the Aristotelian, Neoplatonic and Galenic Theories." In McGinnis, *Interpreting Avicenna*, 62–86.

————. (2006). "The *'Wahm'* in Ibn Sina's Psychology." In Pacheco and Meirinhos, *Intellect et Imagination dans la Philosophie Médiévale*, 533–549.

Hasnawi, Ahmad. (1984). "La Dynamique D'Ibn Sīnā (La notion d'"inclination': *mayl*)." In *Études sur Avicenne*, ed. J. Jolivet and R. Rashed, 103–123. Paris: Société d'édition Les Belles Lettres.

————. (2001). "La définition du mouvement dans la *Physique* du *Šifā'* d'Avicenne." *Arabic Science and Philosophy* 11: 219–255.

Hasse, Dag Nikolaus. (2000). *Avicenna's* De Anima *in the Latin West: the Formation of a Peripatetic Philosophy of the Soul, 1160–1300*. Warburg Institute Studies and Texts vol. 1. London and Turin: The Warburg Institute and Nino Aragno Editore.

————. (2001). "Avicenna on Abstraction." In Wisnovsky, *Aspects of Avicenna*, 39–72.

Ibn al-Haytham. (1983). *Kitāb al-Manāẓir*, Books I–III. Edited by A. I. Sabra. Kuwait: The National Council for Culture, Arts and Letters.

————. (1989). *Kitāb al-Manāẓir*, Books I–III (*Optics*). Translated by A. I. Sabra. Studies of the Warburg Institute, vol. 40, i. London: The Warburg Institute.

Inati, Shams. (1996). "Ibn Sīnā." In Nasr and Leaman, *History of Islamic Philosophy*, 231–246.

Jabre, Farīd. (1984). "Le sens de l'abstraction chez Avicenne." *Mélanges de l'Université St. Joseph de Beyrouth* 50: 281–310.

Janssens, Jules. (1986). "Le Dānesh-Nāmeh d'Ibn Sīnā: un texte à revoir?" *Bulletin de philosophie médiévale* 28: 163–177.

————. (1991). *An Annotated Bibliography on Ibn Sînâ (1970–1989): Including Arabic and Persian Publications and Turkish and Russian References*. Leuven: Leuven University Press.

————. (1997). "Creation and emanation in Ibn Sīnā." *Documenti e Studi sulla Tradizione Filosofica Medievale* 8: 455–477.

————. (1999). *An Annotated Bibliography on Ibn Sīnā: First Supplement (1990–1994)*. Textes et Études du Moyen Âge, v. 12. Louvain-la-Neuve: Fédération Internationale des Instituts d'Études Médiévales.

————. (2004). "'Experience' (*tajriba*) in Classical Arabic Philosophy (al-Fārābī – Avicenne)." *Quaestio* 4: 45–62.

————. (2006a). "Ibn Sīnā, and his heritage in the Islamic world and in the Latin West." In *Ibn Sīnā and his Influence on the Arabic and Latin World*. Variorum Collected Studies Series. Aldershot, UK and Burlington, VT: Ashgate.

————. (2006b). "The Notions of *Wāhib al-Ṣuwar* (Giver of Forms) and *Wāhib al-ʿaql* (Bestower of Intelligence) in Ibn Sīnā." In Pacheco and Meirinhos, *Intellect et Imagination dans la Philosophie Médiévale*, 551–562.

Janssens, Jules and Daniel De Smet, eds. (2002). *Avicenna and His Heritage, Acts of the International Colloquium, Leuven-Louvain-la-Neuve, September 8–September 11, 1999*. Leuven: Leuven University Press.

Johnson, S. A. (1984). "Ibn Sīnā's Fourth Ontological Argument for God's Existence." *Muslim World* 74: 161–171.

Kaukua, Jari. (2007). *Avicenna on Subjectivity: A Philosophical Study*. Jyväskylä, FI: Jyväskylä University Printing House.

Kennedy-Day, Kiki. (2003). *Books of Definition in Islamic Philosophy: The Limits of Words*. London and New York: RoutledgeCurzon.

Al-Kindī. (1950–1953). *Fī l-falsafa l-ūlá (On First Philosophy)*. In *Rasāʾil al-Kindī al-falsafīya*. vol. 1. Edited by Muhammad Abū Rīda. Cairo: Dār al-Fikr al-ʿArabī.

————. (1974). *Al-Kindī's Metaphysics: A Translation of Yaʿqub Ibn Ishaq al-Kindī's Treatise "On First Philosophy."* Translated by Alfred L. Ivry. Albany, NY: State University of New York Press.

Kripke, Saul. (1963). "Semantical Considerations on Modal Logic." *Acta Philosophica Fennica* 16 (1963): 83–94.

Kruk, Remke. (2002). "Ibn Sīnā *On Animals*: Between the First Teacher and the Physician." In Janssens and De Smet, *Avicenna and his Heritage*, 325–341.

Kuhn, Thomas. (1957). *The Copernican Revolution: Planetary Astronomy in the Development of Western Thought*. Cambridge, MA: Harvard University Press.

Laplace, Pierre Simon. (1951). *A Philosophical Essay on Probabilities*. Translated by Frederick Truscott and Frederick Emory. New York: Dover Publications.

Lettinck, Paul. (1999). "Ibn Sīnā on Atomism, Translation of Ibn Sīnā's *Kitāb al-Shifāʾ, al-Ṭabīʿiyyāt 1: al-Samāʿ al-aṭ-ṭabīʿī, Third Treatise, Chapter 3–5.*" *Al-Shajarah* 4: 1–51.

Lindberg, David. (1976). *Theories of Vision from al-Kindi to Kepler*. Chicago: University of Chicago Press.

————. (1978). "The Transmission of Greek and Arabic Learning to the West." In Lindberg, *Science in the Middle Ages*, 52–90.

Lindberg, David, ed. (1978). *Science in the Middle Ages*. Chicago: University of Chicago.

Lovejoy, Arthur O. (1933). *The Great Chain of Being: The Study of the History of an Idea*. The William James Lectures Delivered at Harvard University. Cambridge, MA: Harvard University Press.

Marmura, Michael E. (1960). "Avicenna and the Problem of the Infinite Number of Souls." *Mediaeval Studies* 22: 232–239. Reprint in Marmura, *Probing in Islamic Philosophy*, 171–179.

———. (1962). "Some Aspects of Avicenna's Theory of God's Knowledge of Particulars." *Journal of the American Oriental Society* 82: 299–331. Reprint in Marmura, *Probing in Islamic Philosophy*, 71–95.

———. (1964). "Avicenna's Theory of Prophecy in the Light of Ash'arite Theology." In *The Seed of Wisdom: Essays in Honour of T. J. Meek*, ed., W. S. McCullough, 159–178. Toronto: Toronto University Press. Reprint in Marmura, *Probing in Islamic Philosophy*, 197–216.

———. (1975). "Avicenna's Chapter 'On the Relative,' in the *Metaphysics* of the *Shifā'*." In *Essays on Islamic Philosophy and Science*, ed. George F. Hourani, 83–99. Albany, NY: State University of New York Press.

———. (1979). "Avicenna's Chapter on Universals in the *Isagoge* of the *Shifā'*." In *Islam Past and Present Challenge: Studies in Honour of W. M. Watt*, ed. T. Welch and P. Cachia, 34–56. Edinburgh: Edinburgh University Press. Reprint in Marmura, *Probing in Islamic Philosophy*, 33–59.

———. (1980a). "Avicenna on the Division of the Sciences in the *Isagoge* of his *Shifā'*." *Journal of the History of Arabic Science* 4: 239–251. Reprint in Marmura, *Probing in Islamic Philosophy*, 1–15.

———. (1980b). "Avicenna's Proof from Contingency for God's Existence in the *Metaphysics* of the *Shifā'*." *Mediaeval Studies* 42: 337–352. Reprint in Marmura, *Probing in Islamic Philosophy*, 131–148.

———. (1984a). "Avicenna on Primary Concepts in the *Metaphysics* of the *Shifā'*." In *Logos Islamikos: Studia Islamica in honorem Georgii Michaelis Wickens*, ed. R. Savory and D. A. Aguis, 219–239. Toronto: Pontifical Institute of Mediaeval Studies. Reprint in Marmura, *Probing in Islamic Philosophy*, 149–169.

———. (1984b). "The Metaphysics of Efficient Causality in Avicenna (Ibn Sina)." In Marmura, *Islamic Theology and Philosophy: Studies in Honor of George F. Hourani*, ed. M. E. Marmura, 172–187. Albany, NY: State University of New York Press.

———. (1986). "Avicenna's 'Flying Man' in Context." *The Monist* 69: 383–395. Reprint in Marmura, *Probing in Islamic Philosophy*, 181–195.

———. (1992). "Quiddity and Universality in Avicenna." In *Studies in Neoplatonism*, vol. 5, ed. Parviz Morewedge, 77–87. Albany, NY: State University of New York. Reprint in Marmura, *Probing in Islamic Philosophy*, 61–70.

————. (2005). *Probing in Islamic Philosophy: Studies in the Philosophies of Ibn Sina, al-Ghazali and Other Major Muslim Thinkers.* Binghamton, NY: Global Academic Publishing.

————. (2008). "Some Questions regarding Avicenna's Theory of the Temporal Origination of the Human Rational Soul." *Arabic Sciences and Philosophy* 18: 121–138.

Mayer, Toby. (2001). "Ibn Sīnā's 'Burhān al-Siddīqīn'." *Journal of Islamic Studies* 12: 18–39.

McGinnis, Jon. (1999). "Ibn Sīnā on the Now: Text and Commentary." *American Catholic Philosophical Quarterly* 73: 73–106.

————. (2003a). "Scientific Methodologies in Medieval Islam: Induction and Experimentation in the Philosophy of Ibn Sînâ." *Journal of the History of Philosophy* 41: 307–327.

————. (2003b). "The Topology of Time: An Analysis of Medieval Islamic Accounts of Discrete and Continuous Time." *The Modern Schoolman* 81: 5–25.

————. (2006a). "A medieval Arabic analysis of motion at an instant: the Avicennan sources to the *forma fluens/fluxus formae* debate." *British Journal for the History of Science* 39: 189–205.

————. (2006b). "Occasionalism, Natural Causation and Science in al-Ghazālī." In Montgomery, *Arabic Theology, Arabic Philosophy*, 441–463.

————. (2006c). "A Penetrating Question in the History of Ideas: Space, Dimensionality and Interpenetration in the Thought of Avicenna." *Arabic Sciences and Philosophy* 16: 47–69.

————. (2006d). "Positioning Heaven: the Infidelity of a Faithful Aristotelian." *Phronesis* 51: 140–161.

————. (2007a). "Aquinas' Arabic Sources on the Age of the Universe: A Response to Gerald J. Massey." *Divinatio* 26: 191–204.

————. (2007b). "Making Abstraction Less Abstract: The Logical, Psychological, and Metaphysical Dimensions of Avicenna's Theory of Abstraction." *Proceedings of the American Catholic Philosophical Association* 80: 169–183.

————. (2008). "Avicenna's Naturalized Epistemology and Scientific Methods." In *The Unity of Science in the Arabic Tradition*, ed. S. Rahman, T. Street, H. Tahiri, 129–152. Dordrecht: Kluwer Academic Publishers.

————. (forthcoming [a]). "Natural Knowledge in the Arabic Middle Ages." In *Wrestling with Nature: From Omens to Science*, ed. Peter Harrison, Ronald L. Numbers and Michael M. Shank. Chicago: University of Chicago Press.

————. (forthcoming [b]). "Avicennan Infinity: A Select History of the Infinite through Avicenna." *Documenti e Studi sulla Tradizione Filosofica Medievale.*

McGinnis, Jon, ed. (2004). *Interpreting Avicenna: Science and Philosophy in Medieval Islam*. Leiden: E. J. Brill.

McGinnis, Jon and David C. Reisman, trans. and ed. (2007). *Classical Arabic Philosophy: An Anthology of Sources*. Indianapolis and Cambridge: Hackett Publishing Co.

Meyerhof, Max. (1926). "New Light on Hunain Ibn Ishaq and his Period." *Isis* 8: 685–724.

Mez, Adam. (1995). *The Renaissance of Islam*. Translated by Salahuddin Khuda Bakhsh and D. S. Margoliouth. 3rd edition with new typesetting. New Delhi, India: Kitab Bhavan.

Michot, Jean [Yahya] R. (1984–1985). "Avicenna's 'Letter on the Disappearance of the Vain Intelligible Forms after Death'." *Bulletin de Philosophie Médiévale* 26–27: 94–103.

———. (1986). *La destinée de l'homme selon Avicenne: Le retour à Dieu* (maʿād) *et l'imagination*. Louvain: Aedibus Peeters.

———. (1987). "'L'Épître sur la disparition des formes intelligibles vaines après la mort' d'Avicenne," *Bulletin de Philosophie Médiévale* 29: 152–170.

———. (1997). "La réponse d'Avicenne à Bahmanyâr et al-Kirmânî: Présentation, traduction et lexique arabe-française de la *Mubâhathat III*." *Le Muséon* 110: 143–221.

Montgomery, James E., ed. (2006). *Arabic Theology, Arabic Philosophy. From the Many to the One: Essays in Celebration of Richard M. Frank*. Leiden: Peeters.

Morewedge, Parviz. (1979). "A Third Version of the Ontological Argument in the Ibn Sinian Metaphysics." In *Islamic Philosophical Theology*, ed. P. Morewedge, 188–222. Albany, NY: State University of New York Press.

Musallam, Basim. (1989). "Avicenna: §X, Biology and Medicine." In *Encyclopaedia Iranica*, ed. E. Yarshater, 3: 94–99. Boston: Routledge & Kegan Paul.

———. (1990). "The Human Embryo in Arabic Scientific and Religious Thought." In *The Human Embryo, Aristotle and the Arabic and European Traditions*, ed. G. R. Dunstan, 32–46. Exeter: University of Exeter Press.

Nasr, Sayyed Hossein. (1996). "Ibn Sīnā's 'Oriental philosophy'." In Nasr and Leaman, *History of Islamic Philosophy*, 247–251.

Nasr, Sayyed Hossein and Oliver Leaman, eds. (1996). *History of Islamic Philosophy*. London and New York: Routledge.

Nuseibeh, Sari. (1981). "Avicenna: Medicine and Scepticism." *Koroth* 8₁₋₂: 9–20.

———. (1989). "Al-ʿAql al-Qudsī: Avicenna's Subjective Theory of Knowledge." *Studia Islamica* 69: 39–54.

Owens, Joseph. (1991). "Aristotle and Aquinas on Cognition." In *Aristotle and His Medieval Interpreters*, ed. Richard Bosley and Martin Tweedale. Calgary, Canada: The University of Calgary Press.

Pacheco, Maria Cândida and José Francisco Meirinhos, eds. (2006). *Intellect et Imagination dans la Philosophie Médiévale*. vol. 1. Turnhout, Belgium: Brepols.

Pasnau, Robert. (1997). *Theories of Cognition in the Later Middle Ages*. Cambridge, UK: Cambridge University Press.

Philoponus, John. (1888). *In Aristotelis Physicorum libros tres priores [et] quinque posteriors commentaria*. Commentaria in Aristotelem Graeca, vols. 16–17. Edited by Hieronymus Vitelli. Berlin: typis et impensis Georg Reimer.

———. (1963). *De Aeternitate Mundi contra Proclum*. Edited by H. Rabe. Leipzig: Teubner, 1899; reprinted Hildesheim, Georg Olms Verlagsbuchhandlung.

———. (1987). *Philoponus, Against Aristotle on the Eternity of the World*. Translated and compiled by Christian Wildberg. Ithaca, NY: Cornell University Press.

———. (2005). *Against Proclus' On the Eternity of the World 1–5*. Translated by M. Share. Ithaca, NY: Cornell University Press.

Pines, Shlomo. (1997). *Studies in Atomism*. Jerusalem: The Magnes Press, The Hebrew University.

Plantinga, Alvin. (1974). *The Nature of Necessity*. Oxford: Clarendon Press.

Porphyry. (1975). *Isagoge*. Translated by E. W. Warren. Medieval Sources in Translation, vol. 16. Toronto: Pontifical Institute of Medieval Studies.

Proclus. (2001). *On the Eternity of the World (de Aeternitate Mundi)*. Edited and translated by Helen S. Lang and A. D. Macro. Berkeley: University of California Press.

Quine, W. V. O. (1953). "On What There Is." In *From a Logical Point of View*, 1–19. Cambridge, MA: Harvard University Press.

Rahman, Fazlur. (1975). *The Philosophy of Mullā Ṣadrā (Ṣadr al-Dīn al-Shīrāzī)*. Albany, NY: State University of New York Press.

Rashed, Marwan. (2005). "Natural Philosophy." In Adamson and Taylor, *The Cambridge Companion to Arabic Philosophy*, 287–307.

Rashed, Roshdi. (1984). "Mathématiques et Philosophie chez Avicenne." In *Études sur Avicenne*, ed. J. Jolivet and R. Roshdi, 29–39. Paris: Société d'édition les Belles Lettres.

Reisman, David. C., ed. (2003). *Before and After Avicenna: Proceedings of the First Conference of the Avicenna Study Group*. Leiden: E. J. Brill.

Richardson, Kara. (2008). "The Metaphysics of Agency: Avicenna and His Legacy." Ph.D. diss., University of Toronto.

Sabra, Abdelhamid I. (1980). "Avicenna on the Subject Matter of Logic." *Journal of Philosophy* 77: 746–764.

———. (2006). "Kalām Atomizing as an Alternative Philosophy to Hellenizing *Falsafa*." In Montgomery, *Arabic Theology, Arabic Philosophy*, 199–272.

Sayılı, Aydın. (1984). "Ibn Sînâ and Buridan on the Dynamics of Projectile Motion." In *Ibn Sînâ, Doğumunun Bininci Yılı Armağanı*, ed. Aydın Sayılı, 141–160. Ankara: Türk Tarih Kurumu.

Sebti, Meryem. (2005). "Le statut ontologique de l'image dans la doctrine avicennienne de la perception." *Arabic Sciences and Philosophy* 15: 109–140.

Shayegan, Yegane. (1999). "The Healing: On Time." In *An Anthology of Philosophy in Persia*, ed. S. H. Nasr and M. Aminrazavi, vol. 1, 241–250. New York and Oxford: Oxford University Press.

Simplicius. (1882). *In Aristotelis Physicorum*. Edited by H. Diels. Berlin: typis et impensis Georg Reimer.

Smith, A. Mark. (2001). *Alhacen's Theory of Visual Perception*, 2. vols [with a translation from the Latin of Ibn al-Haytham's *Optics, De aspectibus*]. Philadelphia: American Philosophical Society.

Sorabji, Richard. (1987). "Infinity and the Creation." In Sorabji, *Philoponus and the Rejection of Aristotelian Science*, 164–178.

Sorabji, Richard, ed. (1987). *Philoponus and the Rejection of Aristotelian Science*. London: Duckworth.

Stone, Abraham. (2001). "Simplicius and Avicenna on the Essential Corporeity of Material Substance." In Wisnovsky, *Aspects of Avicenna*, 73–130.

———. (2008). "Avicenna's Theory of Primary Mixture." *Arabic Science and Philosophy* 18: 99–119.

Street, Tony. (2002). "An Outline of Avicenna's Syllogistic." *Archiv für Geschichte der Philosophie* 84: 129–160.

Strohmaier, Gotthard. (1999). *Avicenna*. Munich: C. H. Beck.

As-Suhrawardī. (1999). *The Philosophy of Illumination*. Edited and translated by John Walbridge and Hossein Ziai. Islamic Translation Series. Provo, UT: Brigham Young University Press.

Thom, Paul. (2003). *Medieval Modal Systems: Problems and Concepts*. Ashgate Studies in Medieval Philosophy. Aldershot, UK and Burlington, VT: Ashgate.

Weisheipl, James A. (1978). "The Nature, Scope, and Classification of the Sciences." In Lindberg, 461–482.

Winter, Tim, ed. (2008). *The Cambridge Companion to Classical Islamic Theology*. Cambridge, UK: Cambridge University Press.

Wisnovsky, Robert. (2000). "Notes on Avicenna's Concept of Thingness (Šay'iyya)." *Arabic Sciences and Philosophy* 10: 181–221.

————. (2002). "Final and Efficient Causality in Avicenna's Cosmology and Theology." *Quaestio* 2: 97–123.

————. (2003). *Avicenna's Metaphysics in Context*. Ithaca, NY: Cornell University Press.

————. (2005). "Avicenna and the Avicennian Tradition." In Adamson and Taylor, *The Cambridge Companion to Arabic Philosophy*, 92–136.

Wisnovsky, Robert, ed. (2001). *Aspects of Avicenna*. Princeton, NJ: Markus Wiener Publishers.

Wood, Rega and Michael Weisberg. (2004). "Interpreting Aristotle on mixture: problems about elemental composition from Philoponus to Cooper." *Studies in History and Philosophy of Science* 35: 681–706.

Yaḥyá ibn 'Adī. (1989). "Establishing the Nature of the Possible." In Carl Ehrig-Eggert, "Yaḥyá Ibn 'Adī: über den Nachweis der Natur des Möglichen, Edition und Einleitung." *Zeitschrift für Geschichte der arabisch-islamischen Wissenschaften* 5: 63–97.

INDEX

9 780195 331486